Distant Magnets

Ellis Island Series
Ira Glazier and Luigi de Rosa,
series editors

John Tenhula,
Voices from Southeast Asia:
The Refugee Experience in the United States

Avraham Barkai,
The German-Jewish Immigration to the United States,
1820–1914

Distant Magnets

Expectations and Realities in the Immigrant Experience, 1840–1930

edited by
Dirk Hoerder and
Horst Rössler

ELLIS ISLAND SERIES

Holmes & Meier
New York / London

Published in the United States of America 1993 by
Holmes & Meier Publishers, Inc.
30 Irving Place
New York, NY 10003

Book design by Adrienne Weiss

This book has been printed on acid-free paper.

Library of Congress Cataloging-in-Publication Data

Distant magnets : expectations and realities in the immigrant
  experience, 1840–1930 / edited by Dirk Hoerder and Horst Rössler.
     p.   cm. — (Ellis Island series)
  Includes bibliographical references and index.
  ISBN 0-8419-1302-1 (acid-free paper)
  1. Immigrants—United States—History. 2. Immigrants—United
States—Attitudes. 3. United States—Emigration and immigration—
History. 4. Immigrants—Europe—History. 5. Immigrants—Europe—
Attitudes. 6. Europe—Emigration and immigration—History.
I. Hoerder, Dirk. II. Rössler, Horst. III. Series.
JV6450.D57   1993
304.8'73—dc20   91-33415
                                                              CIP

Manufactured in the United States of America

Contents

Distant Magnets

INTRODUCTION

From Dreams to Possibilities: The Secularization of Hope and the Quest for Independence

Dirk Hoerder

"AMERICA"—the land of opportunity? Or "America"—a place of incessant toil? The expectations of the working men and women who planned to migrate were contradictory. Which sources of information were available to them? What were the experiences following migration that modified their hopes and brought about new modes of perception?[1] What was, in fact, their destination—America, North America, the United States? "Little Chicago" was a large tenement area in a European city, which leads one to wonder: Where precisely was "America"? Many migrated instead to European destinations. Was it therefore the streets of Paris that were paved with gold? Was the Ruhr basin the promised land, with its well-paid jobs?

The Distant Magnet was the title of Philip Taylor's book on migration to North America.[2] Using the concept of migrations within the Atlantic economies as developed by the Labor Migration Project, we find, in fact, many "magnets," which differed greatly in distances expressed in miles, but not in social distance, lifestyle, occupation, and ways of working. Intra-European migrations involved larger numbers of men, women, and children than did transatlantic migrations. But to contemporaries and, until recently, to historians, too, these complex movements were less impressive than the highly visible transportation route across the Atlantic.[3] Similarly, the image of "America" seems to have eclipsed those of all other destinations.

Numerous areas and cities in Europe attracted men and women in search of work, places where industrial investment created a demand for skilled and unskilled labor, or where private incomes permitted the hiring of skilled or unskilled domestics. People migrated internally, that is, within an area of the same language and similar customs, or internationally, either within Europe or across the Atlantic. Was the destination for prospective migrants a particular political entity, with democratic structures, presumably higher wages, and better job opportunities? Or were these migrants aiming for a vaguely perceived distant land? Or merely for a particular job a friend or relative had described in a letter? Were they pushed out by economic forces or were they consciously leaving a social system that offered them no opportunities, however hard they might work?

The metaphor "magnet" may suggest an irresistible force of attraction, but, if the analogy is to be pursued, it must also be recognized that there is no undifferentiated natural law. The "pull" of a magnet does not reach most metals, and affects pieces of iron only with regard to their physical properties. The attractive aspects of distant job opportunities exerted more influence on some than on others. Within the economic constraints of the societies of origin, migration involved an individual or a family decision. It involved the consciousness that "fate," whether social forces or poor soil, could be changed by the active construction of one's own life. For most migrants, the dichotomy between drudgery and misery on earth and—after patient waiting—a better life in heaven was replaced by a different outlook: whatever migrants' perspectives on life after death, they felt now that life could be bettered on earth, either by struggles against oppressive conditions at home or by moving to better parts of the world. This might be termed a "secularization" of hope.

We argue that the particular ways in which individuals sought to improve their condition—or, more cautiously put, the reasons for geographical mobility—can only be understood with reference to the society of origin, in particular with reference to local occupational and social experiences of the prospective migrants. Analysis of their actual conditions of living and working enables us to understand their expectations of a presumably better place, be it in Berlin or in New York, in the mines of the Ruhr or of Pennsylvania. The essays in this volume therefore consider how different premigration expectations, images, and myths are created, how constant opposition between overblown hopes and sober information is reconciled into a seemingly balanced view of the migrants' destinations. These essays further explore how the test of actual living in their new worlds again modifies and transforms migrants' expectations. Postmigration experiences thus not only force the immigrants to adjust the gap between their mental world and the real one, but they also filter back as information in letters to friends and kin in the village of origin, where the process starts anew.

In the minds of many, "America" was once the land of opportunity, in the same way that Germany had been for Swedes or France for Italians. But on the basis of the new research on ethnic groups and documentation such as reports from labor-union newspapers, scholars have also found the opposite picture: Pittsburgh, Berlin, or London were places of exploitation, degrading living conditions, and police attacks on striking workers. Migrants' letters provide a differentiated view of their experiences, but the dichotomy between their "unlimited" hopes and the "limited" opportunities in the postmigration experience is never fully resolved.

Positive Clichés, Secular Religion, and Muted Criticism

Prospective migrants often had a cliché-like picture of Vienna, the emperor's city; viewed Paris, the symbol of the French Revolution, with great awe; or dreamed about America as the land of freedom and boundless wealth. We will take Vienna and Paris as examples of European destinations, and the United States as an example of the "new worlds." For a villager, however, the socioeconomic and cultural "world" was as "new" in Paris as in Chicago. New worlds abounded in the Atlantic economies, which, broadly considered, ranged from the Urals to the North American West Coast. This vast area, for which prospective migrants had to develop a mental map, had been united to some degree by trade connections and capital flows. The emerging capitalist economy, once centered in Western Europe, had spread eastward to Moscow and westward first to the thirteen English colonies and then across the North American continent. Long-distance commerce, an ever-increasing number of manufactured goods, and, finally, factory production expanded the center of this system of production and trade to include Western Europe and eastern North America, along with a peripheral circle of mining frontiers and areas of agrarian expansion and industrial investment. Both in the centers on both sides of the North Atlantic and in the peripheries a constant demand arose for more laborers, domestic servants, and skilled workers. Thus labor markets were internationalized and by means of migration ethnic communities emerged throughout the Atlantic world.

Paris was the city of the Enlightenment and the Declaration of the Rights of Man. It attracted political refugees from all over Europe: German journeymen artisans formed a colony in Paris that numbered many thousands; Polish soldiers and liberals took refuge there after 1830; a century later, Italian refugees from Mussolini's corporatist dictatorship arrived, to be followed by those escaping Nazi terror in Germany. Throughout this period, as well, there was a constant flow of French internal migrants into the capital as workers, journeymen, artisans, and small traders. In the countryside, new forms of production and the depletion of the population through out-migration were destroying many forms of social life, and the diversions of life in a large city began to seem more and more attractive. The ranks of in-migrants were augmented by men and women from Italy and from East European Jewish communities. In addition to obtaining jobs, the latter also achieved a very real civic emancipation. Thus, each of these moves across geographic space was also a move into a new social space. But doubts about the benefits of migration remained. Wasn't Paris just a city of easy pleasures, of shamefully seduced girls, of oblivion for the unsuccessful? The view of Paris, like that of all other points of destination, was ambivalent, even contradictory. The image of a capital city full of attractions was offset by fears of materialism and the danger of moral decay.[4]

As far as Vienna was concerned, the story is equally ambivalent, but somewhat different.[5] The city of Metternich and the imperial court could certainly not evoke any imagery of freedom, rights of man, or equality. Nevertheless, it was the city of the court, the nobility, and an emerging bourgeoisie. This meant employment. Skilled women were needed as cooks, unskilled ones as servants in homes and even as porters on building sites. Men could work in a large number of trades. The thriving commercial hub of the city, linked by the Danube to the Black Sea, with merchants from all over Europe, implied a multitude of job opportunities. Above all, the glitter of the court, the equipages of the rich, and the splendid edifices of the bourgeoisie all suggested great wealth. However, many of those who migrated to Vienna were not moved so much by attraction to the glittering image, but instead were being pushed out from home by parents who could not feed them, on the assumption that they would feed themselves in the city. These migrants' accounts show that fear and bewilderment were more prevalent responses to the city than appreciation of its wealth.

Both the cliché and the dismal experience of industrialization, whether in Europe or in North America, are suggested by the Moravian-born architect and art critic Adolf Loos's description of Vienna as a "Potemkin city."[6] Count Potemkin (1739–91), a Russian army leader, statesman, and influential adviser of Catherine II, had conquered the Crimea in 1783, colonized the area, and founded towns. When the tsarina, jointly with Emperor Joseph II of Austria, came to visit and to inspect the new Black Sea provinces, Potemkin had one-street artificial villages built along the route and produced cheering and contented-looking peasants, that is, recent in-migrants, as "bogus evidence of a nonexistent prosperity," as one history textbook notes.[7] In view of actual colonization efforts, however, we should be more cautious: these village facades were dreams of a prosperous future; the first steps toward that future were being made. Similarly, the development of the rapidly expanding towns in Europe, Vienna among them, and the majestic new buildings along the boulevards in Paris[8] or the Ringstrasse in Vienna suggested a prosperity that for segments of the middle classes was real, but that remained a distant goal for lower-class in-migrants, a bogus prosperity for those who could not make it under existing economic and class conditions and who had to live instead in back alleys, overcrowded tenements, or damp basements. But the latter were not merely less visible. They could, quite literally, not be seen from the places where migrants formulated their dreams and hopes.

Since the new, the exceptional, or the large capture the imagination, whereas everyday experiences are passed over in memory as "routine," their superficial splendor molded the image of cities and lent them their "magnetic" qualities. And those who migrated, whether of their own free will or by compulsion, were of an age, usually between fourteen and twenty-five, when one strikes out on one's own to make one's fortune, to become independent.

There is an underlying similarity between the destinations on both sides of the Atlantic, but one important one was neither in the minds of the migrants nor explored in this volume: in the tales of capital cities "success" mostly came about through marriage, and for women only—the female domestic who became the wife of her noble employer, the girl impressed by the fashionable military uniforms who married a hussar or a guard from the court (a clear case of Potemkin facade). Songs and children's tales provide endless variations on this theme. According to the "success" stories prevalent in the United States—namely, the Horatio Alger novels—hardworking individuals, usually men, achieve upward social mobility not, in the final count, by virtue of work, but rather through marriage to the bosses' daughters whom they had saved from drowning.

A further explanation for the persistence of the positive image or cliché is the selective flow of information back to the areas of origin from which the next group of migrants would come. It was especially the successful migrants who kept up contact with their villages and spread the word, through letters or as returnees. Those who were unsuccessful often lost contact and therefore did not correct the myths that were being perpetuated.[9] Many of the negative experiences were filtered out of the flow of information because migrants were reluctant to report their troubles. Others, especially the infirm and crippled, could hardly afford to spend money on postage. Those who died could, of course, no longer report at all. It was thus the successful who remained conspicuously present in the minds of people at home, while those who went under faded from memory.

This was the case not only for Vienna, but also for all receiving areas, whether in the Ruhr district or in the United States. The Potemkin facades that the areas of destination presented to the hopeful peasant migrants help to explain much of the dreams and grandiose imagery associated with their tales. The labor that went into the construction of both the bourgeois facade and the drab working-class back buildings, as well as the ever-increasing number of workshops and factories, explains the realistic aspect of this image of migration: the availability of jobs. The exploitation at work so vividly described in workers' and domestics' accounts is one negative side of the image.

For the United States as the receiving society, positive images and their implications differed from those of Vienna and Paris. This image developed in three stages from 1776 to 1914: from republican system, to country of free soil, to dynamic industrial society. The content of these images varied considerably between the educated middle classes and prospective settler migrants, on the one hand, and artisanal and skilled craft-worker migrants, on the other. The sequence of the stages in the transformation of this image also varied in Great Britain, northern Europe and Germany, and north- and southeastern Europe. Thus the image of "free soil" or cheap homesteads was an issue in Great Britain from about 1815; it reached peasants in Hungary only from the 1870s onward.

The origins of the positive image of a free country date back to the 1770s. The debates over the American Declaration of Independence and the Constitution deeply influenced European liberal political circles during the entire age of revolution. American political institutions were the reference point for many debates on republican goals among European reformers and revolutionaries.[10] The "orderly" transition from one political status to another became the model for most middle-class reformers. It was assiduously contrasted with the bloodshed of the French Revolution. The plebeian democratic traditions that emerged from the latter remained for a long time in the shadows.[11] As a result, the broad range of literature on America as a land of republican and, later, democratic institutions, once published, took hold in the minds of many. In Eastern Europe, where the American Revolution also served as a point of reference, the appeal was less broad, given the rate of literacy and the more limited size of reformist political elites. An analysis of the use that contemporary admirers of the newly formed United States of America made of the Constitution proves that they interpreted the texts according to their own requirements and knew little about American social and economic realities. The texts became a source for inspirational quotations rather than being understood as a framework for one specific political system.

The young United States as a real political entity thus became an idealized construct in the minds of European reformers. This middle-class image was also to have an impact on the lower classes.[12] With certain corrections, it was in the minds of the refugees from the 1848–49 revolutions who came from the Czech regions, from Hungary, and, in larger numbers, from the German states.[13] Expectations of liberty, considerably toned down, also brought refugees fleeing persecution under the German anti-Socialist laws (1878–90) and from the failed Russian revolution of 1905.[14]

From the 1820s to the 1880s, letters from immigrant settlers confirmed many aspects of the image: most officials could be elected; even the president was "Mister" and not "Your Excellency"; there were no swarms of arrogant tithe-, tax-, and fee-collecting officials. From the letters it is obvious that particularly the latter aspect—in the old countries often economically destructive—was a highly valued part of the acculturation experience of the migrants. The everyday repression and humiliation experienced in Europe from petty officials with high notions of their own importance had been left behind, and this resulted in a very concrete notion of what freedom meant in practice.[15]

The second stage in the development of the image of "America" was the availability of land in sufficient amounts at comparatively cheap prices or for a nominal fee. Pressed for land because of partible inheritance, or with extra sons and daughters to be sent off from areas of primogeniture, threatened by expanding (capitalist-oriented) landlords or by remnant feudal forms of dependence, unable to shoulder the burdens imposed on them through the abolition of serfdom, those European smallholders and their sons and daughters who could sell sufficient possessions to afford the passage and a new farm looked to "America" as the fulfillment of their hopes.[16] Such hopes, and their fulfillment, could not, usually, be entertained by the landless poor, for whom the cost of the move was prohibitive. On the other hand, the move seemed attractive to artisans and skilled workers who had left agricultural pursuits only a short time before and who felt increasing discontent with changing conditions of production.[17]

Again, part of this image was nothing but a mental construct, unrelated to reality, in which there were no swamps, no disease-ridden, mosquito-infested lands, no disputed claims or struggles with cattlemen. The image was modified, but left essentially intact by reports that only hardworking healthy migrants could succeed. There were no chances for the infirm or the elderly. Life in isolated farming areas could be solitary, could involve living in dug-outs for the first year or two, and could imply mere subsistence farming since markets were distant. Women evaluated the opportunities to acquire land more cautiously than men. They, too, wanted a better future for themselves and their children, but they knew that homesteading meant geographical distance from neighbors and few or no social contacts. They also experienced the departure from the culture of origin more sharply than the men, who occupied a more marginal place in social networks. It was the women who held families together and who were emotionally supported by female kin. They had more to lose than men. But they could also win: in America they did not have to work in the fields. Thus the image of America also had gender-specific characteristics.

After the Civil War, during the phase of rapid industrialization, the third stage in the life of the positive image of America emerged. The rapid growth of the cities, the speed of factory growth, and the pace of mechanization merged in the notion that "America" was a country of speed, great size, and huge factories. Just as numerous novels about settler migrants had shaped the previous image, accounts of traveling technicians and engineers now influenced public opinion.[18] Gender-specific aspects again emerged. Women were treated better in the United States. They could get jobs. As domestics, they had regulated hours and wages.[19]

By this time, these several images of the United States had

coalesced into a myth of "America" that encompassed a more desirable state of political affairs, a smaller degree of social differentiation, the possibility of acquiring land, more desirable conditions in general, abundance of opportunities, vastness, and perhaps even a gold rush or a rags-to-riches experience to complete the picture. This myth also began to develop a life of its own, separate from its original geographical location. In Europe, particularly large tenement areas were called "Groß-Amerika"; the rapid expansion of cities was referred to as planning "the American way"; and, in industry, there was production "on an American scale." In the 1920s, when Siberia was opened up, providing fascinating opportunities (along with accommodations in sod houses, primitive log cabins, and the like) it was called "another America." A return migrant from Poland, having now acquired land in his home village, noted that "now there is going to be America." "America" had become a mythical yardstick. Even though growth rates with regard to population influx or industrial output in some European cities, or opportunities on the Siberian frontier, matched those in North America, these developments and achievements in Europe were not evaluated in their own right.[20]

The positive image of America remained intact even when, as in the case of European cities, a countervailing negative, but less powerful, image emerged: America was purely materialistic, a land where nothing but money counted. It was considered dangerous in general, unsafe for women, conducive to the loss of spiritual values, and governed by crass materialism. The image of dangerous living conditions reflected understandable fears about life in distant unknown areas, but also—in the case of migration into cities—an uneasiness about lifestyles there. Unsanitary living conditions had led to extremely high death rates, making constant in-migration necessary in order for a city even to maintain its population at a stable level. But these conditions improved, particularly over the second half of the nineteenth century.[21] Migrants complained about the speed and pace of life. For example, Italian statistics suggest a higher rate of mental disturbance among returnees.

The repeated warnings about the dangers presented by migration to what contemporaries considered female virtues reflect more on gender relations than on migration. Out-migration of women who had violated standards of conduct, unaccompanied travel by women, accommodation on ships not segregated according to sex, and women being accosted by men with dubious intentions in the ports of arrival may all have added to these traditional societal (or male) concerns. The sources reveal only a limited number of complaints by women about sexual harassment. The position of domestics in the homes of their employers and below-subsistence wages in some female occupations, especially the needle trades, substantiated some of the concern. Greater opportunities of choice for women—choices not sanctioned within the standards of parents and the home, deliberate childbearing out of wedlock, and union with a man without the sanction of marriage were under some legal systems an efficient way to avoid descent into marital bondage. In a legal system in which women are subject to the total authority of their husbands, have to give any wages they might earn to their husbands, have to transfer property owned before marriage to their husbands, and lose custody of their children upon divorce to their former husbands—union without the sanction of civil or Church marriage permits women to retain control over their property, wages, and children. The choice of such unconventional roles or behavior demonstrated independent female decision making that was quite rational, but that violated traditional roles.[22]

The third aspect of the negative image—loss of spiritual values and the predominance of new materialistic attitudes—merits considerable attention. Migrants moved not only across geographical space but also into new value systems. As a result, friends and kin often could not understand their new forms of behavior. When migrants failed to contribute to family income in the village of origin this was taken as evidence of a materialistic disregard of family ties. Although such behavior may have stemmed from situations such as poor economic conditions in the regions where migrants settled, technical and legal problems in communication, and new priorities of migrants contemplating quasi-permanent residence, it was labeled as egotistical craving for private gain by those remaining in the culture of origin.

Even more important, settlers and labor migrants aimed to improve their material standard of living. Coming into societies where many if not most relations of exchange were mediated by money, and where neighborly help and kinship systems of support did not exist, led to an emphasis on material success. Some migrants complained that their reputation was dependent only on the amount of dollars they made. But they were certainly not considering return to social hierarchies and deference systems. They might have wished for greater consideration of skills or of cultural achievements, but they did not reject, *per se*, the notion of making money. What seems to have inspired much of the criticism of materialism was the move from the social relations of agrarian and village economies into capitalist wage economies. Thus, the critical attitudes toward migrants' economic behavior and the migrants' own doubts were basically an uneasiness about different economic value systems.

Furthermore, family expectations at home were materialistic, too. The migrant—like others from the village—was supposed to improve the whole family's standing. In extremely poor regions there was the certainty that, however bad the situation of the out-migrated son or daughter might be, he or she could not be fed at home.[23] If the migrants failed to send money, family expectations were destroyed and the family's standing in the village damaged. Historians, too, have taken remittances of money by migrants for granted, and have overlooked migrants' requests for money to help them out of distress.

During the nineteenth century, the construct of an "America" where everything was better—the secularization of hope—became the focus of a kind of new belief, a secular religion: the other, new, world was not a paradise of eternal bliss, but a world in which one's personal condition could be improved through choice, work, and increased opportunities. Those remaining behind and those ready to leave clung tenaciously to their hopes. In their minds, "America" did not merely signify a new country; it meant a better world.

In comparative perspective, "America" was only the best-known of such better worlds, a world that happened to send out recruiting agents, to have a Statue of Liberty in its main port of arrival,[24] and to cultivate an ideology of opportunity and liberty. In this sense the images of "America" and of the nation "U.S.A." interact. People migrated to a myth-shrouded "America" and found themselves in a political entity called the "U.S.A.," where they could gain the vote or join political machines, where some political institutions seemed more responsive than those in the old country. One saying, in the German-language version, often repeated in songs, proclaimed "Auf nach Amerika," "Let's go to America." This phrase reflected the image of the ideal. Another, often heard in Eastern European languages— "to bread"—was different. No country is mentioned, but a very basic economic goal, to have enough food, is pursued. This phrase reflected the sober reality,[25] and reflects differences in the images of America held by various ethnic groups.

Expectations of Labor Migrants and the Differentiated Image of America

By the 1840s, migration for the purpose of finding wage labor already comprised two-thirds of total migration to the United States: one-third of the migrants were artisans and skilled workers, and one-third were unskilled workers. The proportion of farmers shrank from about 33 percent in the 1840s to below 5 percent in the 1890s. Although the "settlement migrants" who planned to buy land and settle permanently had to rely on guidebooks prepared by individual travelers or issued by agents of state governments with the purpose of attracting farmers, the labor migrants who worked for a long term in construction or as industrial laborers could rely on a variety of publications giving detailed information. Trade-union newspapers and letters from earlier migrants, especially, provided migrants from industrializing countries with a much more differentiated image of their new destination than could be inferred from clichés.[26]

An analysis of regional origin, occupational background, cultural values, and time of emigration is necessary to keep in view the complex factors influencing expectations, and an analysis of the manifold sources of information is equally necessary if we are to understand the views held by migrants about the area to which they were moving.[27] The English painters who in the course of a year moved between Scotland, London, and New York, depending on the season, the Italian agricultural workers who traveled each year to Argentina, or the Belgians who moved to France—all had detailed knowledge about relative wages and cost of living, of working conditions and peaks of demand for their labor.

The complexity of the information available to labor migrants in particular is evident from a recent study by John Laslett of the migration of Scottish miners to North America during the second half of the nineteenth century. Laslett analyzes the Lanarkshire culture of origin during a specified period (1850–76). Investigating the views of prospective and actual migrants, who at the beginning were still deeply influenced by pre-industrial values and ways of living, he stresses the role of the miners' union, which considered emigration to be one alternative to strikes, and even established "emigration committees" to initiate or support migration. The role of the labor press (Glasgow Sentinel) in the process of information distribution is significant since this information came directly from migrants (in the form of published letters) and initiated a debate about the advantages and disadvantages of migration. Laslett situates the position of the miners' union within the traditions of the British labor movement. Did migration lead to acquiescence in the area of origin, because the most militant workers left? Did it strengthen transatlantic competition in production? Did it ease the local labor-market situation and perhaps even create a shortage of labor that would, in turn, lead to wage increases?[28]

The lively discussions among Scottish miners also had to do with the alternatives awaiting them in the society of arrival: the return to agrarian pursuits (from which many nineteenth-century workers were hardly a generation removed); work in traditional forms of production, thus avoiding impending changes at home; work in more mechanized forms of production in the hope of concomitant wage increases. Options were many and expectations and intentions varied. These all became part of a rational well-informed decision-making process. Horst Rössler and Franco Ramella follow Laslett's approach in their analysis of the reasons for migration among British potters, and Italian weavers and building-workers, respectively.[29]

Among prospective migrants, such discussions hardly ever dealt with the United States as a political entity. They centered on a particular labor market in a particular location and included an evaluation of living conditions there. Of course, aspects of hope colored the migrants' expectations. But these men and women went neither to "America," nor "to bread." They migrated between similar labor markets dispersed throughout the Atlantic economies in pursuit of consciously determined goals.

This process of the selection of goals and destination was limited by migration traditions. Labor markets to which there had been no "pioneer" migration and about which the labor press provided no information could not be included in the deliberations about the relative advantages of work opportunities. "Opportunity" could mean both the chance to exploit all possibilities for a higher material standard of living ("acquisitive mentality") or the chance to continue to work according to traditional methods that were being eroded at home ("craft consciousness"). Thus, the image of America depended on prospective migrants' attitudes toward their work. Less detailed information was available from the pages of the labor press for most occupations and labor markets in many countries from the 1870s or 1880s onward. We will take the German press as an example, as its stance was comparable to that of other national labor presses.

German-language Social Democrats in Europe and America kept in relatively close contact from the 1870s to the early 1900s, publishing information in *Der Sozialdemokrat*. Trade-union publications followed suit when their umbrella organization, the Allgemeiner Deutscher Gewerkschaftsbund (General German Trade Union Federation) was established in 1890 and began to publish its *Correspondenzblatt* in 1891.[30]

The *Correspondenzblatt* reported regularly about the annual conventions of the American Federation of Labor (AFL). Although criticism was voiced concerning some AFL positions, the reports show a basic admiration for the large organization, a state of affairs that the German unions were just beginning to set as their goal. By the mid-1890s the tone of the reports had changed. The conservative policies of the AFL were criticized; cooperation with the National Civic Federation of progressive capitalists was viewed with derision. Articles in the *Correspondenzblatt* also dealt with working and living conditions in the United States. Higher wages, potential migrants were warned, would be offset by higher living costs.[31] In the 1880s the *Sozialdemokrat* concluded that American society was dominated by capitalism, especially by the monopolies, and, quoting the *New Yorker Volkszeitung*, that nowhere in the world were the differences between exploiters and exploited as great.[32]

Some positive aspects received mention: for example, the productivity of American agriculture. Such evaluations, it should be noted, contained an element of international competition. The interest in a better standard of living for workers was closely entwined with an interest in the division of the world's resources among nations. In view of the advanced position of the United States in some fields, the *Sozialdemokrat* quoted Goethe: "America, you are better off." But this praise for real achievements was paralleled by an implicit recognition that the social ideal (and myth) of "America" was a goal to be achieved everywhere in the world: "a politically and socially liberated Germany, that is our America."[33]

The *Sozialdemokrat* opposed emigration: emigration deflected attention from the causes of the miserable social conditions at home, the ranks of the discontented were thinned, and the most energetic part of the population was lost to the country.[34] The ambivalence toward the United States continued throughout the reporting in the *Sozialdemokrat*. When the struggle for the eight-hour day gained momentum in the United States, it quoted Goethe again, but when German migrants suffered under American economic crises it opined that "emigration is often a change for the worse."[35]

By the end of the 1880s the *Sozialdemokrat* was expressing admiration for technological innovation, thus contributing to the image of a more dynamic society. Analysis, however, followed swiftly: mechanization meant unemployment and reduced wages, on the one hand, increased productivity, on the other. The role of unskilled workers would therefore gain in importance, and they might be used as strikebreakers. Or, as the *Sozialdemokrat* recognized, contrary to the view of most AFL unions, unskilled workers would have to be organized, too. Political activity on the part of workers' organizations was absolutely necessary to avoid forms of wage slavery worse than chattel slavery, according to the *Sozialdemokrat*.[36]

An essay by Philipp Rappaport from Indianapolis, Indiana, published in *Neue Zeit* summarized labor's views by arguing that even during the Haymarket persecution, freedom of speech and of the press was comparatively greater in the United States than in any European country. But he contrasted this advantage with the hierarchical structure of American organizations, especially trade unions and political institutions. The Knights of Labor suffered from the influence and accommodationist position of Powderly; the U.S. president was more powerful than the king of England. Americans themselves succumbed to myths: since the founding period, a national pride had developed that might have been justified then, but that now led to self-conceit: "And this feeling of superiority is encouraged from above so that—and this is hardly an exaggeration—the poorest devil carries his suffering more easily, because it is American suffering."[37]

While this may well have been an overstatement, it points to issues that have not been investigated by migration researchers. Does migration and the process of acculturation lead to an overblown pride in achievements,[38] especially material achievements, thus giving substance to the oft-voiced fears about the materialism of the receiving societies? Does the creation of societies mainly composed of in-migrants lead to insecurity because the forces of tradition and the experience of generations cannot be used as legitimizing factors?

From this summary of information available to labor migrants and the resulting image of America that emerges, the role of women is lacking. It was not discussed in the labor press, and men, including the socialists among them, expected women to remain in the family. German women, however, established their own separate migration networks. Their image of women in America was characterized by higher status, greater freedom to dress as one pleased, which included the right to wear fine dresses, and by opportunity for employment and economic independence. Women who emigrated to America from Germany entered both the labor force and the public sphere, as did women from other countries.[39]

Contrary to the specific expectations of clearly defined groups of skilled workers and the broad information available from the labor press, peasants from Southern and Eastern Europe, who came *en masse* as unskilled workers, had a different approach to the labor market and to the land across the ocean. Their information came from agents who exaggerated the positive features of "America"; from debates in the general press, often critical of emigration; and from warnings by landlords, priests, and local entrepreneurs.[40] Two sets of expectations may be discerned for these groups. One was typical for peasant families who were sufficiently well off that they could expect to buy land in North America, or to use a period of temporary proletarianization to accumulate funds to increase land holdings in the village of origin and thus avoid permanent proletarianization there. The other set was that of men and women who no longer saw any opportunities for themselves in agriculture. They migrated within the norms of a family economy that imposed on them the duty to continue to contribute to family income from afar. It might also impose on them the establishment of a "branch base" for the family: they had to earn enough money to send tickets for other family members and to get them started in the new surroundings. Both the hope for land and the expected regular remittances contributed to a certain proximity of their expectations to the positive cliché outlined above.

Two kinds of influences contributed, both to reinforcement and to differentiation of peasants' hopes. One was counseling "from above," from landlords, the nobility, priests, or local dignitaries; the other was the advice gleaned from the letters of earlier migrants. It is very important to take into account the fact that counseling "from above" came from the perennial opponents of the peasants and agrarian laborers, from those who lived on their labor and demanded from them services, fees, tithes, and taxes. Any advice from this quarter was considered to be dictated by its material interests alone.[41] Thus when landlords advised about poor chances for improvement in "America," lower-class recipients of such advice felt confirmed in their view of better conditions in the new country. Communication from the top down was almost automatically reinterpreted from below. East Elbian landlords, Biellese factory-owners, and Budapest industrialists had to replace out-migrating labor at their own cost. The depletion of the labor force could lead to wage increases and proposals for social reform. In warning potential migrants about poor conditions in other labor markets, the employers and landlords were suggesting that the workers stay at home and continue to be exploited. In these societies no communication across class boundaries was possible. In view of this, the distrust of one's "superiors" was not as irrational as it might appear.

The prevalence of the positive image, at least at the time of departure, is related both to deep hopes about better possibilities of living a decent and "honest" life and to bargaining power gained at home with this new possibility of withdrawing one's labor not by striking, but by leaving.

The letters written home by emigrants came as constant reminders that opportunities were only for the strong and the healthy, for "prime workers," to adopt a designation used in chattel slavery. While many of these letters contained money or prepaid tickets they also contained concrete information about labor-market opportunities, or the lack of them. Although no comparative studies of letters from different ethnic groups exist as yet, the analysis of German letters indicates that migrants presented the evidence for and against emigrating, advised the prospective migrants to make up their minds themselves, and were cautious not to invite anyone because on their arrival newcomers would expect to "cash in" on promises made earlier.[42]

In Ireland, and perhaps in Eastern Europe as well, negative information seems to have had less of an impact than the positive for another reason as well. In areas where it was difficult for rural laborers and smallholding peasants to obtain cash, where cash belonged to village traders and those who were better off, even small cash remittances were an indication that the sender was well-off. What would the impact of the letters have been if, rather than cash, they had contained goods instead—food, clothes, perhaps appliances? Independent decisions as to how to spend the money would have been replaced by dependent consumption, as was common in societies relying on exchange of services and barter.

All reports about exploitation, poor housing, and irregular employment notwithstanding, people continued to move. In view of the conditions in the areas of origin, this is not surprising. Men and women being pushed out of families, friendship networks, and local economies, or—put more actively—making the choice between dependent positions in (below-) subsistence economies and positions in wage-economies, did not need much further inducement. The positive image of opportunities after migration was in many cases but a reflection of the fact that conditions at home could not get much worse.

A Measure of Independence and Its Cost

The improvement that migrants were looking for has been described vaguely as "to America," or, more concretely, as "cerca di lavoro"—in

search of work—and "za chlebem"—"to bread." Migrants were looking for guaranteed subsistence, for a regular income. The dream of
finding gold seems to have been more in the minds of those who
stayed at home than in the minds of those men and women who
actually undertook the move. Opportunities to support oneself and
one's family better by moving to areas with more jobs had to be
seized. As one Italian migrant said, it would have been "dishonest" to
his family had he not taken the chance.[43]

Furthermore, people did not migrate only for bread and work;
they also migrated for social conditions where outward signs of social
rank and social submissiveness were less strong—where any man
might wear a hat, a sign of status and the prerogative of only the
better sort in the culture of origin, and where any woman, even a
servant, might wear a bonnet, at home a sign of insolence to the
employer that would be duly punished. People in America did not
have to cringe before employers, they did not even have to doff their
caps when asking for work, as German, Swiss, and Swedish workers
reported.[44] There was relatively little talk about republican institutions or democratic society in the letters of labor migrants, but much
about these very modest signs of not being chained to one's place in
society. But even these advances often remained slight: the men
waiting for a job in front of the stockyard gates had to tip the
policemen or the foremen, women in the New York garment industries reported that the boss expected "favors," newcomers escaping
the arrogance of the upper classes experienced the scorn of natives.
Still, minute differences were perceptible to the migrants.

Most important to migrants was the feeling of taking one's
"fate," one's life, into one's own hands, the feeling of being able to do
something, the feeling of attaining a measure of independence, albeit
a small one. Migrating English potters emphasized this aspect, as did
New England mill girls. East European peasants cherished this new
experience, as did Finnish women.[45]

This notion of independence had as many specific aspects as
there were occupational, cultural, and gender groups involved. Independence had different meanings for different classes in society. For
the dominant classes, independence (as an aspect of the ideology of
the "self-made man," implying unlimited upward social mobility)
served as a justification of their own economic and political power.
For artisans and skilled workers, it often meant the exertion of control over working hours and pace of work; it meant the opportunity to
establish their own class and ethnic institutions (political parties,
unions, cooperatives, churches, and so on).

For the great mass of the lower classes, perhaps the most widespread notion of independence was that of no longer being dependent (and a burden) on their struggling families. To earn one's own living, even a scanty one, was better than being fed on a small farm with no work, being allowed to sleep in the corner of a hut, being an old maid or a surplus son at home. Earning one's own living also meant freedom of choice: to spend one's own money as one saw fit, and to decide how to spend one's hours off work. Nevertheless, migrants' letters also contained bitter warnings: endless hours of work in tenement sweatshops, interminable drudgery in the Monongahela valley steelworks, the terror of underground work in the mines. Independence? They were being treated in just the same way as beasts of burden were at home, many immigrants complained.[46]

Independent choices were also possible when deciding on careers. Migration permitted skilled workers and artisans to remain in their craft; if not regular employment, it permitted at least employment more regular than that available at home. Skills acquired in an artisan workshop at home could be transferred to a foreman's position in a factory in the new society. While capitalist market structures were penetrating the remotest corners of Europe, while village life was not immutable, unchanging over centuries, industrializing centers everywhere were more dynamic and offered a wider range of choices, and were unencumbered by stifling traditions.

On the whole, the improvements expected by migrants were in many cases so limited that there was no disillusionment upon arrival. They expected jobs to be available and work to be hard. They did not assume that employment would be less exploitative. Only the ballast, the parasitic officialdom, and not the power relationships, would be cast off by migration. But, again, skewed communication structures sometimes garbled the message. A South Slav worker wrote home that he could afford to polish his boots in America, a modest advance indeed. But at home his fellow villagers knew for certain that only the lords polished their boots. From this, they concluded that the migrant lived like a lord, which meant white bread, meat every day, and not having to work.

Independence was not without its costs. Networks of kin and friends had to be left behind and were lost. Peasants who had once tilled the soil in the open air had to work hundreds of feet underground or in the deafening noise of machine-filled factories. The loss of family networks also meant a loss of social security. The infirm, the weak, and the old had no place in the new society, as emigrants never tired of repeating. Was this simply accepted or did it weigh on the minds of migrant men and women? Mental illness among return migrants seems to have been proportionally higher than among first-time out-migrants. Men and women in the 20–40-year age group increased their own hopes when leaving home, but destroyed their parents' hopes of being cared for in old age. The social contract between the generations was broken. Did a feeling of guilt result from this? No money remittances could make up for the care that the old expected.

It is important to try to understand the emotional cost of migration both to those who left and to those who remained. Women's testimony, in particular, expressed sadness about leaving social networks and beloved ones. The Macedonian word for migration also meant "sorrow."[47] At the turn of the century, as opposed to the days of sailing ships, many migrants experienced journeying back and forth in a very matter-of-fact way. But women's letters, systems of social relations, Moberg's Swedish novels, and the Irish experience suggest that the emotional impact of migration, individual and collective, still escapes us. Kerby Miller's concluding essay in this volume superbly comes to grip with these questions.

A Comparative Approach to Migrant Mentalities: Unlimited Hopes and Modest Expectations

In contrast to earlier general studies of the image of America, the essays in this volume analyze migrant mentalities in specific regions and periods, thus permitting a more concrete and comprehensive description than that conveyed by a vague myth. Whenever possible, specific occupational groups are studied in depth to evaluate their collective social as well as individual interests, which influence their perception of opportunities after migration. For example, in East European peasant societies the factor of surplus population and the hope of owning land influence the migrants' expectations and attitudes toward their destinations. Furthermore, by viewing the image of America within a comparative perspective, the qualities of a range of industrializing destinations can be distinguished from those specific to the United States.

In the first part of this volume the images of different industrializing areas within Europe are compared. Two capital cities, Paris and Vienna, serve as examples. Migrants in other cities—London, Berlin, St. Petersburg, or Stockholm—had similar experiences. In the second part, the expectations of Poles and Italians migrating either to

European destinations or to the United States are analyzed and compared. Essays in the third section deal with the overpowering image of America, the detailed expectations of specific groups of migrants, and realistic information about specific labor markets and conditions of work available to migrants from England, Scandinavia, the Magyar areas, the South Slav region, and Italy. Studies of the disillusionments of Italian migrants and East European peasant workers, and the profound emotional experiences of Irish migrants, conclude the volume.

Research on migrants' expectations and clichés draws on a broad variety of sources and demands interpretative integration. Statistics, trade-union materials, and analysis of methods of production elucidate the social, political, and economic circumstances in the society of origin. It was on the basis of their social background and their particular skills—or lack of them—that migrants formulated their specific expectations. Moreover, the emigrants' vague hopes and dreams are expressed through more personal, "everyday" documents. The climate of opinion in the home society and prevailing images of a country, area, or city of destination are reflected in oral traditions, in "trivial" as well as in "high" literature, in letters, diaries, songs and poems, tales and jokes.[48] On the basis of such sources, prospective migrants developed their particular images of the destination they wanted to reach. For historians, migrants' use of these sources may be difficult to interpret and some social scientists have shied away from such "impressionistic" materials for methodological reasons. However, any historiographical approach to the study of mentalities has to rely also on those sources that shaped the migrants' view of the world they wanted to reach. Once migration had assumed massive proportions, information became much more differentiated. In addition to emigration guides and the reports of returnees, two other important sources of information were available: letters from America and reports in the labor press. The letters, in particular, provide individual views of the new society that could have performed a corrective function with regard to the all-encompassing clichés prevalent at the time.

The migrations into expanding European cities were composed of many elements. Men and women from the surrounding rural areas (short-distance migration) originally came on a seasonal basis, or perhaps for a period of several years. But this form of migration became increasingly as permanent as did long-distance, or even transatlantic migration. Both of the essays on Paris and Vienna take up this theme. The industries and mines of the Ruhr Basin, on the other hand, had depleted the local reservoirs of labor, and as a consequence of this Polish miners were recruited.

As transportation improved and the pace of commercial and industrial development accelerated, so too did the distances migrants traveled become less intimidating. The traditional migrations of the journeymen artisans were replaced by those of skilled and unskilled workers. The German artisans' colonies in Paris and London declined in importance. Traditional directions of migration were redirected in the nineteenth century to new destinations. Skilled workers and engineers now migrated into industrializing areas to increase their expertise, as is shown by C. H. Riegler, taking the Swedish migrations to Germany, Great Britain, and the United States as examples.[49]

The labor migrations and those of experts in search of additional knowledge were supplemented by the movements of political refugees also in search of an economic basis for survival: forty-eighters and German socialists in the United States, Italian leftists, and, later, anti-fascists in Paris. These groups were particularly eloquent in voicing their views of the host society and their accounts often overshadowed those of the much more numerous labor migrants. This is clearly true for Paris. By 1911, 15 percent of all foreigners in Paris were Italians, the vast majority of them workers. But the image of the city as reconstructed from the sources available is that of Italian *literati* and union activists. Similarly, German images of the United States were for a long time strongly influenced by the writings of a few thousand "forty-eighter" liberals and socialists who left because of anti-Socialist laws.

One aspect of migration that runs through the essays in this volume is the heterogeneity of the images potential migrants had of large cities and industrializing areas. Labor migrants, "educational" migrants (engineers), and political refugees all contributed varying features to these images, features that in themselves were contradictory. Labor migrants saw job opportunities and exploitation, engineers saw technological potential and discrimination on ethnic grounds, refugees saw liberty as well as the inequalities of the new society.

This raises a further question. Were expectations similar for European and North American destinations? We have argued in our research on migration in the Atlantic economies that conditions throughout this large migration system were comparable. To some degree the essays confirm this interpretation. Hopes for employment, better working conditions, and security of employment were similar on both sides of the Atlantic, and magnets attracting labor migrants were found over the whole area. This is shown by Ramella for Italians in southern France and the northeastern United States. But differences also emerge. As has been shown, the image of the United States not only became stronger than all others, but also had mythical aspects. Such quasi-religious beliefs in a better world did not exist for European destinations. Clichés did differ from continent to continent.

Polish miners going to the Ruhr District had an unemotional, sober image of conditions there, as Anna Reczyńska found. Those coming from the Polish territories occupied by Prussia knew what to expect from the authorities, and the area's image never became mythical: liberty, gold, or fabulous riches were never associated with its smokestacks and underground coal seams. But even for destinations veiled by an image of fabulous riches, this image differed to a considerable degree from that of the United States. In the gold rush in distant California everybody could participate. Wages were so high that, figuratively speaking, the streets in America were indeed paved with gold. Wealth was accumulated by self-made men. Thus everybody had a chance. In the El Dorado of Vienna, which is here explored by Michael John and Albert Lichtblau, fabulous riches also existed, but the gold stayed in the coffers of the nobility, and the wealth was inherited. It was the aristocratic glitter that determined the image rather than imaginary nuggets on the banks of the Danube.

The dominant image, that of "America," is approached from several different perspectives. Horst Rössler analyzes one occupational group, England's Staffordshire potters in the 1840s. These potters, still close both to the soil and to independent artisan work, had begun an intensive discussion on the merits of emigration. Analysis of the labor market in manufacture and industrial production led to a policy of encouraging emigration. The experiences that shaped expectations were the agrarian and artisanal traditions, as well as a growing division of labor in expanding manufacturing production. Accordingly, some of the migrants went back to the land, others cherished their regained artisanal independence, and still others tried to establish manufactories of their own. Few of the migrants fell for any "Eden-like beauty of nature" or other such imagery. The majority relied on information from letters and a sober evaluation of what could be achieved.

The migration of Swedish and Danish workers from the 1870s to about 1910 is explored by Claudius H. Riegler. These migrants were able to form their opinion from the labor press. The "educational migration" of Swedish skilled workers and engineers, for example, led—through return migration—to a broad flow of information about wages in the United States, as well as the dissemination of technological innovations. (This should be compared to Riegler's studies of Swedish labor migration within Europe.) To these two sources have to be added emigrant letters. On the basis of this information, migrants hoped for better educational opportunities for their children, an environment fostering independent decision making about the conduct of their life outside of working hours, and a more democratic political and social structure. Most admitted after migration that their expectations had had to be reduced somewhat, but only in a fourth area, the level of wages to be earned, had they really deceived themselves. On the other hand, they knew about the risks: high accident and unemployment rates, the absence of any kind of social security. The extreme exploitation of female domestics in Sweden and the vulnerability of their position, with no recourse to law or authority, made them the only group that had an overly positive image of opportunities in the United States. In answer to the questions of government interviewers, migrants clearly expressed both their discontent with the old society and their satisfaction with the new society, despite its limitations.

For Italian migrants, whether headed for the South of France or the New Jersey textile industry, the main information channels were kinship, friendship, and village ties and networks, as Franco Ramella points out. For them America is Paterson, New Jersey—not the myth without limits, but one single town with jobs in the silk industry. Expectations changed in the course of their stay. Upon arrival, their main frame of reference consisted of the wage levels and standard of living in their home town, Biella: the move to "Patermerica," their view of Paterson as America, appeared to be an improvement. After a few years they no longer compared themselves with their cousins at home but to native-born Americans, and felt that they were not receiving their due.

Images held by migrants from Eastern Europe were less realistic. Jews going to Paris achieved emancipation, but had only limited opportunities to earn a secure income and often had to compromise in questions of religion and culture, as Nancy L. Green argues below. Polish migrants to North America sometimes even believed that the passage would be free. What people knew about "America" remained vague, at times quasi-religious: a place for good boys after death, as one schoolboy assumed. Anna Reczyńska summarizes the typical views: easier farming, refreshing air, cheap bread, and plenty of money.

The essay by Julianna Puskás on the image of America argues that there was a "battle" over the image: those profiting from emigration propagated overblown accounts of opportunities, while those who wanted people to stay at home, that is, landowners wanting to be able to rely on a large pool of cheap labor, and politicians wanting to prevent a loss of population, deliberately spread a negative counter-image. This battle for the allegiance of the lower classes, however, did not extend to the rural populace. Letters, other information, and especially the remittances of money influenced the images and the specific personal expectations they held. In view of the poverty at home, the incoming dollars suggested an El Dorado, where people got rich quickly. The adjustment to reality was expressed in images of hard work and hard times which, however, eventually would lead to success. Lack of success was never analyzed in terms of the shortcomings of the new society but as an individual failing only.

For Slovene migrants, too—according to Matjaž Klemenčič—the image of America oscillated between a country with mountains of gold and one of terrible suffering in poorly paid industrial jobs. America was a labor market for healthy males, the common view held. It was also seen as a country free from the cultural oppression of the old world. A theme not mentioned in the other essays, but important all over Eastern Europe, and probably in Germany and Sweden, too, was the novel view that businessmen, officials, and the wealthy actually worked. To people who had never seen even small businessmen do any work themselves, this was a sign of equality. But it may also have served to strengthen the misleading impression that it was work that would make people rich.

The essay by Rosoli develops the dialectical character of the myth of America that turns the land of promise into one of bitter disillusionment: migrants who had left their home country, which was unrewarding, ungrateful to its sons and daughters, found America ungrateful, too. Work was extremely hard; the law accorded labor no protection. Opportunities were limited and bore no relation to the hopes that had been entertained. Political activity, if aiming at any fundamental reform of the system, placed many Italians in the role of outcasts, while for two of them—Sacco and Vanzetti—it brought imprisonment and death. The initial promise of the Italian-American communities, which once combined the new—land and work—with the memories of the old relationships—epitomized by naming the new community after the old village—turned conventional: elites and nationalism came to structure their society and ideology. By showing the interaction of the myths of Old and New World, and of these myths with the community of migrants itself, Rosoli is able to chart the dynamics of image transformation. He also takes up the comparative theme again. "America" in Italian usage is "the Americas"—Argentina, Brazil, and the United States.

The experience met by migrants in "America" deflated their dreams immediately. Ewa Morawska shows that they compared their working life to the way beasts of burden were treated at home. The way they were ordered to work overtime and to do shifts on Sundays and on holidays reminded them of how the lords of the manor had treated them at home. Only after establishing a base in an ethnic community and relative job security did they begin to be able to enjoy the food, which was better and cheaper than at home. Perhaps this comparison says something about the dreams before departure, too. If society was divided into high and low with no steps in between, the move to the United States and the better life must be the one, albeit huge, step to a lordly position. Only after arrival did migrants realize the endless steps that had to be climbed, often with no handrail, to reach even an intermediate position.

The migrants thus all had complex expectations: they hoped for economic betterment, they aspired to a better social position, and they knew that they wanted to determine their own life courses—they wanted to be independent. Their image of the new world had both an economic and an emotional aspect.

The emotional aspect is the main concern of Kerby A. Miller's study of the hopes of Irish men and women. The diametrically opposed images of America in Ireland as the "land of gold" or the "land of sweat and snakes" persisted throughout the nineteenth century, reflecting contradictions and tensions in Irish society. Miller concentrates on the structure of rural families in the West. Emotional pressure and psychological strains are reflected in views on emigration and the New World. The Irish "often interpreted migration itself in terms of individual obligation and sacrifice, rather than ambition and opportunity," Miller concludes.

These essays reflect not only the variety of hopes and experiences of immigrants from more than a dozen cultures, but also the scholarly discourse of historians and sociologists from ten different countries. Approaches to source materials differ, as do the sources themselves. In Sweden the memory of migration is still very much present in the minds of the population, whereas in Germany it is almost forgotten. In Yugoslavia, emigration was and is attributed to cultural oppression by the Austrian and Hungarian parts of the Habsburg empire. Hungarian scholars, on the other hand, emphasize social and economic motivation as the background for the desire to emigrate. Scholars in the United States have a concept of acculturation that differs from that of their French colleagues. This pluralism of methods and approaches was, to some degree, grafted upon the overarching theme. Careful editing and exchange of opinions among authors was necessary to shape essays that complement each other. No uniformity, no common structures were imposed by the editors; no single national discourse was considered to be superior to the others. The essays thus also reflect the diverse historical and cultural perspectives of the authors.

The chronological scope of the studies included in the volume extends to the late 1920s. The worldwide depression almost brought to a stop the customary migrations. New U.S. immigration laws restricted admission. The migrants' image of destinations both in Europe and in North America was transformed. While the prospects seemed bleak for workers, and would become even bleaker under fascism in Europe, the labor movement in the United States, particularly with the rise of the Congress for Industrial Organizations (CIO), provided hope to some immigrant workers at least.

Notes

1. The research outline on which this book is based was developed by Dirk Hoerder and Horst Rössler at the University of Bremen, "Ausgangslage und Erwartungshaltung ('Amerikabild') von Arbeitsmigranten, 1815–1914," April 1986. Detailed research on labor migration from Britain and Germany to the United States in the nineteenth century is in progress (Rössler). The project has been supported by a grant from the Deutsche Forschungsgemeinschaft. We are grateful to Michael Meadows, Sean Mullan, and Tim Spence for their translations and stylistic corrections, and to Helga Schröder, Dorothea Heinrichs, and Karin Schindler for typing much of the manuscript.

2. See Philip A. M. Taylor, *The Distant Magnet: European Migration to the U.S.A.* (New York, 1971).

3. See Dirk Hoerder, ed., *Labor Migration in the Atlantic Economies: The European and North American Working Class during the Period of Industrialization* (London and Westport, Conn.: Greenwood Press, 1985); Walter F. Willcox and Imre Ferenczi, eds., *International Migrations*, 2 vols. (New York: 1931).

4. See the essay by Nancy Green, Laura Levine Frader, and Pierre Milza in this volume; Abel Chatelain, *Les migrants temporaires en France de 1800 à 1914*, 2 vols. (Lille, 1976); Isabelle Bertaux-Wiame, "The Life History

Approach to the Study of Internal Migration: How Women and Men Came to Paris between the Wars," in *Our Common History: The Transformation of Europe*, ed. Paul Thompson and Natasha Burchardt (London, 1982), 186–200.

5. See the essay by Michael John and Albert Lichtblau in this volume.

6. *Traum und Wirklichkeit: Wien, 1870–1930* (catalogue of an exhibition in Vienna, 1985), comp. by Kirk Varnedoe (Cologne, 1986; English version: New York, 1985), 40.

7. R. R. Palmer and Joel Colton, *A History of the Modern World* (New York, 1978), 320.

8. The Paris boulevards with their monumental facades were built after the defeat of the Commune in 1871. They were intended to separate workers' (in-migrants') quarters from each other and to provide routes for the movements of troops and lines of fire in the event of further uprisings. In this case the image and the reality were juxtaposed to each other to an unusual degree.

9. See Bertaux-Wiame, "The Life History Approach."

10. See Jaroslav Pelenski, ed., *The American and European Revolutions, 1776–1848: Sociopolitical and Ideological Aspects* (Iowa City, Iowa, 1980); *La Révolution Américaine et l'Europe*, ed. Claude Fohlen and Jacques Godechot (Paris, 1979); *The Impact of the American Revolution Abroad*, Library of Congress Symposium on the American Revolution (Washington, D.C., 1976); Horst Dippel, *Germany and the American Revolution, 1770–1800* (Chapel Hill, N.C., 1977); Erich Angermann, "Der deutsche Frühkonstitutionalismus und das amerikanische Vorbild," *Historische Zeitschrift* 219 (1974): 1–32; Eckhart G. Franz, *Das Amerikabild der deutschen Revolution von 1848–49* (Heidelberg, 1958); Aladár Urbán, "A Lesson for the Old Continent: The Image of America in the Hungarian Revolution of 1848–49," *New Hungarian Quarterly* 17, no. 63 (1976): 85–96; Zofia Libiszowska, "American Thought in Polish Political Writings of the Great Diet (1788–1792)," *Polish-American Studies* 1 (1976): 41.

11. Bruce Levine has begun work on this comparison, with reference to German Americans, in "In the Heat of Two Revolutions: The Forging of German-American Radicalism," in *"Struggle a Hard Battle": Essays on Working-Class Immigrants*, ed. Dirk Hoerder (DeKalb, Ill., 1986), 19–45; see also E. P. Thompson, *The Making of the English Working Class* (1963, rpt. Harmondsworth: Penguin Books, 1974), 94–107, 111–203; and the whole discussion of Jacobin literature initiated by Walter Grab in West Germany: Gert Mattenklott and Klaus R. Scherpe, eds., *Demokratisch-revolutionäre Literatur in Deutschland: Jakobinismus* (Kronberg/Taunus: Scriptor, 1975); Walter Grab, *Radikale Lebensläufe: Von der bürgerlichen zur proletarischen Emanzipationsbewegung* (West Berlin: Ästhetik und Kommunikation, 1980).

12. A differentiated analysis of this early image of "America" and the changes it went through is provided by Horst Rössler in "British Chartism, American Republican Institutions and Constitutions"; Juliane Mikoletzky,

"U.S. Political Institutions as Depicted in Nineteenth Century German Popular Fiction"; Jozsef Gellen, "The Reception of the American Constitution in East-Central Europe, 1789–1848" (papers given at the Congress of the Association Française d'Études Américaines, Chantilly, 1988).

13. See Richard Schneirov, "Free Thought and Socialism in the Czech Community in Chicago, 1875–1887," in Hoerder, *"Struggle a Hard Battle,"* 121–142; Paul Krause, "Labor Republicanism," in Hoerder, *"Struggle a Hard Battle,"* 154; A. E. Zucker, ed., *The Forty-Eighters: Political Refugees of the German Revolution of 1848* (New York, 1950).

14. See Heinzpeter Thümmler, *Sozialistengesetze §28: Ausweisung und Ausgewiesene, 1878–1890* (East Berlin, 1979); Hartmut Keil, *Deutsche sozialistische Einwanderer in den USA im letzten Drittel des 19. Jahrhunderts: Lebensweise und Organisation im Spannungsfeld von Tradition und Integration* (Habilitationsschrift, University of Munich, 1986).

15. Hans Herder, ed., *Hessisches Auswandererbuch* (Frankfurt, 1983), 21, 22, passim. See also the essay by Horst Rössler in this volume.

16. Earlier some European smallholders had looked to "Russia" or the Danubian areas vacated by the Ottoman Empire. In both cases they received privileges and thus went off to a society they had constructed in their minds from information and hopes. Many left when the privileges were revoked and the local socioeconomic reality impinged on them.

17. See Wolfgang Helbich, ed., *"Amerika ist ein freies Land . . .": Auswanderer schreiben nach Deutschland* (Darmstadt, 1985), and similar collections for other ethnic groups. Horst Rössler is investigating such moves back to the land (cf. note 1).

18. Juliane Mikoletzky, *Die deutsche Amerika-Auswanderung des 19. Jahrhunderts in der zeitgenössischen fiktionalen Literatur* (Tübingen, 1988); Stephan Görisch, "Träume von Besitz, Arbeit und Unabhängigkeit: Die Vereinigten Staaten im Spiegel deutscher Informationsschriften für Auswanderer im 19. Jahrhundert" (John F. Kennedy-Institut für Nordamerikastudien, Working Paper no. 11, West Berlin, 1988).

19. Helbich, *"Amerika ist ein freies Land,"* 110–58; Wolfgang Helbich, Walter D. Kamphoefner, and Ulrike Sommer, eds., *Briefe aus Amerika: Deutsche Auswanderer schreiben aus der Neuen Welt, 1830–1930* (Munich, 1988); H. Arnold Barton, ed., *Letters from the Promised Land: Swedes in America, 1840–1914* (Minneapolis, Minn., 1975).

20. Klaus Goebel and Günther Voigt, eds., *Die kleine, mühselige Welt des jungen Hermann Enters* (Wuppertal, 3d ed., 1979), 28; Walter Köpping, ed., *Lebensberichte deutscher Bergarbeiter* (Frankfurt a.M., 1984), 110. Otto Heller, *Sibirien, ein anderes Amerika* (Berlin, 1930); Adam Walaszek, "Return Migrants from the United States in Poland, 1919–1924" (unpublished paper, 1990).

21. For the German case, see, for example, Peter Marschalck, *Be-*

völkerungsgeschichte Deutschlands im 19. und 20. Jahrhundert (Frankfurt a.M.: Suhrkamp, 1984).

22. Such fears were demonstrated in posters warning women to beware of dangers. See, for example, Günter Moltmann, comp., *Germans to America: 300 Years of Immigration, 1683–1983* (Stuttgart, 1982), 120, 121. These concerns also surfaced in the intense debate about the importation of prostitutes to America, the intense fear of "white slavery" that was expressed around the turn of the century in debates about exclusionary measures. The statistics of the Commissioner of Immigration demonstrate that the percentage of female migrants excluded for this reason was miniscule. For conscious decision making, see Margareta R. Matovic, *Stockholmsäktenskap: Familjebildung och partnerval i Stockholm, 1850–1890* (Stockholm, 1984).

23. Letters from America containing no money were hidden from neighbors in some areas; see Kerby A. Miller, "Emigration and the Popular Image of America in Rural Ireland," in *Emigration: The Irish Experience*, ed. Joseph J. Lee (Dublin and Cork: Mercier Press, forthcoming); see also Miller's essay in this volume. For children sent away, see the essay by John and Lichtblau in this volume.

24. The image of the Statue of Liberty, too, is a construct. It was meant by the French donors to be commemorative of past struggles for liberty, not a description of the present in the 1880s or a beacon for the future.

25. German emigrant songs extolling "America" are reprinted in Lutz Röhrich, "Auswandererschicksal im Lied," *Hessische Blätter für Volks- und Kulturforschung* 17 (1985): 71–109; Krause, "Labor Republicanism"; Victor Greene, *The Slavic Community on Strike* (Notre Dame, Ind.: Notre Dame University Press, 1968), 28–29.

26. See Miller, "Emigration and the Popular Image"; Helbich, *Briefe aus Amerika;* Dirk Hoerder and Christiane Harzig, eds., *The Press of Labor Migrants in Europe and North America 1830s to 1930s* (Bremen, 1985).

27. See also "The Image of Labor-Importing Countries in the Labor Press of the Cultures of Origin" by John H. M. Laslett, Lars-Göran Tedebrand, and Hannes Siegrist in Harzig and Hoerder, eds., *The Press of Labor Migrants*, 521–79.

28. See John H. M. Laslett, *Nature's Noblemen: The Fortunes of the Independent Collier in Scotland and the American Midwest, 1855–1889* (Los Angeles, 1983); and idem, "Acculturation and the New Immigrant History: Some Methodological Considerations," in Harzig and Hoerder, eds., *The Press of Labor Migrants*, 581–92; Charlotte Erickson, "The Encouragement of Emigration by British Trade Unions, 1850–1900," *Population Studies* 3 (1949): 248–73; Rowland T. Berthoff, *British Immigrants in Industrial America, 1790–1950* (Cambridge, Mass., 1953).

29. See their essays in this volume.

30. The following analysis is based on D. Hoerder, "German Immigrant Workers' Views of 'America' in the 1880s," in Marianne Debouzy, ed., *In the Shadow of the Statue of Liberty: Immigrants, Workers and Citizens in the American Republic, 1880–1920* (Vincennes, 1988), 17–33.

31. See Dirk Hoerder and Hartmut Keil, "The American Case and German Social Democracy at the Turn of the Twentieth Century, 1878–1907," in *Why Is There No Socialism in the United States?* ed. Jean Heffer and Jeanine Rovet (Paris, 1988), 141–65.

32. The following paragraphs are based on a close reading of the *Sozialdemokrat* from the years 1880, 1885, and 1890. Many articles were reprinted from the German-American labor press.

33. *Sozialdemokrat* (hereafter quoted as *Sd*) 24 Oct 1880, 16 Jan 1881 (trans. D.H.)

34. See *Sd*, 16 Jan 1881.

35. *Sd*, 23 July 1885.

36. See *Sd*, regular column "Sozial-Politische Rundschau," 1890, passim; *Sd*, 22 Feb, 11 July, 28 Nov 1880.

37. *Neue Zeit* 7 (1889): 63–69, esp. 66.

38. The travel literature of the nineteenth century points again and again to the fact that Americans constantly extolled the virtues and advantages of their own country. See, among many others, *A Russian Looks at America: The Journey of Aleksandr Borisovich Lakier in 1857*, ed. and trans. Arnold Schrier and Joyce Story (Chicago, 1979), and the summary of German travel reports: Gerhard Armanski, Renate Grunert, and Marianne Suchan, "Aufbruch in die Neue Welt: Entstehung des deutschen Amerikabildes im Spiegel der Auswanderer- und Reiseliteratur," *Dollars & Träume* 4 (September 1981): 19–48; 5 (March 1982): 135–51.

39. See Christiane Harzig, "The Role of German Women in the German-American Working-Class Movement in Late Nineteenth-Century New York," *Journal of American Ethnic History* 8 (1989): 87–107, and her ongoing research project, "Women in the Migration Process: A Comparative Perspective: German, Irish, Polish and Swedish Women in Chicago, 1900"; Varpu Lindstrom-Best and Allen Seager, "*Toveritar* and Finnish-Canadian Women, 1900–1930," in Harzig and Hoerder, eds., *The Press of Labor Migrants*, 243–64; Dorothee Schneider, "'For Whom Are All the Good Things in Life?' German-American Housewives Discuss Their Budgets," in Hartmut Keil and John B. Jentz, eds., *German Workers in Industrial Chicago, 1850–1910: A Comparative Perspective* (DeKalb, Ill., 1983), 145–60.

40. See the essays by Anna Reczyńska, Julianna Puskás, and Matjaž Klemenčič in this volume.

41. See the essays by Reczyńska and Ramella below.

42. Helbich et al., *Briefe aus Amerika*, 33–34.

43. Quoted in Anna Maria Martellone, "Italian Mass Emigration to the United States, 1876–1930: A Historical Survey," *Perspectives in American History* n.s. 1 (1984): 379–423, esp. 410.

44. This particular remark was made by a German immigrant in 1861 (Helbich, *"Amerika ist ein freies Land,"* 116); by a Swedish immigrant, 1903 (David M. Katzman and William M. Tuttle, Jr., eds., *Plain Folk: The Life Story of Undistinguished Americans* [Urbana, Ill., 1982], 33); and by a Swiss technician (quoted in Hannes Siegrist, "Images of Host Countries: The U.S. and Germany in the Press of Swiss Technicians [1904–1935]," in Harzig and Hoerder, eds., *The Press of Labor Migrants*, 565).

45. See Lindstrom-Best and Seager, *"Toveritar* and Finnish Canadian Women," 243–64; Thomas Dublin, *Women at Work* (New York: Columbia University Press, 1979); Jacqueline Hall, Robert Korstadt, and James Leloudis, "Cotton Mill People: Work, Community, and Protest in the Textile South, 1880–1940," *American Historical Review* 91 (1986): 246–86; see also the essay by Horst Rössler in this volume.

46. See Ewa Morawska, *For Bread with Butter: Life-Worlds of East Central Europeans in Johnstown, Pennsylvania, 1890–1940* (New York and Cambridge: Cambridge University Press, 1986); David Montgomery, "Nationalism, American Patriotism, and Class Consciousness among Immigrant Workers in the United States in the Epoch of World War I," in Hoerder, *"Struggle a Hard Battle,"* 327–51.

47. See Milorad Ekmečič, "The International and Intercontinental Migrational Movements from the Yugoslav Lands from the End of the XVIIIth Century till 1941," in *Les migrations internationales de la fin du XVIIIe siècle à nos jours* (Paris, 1980), 581.

48. See Mikoletzky, *Die deutsche Amerika-Auswanderung;* Agnes Bretting, "Deutschsprachige Auswanderliteratur im 19. Jahrhundert: Information oder Spiegel der Träume?" *Gulliver: German-English Yearbook* 22 (1988): 63–71.

49. See Claudius H. Riegler, "Transnationale Migration und Technologietransfer: Das Beispiel der schwedisch-deutschen Arbeitswanderung von Technikern und Ingenieuren vor dem Ersten Weltkrieg," in *Auswanderer, Wanderarbeiter, Gastarbeiter: Bevölkerung, Arbeitsmarkt und Wanderung in Deutschland seit der Mitte des 19. Jahrhunderts,* ed. Klaus J. Bade (Ostfildern: Scripta Mercaturae, 1984), 506–26.

PART I
Expectations in Europe

2

Paris: City of Light and Shadow

Nancy L. Green, Laura Levine Frader, and Pierre Milza

IN tracing the migrant's path backward from the point of destination to the point of departure in order to explain the path taken from homeland to adopted country, historians look for causal relations while possessing foreknowledge of effect. This is an inevitable weakness of historical method. Why, we ask, did people leave the land of their birth? This question refers only to those who left; we do not ask about the motives of those who stayed behind. What were the migrants' expectations concerning their destinations? Again, it is not only our questions, but also our sources that focus on those who completed the journey. Rarely, however, do we ask of immigrants to Paris why they did not go to New York, or vice versa. Such an approach could be counterfactual, although inclusion of a comparative dimension could prove to be very fruitful.

We have chosen a comparative approach to the migrant "magnet" question. Two such lines of inquiry are pertinent. It is possible to trace one population migrating toward different destinations, in order to distinguish differences in expectations and experiences.[1] Or, as we have done here, we can confront the images of three different populations converging on one destination. In this way we can examine different groups' perceptions of a common undertaking. French peasants, Italians, and Jews heading to Paris in the nineteenth and twentieth centuries seem to form part of a common movement toward the Seine. Each group, however, took a separate path and had distinct motivations, which may converge in broad outlines but differ in important ways as to detail.

Furthermore, we have tried to be sensitive to the counter-arguments along the migration trail. The post facto linear model of migration should not blind us to the ambiguities of the decision-making process. It is never easy to leave family and friends, even if the whole village eventually follows. And, although chain migration often determined migration patterns, migrants did not necessarily hold uniformly positive images of their ultimate destination. In starting, as in so many migration studies, from the point of arrival, we nevertheless want to insist upon the varieties of representation that make up "destination imagery." Even Paris, the renowned City of Light, had its detractors, both among those who never left their home towns and among those who did. Yet its symbolic and real attraction remained strong. It is the complexity of the migration move that merits renewed consideration.

Peasant Migration to Paris

From the very beginning of the nineteenth century, peasants migrated to the new cities. In the 1830s and 1840s, some 40,000 men and women left France's poor agricultural regions annually, most of them for Paris. This did not necessarily mean a permanent move: many returned home for seasonal work. However, the slow process of population exchange between the countryside, on the one hand, and towns and cities, on the other, gradually became more unidirectional over the course of the century. Peasants settled into the cities and returned less and less frequently to their farms and villages.

Thus, in the early 1830s, the young Martin Nadaud followed in the footsteps of his mason father and grandfather, and left his rural origins in the department of Creuse in central France for seasonal work on construction projects in Paris. Men like Nadaud made their first journey to Paris on foot, walking 170 miles to Orleans, where wagons would take them to their destination in a five-day trip. In 1833, migrants from the Creuse and the departments of the Cantal and the Aveyron further south made up about 5 percent of the Parisian population.[2]

As construction work boomed on Napoleon III's public-works projects in the 1850s and 1860s, greater and greater numbers of rural dwellers traveled to Paris, benefiting from the rail links in the mid-1850s that permitted them to reach the capital in a mere twelve or thirteen hours. By the end of the 1860s as many as half of the men in the Creuse had "gone up" to Paris, in some areas as many as two-thirds. A major wave of departures from rural France occurred between 1851 and 1856, when some 115,000 French men and women left each year for urban destinations. During the Second Empire, Paris experienced massive immigration from rural areas, with some 510,000 men and women arriving in the capital from the provinces. The majority of these migrants came from the Massif Central, from Savoy in the east, and, later in the nineteenth century, from Brittany in the west of France. By 1881, 63 percent of the population of Paris had been born outside of the city. Ten years later, Breton migrants counted for 4.5 percent of the Parisian population. Fewer peasants came from the south, as well.[3]

In 1857, an agricultural laborer in the Aude, in the south of France, received a letter from a friend who had recently migrated to Paris:

> What are you doing now at home? You earn 25 or 30 *sous* per day; you're badly fed and when you're sick, you have only a thin soup to restore you; you don't have the money to pay for medicine and a doctor. Here we earn 3 francs 50 daily. We eat good, thick soup, good meat, good bread, and we drink good wine. When we are sick we are well cared for in the hospital. . . . Come and join us instead of staying in the country.[4]

In this brief letter the migrant summed up several good reasons for French peasants to abandon their fields and farms for the capital. Higher wages in Paris were a determining factor for all three of our migrating populations. The Auvergnats from central France, who made their way up to Paris in the first half of the nineteenth century and managed to become skilled workers there, could hope to earn 500 francs a year, considerably more than the 150 or 200 francs that their compatriots who migrated south and west might earn.[5] Similarly, a woman from the eastern Haute-Saône who earned 100 or 200 francs as a domestic servant could hope to earn 300 francs in Paris.[6] Not only wages drew peasants to Paris, but also the possibility of more regular employment and sometimes even a lower cost of living; in some areas of France, the cost of living was actually higher than in the capital.[7]

Most important, decisions to leave for the city were not necessarily individual ones but more often part of family strategies designed to provide extra family income or to avoid Napoleonic inheritance laws.[8] In many regions of France, such as the Auvergne and neighboring Limousin, demographic pressure weighed so heavily upon peasant families well up to the turn of the century that many defied the Civil Code, passed on their lands to the eldest son alone, and sent the other sons to Paris to make their way as apprentices.[9]

Similarly, "surplus" daughters, whose poor peasant families could not afford to provide them with a dowry, often had little recourse but to migrate and hire themselves out as domestic servants in a large city such as Paris. Indeed, such migrants usually chose to leave the land because of the "pressure of need, the endless search for a bit of cash to make ends meet. . . . [G]oing away from home . . . was the only way to keep the home going."[10] As late as the eve of World War I, women from the south of France went to the capital to work temporarily as cooks and maids in order to help sustain their families. Thus, Anastasie Vergnes balanced her work as a vineyard laborer with occasional trips to Paris to earn extra cash during the turn-of-the-century depression in the southern wine markets.[11]

Finally, to these traditional reasons for migration to the capital must be added those that were themselves a product of the rural exodus: the exasperation at living in progressively depopulated, isolated areas, where social customs such as the evening get-togethers *(veillées)* were dying out and no longer provided relief from the interminable, lonely winters.[12]

Those who went back to their native villages became objects of public curiosity—called "les Parisiens"—as neighbors clustered around them, eager for news of the capital.[13] Migrants who returned to more remote villages sporting the new clothes they had bought with their urban wages and relating stories of the excitement of Paris were undoubtedly more convincing as an advertisement for the promise of urban life than the press may have been.

Yet migration for French peasants, as we shall see for Italian and Jewish migrants as well, comprised a mixture of both apprehension and adventure. The anxiety of finding oneself in unfamiliar, perhaps unmanageable surroundings, caught up in the speed and constant movement of the urban world whose hum resembled that of a great machine in perpetual motion, was true for all those new to the city. It added to worries about finding work and being accepted. It was well known, for example, that regional accents, qualified as "foreign," were just as often the subject of ridicule in Paris as accents from other countries.

A drawing in the January 15, 1882, edition of *La Semaine agricole* is suggestive of the representation of the city in the mind of the French peasant migrant. A young girl sits with a bundle in her lap as her mother, with finger raised, seems to issue a silent warning of the urban dangers that lie ahead. The girl's eyes are wide; she stares straight ahead, her expression a mixture of anxiety and resolution. One imagines that she has read Michel Greff's *La Fermière* (1859) or Louis-Eugène Berillon's *La Bonne menagère agricole* (1862), both of which urged young peasant girls like this one to remain on the farm and shun the evils of the city.[14]

Indeed, much of the literature on domestic economy that addressed women portrayed the city as a dangerous place and condemned urban life for its destructive influence on the family.[15] This was true not only with respect to daughters. As Leslie Moch reports, "In the words of an old woman who hastened to Paris from her village to attend the trial of her son, 'It's Paris that's to blame; I'm taking my son out of it and I'll make sure he never sets eyes on it again!'"[16] Those who stayed behind sometimes saw the city as inherently evil and blamed the urban world when peasant migrants became involved in or victimized by urban crime. Moreover, the misery of unemployment in the capital could be cruel. If some peasants left the land with the expectation of steady work, those who returned to Paris a second or third time were more often than not disabused of that notion. Martin Nadaud's comparison of unemployment in the countryside with that of Paris left no doubts:

> [Unemployment in] the city is much more horrible; it wastes the body and mind . . . it is death preceded by a long and cruel agony. . . . In the city, there are no resources when the worker can't find work, no more shelter, no more clothes, no more bread. . . . [C]harity alone, contemptuous, insulting, too often insufficient, is his only refuge.[17]

Indeed, one might add to this picture the dramatizations of urban crime and poverty that filled the novels of Hugo, Balzac, Zola, and Sue—imagery that conjured up a dangerous, threatening Paris.[18]

Yet, at the same time, Paris held a magical appeal. To Breton peasants, "Paris was like [an] enchanted fairy-tale city," an "unending fair or feast," a city of cheap amusements, forbidden pleasures, and light.[19] In the minds of many rural folk, in addition to the higher wages it offered, city life seemed easier, work more regular and less physically demanding, diversions like theaters, cafés, and music halls more accessible. It was a great temptation and far indeed from the relative drabness of rural hamlets and villages.

The insistence on the part of contemporaries that women and girls migrated more frequently than men because they were more quickly drawn to the bright lights and perceived luxuries of the capital (such as running water) was probably exaggerated. For women as for men, the image of the city as the great provider of work was crucial. It is true, however, that hardworking farm girls, armed with fundamental domestic skills, could perhaps more easily find work as servants, seamstresses, or laundry workers in the homes of the Parisian bourgeoisie. Young Breton peasant girls thus left the poverty of their rural existence for a starched uniform, better diet, clean sheets, and regular wages "in service."

After the early 1880s and Jules Ferry's laws on obligatory primary schooling, the schools themselves contributed to forming the images and expectations of the city for peasant youths. Works such as G. Bruno's (Augustine Tuillerie Fouillée) *Le Tour de France par deux enfants*, could not but have influenced rural dwellers' dreamlike images of the City of Light. In this popular, schoolchildren's bird's-eye view of France, first published in 1877 but reprinted in numerous editions thereafter, André and Julien, in their travels around the Hexagon (as France is dubbed, after its shape), finally make their way to Paris. The splendors of the great city lie before them: shops filled with enticements, monumental buildings, streets sparkling with light at night, the famed state schools, the libraries, restaurants, the zoo. On parting to go home, Julien admits that he is happy to leave the hustle and bustle of the big city for the fields and cows of his rural home; but he confesses that he loves Paris with all his heart, for it is the capital of France.[20]

All the glitter and movement aside, Paris was in one important way very likely a more manageable and less alienating place for peasant migrants than some of the dire warnings suggested. Like foreign migrants, most rural newcomers came to the city through contacts of kin or friendship, or through professional associations, as in the case of artisans like Nadaud. These individuals immediately found themselves surrounded by *compagnards* in the Auvergnat colonies near the place de la Bastille or in the Alsatian communities near the slaughterhouses of La Villette.[21] In these villages within the city, whose traces are still found in the Auvergnat specialty shops in the rue de Lappe and the rue de la Roquette, or in the Breton restaurants near the Gare Montparnasse, the overwhelming nature of the capital was reduced to life-sized proportions. The knowledge that there was a congenial community of regional compatriots where one could speak the *patois* (regional dialect) and feel at home helped make expectations of the city less forbidding.

Fascination, fantasy, and fear all structured the image of Paris for potential migrants. Financial need, demographic pressure, and family strategies fed the most important expectation—that of better jobs. For rural and foreign migrants alike, the attraction of economic opportunity was combined with that of bright city lights. However, both were contrasted in turn with ominous warnings about the dangers of the city. We do not know how many young girls with bundles on their laps ultimately stayed home because of those fears. But, as we shall see, a composite image also held true for Italians and Jews.

The Italian Relay

By the end of the nineteenth century, peasant movement to the cities began to slow, largely due to a leveling off of the French birthrate. Demographers, economists, and public officials began to worry about how to "fill the void."[22] Foreign migration was a complementary factor in the long-term process of urban growth. Rural migration of both men and women continued, of course, to come from the French countryside. But, soon, growing numbers of foreign workers began to come as well. From the late nineteenth century into the interwar period, France became a country of immigration much like the United States.[23]

The Italian colony in Paris itself dates back to the early part of the nineteenth century. Approximately 3,650 Italians lived in the French capital in 1833; by 1851, the year of the first census, there were 8,512 in Paris, out of a total of 63,000 Italians living in France.[24] This figure remained fairly stable until the period 1876–81, years when in Paris, as elsewhere in France, the "take-off" of the second phase of the Industrial Revolution meant a "take-off" in foreign inmigration. The Italian colony doubled in size in those five years, and, in spite of a decline during the depression years from 1886 to 1896, the percentage of Italians among foreigners in the capital continued to grow up to World War I: 9.6 percent of all foreigners in 1876, 11.8 percent in 1896, nearly 15 percent in 1911. The Italians nonetheless represented only 0.7 percent of the total population in the Seine Department, a far cry from the 18 percent (90,000) they constituted in the city of Marseilles. A sentiment of "invasion," felt in the South of France as part of daily coexistence, was in the North a more or less abstract mental construct, one fed by the nationalistic press. Italian migration to Paris did increase spectacularly after 1921, due to economic, psychological, and, of course, political reasons. From 1924 to 1926, with the rise of Mussolini and the radicalization of his regime,

Paris became the European capital of anti-Fascist exiles. By 1931 there were over 50,000 Italians in Paris and even more in the surrounding suburbs: 148,334 in the entire Paris region.[25] Paris overtook Marseilles and became the most important "Italian city" in France. Between the wars, one out of every four foreigners in the Paris metropolitan area was Italian, even if the Italians still represented only 2.3 percent of the city's total population.

Several characteristics of the Italian population correspond to the classic image of economic migration: the migrants were for the most part young, male, and working-class. However, we can note significant differences from the other two populations being studied. The Italian group was more predominantly male than that of the French peasants or the Jewish migrants. There were fewer domestic servants and more laborers, with about the same percentage of skilled workers as among the Jewish immigrant population.[26] The Italian population in Paris was also particularly mobile, not through seasonal migration, like the French peasants, but due to a high turnover. Even more so than in the South of France, Italian migrants in Paris exercised a "nomadism" that lasted into the 1930s. As was the case for almost all migrants, the path taken was determined primarily by kin and regional affinities. The Italians coming to Paris were mainly from the northern Piedmont, Emilia-Apennine, and Friuli regions, and they settled together mostly in the eastern part of Paris and its suburbs—in the Villette, Pont de Flandre, Roquette, Quinze-Vingts, Charonne, and Picpus districts, and in the suburbs of Aubervilliers and Saint-Denis in the North, Fontenay-sous-Bois in the East, Ivry, Vitry, and Boulogne in the South.

A mixture of economic opportunity, myths, and cultural references drew the Italians to the French capital. The city struck their imagination with an ambiguous fascination. Contrasting signals corresponded to two distinct politico-cultural traditions. On the one hand, the far Left and the Cavourian, liberal Right joined in admiration for the France of the Declaration of the Rights of Man: a generous and humane France, spreading the seed of liberation. On the other hand, both the nationalist "Left" and the clerical conservatives were hostile to their decadent "Latin sister," seen as completely absorbed by hedonistic craving. Paris symbolized this contradictory mythology: on the one hand, the Paris of the barricades and of Liberty triumphant, where the people had risen up against tyranny over and over again: on the other, a "city of light" in the literal sense: a city of easy living, of a *dolce vita* that had not yet come to the banks of the Tiber.

Even a friend of France such as the leftist Edmondo de Amicis could be very critical of the Parisians. In his *Souvenirs de Paris*, published in 1872, he wrote:

> This idea of having been born in Paris, of having received a sign of preference from God, is an idea that dominates the thoughts of the Parisian, like a star which illuminates his whole life with a celestial consolation. The kindness which he shows to foreigners is largely inspired by a feeling of commiseration.[27]

For the foreign migrant, Paris was France. Just as French travelers to Italy saw all Italians through the distorting mirror of the *popolino romano*, Italians to Paris saw the vanity of the capital as the vanity of the country. Paris was the "ville-miroir" (the mirror-city), symbol of a deteriorating society whose model continued to have a deleterious effect on other nations.[28]

The negative side of the Italian opinion of France reflected the rural, clerical, and traditional backgrounds that characterized much of the migration. France was condemned as corrupt, decadent, and unworthy of its past. The Prussians had given the French a "good lesson" in 1870.[29] Germanophilia on the part of some—admiration for a young, dynamic country of serious and "virtuous" people (in the Italian sense of *virtù*)—which was later to play a part in Fascist discourse in Italy—corresponded to a gallophobia that viewed the French, in contrast, as frivolous, libertine, and pleasure-seeking. For the "party of order," Paris represented disorder.[30]

However, if Left and Right sometimes joined in a cultural critique of the French before World War I, for the Italian Left there was a symmetrical cliché of Paris that emphasized its political heritage. Capital of liberty and of progress, symbol of *the* Revolution (1789), Paris incarnated those universal values for which some Italians were even ready to come and fight. Thousands of volunteers—either already in Paris or having come just to join the "Garibaldian Legion"[31]—enrolled during the winter of 1870–71 and again in August 1914. Whether "economic" or "political" migrants,[32] they were joining the force of "progress" in order to combat a Germanism that was, in their eyes, a synonym of obscurantism and reaction. One of them, Camillo Marabini, explained his symbolic gesture as follows: "That which extends from the sea to Switzerland is not a mass of armies; it is a formidable barricade, where the second revolution is being fought. In 1789, for the Rights of Man. In 1914, for the Rights of

Nationalities."³³ And he added, making clear the reference to the myth of revolutionary Paris:

> Two eras, past and future, and two ideas, confront each other: One was born with the tribune of Rome and triumphed in Paris at the Bastille; the other gleamed in the eyes of the barbarians who, more than once throughout the centuries, have marched towards the South, avid for sun and booty.³⁴

From 1871, when they fought alongside the Communards, to 1944, when many joined the French resistance, the Italians contributed to the image and the cause of revolutionary France.

Are the contradictory representations of a frivolous or a revolutionary Paris necessarily irreconcilable? We find this duality in several oral histories, and the "easy" adventures that could lighten the exile of young antifascists in the 1920s and 1930s also created a sense of lightness, if not of liberty.³⁵ The city of lights can thus represent the (bright) light of liberty or the (dim) lights of perdition. Ultimately, the ambiguities of the migrant imagination are perhaps less contradictory than they may seem: the two images are telescoped within each migrant because they arise from a common source—that of the liberty of action.

The East European Jews in Paris

Jews, too, sought a double emancipation in heading toward Paris: a civic emancipation as well as a psychological one. Whether the Jews were derogatorily lumped together with Auvergnats or contrasted to the "good" Breton peasants,³⁶ their migration to Paris comprised elements similar to that of both the French rural migrants and the Italian newcomers. Attracted to Paris in anticipation of job opportunities, creating their own mutual aid and other networks to ease the cultural shock, Jewish migrants followed a general pattern common to most migrations. They, too, were drawn to the city for both symbolic and realistic reasons. The City of Light charmed and fascinated Jews in the far-off Pale of Russia just as it did Auvergnats and Piedmontese "only" 350 or 700 kilometers away.

Yet if all three migrant groups shared similar expectations with regard to work and leisure in the French capital, the Jews, like the Italians, added another, different political component to their representation of the city. Paris was the embodiment of France, not just any France, but the France of the Revolution. The Revolution of 1789 also possessed particular significance for the Jews.

Roger Ikor, in his prize-winning novel about the arrival and settlement in Paris of the capmaker Yankel Mykhanowitzki, suggests why other destinations may have been rejected in favor of Paris for the 35,000 Jewish migrants who arrived there between 1881 and the start of World War I. America's streets were paved with gold, or so the story went. But the other side of the coin for this American legend was just as widespread in premigration circles: a disdain for an uncultured, materialist society.[37] As for Germany, the anti-Semitism of the 1880s discouraged many potential migrants from going there. For Yankel, Germany was simply still too close to Russia, and the names of Bismarck, Nietzsche, and Wagner compared poorly with Tolstoy, Yankel's hero. But why not England, for example? "Liberals, you say? Of course, liberals! But rotten with prejudice, with tradition, full of monocled dukes. . . . And, besides, why do they need a king, even a decorative one? What's he good for, this parasite?"[38]

A posteriori literary rationalizations can only be suggestive. Paris was perhaps quite simply closer than the United States, and migration to Paris did not entail the uncertainties of sea travel. Many historians, following Michel Roblin, argue that Paris was but a stopping point on the way to America, a transit point that ultimately became a final destination.[39] However, there were also explicit, positive reasons for the choice of Paris.

The migrant "magnet" is both economic and ideological, even if jobs often speak louder than words. The letters home, the newspaper accounts, the guidebooks in Yiddish for the migrant,[40] and the occasional returnee all made it clear that jobs were available in Paris. The growth of the ready-to-wear clothing industry provided opportunities for former as well as future tailors. The cap industry was expanding, thanks both to the Russian Jews and to an increased demand for sportswear to clothe the growing number of new bicycling and automobile adepts.[41]

As Jews fled both the bloody and the "dry" (legislative) pogroms of late nineteenth-century tsarism, they sought both jobs and freedom. They were sometimes disappointed in the former. The fictitious Yankel Mykhanowitzki, like the very real Martin Nadaud, ended up complaining about his new economic condition. However, it was de-skilling rather than outright unemployment that frustrated him:

> Just yesterday, wasn't the least gesture of his trade a constantly renewed source of pleasure? To appreciate from afar a fresh piece

of material, to appreciate in advance the suppleness of the cloth, its texture, with a squint in order to carefully judge the color. . . . No: that was in the old days, in the Rakwomirian days. Now Yankel's work was mechanized. He no longer jokes, he no longer smiles at jokes.[42]

Ikor's hero reminds us that dissatisfaction over jobs mingled with the predominant image of job opportunity.

Another reason favoring the choice of Paris for the Eastern European Jews was the presence of the French Jewish community that was centered there. Although the latter feared attracting too many of their less fortunate brethren from the East, knowledge of the French Jewish institutions—the world-renowned Alliance Israélite Universelle, with its headquarters in Paris, the Consistoire and its welfare office, the Comité de Bienfaisance—circulated in Eastern Europe, acting as an implicit "pull." Potential migrants could thus imagine a safety net into which to fall if the reality of migration did not live up to the myth. Little by little, their own networks, like those of French peasants and Italian immigrants, would also serve this function.

Yet, in the end, the ideological component in Paris's appeal may have been the determining factor for those who chose to make caps in Paris rather than in London or New York. "Lebn vi Got in Frankraykh" goes an old Yiddish saying—to live like God in France.[43] Very similar to that of the Italians, the "Jewish" Parisians' myth was a French myth, but above all it was a composite one. "C'était la Lumière qui régnait, la Liberté, la Civilisation, la Vie!"—"It was Light that reigned, Liberty, Civilization, Life!"[44]

The representation of France and Paris thus revolved essentially around three poles—French civilization, the combined notions of light and liberty, and a further link of liberty to revolution. The French civilization to which these representations referred came not from just any period of French history. Rarely, in the Jewish (or Italian) migrant literature is there reference to Louis XIV and the splendors of Versailles. It is invariably the eighteenth-century philosophers and the nineteenth-century social critics—Pascal, Montesquieu, Voltaire, Rousseau, Balzac, Hugo, Zola—who are reverentially cited. Books, French teachers, history teachers, even Hebrew teachers, and the occasional murder mystery, are mentioned as information vectors with respect to France. Many sons and daughters of immigrants have told of their grandfathers' introduction to France through the Yiddish translation of *Les Misérables*. Others referred to different symbols of French civilization: Sarah Bernhardt, French-style bread (made in Russia), or the French perfume stands at the Nizhnii fair.[45]

This civilization, and the city of Paris itself, were symbols of light, a light that contrasted with the "obscurity," "barbarity," and "gloom" of the tsarist regime, or with the suffocating atmosphere within the traditional Jewish community itself.[46] The light to which the migrants were drawn was thus a light of liberty, a light of emancipation. This emancipation was both individual and collective, from the confining Pale of Russia and from the Jewish *shtetl*. But for the Jews it also had a special, historic meaning. France represented very real, legal emancipation—the granting of full rights of citizenship to the Jews in 1791–92. This date in French history had a particular impact on Jewish migration to France. Revolutionaries or not, those heading toward Paris identified it with the Revolution and its great gift of liberty to the Jews.

Ikor's capmaker Yankel marched symbolically to the silent hum of *La Marseillaise* as he crossed the Russian border heading towards France. For the real militant, Hersh Mendl, the revolutionary attraction of Paris was even more explicit. He had read in Gorki that every good revolutionary should go to Paris at least once to visit the Bastille, and so he did, just as Jacques Tchernoff, upon his arrival, imagined himself following the path of Alexander Herzen on the trail of Camille Desmoulins.[47] The French Revolution, like the Paris Commune, presented strong images to the Russian revolutionary imagination.

The accounts of those who emigrated provide a fairly strong consensus on what attracted the Jews to Paris. There are even *a posteriori* explanations of why the Dreyfus Affair was not a particularly inhibiting factor: French anti-Semitism, after all, could hardly be compared to tsarist pogroms.[48] However, there were also those who argued against migration. A counter-myth existed, extending from revolutionaries to rabbis. Those revolutionaries who preferred to remain in Russia to continue the struggle there rather than in exile complained about their ex-comrades who had gone abroad and been lost to the cause through "bourgeoisification."[49] Trotsky—one who was surely not lost to the Russian revolutionary cause, but also not the average Jewish refugee—made the simple comment upon arrival in Paris, "It looks like Odessa, but Odessa's better."[50]

The religious argument, on the other hand, reflected the recognition that many young Jews were leaving precisely to escape from a stifling, traditional environment. Going west was perceived as going into Babylon, of which Paris represented but one of the most dangerous manifestations. For old Sarah, in Moïse Twersky's semi-auto-biographical account, Paris was a place where you could not even tell a French Jew from a non-Jew. Bakeries stayed open on the Sabbath. Worse yet, Parisians ate forbidden foods such as frog's legs and escargots. No one went to the synagogue except a few old people. And Paris itself was dangerous: crime in the streets (the Gobelins Stranglers!), policemen pestering girls. Worst of all, there were even Jewish pimps![51] Literary embellishment may ridicule the detractors who are outnumbered and necessarily minimized in a migration tale. But the spoilsports spoke partial truths and provide insight into the forgotten reverse-side of the migrant myth.

Conclusion

The three migration streams fulfilled somewhat different, yet complementary, roles in the development of Paris. Peasant girls came as domestic servants, their brothers were recruited to unskilled manufacturing positions, to be replaced by Italians in the latter part of the nineteenth century. Jews largely went into light industry and peddling. All in all, by 1896 almost two-thirds of the Parisian inhabitants had been born outside the city limits.[52]

These immigrants brought with them similar, composite expectations of the city, ranging from fear to excitement. If the latter is sometimes recounted in embellished, even ecstatic terms, this probably served to overcome and erase the anxiety that had accompanied the move. The migrants had real cause for concern. "What if no one wears caps in Paris?" worried our Jewish capmaker, afraid of not finding employment. "You will be lost to Babylon," argued those who stayed behind, whether in French farms or Italian villages or Jewish *shtetls.* Paris epitomized the secularization of nineteenth-century French society, instilling fear in the hearts of good French and Italian Catholics and in those of Orthodox Jews as well.

All the migrants received mixed signals: the availability of jobs, but the dangers of unemployment or de-skilling; excitement, yet danger; the Bastille versus Babylon. Yet all seem to have been motivated by a similar series of perceived dichotomies: jobs versus temporary or chronic unemployment; city lights versus the humdrum habits of home life; being freed from a stifling, traditional atmosphere. Each group had its specific set of expectations and worries. If some Jews came to Paris in symbolic search of (nonkosher) oysters, Breton peasants perhaps went there to—figuratively, at least—escape the regional delicacy. If some Jewish and Italian migrants went to Paris seeking revolutionary France, some Auvergnats or Limousins left home to avoid the consequences of the land-splitting Napoleonic laws. Jews from tsarist Russia and (particularly later, anti-Fascist) Italians sought the political and civil freedom that the French provincials already had. But the latter joined the former in search of a personal emancipation from the watchful eyes of the village square. We have only hints of puckered disapproval on the part of those who remained home, or of disappointments on the part of those who arrived. But if migration is almost always an *a posteriori* "success," the ambiguities of apprehension and adventure should not be underestimated.

Notes

1. See, for example, Robert Foerster's classic, *The Italian Emigration of Our Times* (Cambridge, Mass.: Harvard University Press, 1919); John Briggs, *An Italian Passage: Immigrants to Three American Cities, 1890–1930* (New Haven, Conn.: Yale University Press, 1978); Samuel L. Baily, "The Adjustment of Italian Immigrants in Buenos Aires and New York, 1870–1914," *American Historical Review* 88 (April 1983): 281–305; Herbert S. Klein, "The Integration of Italian Immigrants into the United States and Argentina: A Comparative Analysis," *American Historical Review* 88 (April 1983): 306–29 and comments, 330–46.

2. See Martin Nadaud, *Les Mémoires de Léonard, ancien garçon maçon* (Paris: Librairie Charles Delagrave, 1912); David Pinkney, "Migrations to Paris during the Second Empire," *Journal of Modern History* 25 (March 1953): 5; Philippe Ariès, *Histoire de la population française et leurs attitudes devant la vie depuis le XVIIIᵉ siècle* (Paris: Editions Self, 1948), 319.

3. See Pinkney, "Migrations to Paris," 2; Maurice Agulhon, Gabriel Desert, and Robert Specklin, eds., *Apogée et crise de la civilisation paysanne*, vol. 3, in *Histoire de la France rurale*, ed. Georges Duby (Paris: Seuil, 1976), 222–23; Daniel Courgeau, *Study of the Dynamics, Evolution, and Consequences of Migrations: Three Centuries of Spatial Mobility in France* (Paris: Unesco, 1982), 26–27, 30: Ariès, *Histoire de la population française*, 320. The 63 percent non-Parisian born obviously included foreign immigrants, but in 1881 their numbers were still small.

4. Quoted in Pinkney, "Migrations to Paris," 12.

5. See Françoise Raison-Jourde, *La Colonie auvergnate de Paris au XIX siècle* (Paris: Ville de Paris, Commission des travaux historiques, 1976), 87.

6. See Pinkney, "Migrations to Paris," 8.

7. Ibid., 11, reports that the cost of living in the Seine-et-Marne, for example, was higher than that of Paris in the 1850s.

8. According to Napoleon's Civil Code, all land had to be equally divided among heirs. See, for example, Louise A. Tilly, "Individual Lives and Family Strategies in the French Proletariat," *Journal of Family History* 4 (Summer 1979): 137–52; Leslie Page Moch, *Paths to the City: Regional Migration in Nineteenth Century France* (Beverly Hills, Calif.: Sage, 1983); Louise Tilly and Joan Scott, *Women, Work and Family* (New York and London: Methuen, 1986, 2d ed.), passim. See also Leonard Berlanstein, *The Working People of Paris, 1871–1914* (Baltimore, Md.: Johns Hopkins University Press, 1984).

9. See Raison-Jourde, *La Colonie auvergnate*, 182.

10. Eugen Weber, *Peasants into Frenchmen* (Palo Alto, Calif.: Stanford University Press, 1976), 278.

11. Laura Frader, Interview with Anastasie Vergnes, Coursan, Aude, July 1974; see Leo Loubère, Laura Frader, Jean Sagnes, and Rémy Pech, *The Vine Remembers* (Albany, N.Y.: SUNY Press, 1986).

12. See Raison-Jourde, *La Colonie auvergnate*, 183–84.

13. See, for example, Nadaud, *Les Mémoirs de Léonard*, 80, 84–85; and Pinkney, "Migrations to Paris," 6.

14. See reproduction in Agulhon et al., *Apogée et crise*, 399.

15. See, for example, Comtesse Kéranflech-Kernezne, *Causeries et conseils aux mères de famille* (St. Brieuc: n.p., 1911); and Linda Clark, *Schooling the Daughters of Marianne* (Albany, N.Y.: SUNY Press, 1984), 56.

16. Moch, *Paths to the City*, 22.

17. Nadaud, *Les Mémoirs de Léonard*, quoted in Louis Chevalier, *Classes laborieuses et classes dangereuses* (Paris: Plon, 1958), 550.

18. For a discussion of representations of the city in the nineteenth-century novel, see especially Chevalier, *Classes laborieuses*.

19. Weber, *Peasants into Frenchmen*, 285–86.

20. See G. Bruno, *Le Tour de France par deux enfants*, (Cours moyen) (Paris: Librairie Classique Eugène Belin, 1970), 288.

21. See Weber, *Peasants into Frenchmen*, 282; and Raison-Jourde, *La Colonie auvergnate*, passim.

22. See Nancy Green, "'Filling the Void': Immigration to France before World War I," in *Labor Migration in the Atlantic Economies*, ed. Dirk Hoerder (Westport, Conn.: Greenwood Press, 1985), 143–61.

23. See ibid.; Pierre Milza, "Un siècle d'immigration étrangère en France," *Vingtième siècle* 7 (special issue: "Etrangers, immigrés, français") (July–September 1985): 3–18; Gérard Noiriel, *Le Creuset français* (Paris: Seuil, 1988).

24. We are speaking here only of the city of Paris itself and the Seine

Department. A more complete study of Italians in the Paris region should include the neighboring departments of the Seine-et-Oise and the Seine-et-Marne.

25. See Pierre Milza, ed., *Les Italiens en France de 1914 à 1940* (Rome: Ecole Française de Rome, 1986).

26. See Nancy L. Green, *The Pletzl of Paris: Jewish Immigrant Workers in the Belle Epoque* (New York: Holmes & Meier, 1986), 122; table comparing the occupational structures of different immigrants in Paris in 1901, drawing on K. Schirmacher, *La spécialisation du travail—Par nationalités, à Paris* (Paris: Arthur Rousseau, 1908), 171–74.

27. E. de Amicis, *Ricordi del 1870–1871* (Rome, 1872), 238–39.

28. Several articles were published on this theme in the *Corriere della Sera* in July–August 1914.

29. See, for example, N. Marselli, *Gli avvenimenti del 1870–1871* (Turin and Rome, 1873); G. Mazzini, *Il comune e l'assemblea*, in idem, *Scritti editi e inediti* (Rome, 1887), 17: 37.

30. See B. Vigezzi, "L'opinione pubblica italiana e la Francia nell'estate 1914," in *La France et l'Italie pendant la première guerre mondiale* (Grenoble: Presses Universitaires de Grenoble, 1976), 34ff.

31. This was in fact the fourth "régiment de marche du 1er étranger."

32. On the very hypothetical distinction between "economic" and "political" Italian immigrants, cf. Pierre Milza, "L'immigration italienne en France d'une guerre à l'autre: interrogations, directions de recherche et premier bilan," in Milza, ed., *Les Italiens*, 1–42.

33. C. Marabini, *Les Garibaldiens de l'Argonne* (Paris, 1917), 33. Later, in the 1930s, Marabini, a Garibaldian and republican, headed a veterans (of the French army) league called the Fascio de Paris.

34. Ibid., 32.

35. See, for example, the memoirs of the Communist leader Giorgio Amendola, *Un'Isola* (Milan: Rizzoli, 1980).

36. As Balzac wrote in *Le Cousin Pons*, reflecting suspicion of peasant and other migrants to the city: "The Jews, the Auvergnats, the Savoyards, these races of men all have the same instincts: they make their fortunes by every means possible. They spend nothing, they make profits and accumulate interest." Quoted in Raison-Jourde, *La Colonie auvergnate*, 103. As for the outcry in 1938 when Marx Dormoy tried to defend the Jews by saying they were as good as Bretons, see Pierre Birnbaum, *Un mythe politique: la "République juive"* (Paris: Fayard, 1988), 153–60.

37. See Roger Ikor, *Les Fils d'Avrom: Les Eaux mêlées* (Paris: Albin Michel, 1955), 92–93; see an editorial by Abraham Cahan in 1911, quoted in Ronald Sanders, *The Downtown Jews* (New York: Signet, New American Library, 1976), 344–45: "A land of skyscrapers and yellow journalism, a huge

circus of business dealing and bluffing—this is all people there know about the United States." See also, on Germany, André Billy and Moïse Twersky, *L'épopée de Ménaché Foïgel*, vol. 1 (Paris: Plon, 1927–28), 243–44.

38. Ikor, *Les Fils d'Avrom*, 93.

39. See Michel Roblin, *Les Juifs de Paris: Démographie, économie, culture* (Paris: A. et J. Picard et Cie., 1952).

40. See Wolf Speiser, *Kalendar* (Paris: n.p., 1910).

41. See Maurice Lauzel, *Ouvriers juifs de Paris: Les casquettiers* (Paris: Edouard Cornély et Cie., 1912).

42. Ikor, *Les Fils d'Avrom*, 159, 161.

43. See Billy and Twersky, *L'épopée de Ménaché Foïgel*, 1:243, on the origins of the myth. David Weinberg, "'Heureux comme Dieu en France': East European Jewish Immigrants in Paris, 1881–1914," *Studies in Contemporary Jewry* 1 (1984): 26–54.

44. Ikor, *Les Fils d'Avrom*, 66; see Billy and Twersky, *L'épopée de Ménaché Foïgel*, 1:224; and Amendola, *Un'Isola*, 28.

45. See Jacques Tchernoff, *Dans le creuset des civilisations*, vol. 1 (Paris: Editions Rieder, 1937), 174; and Amendola, *Un'Isola*.

46. "De l'air! J'étouffe!"—"Some air! I'm suffocating!"—Tchernoff, *Le creuset des civilisations*, 1:176 and 2:2; see Ikor, *Les Fils d'Avrom*, 66–67; Lionel Rocheman, *Devenir Cécile* (Paris: Ramsay, 1977), an amusing, biographical account of his mother's immigration, 150; and Nancy L. Green, "L'émigration comme émancipation: Les femmes juives d'Europe de l'Est à Paris, 1881–1914," *Pluriel*, no. 27 (1981): 51–59.

47. See Hersh Mendl, *Mémoires d'un révolutionnaire juif* (Grenoble: Presses Universitaires de Grenoble, 1982), 130; Tchernoff, *Le creuset des civilisations*, 2:1–3, 75–84; 4:142–43. Although, where Tchernoff expected to see the revolutionary masses on the street, he was somewhat disappointed to find just ordinary people.

48. See, for example, Rocheman, *Devenir Cécile*, 172, in his tongue-in-cheek treatment of the "subtilités . . . par trop hermétiques"—"excessively esoteric . . . subtleties"—of French anti-Semitism.

49. See Henry J. Tobias and C. E. Woodhouse, "Political Reaction and Revolutionary Careers: The Jewish Bundists in Defeat, 1907–10," *Comparative Studies in Society and History* 19 (July 1977): 367–96.

50. Leon Trotsky, *Ma Vie*, vol. 1 (Paris: Rieder, 1930), 233.

51. See Billy and Twersky, *L'épopée de Ménaché Foïgel*, 1:163–68.

52. See Louis Chevalier, *La formation de la population parisienne au XIXe siécle*, Institut National d'Études Démographiques—Travaux et Documents 10 (Paris: Presses Universitaires de France, 1950), 46.

3

Vienna around 1900: Images, Expectations, and Experiences of Labor Migrants

Michael John and Albert Lichtblau

INVESTIGATIONS into the psychology of perception and the construction of reality have shown that stereotypes function as part of the general process of orienting oneself to the world in which we live. Through selective overemphasis, a sense of "order" is established in what is being perceived. Reality is comprehended by means of models and patterns of meaning, so that the formation of clichés, images, and stereotypes represents a normal and universal process.[1]

Clichés about Vienna have a long history, as two examples will show. In the thirteenth century it was hailed as a glorious, renowned city with clean air, one pleasantly situated by a river, densely populated, abounding in affectionate ladies, surrounded by fertile land, numerous vineyards, and a wooded environment "where living is most heavenly." In 1450, Aeneas Silvius Piccolomini emphasized mainly the negative aspects. The students were interested only in eating, drinking, and women. Unbelievable amounts of wine were consumed in Vienna, and vast quantities of groceries were delivered to the city daily. The population was gluttonous and squandered on a Sunday what it took all week to earn. Prostitution was rife and marriage a scandal.[2]

At the turn of the century, during the reign of Franz Josef I (1848–1916), Vienna's position as a cultural, political, administrative, and economic center corresponded to Austria's position as a world power. Literature, travel guides, newspapers, folk songs, and oral traditions contained a profusion of clichés and images, in which the city was seen and described variously as an imperial city, seat of the powerful Habsburg dynasty; as the center of enormous military might; as a city of splendor, economic riches, and thriving architecture; as an enormous cultural temple; as the city of the waltz and center of fashion; as a metropolis exuding vivacity, hedonism, and *Gemütlichkeit*, a city of tantalizing eroticism, but also of prostitution.[3] On the other hand, Vienna was also seen as a breeding place for poverty, misery, and the "Viennese disease," tuberculosis. It was described by others again as a city of ethnic miscegenation and of increasing Jewish influence. For a racist world view, as exemplified here by Hitler, it was "a city of racial disgrace and incest." Finally, Vienna was considered to be a city of decadence, morbidity, and death.[4]

Who were the migrants that came to the city, and which sources inform us about their image of Vienna? After answering these questions, we will analyze migrants' experiences in leaving their hometowns and coming to Vienna. The next section will deal with the motives for migration and migrants' expectations. In a final section we will relate individual migration to the labor movement's view of the migrants, and suggest that for class-conscious workers it was not the physical aspects of the city, but rather the strength of the labor movement there that lent Vienna a positive image.

Origin, Composition, and Sources of Migrant Experiences and Expectations

"The city of Vienna is a magnet, it attracts people," declared a song from the turn of the century.[5] In 1830 the Viennese conurbation[6] had a population of 401,200. In 1857 the figure was approximately 683,000, and by 1910 the population had grown to 2,083,630 people. Vienna was thus in the upper range of the fourteen largest cities in Europe. Within the monarchy it was surpassed only by Budapest, which had increased its population more than eightfold in the same period.[7] The proportion of residents who had been born in Vienna was consistently under 50 percent during the era of Franz Josef, while the proportion of those who had been born in the Alpine provinces was approximately 15 percent, the overwhelming majority of whom were from Lower Austria.[8] Approximately one-quarter of the population came from Bohemia and Moravia, the main reservoir of migrants. Of these, 75 to 80 percent were Czech-speaking, the remainder German-speaking. Between 5 and 10 percent came from what was then Hungary, and about one-third of these were Slovaks.[9] About 2 percent immigrated from the northeastern provinces of Galicia and Bukovina; only slightly fewer came from Silesia. The level of migration from countries outside the Austrian Empire was very low, amounting to only 5 percent in 1856; later, it was relatively constant at 2 percent.

During the first phase of migration, a large number of the migrants in trade, industry, or the service professions were dependent wage-earners or seemingly self-employed people doing sub-contracted work at home.[10] In 1880, 92.3 percent of all servant girls were migrants, 46.8 percent of them from the provinces of Bohemia and Moravia; ten years later, the number of servant girls who had been born in Vienna had increased somewhat, although the percentage of migrants among them, at 87.6 percent, was still high.[11] Migrants similarly dominated the cobbler and tailor trades, the building industry, and brickmaking.[12] In an analysis of the censuses of 1857, 1880, and 1890, Heinz Fassmann was able to differentiate further: the lower social classes in Vienna consisted mainly of Lower Austrian migrants from the direct vicinity of the city and migrants from the nearby provinces of Bohemia and Moravia, and, to a much lesser extent, from the Alpine regions. On the other hand, migrants from Galicia, Bukovina, and abroad belonged to a greater extent to the upper classes.[13] Jewish migration cannot be included primarily under labor migration.[14] Croats and Slovaks belonged to the group of very poor migrants: peddlers, greengrocers, market women. Slovaks and Italians worked seasonally in large construction projects, such as the building of canals, the regulation of rivers, road construction, or the erection of the numerous monumental buildings. Most of the seasonal workers did not appear in the official statistics, since the census was taken on December 31, when they had already left the city.[15]

Migration was a continuous process that peaked in the period between the late 1850s and the end of the boom period in 1873. After a temporary decline, the heaviest migration in absolute terms occurred between 1890 and 1900.[16] Vienna represented a central, high-quality location and surpassed other, local centers in its power of attraction.[17] Internal migration also far surpassed migration to other countries, especially migration to America. In 1890, only 240,000 citizens from old Austria were counted in the United States, and only 490,000 in 1900. In 1900 there were 900,852 migrants living in Vienna. In 1899 and 1900, a mere 6,800 people migrated to America from Bohemia and Moravia; from the Austrian Alpine regions the figures amounted to 14,800. It is obvious that up to the turn of the century, America's pull on the Austrian regions that had traditionally sent migrants to Vienna was relatively insignificant. This changed considerably in the following decade, and in 1910 1.2 million Austrians were counted in the United States.[18] However, subsequent transatlantic migration from Lower Austria, Bohemia, and Moravia remained of below-average importance.[19]

The gender composition of migration to Vienna shows that women were clearly underrepresented during the middle of the nineteenth century, but accounted for about half of the migrants at the end of the century. At the same time, family migration gained in importance among labor migrants. This migration was predominantly from rural regions, although urban migration from Bohemia and Moravia developed disproportionately from 1857 to 1869 and from 1890 to 1910. Migration to cities and towns was primarily due to the comparatively higher wage levels to be found there.[20]

All migrants had some expectations upon arriving in the imperial metropolis. Analysis of this issue is difficult, however, because no systematic collections of letters from the lower social classes exist. Manuscript collections are restricted to correspondence from prominent persons. This is explained not only by the negligence of archivists and scholars, but also by the higher illiteracy rates in Austria as compared with Ireland, Holland, or England.[21] Thematic access is possible mainly through the "Life History Documentation" in Vienna[22] and a similar life-history collection in Prague,[23] through the Vienna city council's historical manuscripts,[24] through privately owned memoirs, and through material in magazines, daily newspapers, or printed autobiographies. These sources have to be used with caution: with the exception of diaries, autobiographical records are characterized by strong selectivity, self-justifications, and self-assertions. This is particularly true for printed memoirs, less so for handwritten records from the lower social classes. However, individual life stories are always structured self-portraits.[25] It is often difficult to distinguish between personal experience and preexisting clichés that have been adopted: some memoirs, for example, reproduced clichés of the sentimental *Heimatroman*, the sentimental "Home-Sweet-Home" novels in which "pure," healthy migrants from the countryside came to strange but fascinating big cities. In general, the source materials allow only cautious hypotheses to be made about the development and tendencies of migrants' views. Since only a few sources exist for the 1850s and 1860s, this study will focus on the third quarter of the nineteenth and the beginning of the twentieth century.

In 1854 Josef Jireček wrote in *Perly české* (*Bohemian Pearls*):

> It is almost unbelievable how many people go to Vienna to make their fortune. They usually come with empty hands, and after several years of activity many of them attain, if not exactly riches, then a certain degree of comfort. . . . Many a Bohemian also comes to Vienna and finds a starving city instead of an El Dorado.[26]

To understand whether this general picture is a cliché, an illusion, reality, or all three, we need to draw on individual life histories.

Migrants in Life Histories

The migratory process as experienced by Karel Šimonek, reported in his fastidiously kept private diary, was quite complex.[27] Karel Šimonek was born on August 9, 1875, in Mezeřič, Bohemia, the youngest son of Václav Šimonek, a "domkář" (poor farmer, who possesses only a tiny cottage, very few farm animals and very little land). His mother bore eleven children, of whom five—two girls and three boys—survived.

Even as a child, Karel had a full role to play in the family economy: "I was only happy at school. I had hardly got home when there was hard work in the field or house already waiting for me." Although he received an excellent school report in 1889, with a suggestion that he should continue his education, he had to begin as an apprentice cooper at his older brother's shop. "[I] had to work very hard; there was often trouble with my sister-in-law, who put on airs as if she were the mistress of the workshop." Afterward, he worked on the farm, usually until dark. On June 15, 1890, he noted, "I often have to cry and do not know what to do to get out of this hell. I've heard that one can voluntarily register for training in military music."

In 1890, Karel, who had learnt to play the trumpet, volunteered in the Slovak town of Trenčín and became an army musician. A letter from his brother Josef, a labor migrant in Budapest, informed him, "Don't go to Vienna; although it's a wonderful city, they don't like the Czechs. They treated me badly. Here in Budapest it is much better. When I have earned enough money, I am going to travel on."

However, Karel had "heard wonderful things about Vienna" from another migrant, and in 1893 he began to learn "German diligently, it's necessary." His wish to be in the *Kaiserstadt* (City of the Emperor) on this twentieth birthday came true: on October 3, 1894, his military company was moved to Vienna. "What hopes, what desires I had when I got onto the train!" He recorded no further details about his expectations in the several hundred pages of his diary.

His room in the Heumarkt barracks was on the third floor, a fact that frightened the villager: "My first steps at this height were not exactly pleasant. Hopefully nothing will fall in. I don't feel very safe!" He was not safe in bed either: "1000 fleas and bedbugs sucked our blood. That's not how it is at home. We also heard terrible noise coming from the street. We left the peaceful life in the country for the din of the big city!"

Karel remained in Vienna until the end of his military service, but was worried about his future. When he asked his parents for advice, his father merely sent back four blank sheets. "I cried bitterly. I can't stay in Vienna, I won't stay, I'll go home to my parents." He had a suit made with the money saved from tips, and, in 1895, when his military service was over, he left Vienna.

The return migrant was not welcome. "Father greets me in astonishment. What now? Why are you here?" Karel found work with a farmer through a friend and then became a poorly paid warehouse assistant at the railway in nearby Vrtice. Asked by a friend if he wanted to go to the United States with him, he remarked: "America!! But where will I get the money for the trip?" Rather than go to America, he returned home, but his "father said, Son, I'm worried about you. Go out into the world. God won't forsake you or us." So, at the age of 22, he went to Prague to apply for a job with the police.

Turned down temporarily, he migrated to Vienna again. This time acculturation was easier: "I feel as though I've always been in Vienna." He first looked for a schoolfriend, then tried his married sister in the sixteenth district, who "greets me pleasantly and lets me sleep here." By coincidence, he again obtained a position with the military band. Three times he sent small sums of money to his parents but could not even buy himself a decent shirt to visit his friend, the servant girl Božena Kohoutkova. "So I shall have to wear my uniform again when I go to Božka [nickname for Božena]. But she likes it." That summer he fell ill and lost both his job and his share of the band's revenues.

In September 1898, he again planned to apply to the police in Prague. "But where will I get the money for the trip?" His sister sent him the necessary sum. Refused again, he returned home a second time. "Father, please let me sleep here. I won't come again." "But where shall I go? To Vienna. But where can I turn, so that I won't be a burden to anyone?" "I walk around the streets day and night looking for work. I have 19 *Kreuzer.*" On October 7, he went to Antonín, his schoolmate, to ask if he could stay there to write job applications. "I could stay at Antonín Hauser's. On the 8th day I slept in a bed again. He knows of a job for me with Inspector Hinke at the gasworks." The next day he got a job as a helper at the gas works. On starting this job he was given a suit from Hauser's sister and her husband, a mason. He was "not especially happy" with his work, receiving only 20 *Gulden* per month, a very low salary. "I sit here surrounded by Germans and long for my homeland." He advanced to lantern-lighter, and later to assistant clerk at the gas works, where he remained until his retirement in 1933. He lived in Vienna until his death.

This life history illustrates the wide gap between expectations and real job opportunities, the repeated moves in disillusionment to other places in search of a job or at least a place to stay. This experience was no exception. For many rural migrants, living conditions were very hard.[28] Eighteen-year-old Jan Mařík, born into a ten-member family in 1885, was handed a bag, a blanket, and 50 *Gulden* by his father, who said, "Go out into the world, you can't stay here." Arriving in Vienna, Mařík leaned against a pier on the Tabor Bridge and cried, "What am I to do here?"[29] Jakob Štefan, born in 1863, from Klein-Seinitz in Moravia, was one of six children of a *Kleinhäusler* (cottager). Migration was to be his fate, too. Immediately after he finished school, his father told him "Son, you have to go to Vienna," but his mother helped him postpone the departure. He became an apprentice with a neighborhood locksmith. Once his apprenticeship was completed, however, he was sent off. His father at least was able to arrange for a job through the father of an acquaintance who had gone to Vienna earlier. Jakob Štefan left on October 14, 1880:

> I put on my best clothes, . . . the only ones I had besides my work clothes, . . . and a sprig of rosemary that mother also packed as a decoration because it was the Emperor's birthday. I left my beloved home with a small wooden suitcase containing my few possessions and my boots tied together over my shoulder.

Deeply moved, his mother delivered him to God's care. At four o'clock in the morning he arrived in Vienna where he calmly waited until "Mr Zadráhal came and asked if I was Štefan. We went to the wagon factory right away, and quarters had already been rented, so I was able to move in immediately." While he was thus assured of a live-lihood, there was distinctly less royal splendor than he had expected. "In the imperial city you couldn't tell that it was the Emperor's birthday, so there was no need for the sprig of rosemary."[30]

Just as the young men were sent away by their impoverished parents, so too were many young women. In many cases there seems to have been no image of something new, interesting, or rewarding. Often no expectations were voiced at all, just fear about the strange surroundings and the absence of friends. Most of these life stories show survival strategies rather than any form of upward mobility. Marie Svedláček, for example, was sent by her parents to Vienna from a small town in central Bohemia. The family farm had to be sold, and Marie had to leave at the age of fourteen. She had to sell her featherbed to afford the train. She worked in Vienna and married Franz Meduna, who had been sent to Vienna at the age of fifteen to become a shoemaker.[31] Therese Liegenfeld, from a German-speaking family in southern Bohemia, was one of eight children in a shoe-maker's family:

> When I was twelve years old, I unfortunately had to go to stran-gers. I had to tend cows on a farm, an hour away from home. That's where I learned about homesickness. . . . On All Saints' Day mother came and I was allowed to go home again. The following year, as soon as I got out of school, I had to leave again, from July until December, to work as a nanny. . . . My brothers and sisters and I had all done well in school, but unfortunately none of us was able to continue learning. We all had to go to work. The farmers always got their working girls from our region. Father said, "You already know about farming, so go to the city so that you can learn how to keep house and cook."[32]

Maria Wortner, born in 1894, migrated to Vienna in 1909 from the Budweis region, the predominantly Czech-speaking Trhové Sviny. She was one of six children. Her father, a shoemaker, also tilled a small plot of land. He prepared his children for migration by making them take special German lessons. After completing her school edu-cation, she was put on a train to Vienna and given the address of a relative who had a job for her.[33]

Anna Jäger, born in 1894, lived close to the Austro-Hungarian border. Her sister got married in Vienna and she, too, was sent away, in 1911. She did not want to stay at home since her stepfather was very rough and often drunk. I got my first position from an agency for servant girls on Sperlgasse, working for a Mr. Jelinek, who was also Hungarian. And while I was working for him, my mother came every month to pick up my wages. So I didn't even have a *Kreuzer*, my mother always took the money.[34]

Thus, surplus daughters were sent off to work as maids on farms or, more often, as domestics in Vienna. Some wanted to escape from violence in the family; most were pushed out at an early age. They seem to have looked for work and something to eat rather than the glitter of a metropolis.

Men and women had to rely on networks of friends, acquaintances, and relatives to find work in Vienna or elsewhere, to help each other in periods of unemployment. Johann Hallawitsch was born in 1879, the son of a *Kleinhäusler* in Fröllersdorf, in a predominantly German-speaking area in southern Moravia. In order to find a job he first moved to a small village, seven kilometers from his hometown, where he worked in a sugar factory. He washed beets and labored in the sugar cellar, at temperatures of up to 40 degrees centigrade, in a group with three friends. "There were good wages," but the thirty-six-hour weekend shift was too much for him. "Since there were already quite a few people from Fröllersdorf who were working and earning in Vienna, I decided to go to Vienna, but I first looked around for an agent." Rather than leave, he took odd jobs at the age of sixteen, but the "pay was quite low." When the sugar-beet work began, the "old four-man group immediately got together" and went to a large estate:

We stayed there all week, sleeping in the hayloft with a number of old horse blankets. There was no personal hygiene whatsoever. The return trip was often spent in the cattle wagon. . . . Among other things, there was once a wedding ride to Gutenfeld. I always liked to be a guest in Gutenfeld. . . . I had several friends there.

He usually asked there for help in getting a job in Vienna:

My father's cousin, Johann Slunsky, had also become a friend; his brother Josto and his uncle Josa had jobs in Vienna-Floridsdorf in the St. Georg Brewery. I took this opportunity and asked Johann Slunsky to put in a good word for me with his brother. He agreed that he would, as he already had the assurance of a job himself in the St. Marx Brewery.

But there was no work, and more odd jobs followed. Finally, at the age of seventeen, friends sent word from Vienna that a brewery job was available. "I couldn't believe it." In July 1896 he obtained a workbook and several other things for the trip and left.[35]

Family arrangements were often difficult: resources were meager and contacts limited. Johann Böhm's father was a mason and a forester during the winter; his mother kept a very small farm on the side. He had to begin a masonry apprenticeship three hours away from his hometown, but physically could not stand the very strenuous unskilled labor. "Every day right after work I sank completely exhausted onto my bed of straw." His father then accompanied him to Vienna. "This turn of affairs made me very happy at the time, since I had heard so many nice things about life in Vienna that I thought all my troubles were over." It was a "trip into the unknown," but a colleague of his father "had arranged for places for himself and for us to sleep."[36]

Johann Böhm can be considered privileged in that his father accompanied him. In Bohemia, many adolescents were handed over to professional male or female *Schlepper*, who were paid in the 1850s, 1860s, and 1870s to take groups of 30 or 40 boys or girls to Vienna, initially on foot, but later by train. Here they were delivered to their masters in return for a commission. Contemporaries spoke of a slave trade. Even as late as the turn of the century, the Franz Josef Railway Station reminded a local politician of a "slave market."[37] At a conference in 1893, a shoemaker explained the practice of bringing Czech apprentices to Vienna through a male agent:

> The masters complain that the shoemakers here cannot get apprentices, because the exploitation is so well known that the Viennese do not allow their sons to become shoemakers. For this reason, most of the apprentice boys are imported from Bohemia and Moravia.[38]

Market-like conditions could also be found in various areas of the female professions: in Olmütz there were effectively markets for wet nurses, where the persons up for offer—boldly expressed—did not know in the morning where they would be in the evening; it could be Prague, Brünn, Linz, Graz, Vienna, or elsewhere.[39]

Motives and Expectations

The causes for migration are to be seen in the change from agrarian-feudal economic and social structures to market-oriented industrial production and capital accumulation. This resulted in the restructuring of the population by professions and by regions, and in increasing urbanization and the emergence of a wage-dependent class.[40] During the pre–World War I years, Vienna, that "modern, industrial metropolis,"[41] stood in sharp contrast to the predominantly agrarian society around it. The establishment of industry in Vienna necessitated a large influx of potential job seekers from provincial areas. Supraregional mobility of the workforce as a mass phenomenon in the nineteenth century was conditioned primarily by two factors: the pauperization of the rural population and the needs of the labor market. After the revolution of 1848, capitalism began to permeate the agrarian economy. Dependence on market forces had drastic consequences during the 1880s because of the fall of grain and sugar prices. In the period from 1878 to 1892, auctions of real estate in Bohemia and Moravia following the forfeiture of mortgaged property reached peak levels.[42] The rural population in southern and southwestern Bohemia was particularly hard-hit, as it was primarily dependent on grain sales. A further structural change was an increase in the number of farms so small that they could hardly sustain their owners, who were then forced to find additional employment. The number of medium-sized farms had decreased through partition.[43]

As opposed to the northern Bohemian region, no industry of note developed in the southern Bohemian or southern Moravian regions.[44] The situation in the Lower Austrian *Waldviertel* and in the Upper Austrian *Mühlviertel* was similar. In all these regions, in the second half of the nineteenth century and up to the outbreak of World War I, one could speak of a tendency toward virtual depopulation. A statement issued by the Diocese of Budweis spoke of a "general exodus" even after the turn of the century: "Whole groups left in 1907. . . . Some houses were left empty, in some only old people and small children remained. In some districts all of the young people have left, so that the farmer can find neither a servant boy nor a maidservant."[45] About 55 percent of all migrants from Bohemia and Moravia were only twenty years old or younger, those aged thirty and less constituted 77 percent, while these figures were 40 and 67 percent, respectively, in 1910.[46] As our examples show, these people were often forced into migration, sent to relatives or acquaintances, deposited with agents, or hired out.

Whatever specific expectations a migrant might have had, economic circumstances became the determining factor. Motives for migration and expectations were often not identical: finding work was the single crucial issue. In the space of a decade, hundreds of thousands of migrants poured into Vienna. Their status there fluctuated: they commuted, returned home then came back, or simply remained in the city. In addition to the search for work and subsistence, there were other motives for coming to Vienna. Girls were sent to Vienna as servants to find husbands, or to prepare for married life.[47] Further motives were curiosity, emancipation, or family problems. Friederike Mojka, born in Moravia in 1896, recalled:

> There were six children, of whom I was the oldest; and of course I had a lot of work to do at home, like doing the washing with mother at night. She had to work during the day and couldn't do it then. . . . When my father came home from work, he would go to the neighborhood tavern for a beer. . . . I said to mother, "I can't stand it anymore!" And then I went to Vienna.[48]

To place the cliché of the "imperial city of Vienna" in the foreground as the motive for migration would mean to exaggerate the "pull" and to detract from the "push" factors involved. This is amply demonstrated in the reminiscences of labor migrants. In the extensive resources of the "Life History Documentation," not a single example can be found in which labor migrants discuss or analyze their specific expectations, which they must certainly have had. They obviously did not deem them to be relevant.

Upon arrival in the cities, hopes vanished in the face of the bewildering hustle and bustle. The migrants had once had dreams about the imperial city, but not expectations beyond earning a living. Ferdinand Hanusch, for example, a former traveling journeyman and later, from 1918 to 1920, Austrian social minister, wrote in his memoirs about his arrival in Vienna in 1885:

> I stood on the Danube Bridge and watched the majestically flowing river. . . . Since no one else did it I tried to tell myself to be brave, and now steered straight over the bridge towards the labyrinth of streets and alleys. Now I, too, was an ant in this great ant heap, and would first have to find my way, while those hurrying by knew it already. The large buildings, the big store windows, the many people who hurried by without paying any attention to me, the carriages rushing by and the buses rumbling by on the cobblestones, the horse-drawn tramway and the cursing carrion drivers; all of that makes such noise, that the city folk are probably used to it, but for someone coming to the big city for the

first time it is so oppressive that he loses his last bit of courage, because it seems like it's going to be impossible to make one's way in this life and in all this bustle. . . . To go to Vienna and make my fortune, that had been my dream since early boyhood, just as it is the dream of so many others. Now I was in Vienna, in this city of millions, and felt lost and lonely, lonelier than I had ever been in my life. I could still picture my mother crying at my father's grave, and the tears, that wouldn't come as I bid farewell, fell now on the old, wooden table.[49]

In the "Kleplova sbírka" life-story documentation in Prague, too, there is very little direct mention of expectations. Jan Waldauf, a brushmaker, wanted to leave home "to gain experience, could not get a job in Vienna and returned to Bohemia"; Františka Pelzlová went to Vienna "to earn more money." Karel Přibyl, a carpenter, came to Vienna in 1905 after a strike and the loss of his job: "There was no work. So I set off for Vienna. Well, they cursed me and chased me away—because I'm from Prague, because we're on strike, because we're not working." He had no money, but he "found a job working for a woman in the third district. She was a Czech."[50] In the entire life-story documentation nothing more can be found.

In the source material relating to emigration to the United States, however, numerous clichés of "El Dorado" and the "Golden West" are recorded and cited as motives. A contemporary review in the Budweis region considered the emigrants' letters that portrayed a euphoric picture to be a conclusive motive for emigration. In Vienna, agents of shipping companies stated in their reports that they used talk of "El Dorado" and riches to persuade high-school students—especially those with poor grades—to buy tickets to America.[51] In the case of Vienna, middle- and upper-class migrants were far more ready to believe the common, positive clichés. Bourgeois memoirs often mention culture, prominence, and greater riches as motives for migrating to Vienna; proletarian memoirs seldom do this.[52] The aim of lower-class people in coming to Vienna was to find work, any work, in order to survive.

Other needs and expectations did exist but were of less importance. The journeyman shoemaker, František Klupák, for instance, who came to Vienna in the 1880s, recalled retrospectively: "What I loved the most was that I learned to read and write, something I had longed to do." He had joined an educational club.[53] Fashion also played a role. As early as 1854, in *Perly české*, Jireček recalled the myth that servant girls in Vienna were more elegantly dressed than their mistresses.[54] Among the rural population, clichés about dress were deeply rooted: Anna Wortner, who migrated shortly before 1910, found people in Vienna particularly well dressed, especially the "handsome" soldiers. This she related on her first visit home.[55] The young female milliner, Pelzlová, dressed up for the trip from Prague to Vienna. But when she inquired about a bed at a convent that offered poor travelers shelter, she was suspected of being a prostitute.[56] Migrants often bought themselves new clothing with the first money they saved.[57] Dress elevated the migrants over the poorly attired villagers, and city dress protected them from being considered country bumpkins. But education and fashion were not primary motives for migration. Moving to Vienna "was a custom." "Of course we went to Vienna" is a typical remark in workers' reminiscences.[58] To avoid odd jobs and poor wages in the rural areas, men and women were lured away by agents, or followed the calls of acquaintances, relatives, or friends.

The written memoirs of the journeyman shoemaker Klupák provide a description of information channels among the migrating lower classes—leading to work and living quarters—and of secondary motives for migration, such as looking for a marriage partner or amusement. Klupák's journeyman status was the primary cause for his labor migration in the second half of the nineteenth century. Journeymen artisans still had to wander. Vienna was not only the largest labor market but also the largest matchmaking market in the Habsburg monarchy:

> It was in the eighties that I went wandering. First to Prague, then in the direction of Benešov, and from there to Písek, where I met Božena and Libuše. They also wanted to go to Vienna, and when I told them that they should go with me, they objected that that wasn't possible, and I should write to them in Písek from where they would go to Vienna. . . . I went via Telč, Moravské Budějovice, Znojmo, Korneuburg, Tolenzdorf. From Tolenzdorf we went in groups and with music—accordions and whistles. I was the band leader with a baton. We sang "Když jsem vandroval, musika hrála . . ." (When I wandered the music played). Then a policeman came and chased us about, because we were singing in Czech. We reached Vienna and I got work in Ottakring. The wife of the master there introduced me to Greta. She was beautiful, but couldn't speak Czech. . . . So I taught her Czech and had a lot of laughs in doing so. Otherwise she was very good-natured and brought my supper to the window. . . . But I thought about

Božena and Libuše, and since I couldn't write, I told Pepa, my colleague, and he wrote to them. Four days later I got a card from Božena; I should find a place for them to sleep, they would be leaving Písek early in the morning. I went to meet them at the train station and brought them to Pepa's sister. She went with them to the agent who got them positions, one on Liechtensteinstraße and one in Alsergrund. Afterwards I went dancing with them in the Prater. In July Božena's employers went on vacation to Kotor for four weeks, and Božena was afraid to stay alone, because at that time Hugo Schenk and Šlosárek (two women-killers) were doing their evil deeds. So I did as Božena wished and slept there. Of course I was very obliging. Božena showed me the bedroom. It was very beautiful. That was the first time I had ever seen such a beautiful bedroom. I objected that I had never slept in such a white feather bed. That was really true— neither at home, nor at a master's. Božena put me to bed in the master bedroom.

Klupák stayed in Vienna for two years, then wandered via several other places to Trieste. He returned to Vienna on two other occasions and finally lived in Teplice in Bohemia.[59]

Many others migrated back and forth like Klupák. An enormous mobility and fluctuation prevailed during the entire Franz Josef era. For example, within one or two years, the membership of several large Czech associations in Vienna changed almost completely but remained at a constant level.[60] According to the census of 1910, of every five migrants that came, only one took up permanent residence in Vienna.[61] Migration distances of 100 to 300 kilometers were more conducive to "trial and error" than transatlantic migration. For those trained male and female workers who came to Vienna after reaching the age of twenty, the possibility of correcting possible false expectations was large; this was even more true for the younger migrants, who had been forced into going to Vienna. The importance and relevance of expectations about specific locations was low, since migration became a way of life. The role of the cliché about Vienna for labor migrants cannot be equated with the image of America, as Fassmann argued, nor did Vienna appear to be as much of an "El Dorado" as Glettler has described it to be.[62]

After the collapse of the Habsburg empire in 1918—a political and most important, economic catastrophe for Vienna and Austria— approximately 150,000 migrants returned to the newly founded Czechoslovak Republic. Yet, in the minds of many, Vienna remained

Vienna—city of the waltz, city of culture; the splendid buildings of the Habsburgs remained, even if the emperor had vanished. In this sense, the city had lost little of its attraction. Bohemians and Moravians came back, not as laborers but as tourists. Czechoslovaks were the most frequent visitors to Vienna in the period between the wars.[63] Vienna was no longer a magnet for workers, but the popular lore about it remained.

The Image of Labor Migrants among Organized Labor

The relationship of labor migrants to the domestic labor movement was more important for their acceptance and integration into society than either expectations, on the one hand, or images and dreams, on the other. The organized labor movement did not reflect on the problems of migration until the 1890s. With its rather hesitant relationship to labor migration, it developed a tradition that has remained effective to the present.[64]

Paralyzed by ideological quarrels and restrictive laws, the Austrian labor movement did not succeed until the end of the nineteenth century in changing the form of workers' protests from spontaneous reactions to organized, planned action.[65] According to the strike concept, labor migrants were supposed to act in solidarity with their locally born colleagues. But migrants were also considered potential rivals, as strikebreakers. Both aspects are reflected in the reports about the large-scale, successful strikes in Vienna waged by the Wienerberger brickmakers from April 16 to 27, 1895. Approximately 10,000—for the most part Czech—brickmakers took part. The central organ of the Austrian Social Democratic Party, the *Arbeiter-Zeitung*, warned both strikers and potential strikebreakers:

> Attention! We have news that agents of the Wienerberger Company are traveling around in Moravia hiring workers, under the pretence of getting people for Wiener-Neustadt. We were informed that a group of such workers was transported from Znaim yesterday. A musician was added to the group to keep the people in good spirits. We are convinced that when these workers find out that a strike is underway, they will immediately return to their homes.

After the successful outcome of the strike, the *Arbeiter-Zeitung* praised the behavior of the workers of different "nationalities" thus:

One must know what it means when thousands of workers and their families that belong to three different nationalities subject themselves to the same discipline. The behavior of the Italian workers can be particularly commended. This is not their home, they are separated from the others by their language; to some extent they have better wages, yet despite this they showed unquestionable solidarity.[66]

Resistance to migrant strikebreakers and the solidarity of foreign-language migrants were considered decisive for victory in industrial disputes.[67]

In the early phase of strike history, strikers often took to "direct action" against labor migrant scabs, and fights erupted between the two groups.[68] Later, the labor movement used available media to prevent the importation of strikebreakers. They constantly listed occupations and firms or cities that should be avoided by migrants because of ongoing strikes. This concerned not only the domestic, but also the international labor market, for strikebreakers were being recruited outside Austria.[69] In large, planned strikes, trade-union functionaries would issue warnings against migration before the dispute began. These were published in the areas where potential migrants or strikebreakers were usually recruited. During the dispute, union leaders urged migrant workers who had arrived inadvertently to return home.[70] Successful recruiting of strikebreakers by employers was attributed in the trade-union and social democratic press to the low cultural, that is,—economic—level of the recruits. In the case of a metal-workers' strike in the Lower Austrian town of Traisen, the trade-union journal spoke of people from "partly Asiatic areas"—Slovakia and Hungary were meant—as well as of a "horde of Croats."[71]

According to the theorists of the German-Austrian labor movement, the cultural standard—intellectual, mental, and material—of the labor migrants, which was related to the level of development of the productive forces in the area of origin, had an indisputable influence on their attitude toward strikes and organizations.[72] Otto Bauer, the Austro-Marxist, drafted a model of comparative levels of labor migration and its effects for discussion within the Second International: the lower the cultural standard of the migrants, the more "dangerous" the migration for the organized workers in the target area. Migrants who came from areas dominated by agriculture and cottage industry would easily accept arbitrary wages and behavior of the employers.[73] In the party's discussion, migrants to Vienna were hardly mentioned. For the migration of Czechs to Vienna, Bauer noted in 1907 that the early "agrarian-domestic" phase was past: "The Czech emigrants come to Vienna no longer as boorish wage slaves, but as confident laborers, who have integrated part of their national culture."[74]

This conclusion was probably also related to the decline of internal tensions within the Austrian Social Democratic Party, which had previously been organized on a multinational basis. After 1905, the multinational organization found itself increasingly under the influence of separatist ethnic forces. With the foundation of the Czech Social Democratic Workers' Party in May 1911, the so-called "Small International" broke apart.[75] If the candidacy of Antonín Němec, the Czech Social Democrat, and the positive reaction to his campaign in a Viennese electoral district in 1897, can be considered as evidence of this good understanding, the refusal to nominate a Czech candidate for the parliamentary election in 1907 marks new dividing lines.[76]

Vienna, where the Christian Social city council had a fixed policy of assimilation, was one of the centers of national tensions among sections of the labor movement. It did its best to wage a bureaucratic war on the emerging Czech private school system.[77] While Czech nationalists and Czech Social Democrats argued that the process of assimilation could be prevented, the attitude of German-Austrian Social Democracy differentiated between levels of economic development in the areas of origin.[78] Within the framework of his theoretical writings, Otto Bauer attempted to develop a specific "Assimilation Law of the Proletariat," according to which

> proletarian immigrants of the agrarian-domestic type assimilate more easily, proletarian immigrants of the industrial-capitalist type with more difficulty, the further the economic development in their country has progressed; the higher the qualification of their work, the higher is their cultural standard.[79]

According to Bauer, the industrial-capitalist migrant movement was commendable because of its raised level of class consciousness, but at the same time it presented new potential for conflict because these migrants would be more difficult to integrate into the resident working class. Any such process of "national assimilation" could take place only within a long-term perspective:

> The self-confident Czech worker, who in his homeland already learned to know and love a piece of the history of his nation, its

culture and ideas, clings much more tightly to his language and nationality than the boorish wage-slave of earlier times. Even in his new environment he is closely organized and in constant contact with his national and class comrades; he reads Czech newspapers and books, belongs to Czech organizations and goes to Czech gatherings.[80]

In this phase, any image of Vienna had less impact on acculturation processes than the ethnically rooted class consciousness of the culture of origin.

According to Bauer, those migrants who lived and worked with German speakers, particularly the servant girls, could be assimilated, while the Czech brickmakers on Vienna's periphery, due to their numbers and the closed nature of their settlements, could not. The "German-Austrian" Social Democrats expected assimilation to occur over the long term, and they considered it to be absolutely positive. This was due partly to the German nationalist views of many social democratic functionaries, as well as to the dislike of any minority consciousness that might become a "dividing wall" between workers. Neither Karl Renner nor Bauer doubted the superiority of the "German nation" in the free and peaceful competition of national cultures that they promoted. This attitude left their Czech comrades with little room for compromise.[81]

Toward the end of the century, when autobiographical documents from the lower social classes slowly drew the attention of the public, the social democratic *Arbeiter-Zeitung* published Josefine Joksch's memoirs of her experiences as a servant girl in 1885:

> It was a dreary winter day when I made my first trip to Vienna to take up a position as nanny. I was glad to leave home. First, because everyone who was in a position to work as a servant went away, so that they wouldn't lose the bit of esteem that they had enjoyed at home; and then because Vienna had been the subject of my longing for a long time. "There's just one imperial city, there's just one Vienna! There it must be splendid, that's where I must go!"—this I sang even as a very small girl, later with ever-increasing conviction and ardent desire. And as I now sat shivering in the compartment corner and looked out into the dim winter morning, I thought about how dreary and boring such a winter's day in my home town was, and how nice it was to have escaped from that eternal monotony. At the same time my heart was filling with doubt. They told me that I would suffer much at the beginning.

Josefine was met by an acquaintance and brought to a prearranged place, where she was to work as a nanny. After a short time, she contracted a minor illness, an inflammation of the throat, and was immediately dismissed: the children, she was told by her employer, were not to be infected. In a servants' dormitory for unemployed girls she tried several times to get a bed for the night. But she did not have enough money and was sent away:

> So that was our humane era, where the Viennese with their famed "golden hearts" had the saying "live and let live" as their slogan! It appeared to me that I was really being left to die. I didn't have any means to make the trip home, and I couldn't agree to the disgrace of being exported home at the expense of the state. And yet I got out of that very sticky situation in one piece, with the help of a servant girl who was also from my home town, and whom I remembered at the last minute. Everyone disapproved of what I was doing, but she didn't. She only nodded her head when I told her of my suffering, comforted me as best she could, and helped me to get home.[82]

Publication of this migrant drama in the *Arbeiter-Zeitung* does not appear to be a coincidence. The labor movement's relationship to and image of the Viennese metropolis was at best ambivalent. Until the turn of the century, the metropolis embodied not only the progress of industrial production as desired by Social Democracy, but also, according to the impoverishment theory, the pauperism and depression caused by the development of capitalism. The "Moloch Metropolis" as a symbolization of "the capitalism that destroys humanity" found a daily reflection in the suicide reports.[83] Max Winter, for example, editor of the *Arbeiter-Zeitung*, well-known journalist and later a parliamentarian, wrote specific Viennese social commentaries—true accounts of misery and poverty, in which homeless Bohemian and Slovak migrants had to sleep out in the open, went to asylums, or lived in miserable shacks.[84]

The regular reports of misery, which can be followed in social democratic publications until the collapse of the monarchy, would certainly not attract any labor migrants into the city. On the other hand, Social Democracy developed activities at different levels for social reforms that were diametrically opposed to the apocalyptic scenarios of poverty.[85] The emancipation potential of the metropolis was also discussed:

Capitalism has destroyed the old life and created a new life. It has uprooted masses from their homes, driven them into monstrous tenements. Here they gain new support: from their brother's arm, from their comrade's spirit; in a supporting and uplifting community. They have become free from the narrow horizon of the village; they have learned to desire greatness. And so they will wait, until the day comes that will give their community power, to arrange the world according to their own will—with clear minds and clenched fists.[86]

Vienna was of extraordinary importance for the labor movement: 37.3 percent of the party and trade-union members lived here. Working-class voters were extremely disadvantaged by the communal *Kurienwahlrecht*—suffrage based on property qualifications—which impeded the participation of Social Democracy at community level. The weight of identification with Vienna therefore lay less on the city itself than on its movement.[87] For labor migrants the labor movement in no way projected a euphoric picture of Vienna, which would have implicitly meant the promotion of migration. Ruined existences, poverty, housing shortages, and misery were much more prevalent in the workers' press and in social democratic publications than were examples of social ascent or prosperity. This, too, is an aspect of the differences between dream and reality: Do not succumb to desperation, but bring reality into line with your images and expectations.

Notes

We are grateful to Meredith Schneeweiss (B. A., University of Vermont, 1975), who translated this manuscript from German.

1. See Peter R. Hofstätter, *Einführung in die Wahrnehmungspsychologie* (Stuttgart: Kroener, 1973), 364–68.

2. See Alphons Lhotsky, "Mittelalterliche Lobsprüche auf Wien," in idem, *Aufsätze und Vorträge*, vol. 4 (Vienna: Verlag für Geschichte und Politik, 1974), 11–13; Theodor Ilgen, *Die Geschichte Kaiser Friedrichs III, von Aeneas Silvius* (Leipzig, 1899), 14–18.

3. See Wolfgang Mantl, "Wien um 1900—ein goldener Stachel," in *Wien um 1900: Aufbruch in die Moderne*, ed. Peter Berner, Emil Brix, and Wolfgang Mantl (Vienna: Verlag für Geschichte und Politik, 1986), 249–58; Carl Schorske, *Wien: Geist und Gesellschaft im Fin de siècle* (Frankfurt a.M.: S. Fischer, 1982); Käthe Leichter, *Leben und Werk* (Vienna: Europaverlag, 1973),

241; Edward Timms, *Karl Kraus, Apocalyptic Satirist: Culture and Catastrophe in Habsburg Vienna* (New Haven, Conn., and London: Yale University Press, 1986), 28–30, 83.

4. See Otto Gerber, *Die Boden- und Wohnungsfrage in Beziehung auf die Tuberkulose mit besonderer Berücksichtigung Wiener Verhältnisse* (Vienna, 1918), 15; Timms, *Karl Kraus;* Norbert Leser, "Der zeitgeschichtliche Hintergrund des Wien und Österreich im Fin de siècle," in *Theodor Herzl und das Wien des Fin de siècle,* ed. Norbert Leser (Vienna: Böhlau, 1987), 32–33; for Adolf Hitler see *Mein Kampf* (Munich, 1937), 135: "The conglomerate of races that could be seen in the monarchy's capital was repugnant to me, this whole mixture of nationalities, of Czechs, Poles, Hungarians, Ruthenians, Serbians, Croatians, etc., was repugnant to me. And among all of them as a bacterium eternally dividing humanity—Jews and more Jews. The huge city seemed to me to be the embodiment of race defilement" (translated by M.S.).

5. Franz Stuiber, "Die Wienerstadt ist ein Magnet," in *Das Wiener Volkslied,* ed. Josef Blaha, op. 30. 1. Nr. 24201 (Vienna, n.d.).

6. In portraying the development of Vienna's population, the respective city boundaries are frequently referred to: they vary considerably and should actually not be taken as a basis for comparison. The city expansion of 1890 had a particularly distorting effect. The incorporation increased the number of city districts from ten to nineteen and increased the population by more than half a million. For comparison, it is appropriate to use the current city boundaries, and convert the historical data to this area, which is what we have done here.

7. For the development of Vienna's population from 1830 to 1910, see *Statistisches Handbuch für die Republik Österreich,* 1983 (Vienna: Österreichische Staatsdruckerei, 1983), 13; Felix Olegnik, *Historisch-Statistische Übersichten von Wien,* 1 (Vienna: Magistrat der Stadt Wien, 1956), 22–23, 59, 81; *Statistik der Stadt Wien,* no. 2 (Vienna, 1861), 80.

8. The breakdown according to the individual Austrian Alpine provinces varied only slightly during the observation period. The birthplaces of Vienna's 1,674,957 residents in 1900 were as follows.

Vienna	774,105	(46.40%)
Alpine provinces		
Lower Austria	188,493	(11.20%)
Upper Austria	24,250	(1.44%)
Other parts of the empire		
Styria	21,960	(1.32%)
Salzburg	2,670	(0.16%)
Carinthia	6,826	(0.41%)

Tyrol	5,632	(0.33%)
Vorarlberg	1,026	(0.06%)
Bohemia/Moravia	411,037	(24.54%)
Galicia/Bukovina	36,763	(2.50%)
Silesia	27,658	(1.65%)
Other parts of Cisleithania	8,958	(0.53%)
Other countries, including Hungary	162,579	(9.71%)

See *Statistisches Jahrbuch der Stadt Wien im Jahre 1901* (Vienna, 1903), 34–41. The foreign citizens came from Hungary (including Slovakia, Transylvania, and German-speaking West Hungary): 129,081; the German Empire: 21,733; other: 17,660; see *Österreichische Statistik* 59, no. 2 (Vienna, 1905), 2. A good survey of total migration to Vienna can also be found in Harald Praschinger, "Bemerkungen über die wirtschaftliche und soziale Rolle der im franzisko-josephinischen Zeitalter nach Wien zugewanderten Bevölkerung," in *Österreich in Geschichte und Literatur* 29 (1985): 19–34.

9. See Monika Glettler, *Die Wiener Tschechen um 1900: Strukturanalyse einer nationalen Minderheit in der Großstadt* (Munich: Oldenbourg, 1972), 33–36. In 1900, 42,896 people lived in Vienna from chiefly Slovak-speaking regions of what was then Hungary; in 1910, there were 46,210. See Michael John and Albert Lichtblau, "Česká Vídeň: Von der tschechischen Großstadt zum tschechischen Dorf," in *Archiv 1987: Jahrbuch des Vereins für Geschichte der Arbeiterbewegung* (Vienna: Eigenverlag, 1987): 36.

10. See Heinz Fassmann, "A Survey of Patterns and Structures of Migration in Austria, 1850–1900," in *Labor Migration in the Atlantic Economies: The European and North American Working Classes during the Period of Industrialization*, ed. Dirk Hoerder (Westport, Conn.: Greenwood Press, 1985), 84–87.

11. See Stephan Sedlaczek, *Die k.k. Reichshaupt- und Residenzstadt Wien: Ergebnisse der Volkszählung vom 31.12.1880*, pt. 3 (Vienna, 1887), 247–48; Glettler, *Wiener Tschechen*, 230.

12. In 1880, 58.3 percent of the journeymen carpenters, 68.8 percent of the cobblers, and 71.8 percent of the tailors came from Bohemia and Moravia; Sedlaczeck, *Volkszählung 1880*, 246–47. For the structure of the professions, see also Glettler, *Wiener Tschechen*, 60–68, and Erika Iglauer, *Ziegel— Baustoff unseres Lebens* (Vienna: Berger & Söhne, 1974).

13. See Fassmann, "Migration in Austria, 1850–1900," 80, 84–87, 91. Fassmann categorizes the migration to Vienna into short-distance, middle-distance, and long-distance migrants, although he defines these categories only roughly; not all who came from Bohemia and Moravia were penniless. This can be seen in the relatively high number of house-owners from

Bohemia and Moravia, which amounted to approximately 1,000 persons in 1862—12 percent of all house-owners. See P. Polan (Pseudonym for Karl Matal), *Die Wiener Hausherren aus dem Jahre 1862 im Lichte einer nationalen Statistik, Bohemica Viennensia, no. 2* (Vienna, 1948), 7–14.

14. For Jewish migration to Vienna see Marsha Rozenblit, *The Jews of Vienna, 1867–1914: Assimilation and Identity* (Albany, N.Y.: State University of New York Press, 1983). The Jewish population of Vienna increased from 15,116 in 1856 to 175,318 in 1910. See *Statistik der Stadt Wien*, trial issue (Vienna, 1857), 44–45.

15. In 1856, the number of seasonal workers was estimated at 15,000, and at many times that number at the turn of the century; Karl Freiherr v. Czörnig, *Ethnographie der österreichischen Monarchie*, vol. 1, sect. 1 (Vienna, 1857), 675. For fluctuations of the Bohemian and Moravian labor migrants at the turn of the century see Glettler, *Wiener Tschechen*, 41–43.

16. See *Statistisches Handbuch*, 1983, 18.

17. See Fassmann, "Migration in Austria, 1850–1900", 71–78.

18. See *Österreichische Statistik*, n.s., vol. 2, 3 (Vienna, 1919), 37; *Statistisches Jahrbuch der Stadt Wien*, 1901 (Vienna, 1903), 34–41; *Zeitschrift für Demographie der Juden* 1, no. 7 (Berlin, 1905): 13.

19. See Hans Chmelar, *Höhepunkte der österreichischen Auswanderung: Die Auswanderung aus den im Reichsrat vertretenen Königreichen und Ländern, 1905–1914* (Vienna: Verlag der österreichischen Akademie der Wissenschaften, 1974), 108–11. In the decade from 1900 to 1910, the provinces of Galicia and Bukovina made up the largest contingent of migrants to America, relatively speaking. These provinces played only a minor role in labor migration to Vienna. A detailed survey of transatlantic migration can be found in Dirk Hoerder, "Arbeitswanderung und Arbeiterbewußtsein im atlantischen Wirtschaftsraum: Forschungsansätze und -hypothesen," in *Archiv für Sozialgeschichte* 28 (1988): 391–425.

20. See Glettler, *Die Wiener Tschechen*, 44–51; Fassmann, "Migration in Austria, 1850–1900," 81; Michael Mesch, *Arbeiterexistenz in der Spätgründerzeit: Gewerkschaften und Lohnentwicklung in Österreich, 1890–1914* (Vienna: Europaverlag, 1984), 201.

21. From an international comparison at the beginning of the 1880s, it has been established that the rate of illiteracy in the male population over six years of age was 10.4 percent in Holland, 13.2 percent in England, and 20.8 percent in Ireland, but was 38.9 percent in Austria and 43.3 percent in Hungary. See "Über Analphabeten" in *Statistische Monatsschrift* 12 (Vienna, 1886): 290.

22. The "Dokumentation lebensgeschichtlicher Aufzeichnungen," Prof. Michael Mitterauer, Director of the Institute for Economic and Social History, University of Vienna, comprises a total of 600 records, of which only

a small portion was relevant to our questions. We are grateful for permission to use this collection.

23. The collection "Kleplova sbírka" is located in the archive of the Musuem of Technology and Trade in Prague. A team of chroniclers collected thousands of reminiscences of former workers. Excerpts were published in Adolf Branald, ed., *Hrdinové všedních dnů: Jejich příhěby, vzpomínky a vypravění* (Heroes of Daily Life, Their Experiences, Recollections, and Accounts), 2 vols. (Prague, 1953). We are grateful to Mira Klebel for the translation.

24. This is the collection from the "Historical Commission of the City of Vienna," which can be found in the Vienna City Hall.

25. See Andrea Schnöller and Hannes Stekl, "Bürgerliche Kindheit in Autobiographien: Forschungsprobleme," in *"Es war eine Welt der Geborgenheit . . .": Bürgerliche Kindheit in Monarchie und Republik*, ed. Andrea Schnöller and Hannes Stekl (Vienna: Böhlau, 1987), 9–12.

26. Josef Jireček, "Die čecho-slavische Bevölkerung in Wien: Einige Skizzen" (translated from "Perly české"), *Jahrbücher für slavische Literatur, Kunst und Wissenschaft* n.s. 2 (1854): 580.

27. Karel Šimonek (1875–1947) kept a more or less regular diary from the end of his school education at the age of fourteen onward; he wrote retrospectively about the time prior to that. Šimonek kept the diary only for himself; no one knew of its existence. It was found by his son and daughter-in-law after his death. We are grateful to Anna Simonek for translating the diary from the Czech.

28. The following recollections were all either written by hand or transmitted orally. They have been examined for their reliability and contain the most important elements of the migration process.

29. Reminiscences of Jan Mařík, privately owned by Johann Marik, Vienna.

30. Jakob Štefan, "Mein Lebenslauf: Erlebnisse und Erinnerungen," handwritten notebooks (Vienna, 1939), 1–3, 30–32.

31. Interview with Franz Meduna, born in 1908 (by Helmut Fielhauer). Transcript, 1–16. Excerpts in Helmut Fielhauer, "Geschäftsleute in Währing (1). Franz Meduna, Schuhmachermeister," *Unser Währing: Vierteljahresschrift des Museumsvereins Währing* 19 (1984): 184–89.

32. Therese Weber, ed., *Häuslerkindheit: Autobiographische Erzählungen* (Vienna: Böhlau, 1984), 184–89.

33. Recollections of Maria Wortner, privately owned by the Wortner family, Vienna.

34. Interview with Mrs. Juliane Jäger (by Albert Lichtblau). Transcript, 1–3.

35. Johann Hallawitsch, "Familienchronik: Mein Lebensweg," type-written notebooks (Vienna, 1950), 9–10.

36. Johann Böhm, *Erinnerungen aus meinem Leben* (Vienna: Europaverlag, 1964), 22–24.

37. See František Soukup, *Česká menšina v Rakousku* (The Czech Minority in Austria) (Prague, 1928), 501; Glettler, *Wiener Tschechen*, 218–19; *Bericht über den Ersten Österreichischen Schuhmachertag in Wien*, ed. Johann Andritzky (Vienna, 1873), 38; Eduard Sueß, *Erinnerungen* (Leipzig, 1916), 341.

38. *Stenographisches Protokoll der durch die Gewerkschaften Wiens einberufenen Enquete* (Vienna, 1895), 38.

39. See Susan Zimmermann, "Brauchen wir Anwältinnen der Frauen," *AUF: Eine Frauenzeitschrift*, no. 51 (May 1986): 6.

40. For a detailed cause-analysis study regarding labor migration to Vienna, see Michael John and Albert Lichtblau, "Assimilation und Integration der Arbeitsmigrantinnen in Wien: Eine Skizze politischer, sozialer und kultureller Faktoren: Rückblick, Bestandsaufnahme, Prognose," in *Über den Umgang mit Minderheiten*, ed. Rainer Bauböck, Gerhard Baumgartner, Bernhard Perchinig, and Karin Pinter (Vienna: Verlag für Gesellschaftskritik, 1988); see also Michael John and Albert Lichtblau, *Schmelztiegel Wien—einst und jetzt: Geschichte und Gegenwart der Zuwanderung nach Wien* (Vienna: Böhlau, 1990).

41. Renate Banik-Schweitzer and Gerhard Meissl, *Industriestadt Wien: Die Durchsetzung der Industriellen Produktion in der Habsburgerresidenz* (Vienna, 1983), 38.

42. See Jan Havránek, "Die ökonomische und politische Lage der Bauernschaft in den böhmischen Ländern in den letzten Jahrzehnten des 19. Jahrhunderts," in *Jahrbuch für Wirtschaftsgeschichte*, pt. 2 (Berlin, 1966): 123; according to official statistics, the number of execution sales of real estate entered in land registers in Bohemia and Moravia amounted in the following years to: 1868–72: 11,651; 1873–77: 11,627; 1878–82: 26,836; 1883–87: 25,021; 1888–92: 32,756; 1893–97: 19,490; 1898–1902: 18,290. See ibid., 110.

43. See Glettler, *Wiener Tschechen*, 32–44; for the economic development of Bohemia in general: Karl M. Brousek, *Die Großindustrie Böhmens, 1848–1918* (Munich: Oldenburg, 1987).

44. Small industrial islands could only be formed in the towns with wood and lumber industry and around Budweis; ibid., 45–84.

45. Quoted in Leopold Caro, "Auswanderung und Auswanderungspolitik in Österreich," *Schriften des Vereins für Sozialpolitik*, vol. 131 (Leipzig, 1909), 58.

46. See Glettler, *Wiener Tschechen*, 45.

47. See Marina Tichy, *Alltag und Traum: Leben und Lektüre der Dienst-mädchen im Wien der Jahrhundertwende* (Vienna: Böhlau, 1984), 16–27.

48. Interview with Friederike Mojka (by Albert Lichtblau). Transcript, 8.

49. Ferdinand Hanusch, *Aus meinen Wanderjahren: Erinnerung eines Walzbruders* (Reichenberg, n.d.), 8–10.

50. Branald, *Hrdinové všednich dnů*, 20, 327, 173.

51. Caro quotes from the review on economic conditions in the Bud-weis area: "America appears to everyone to be the promised land, the true paradise, an idea to which the American Czechs contribute to a great extent by their letters to relatives and friends, generous gifts, frequent trips to the old homeland and by the Czech-American newspapers." Caro, "Auswanderung und Auswanderungspolitik," 59; see also Chmelar, *Höhepunkte der österreichischen Auswanderung*, 111.

52. See, for instance, Leichter, *Leben und Werk*, 240–43; Joseph Wechsberg, *The Vienna I Knew: Memories of a European Childhood* (Garden City, N.Y., 1979), 137. Otto Simon, high school teacher in the provinces, wrote emphatically in an application for a similarly qualified position in Vienna: "Better to work paving the streets of Vienna than to be a principal in Un-garisch-Hradisch!" Joseph T. Simon, *Augenzeuge* (Vienna: Wiener Volks-buchhandlung, 1979), 10.

53. Branald, *Hrdinové všednich dnů*, 301–9.

54. See Jireček, "Die čecho-slavische Bevölkerung in Wien," 579–82.

55. Recollections of Maria Wortner.

56. See Branald, *Hrdinové všednich dnů*, 327–32.

57. See Šimonek, "Diary," 110; Hallawitsch, "Familien chronik," 12; Štefan, "Lebenslauf," 40.

58. Interview with Johann Diwisch, born in 1900 (by Albert Lichtblau and Michael John). Transcript, 3.

59. Branald, *Hrdinové všednich dnů*, 301–9. See Chmelar, *Höhepunkte der österreichischen Auswanderung*, 88.

60. See John and Lichtblau, "Česká Vídeň," 34–35.

61. The average migrational increase was 15,170 persons in the decade 1900–10, *Statistisches Handbuch 1983*, 18. After the census of 1910, there were 127,770 people who had lived in Vienna for less than a year; after deducting the 46,128 newborns of the year 1910 (see Olegnik, *Statistische Übersichten*, 92), approximately 80,000 people were left, who can be divided into rough groups of 15,000 (permanent) and 65,000 (fluctuating), *Statistisches Jahrbuch*, 1912 (Vienna, 1913), 911.

62. See Fassmann, "Migration in Austria, 1850–1900," 79; Glettler, *Wiener Tschechen*, 40–41.

63. See John and Lichtblau, "Česká Vídeň," 41, 53.

64. See John and Lichtblau, "Assimilation und Integration der Arbeitsmigrantinnen in Wien," 18.

65. See Fritz Klenner, *Die österreichischen Gewerkschaften: Vergangenheit und Gegenwartsprobleme* (Vienna: ÖGB-Verlag, n.d.), 1.

66. *Arbeiter-Zeitung: Zentral-Organ der österreichischen Sozialdemokratie* (hereafter quoted as *AZ* (Vienna), 22 and 27 Apr 1894. By "three different nationalities" the Italians, Czechs, and supposedly "German-Austrians" were meant.

67. A summary of the outcome of the butchers' strike of 1892: "It would have been a shining victory, if there hadn't been the usual strikebreakers." *Österreichischer Metallarbeiter: Organ der Eisen-und Metallarbeiter Österreichs* (hereafter quoted as *ÖM*), Vienna, 20 May 1892.

68. See Otto Bauer, "Proletarische Wanderungen," *Die Neue Zeit: Wochenschrift der deutschen Sozialdemokratie* (Stuttgart) 25 (1907): 491; *ÖM*, 8 and 22 June 1905. See also Eva Viethen, "Wiener Arbeiterinnen: Leben zwischen Familie, Lohnarbeit und politischem Engagement" (Ph.D. Diss., Vienna, 1984), 169: "A police report stated . . . that on the said day [29 Aug 1906, E.V.] at 9:30 in the evening, eight wagons filled with Slovak workers, whom the owner of Fa. M. Edlingers Witwe & Sohn, Silk Dying Company in Vienna II, had hired to replace workers who had been on strike since July 24, 1906, drove through the Linnegasse and Schiffmühlgasse. They were met by an agitated crowd of hundreds with shouts, curses, and a barrage of stones, which resulted in shattered car windows and numerous injured workers and security guards. Not only were stones thrown by the crowds in the streets, they also came from gardens, excavations, why even from windows of some of the buildings."

69. Besides the constant warnings against migration, the newspapers of the labor movement also reported on agents who were recruiting workers outside of Austria. See, for instance: *Gleichheit: Sozialdemokratisches Wochenblatt* (Vienna), 5 Apr 1899; *ÖM*, 6 Mar 1905.

70. See Böhm, *Erinnerungen aus meinem Leben*, 48.

71. *ÖM*, 3 Aug 1905; Wolfgang Maderthaner, "Die Metallarbeiter der ländlichen Großindustrie und die militante Aktion: Eine Streikanalyse" in *Berichte des 16. österreichischen Historikertages in Krems 1984* (Vienna: Verband österreichischer Geschichtsvereine, 1984), 758–68.

72. A "classic" in deeming the cultural origin of migrants inferior is a text of the young Engels about the migration of the Irish to England. Friedrich Engels, *Lage der arbeitenden Klassen in England,* in Karl Marx and Friedrich Engels, *Werke,* vol. 2 (Berlin: Dietz, 1980), 320–23. See also Hans Mommsen, *Die Sozialdemokratie und die Nationalitätenfrage im habsburgischen Vielvölkerstaat* (Vienna: Europaverlag, 1963), 32–40.

73. Bauer, "Proletarische Wanderungen," 476–94.

74. Ibid., 481; Otto Bauer, "Nationale Minderheitenschulen," *Der Kampf* 3 (1910): 255.

75. See Otto Bauer, *Die Nationalitätenfrage und die Sozialdemokratie, Werkausgabe* edition (Vienna, 1975), 293–94; Raimund Löw, *Der Zerfall der "Kleinen Internationale": Nationalitätenkonflikte in der Arbeiterbewegung des alten Österreich (1889–1914)*, Materialien zur Arbeiterbewegung 14 (Vienna: Europaverlag, 1984), 32–33; Hans Mommsen, *Arbeiterbewegung und nationale Frage* (Göttingen: Vandenhoek & Ruprecht, 1979), 127–217.

76. In 1907, the Czech Social Democratic Party had 4,800 members in Lower Austria. At that time, Vienna was part of Lower Austria. See Löw, *Der Zerfall der "Kleinen Internationale,"* 10, 30, 56; see also Mommsen, *Sozialdemokratie,* 403–6.

77. See Karl Brousek, "Hundert Jahre tschechische Schulen in Wien," *Slovanský Přehled 1983–84* (Prague, 1984), 209–17.

78. See Mommsen, *Arbeiterbewegung,* 210–11. In *Der Kampf* the minority school question was discussed in great detail in 1909 and 1910, although without yielding any conclusions. The practical demand of solving the question aroused fewer emotions than the proposals for assimilating the new urban minority. See the contributions by Bauer, Hartmann, Tomašek, Pistiner, Wesely, Prachensky, Renner, Meissner, and Seliger.

79. Otto Bauer, "Die Bedingungen der nationalen Assimilation," *Der Kampf* 5 (1912): 256. As further factors, Bauer names: the dimension of the migration, the immigrants' degree of segregation, their social position, and the "difference" of their race.

80. *AZ*, 15 Aug 1909.

81. See Mommsen, *Arbeiterbewegung,* 212; Bauer, "Bedingungen der nationalen Assimilation," 261–62; *AZ*, 15 Aug 1909; Bauer argued against the view that the Czech migrant should learn the German language but not give up his national identity: "It seems to me that this reasoning is not incontestable. First of all, it is in no way certain that the worker who keeps his national identity in a foreign city does not suffer when he learns only the language of the minority. I fear that even if he is not hurt economically, he will be hurt culturally, because he will be cutting himself off from the rich life of the majority and from the great struggles of the community, and will be moving only in the tight circles of an uprooted minority." *Der Kampf* 4 (1911): 204.

82. *AZ*, 10 and 17 Jan 1897, quoted in *Arbeiterinnen kämpfen um ihr Recht: Autobiographische Texte rechtloser und entrechteter "Frauenspersonen" in Deutschland, Österreich und der Schweiz des 19. und 20. Jahrhunderts,* ed. Richard Klucsarits and Friedrich G. Kürbisch (Wuppertal: Hammer-Verlag, n.d.), 86–92.

83. *AZ*, 4 Apr 1889. For reference to suicide and perception see also Hans Kuttelwascher, "Selbstmord und Selbstmordstatistik" in *Statistische*

Monatsschrift, n.s. 18 (Brünn, 1912): 267–350; also Wiener Stadt- und Landesarchiv, Historische Kommission, 40-a, interview with Emma Studynka (born in 1905), 4–5.

84. See Stefan Riesenfellner, *Der Sozialreporter: Max Winter im alten Österreich* (Vienna: Verlag für Gesellschaftskritik, 1987); for a negative view of Vienna, see, in particular, 145–99.

85. See Siegfried Mattl, "Politik gegen den Tod: Der Stellenwert von Kunst und Kultur in der frühen sozialdemokratischen Bewegung. Eine Skizze," ed. Wolfgang Maderthaner, *Sozialdemokratie und Arbeiterstaat. Sozialistische Bibliographie 1* (forthcoming).

An impressive example of an intensified picture of the pauperized migrant can be found in: Wiener Stadt- und Landesarchiv, Historische Kommission, 3a-i, Johanna Lewandoske, Schicksale in Wien (life story of a 72-year-old Viennese woman), 1.

86. *Arbeiterinnen-Zeitung: Socialdemokratisches Organ für Frauen und Mädchen* (Vienna), 2 July 1912.

87. See *Protokoll der Verhandlungen des Parteitages der deutschsozialdemokratischen Arbeiterpartei in Österreich: Abgehalten in Wien vom 31. Oktober bis zum 4. November 1913* (Vienna, 1913), 25. A direct reference to the practice of identifying "Red Vienna" as the city itself can be seen in *Die Wiener Arbeiterbewegung: Den Mitgliedern des Internationalen Sozialisten- und Gewerkschaftskongresses Wien 1914 gewidmet* (Vienna, 1914).

PART II
Comparative Expectations: Europe and North America

4

America and the Ruhr Basin in the Expectations of Polish Peasant Migrants

Anna Reczyńska

IN the second half of the nineteenth and at the beginning of the twentieth century Polish mass migration flowed predominantly in two directions: to the United States of America and to the Ruhr Basin in Germany.[1] Migration of Poles to the United States began in the Prussian-held territories, which are the focus of my study here. Migration began to assume a mass character in the 1880s. Migrants left their native country "in search of bread" and "to improve their existence." For the majority of the Polish peasants and farmworkers who left for the New World, these expectations and deeply felt hopes were closely connected with a mythical image of America: a country of abundance with free land, where even the passage to it cost nothing.

America: A Paradise on Earth?

The spread of an exaggerated and stereotyped image of America was usually ascribed by the Polish-language press (and by playwrights) to the German agents of the shipping companies and to the Jewish innkeepers who acted on their behalf. These were accused of luring naive peasants into emigration by describing America as a promised land, a paradise, and a gold-mine rolled into one, and of doing it for profit (they were said to receive a commission for each traveler to the United States).[2] However, the role played by the agents has been grossly exaggerated. They merely encouraged migration, and provided migrants with a sense of direction. These intermediaries, however, could neither initiate migration—its bases were the socioeconomic conditions—nor win the peasants' confidence. Peasants were suspicious of strangers, especially Jews. The picture painted by shipping agents confirmed the information that had already reached peasants through other channels, especially in letters from earlier migrants and in the press. The image was counteracted by some writers and playwrights. But because it thrived on the peasants' innermost hopes, factual information and satire had little influence. The image consisted of the availability of free land and later of jobs, of easy (or even free) transportation to the United States, of a higher status for women.

For Polish peasants, promises of obtaining land had a magnetic quality. To obtain land they had been ready to make many sacrifices. Now they found that they could become landowners for almost nothing. In the 1860s this dream could indeed come true. The Homestead Act (1862) offered land to every immigrant male over the age of 21 for nothing but a small fee, on condition that he become a U.S. citizen. The existence of this condition was often overlooked. Numerous articles about the decreasing amount of free land, more difficult access to it, and its price were also available, but could not destroy the myth.[3] Only gradually did prospective and actual migrants realize that the road to owning a piece of land was replete with obstacles, and demanded hard work as well as savings. In spite of these obstacles, migrants' hopes of obtaining farmland survived for a long time. In 1877 a campaign to start an all-Polish settlement in Arkansas after purchasing a large area of fertile land called forth "an expectedly high number of Poles [who] volunteered to buy the land."[4]

Exact reconstruction of all the hopes that Polish peasants attached to migration is not an easy task. The myth grew gradually to include those eternal needs: prosperity, justice, and a happy life. However, the vaguely imagined, distant America also had to meet more immediate needs. And so, gossip promised there would be an abundance of goods in America, goods that were in short supply or not available at home. The way to America was long. And so, rumors promised a free passage.[5]

The belief that traveling to America was free is a good example of the "mythical" thinking that incorporates only those bits of news that support its preconceptions and dismisses everything else. For example, at mid-century, the rumor spread throughout Prussia that "a Prussian Prince" had bought land in Australia and America and that he was offering free passage to potential migrants. Owing to this, many credulous but penniless Polish peasants made their way to Bremen. (Behind the imaginary prince were probably emigration agents anxious to lure cheap contract labor overseas.)[6] In 1880 other unfortunate migrants, convinced that they would be sent to Galveston by a Frenchman who owned farmland in Texas, were to beg for money in Bremen or to return home on foot.[7] Although some sources claim that such cases were not rare, by no means were they frequent. Above all, the American Immigration Act of 1864 seems to have led to the belief in the possibility of free passage, as it permitted an advance of travel expenses to migrants by their future employers. But this "contract labor" clause was revoked in 1885; whether Polish peasant migrants profited from the 1864 Act remains an open question. Some of them probably did, and this may have led their compatriots to believe that they, too, could travel to the United States without immediate payment. Afterward it may well have been that poor Polish peasants thought of prepaid tickets sent by countrymen who had migrated earlier (on behalf of their employers?) as free passage. Thus, in the 1890s Father Jaskulski in Poznań warned: "The poorest and the most pitiable are those who will get here a free ticket to America: they will become slaves [and work] under the yoke of a ruthless farmer or factory owner, entirely at their mercy."[8] In the 1890s a limited offer of free passage to Brazil and Argentina, as well as a misreading by credulous migrants of a publication by a well-esteemed Polish expert on migration, contributed to the belief that passage was free.[9]

In addition to expectations shared by all emigrants, others were held by specific groups of people. For instance, many young females—according to popular biases, particularly those without any natural talent—expected to find rich husbands: "We hear from Lidzbark about numerous cases of emigration to America, from where invitations and boat tickets are sent. . . . The first to emigrate are young single girls, hoping to get married."[10] Tales from America included information about the higher status of women there in comparison with their status in their home country and about the better conditions for American wives. All this encouraged women's hopes, and the number of those wishing to emigrate increased. An element of personal happiness became part and parcel of the "American dream."

The kind of knowledge about America disseminated by schools was of a very elementary nature. In the part of Poland under Prussian rule, its influence was paramount, due to compulsory schooling introduced as early as 1819 in Silesia, in 1825 in the Poznań district, and in 1845 in West Prussia.[11] A diary writer who attended school in 1868 noted that instruction at school included knowledge of five continents (including America), of the rivers, lakes, and seas of the entire world.[12] However, as the following example shows, even among schoolchildren the image of America as the land of promise had not yet been replaced by sound knowledge. At the beginning of the twentieth century a visitor to a Galician village school asked the best pupil "Where was America? He hesitated a moment, then he said he did not know, except that it was a country to which good Polish boys went when they died."[13]

The image of America adopted by Polish peasants emerged under the influence of letters written by relatives, friends, or neighbors staying in the United States. They were treated as the most reliable sources of information. The earliest Polish emigrants from Silesia were no doubt attracted by the news spread by German migrants regarding favorable farming conditions (because of the moderate climate), lack of taxation, and lack of dependence on landowners and officials.[14] News of this kind was confirmed by letters and first-hand accounts of people like Father Leopold Moczygemba, a Franciscan priest, who came from Silesia, worked in Texas among German settlers, and encouraged his compatriots to migrate to the United States. The first who came were mainly wealthy peasants and their sons, who could afford to pay for the fare and for at least part of the farming equipment. They wanted to obtain large tracts of farmland for individual farming and, judging from their accounts, could make their expectations come true, due—among other things—to mutual assistance. Their optimistic letters encouraged other Silesians to emigrate. They described the large farms, land that required a lot of work but was fertile, and cattle-breeding supported by an "abundance of fodder growing everywhere"[15]:

> The land is big and there is plenty of space, with settlers few and far between; for example, the distance between Indijonol and Victoria is 50 miles. . . . and only ten people live there; they are all prosperous and wealthy as some raise 2000 cattle, pigs and innumerable other animals. . . . [T]hey love only cattle but live like lords.[16]

All these letters had one common element: their authors claimed unequivocally that life in America was better and easier than life in Silesia, with good prospects for the future, considering the number of inhabitants, who were few but well-off.

In another letter, the same author wrote that farming was

similar to that in Silesia, but that raising cattle was a bit easier.
Because cattle can graze unattended,

> cows and oxen are bigger in size. . . . There are plenty of trees on
> the farm . . . both for building and burning. . . . [A]mong the trees
> a lot of ivy can be found . . . with grapes tasting like the best
> grapes in Silesia that can be used for feeding pigs in summer and
> for homemade marmalade, vinegar and wine.[17]

Letters carried descriptions of fertile fields and meadows full of
sweet-smelling flowers:

> The climate is always healthy; although there are heat waves in
> summer, cool, refreshing winds blow continuously. . . . Winters
> are cold. . . . [N]ortherly winds cool the air so that we have to
> burn coal in stoves for several months. All in all living in Panna
> Maria (Virgin Mary) [Texas] is pleasant, nice and merry; we are
> never hunger-stricken, on the contrary, we prosper both mate-
> rially and spiritually.[18]

Optimistic accounts of this kind played a significant role in sustain-
ing the "American dream." And so did letters written on top-quality
stationery, which often contained prepaid tickets.

All this strongly affected the reader's imagination. Later warnings and stories of failure (or even death) were ignored. Prospective
migrants had confidence in their resourcefulness, strong arms, and
ultimate success. Viewed from Polish villages, "this distant America
had a magnet-like property." Since village people could not make
ends meet,

> the dollars sent by relatives from the States helped create the
> image of this country as a dollar country. Even the [news of the]
> death of several girls who gained nothing but tuberculosis did not
> destroy the image. Year by year, the number of emigrants in-
> creased.[19]

And every year the letters from America that reached the eastern
provinces of Prussia became more numerous.[20] They were read by
family and friends, and reports were embellished from other sources.
Sometimes the tales were completely untrue, for people wanted to
keep news of failure to themselves. However, as a rule, letters from

America did in a realistic way encourage hopes of improving living standards, especially if the addressees were poor peasants.

Emigration spread and affected Greater Poland, Pomerania, and Prussia. Hopes of getting rich and becoming independent strongly roused the imagination, especially when a migrant had little to lose:

> [I saw] crowds of people in Czerwińsk, Warlubie, and at other railway stations all leaving for America. Among them were farmworkers' families with very small children, even breast-fed babies. . . . Ten fingers, a desire to improve their fate, confidence in promises made by relatives and friends in America, and above all discontent with local conditions, feelings of frustration and depression—this was their luggage and the things they wanted to escape from. . . . They live in a state of intoxication, afraid of the future and sad at the prospect of leaving their motherland, consoling themselves that their life there cannot be worse than life here and the lives of those that had emigrated before them and who are now full of praise.[21]

The role of the Polish-language press regarding migration and the image of America presented by it is quite contradictory. On the one hand, with the intensification of mass migration in the 1880s, scores of appeals and warnings aimed at prospective migrants were published in the press. These publications included very vivid accounts of the dangers, often resulting in poverty and death, that awaited adventurers off to the unknown. Articles and accounts of this kind were published in *Gazeta Gornosląska* (Upper Silesian Gazette), *Gazeta Toruńska* (Torun Gazette), *Katolik* (The Catholic), *Gazeta Opolska* (Opole Gazette), *Gwiazdka Cieszyńska* (The Cieszyn Star), and other newspapers for the common people. The press also published letters by disappointed emigrants that painted a gloomy picture or presented arguments supporting the claim that emigration would result in losses of all kinds. "Agitation" of this kind aroused peasant suspicions concerning the intentions of the agitators. Here is an example of one peasant's reaction to the anti-emigration campaign:

> They depict America as if it were a nightmare, wild rocks and swamps, and the people who read this ask themselves how it is possible that in the same America there is such an abundance of lard and flour that they send them over to Europe. As a result,

people began to exhibit distrust of the press, instead of distrust of America.[22]

Similarly, the activities of the St. Raphael's Society, directed at protecting emigrants, created illusions:

[T]hey imagined a law whereby a priest should visit a community of twenty or more people at least once a year. . . . Thus they assumed that Polish priests would be awaiting them in America and because I gave [one] a letter of reference, they said: ah, the gentlemen are sending us, so they will follow us soon and outright I had seventeen of them requesting similar letters.[23]

Misguided hopes of migrants and their visions of America as paradise on earth were presented by the press with all seriousness and concern, although not without some condescension and disapproval of the peasants' stupidity: "Like many others, this poor man thought that America was a promised land, that he would amass wealth and return to his motherland as a happy man. However, he was greatly disappointed, as were numerous others."[24]

On the other hand, the Polish as well as the Silesian press— which had a large readership and was very popular, as can be seen from the number of titles, circulation, number of subscribers, letters from America requesting subscription, and letters to the editor[25]— depicted America as a land of opportunity for people who wanted to work, as a country of prosperity, religious tolerance, and fair wages, a country where workers were treated justly. This is borne out by the following excerpts: "We work only six days a week. . . . A loaf of bread costing 10 cents at home costs 3 cents here, and 8 cents will buy 12 large rolls."[26] "In America, it is impossible to suffer from poverty because workers are well paid, but one has to be careful when spending money."[27] "Everybody has plenty of bread and meat and we do not have any shortages; also, no one stands behind you with a stick in his hand."[28] Those who worked could amass quite a fortune, like Tomasz Wegrzyk of Evansville: "I had plenty of money; I would have brought 4,000 Prussian thalers with me, after a nine-year stay here . . . but . . . I bought a house for $1,100, with four rooms and painted walls. For furniture I paid $230. All floors are covered with carpets."[29] America provided—above all—plentiful food as well as housing for hardworking and resourceful people.

Some papers printed translations of popular American literature—including *Uncle Tom's Cabin*—love stories, and other works.

The press carried news of the Civil War, presidential elections, and important political events. The most significant items were accounts of meetings with Poles, Polish shopkeepers, innkeepers, and butchers, and with Polish Jews who had their own businesses: "The city of Detroit now has 150,600 inhabitants, 15,000 of whom are Poles."[30] Such information gave readers a sense of security and contributed to another important aspect of the image: America as a land full of one's fellow-countrymen.

Certain elements contained in migrants' tales were regarded as success symbols by the peasants. One of the most fundamental elements was the abundance of food:

American soldiers get $16 per month and free board. . . . [F]or breakfast, we get as much coffee as we wish, a steak with potatoes and delicious white bread, resembling coffee rolls that some of our town bakers bake. For lunch we have roast beef with potatoes, bread and coffee,

wrote one author in his letter home.[31]

Particular attention was paid to the quality of clothing and housing that could be seen in the photographs sent home. The addressees were highly impressed by house and apartment interiors, as these could not be compared with anything available at home. Peasant families were also impressed by tales of savings and investments:

Our compatriots kept arriving here for fifteen years. Mr. Lempke was the first to set up a Polish business and has saved $20,000. . . . Mr. Lorkowski has had similar business for twelve years and has $5,000. . . . Mr. Żółtkowski has saved $25,000 (100,000 marks) during seven years. Where there is reason and resourcefulness, there is no poverty.[32]

In the eyes of peasants, such fabulous wealth further enhanced the image of America as a paradise on earth.

For peasants-turned-industrial-workers, however, the "American dream" often meant nothing more than satisfying simple, everyday needs. Many of them believed that improvements would be real: "As far as better food, drink, clothing and freedom are concerned, America is more lavish to her children than the old country."[33] Although freedom was often mentioned, it was defined very imprecisely. It referred, among other things, to a free choice of school for children and to freedom of religion. Migrants' hopes were also raised by information on industrial relations, especially the respect with which workers were supposedly treated and the different relationship between manager and employee.[34] Data on the prospective migrants' reactions to this kind of information are scarce, and indicate only that migrants did not pay attention to the type of work they were going to undertake. They also remained ignorant of the exact nature of changes awaiting them in their new jobs: different discipline, organization, and the presence of piecework. These attitudes can be partly explained by the migrants' lack of comparable experiences in the home country.

This image and overblown expectations were sometimes ridiculed in poems written by emigrants. One such poem, entitled "America," contrasted the easy lies and the hard work:

Jest tu takich bardzo wiele	There are many people here
co fałszywie twierdzą śmiele	who boldly but falsely claim
Pisując listy do kraju	Writing in their letters home
Powiadają, że są w raju	That they live in paradise
Że ubrany, jakby panicz	Dressed like dandies
Nie wróciłby do dom za nic,	They'd never returned home,
Kapeluszyk na nim modny	Wearing fashionable hats
Napity i też niegłodny	Never thirsty, never hungry,
. . . .	. . . .
Prawda, że dobrze ci płacą,	It's true how well they pay you
Ale wiedzą też i za co,	But they know what for,
Bo nikt jak mówią bez pracy	For you can never earn money
Nie zjadał darmo kołaczy.[35]	Idling away your time.

The clumsy way with which peasants formulated their expectations provoked the reactions of writers and journalists as well. Henryk Sienkiewicz's emigration novel *Za chlebem (In Search of Bread)*, which was published in 1880, was widely discussed. But, according to contemporaries, the author's warnings, despite his intentions, often acted as encouragement: "They only made things worse." The novel "impressed many people who, before reading it, had never thought of emigrating. When some of my workers, who were quite prosperous, quit work, I asked them: Why are you doing it? Because we are going to America."[36]

On the other hand, plays on emigration written and performed by amateur troupes worked by exaggerating the hopes of potential migrants.[37] Some of them were never printed. Those that were preserved, like Władysław Anczyc's *Emigracja chłopska* (Peasant Emigration) and Władysław Łembiński's *Amerykanie* (The Americans), were among the most popular ones in Greater Poland and Silesia. Both plays present German agents and Jewish innkeepers whose lines synthesize all the myths that were in circulation in those times.

> *Mendel:* To America. . . . There you'll be given land for which you'll be paying for 20 years, as well as cattle and timber for building a house; . . . I have just heard from my brother-in-law who's in America that all our peasants who emigrated became very rich. . . .[38]

> *Schultze:* . . . There are no taxes there. . . . No man will be drafted. . . . There is no king and there are no noblemen, as all people are equal. . . . And if someone has little money or no money at all, but wants to go there, I'll give him everything for free, in return for signing a contract, where he'll declare that he will work on a farm for two years.[39]

And, in a still greater exercise of fantasy:

> *Kasztan:* I know a country where gold is dug out like clay here and where all potters become goldsmiths. People live there as in paradise. They go there from all parts of the world. . . . Gold is not deep underground, on the surface golden wheat grows, its grains are as big as noodles, it's pot-ready, it only needs boiling, buttering and can be eaten—real paradise.[40]

These exaggerations are versions of peasant hopes, as perceived and recorded by the intelligentsia of the time.

If such naive hopes suggest that migration was an impulsive rush of reckless and uneducated peasants, emigrants' letters and diaries present a different picture. Decisions on whether to migrate or stay were made after lengthy deliberations, during which all the pros and cons were carefully weighed, and after it had been firmly established that gains would outweigh losses.[41] During their journey, migrants expressed their fear of the new world and tried to learn more about their destination. They asked fellow passengers, who were traveling for the second time, what life was like in America.[42] After the initial—and usually difficult—period, living standards of the immigrants were generally higher than those at home. Different living conditions, the alien environment, the novelty of many situations and phenomena in America—all these factors often made it impossible to compare the United States with anything remembered from the old country. The emigrants' points of reference were a wealthy neighbor, the landlord, and the parish priest. To compensate for the lack of comparative experience and terminology, migrants used biblical and religious terms. As a result, letters and written accounts of migrants were full of expressions like "paradise," "promised land," and "land of milk and honey," which made descriptions more vivid. To many addressees, the reality described in this manner seemed to be a true paradise. They understood the folk religious metaphors as something concrete and tangible.

High Wages in the Ruhr Basin

Since the 1870s the Ruhr Basin had been a new destination for Polish migrants. Among the coal mines and steel mills, a Polish community numbering several hundred thousand people emerged. As most of them arrived from the eastern part of the Prussian monarchy, the journey to the Rhineland and Westphalia was in fact an internal migration. An attractive image of Rhineland-Westphalia was first created as a result of the participation of many draftees from Silesia, Greater Poland, and Pomerania in the Franco-Prussian war of 1870–71:

> During the German-French war the Poles also marched through Westphalia, . . . especially through the coal mining area. . . . They saw the affluence of the inhabitants of this land, and some of them thought of resettling here, regarding it as a country of abundance.[43]

Military service in urban garrisons in the heart of Germany and earlier seasonal migration to Saxony also contributed to peasant migration.[44]

As a result, agents who recruited Polish peasants for work in Westphalian coal mines found favorable conditions for their work. To gain the confidence of the prospective colliers and to overcome the language barrier, mine-owners sent agents who were Poles or spoke Polish: "In May 1871 a new agent left, . . . a Pole called Karol Sliwka, who worked as a pit delegate in the Prosper I mine. He brought with him 400 Polish miners to Bottrop."[45] In 1872 the same man recruited another 500 workers, this time from the Rybnik area. A few other groups of Poles were also recruited to work in Westphalia. From that point on no further recruitment campaigns were necessary. The encouragement or persuasion of those who had left earlier was sufficiently attractive. Recruitment was carried out only in areas where there had been no earlier emigration (e.g., the Masurian Lakes district).[46]

The main source of information about life and work in the Ruhr Basin were the letters and oral accounts of relatives and neighbors who returned home for good or who came as visitors. When several peasants from one village settled in a mining community or worked in the same colliery,[47] news that reached home came from different men and women and was relatively easy to verify because details of one's success or failure soon became common knowledge. Peasants in Poland were well informed about Westphalia, as one diary entry shows:

> When industry in Germany developed, they needed a lot of coal for their steel works and a lot of miners to dig the coal. Younger sons of poor peasants, who stood no chance of owning their father's land, left home to work in Westphalia. When they earned 6,000–10,000 marks and became wealthy, they came back and got married in the Poznań district. Some of them never quit their work as miners, but got wealthy, bought houses and died in Germany, where their children became Germanized. Poles [lived] in Polish ghettos, their faith and love of their motherland being maintained by priests and activists, in choirs and sport clubs. Those who drank liquor never became wealthy.[48]

The author of this account had never been to the Ruhr Basin, but his three sons and several of his neighbors had lived there, and his wife received letters from a sister living in Westphalia.

To prospective migrants, money was the greatest attraction. Their information on the differences between wages in the eastern and western parts of Germany was detailed and accurate. They also knew that costs of living in the West were higher than in the East. "German settlers in the Poznań area pay 150 marks a year, whereas in a forge in Westphalia you can get 4 marks a day,"[49] wrote one of the diarists. In Silesia wages were also lower than those in Westphalia. For example, in 1888 the annual income of a Silesian miner working ten hours a day was 574 marks, while in Westphalia, where the shifts were eight hours long, miners earned 910 marks a year.[50] German employers were fully aware of the attractiveness of the earnings they offered. A recruitment poster addressed to the inhabitants of the

Masurian Lakes district advertised earnings from 3 marks per day for pit hands to over 6 marks per day for hewers and almost 8 marks for coke loaders.[51]

The dominant topic in the accounts of those who made it in Westphalia was the amount of money earned and saved. Higher wages were made possible by working overtime. In his memoirs, a miner wrote: "By digging . . . one can earn 11 marks during one shift. . . . If you work 30–32 shifts per month you can earn 270–290 marks."[52] In 1906 Antoni Podeszwa returned home with 4,000 marks in his pocket.[53] Tomasz Skorupka, the father of three sons working in Westphalia, recorded that the oldest son saved 10,000 marks after eight years of work, the younger one, working shorter hours, 3,300 marks, whereas the youngest son saved 600 marks in the years 1912–14.[54] Cases like these were not uncommon, and so the experience of returnees induced prospective migrants to believe in a Ruhr Basin where a maximum amount of money could be earned in a minimum of time. Poles were always ready to undertake the hardest and the most dangerous work, if well-paid. In order to save more, Polish workers did not pay trade-union fees and were not insured. In search of higher earnings they often changed work whenever the jobs they had fell short of their expectations:

> In 1897 I started work as a miner in the Carolinenglück mine near Bochum but not for long, only 2 days, when I spoke to the pit delegate on the third day I asked him how much I'd get for driving a pit pony . . . and he said 2 marks 50 pfennigs, to which I said I would not work for this money . . . so I started working in another mine where I got 50 pfennigs more.[55]

When people decided to emigrate, they did so with the intention of returning to the home village. With the money saved they planned to buy more land or a new farm or to pay their debts. Because traveling costs were low, even poor peasants who had no land of their own could set off to Westphalia. Entire generations of Polish migrants to the Ruhr Basin dreamed of farming their own land. They built their future on this dream and discussed ways of achieving it: "They said that when they saved enough money, they would marry daughters of farm owners."[56] Visions of future affluence forced emigrants to live very sparingly. Germans who lived among the Westphalian Poles were surprised to see that to satisfy their basic needs Poles "spend [so] little money. . . . Every month they put away a large part of their earnings in the savings bank or, more often, mail the money home."[57] This opinion is borne out by figures showing the amount of cash mailed from Westphalia to the Poznań region and to the Gdańsk part of Pomerania. In 1907 the amount was estimated at about 15 million marks, in 1910 at 25 million marks.[58] The Settlement Act of 1886 resulted in an increase in the price of land, especially of small farms. For some time it looked as if migrants' hopes would have to be abandoned. However, the percentage of those who returned home remained high, and a majority of them invested money by purchasing land. One man, who returned home in 1901 and married the only daughter of an eighty-acre-farm-owner, wrote: "So my dreams have come true. Since I was young I have been striving for my own farm. Finally, I have succeeded. I would not have made it if I had not had my savings."[59]

Hopes connected with emigration to Westphalia were best expressed by the author of a poem published in *Wiarus Polski:*

> I am a miner, miner am I
> born in Poland
> driven from my country
> by repression and hunger
>
> . . . .
>
> When I collect here
> a sackful of money
> I'll come back to Poland
> to buy what miners lost[60]

In cases where migrants planned to return after earning enough money, they did not attach much significance to living conditions in the towns on the Ruhr. They expected to find a higher standard of living, higher earnings, and better food, and, in the poster cited above, much space was devoted to the advertisement of good accommodations. Families of immigrants were offered three- and four-room flats, and rooms were high and spacious, often with a cellar, a small shed, and a garden.[61] Such offers surpassed anything that was available at home. However, the migrants soon learned that to save extra money they would have to sublet a part of the flat, with subtenants paying not only for lodging but also for board. The flats found by migrants were usually the cheapest ones available.[62]

Foreign clothes affected the imagination to a greater degree than news of accommodation. Migrants who visited their homes brought clothes as presents, and they themselves wore well-cut, quality clothes:

Whenever a Westphalian . . . came home, he immediately became
the focus of attention of an entire village: he wore better clothes
and was regarded by all as a superior person. As a result, people
became interested in the foreign land, where life was (though only
apparently so) better.[63]

Clothes were a status symbol to Polish migrants in the Ruhr Basin,
too. "Workers here lived satisfying lives, those who lived economically could eat and drink well and wear smart clothes."[64] A well-cut,
made-to-measure suit was among the first things a migrant bought
on arrival,[65] thus attempting to acquire higher prestige in the eyes of
the Polish community.

Tales of Polish tailors, of Poles renting flats to compatriots, and
of a Polish-language newspaper printed in Westphalia helped to establish the image of the Polish community as well-organized and
differing from the other communities. Awareness of these facts enhanced the migrants' sense of security and attracted new emigration.
This is similar to the effects of migration to America in the home
environment.

Unlike those who emigrated to America, those who left for
Westphalia knew much about their future work: it would be underground work, and there were accidents[66] and unemployment. Tomasz
Skorupka compared the lot of his older sons working in Westphalia to
that of his youngest son, who was sent to a grammar school: "Despite
everything, his life was the easiest one. He was lucky not to become a
miner in Germany. . . . [H]e witnessed their hard work . . . and was
then more willing to work with his brain."[67] That life underground
was detrimental to health was also common knowledge: "When I saw
the miners, pale like ghosts, their eyes staring. . . . Even young men
had gnarled legs, so that a dog could pass between them, and then I
thought: this must be how the people of Westphalia are punished by
God."[68] Fears were uncommon, curiosity and self-confidence
stronger. "Some people tried to terrify me, saying that coal might fall
on me, but a friend of mine said that it is not as bad as that, that
accidents happen, but there are people who have been working for
twenty years and to whom nothing has happened."[69]

Polish peasants working in Westphalia felt a relative improvement of their situation. Working in coal mines to them was a kind of
social promotion. Also, relations between employers and employees
met their expectations. Admittedly, migrants were ignorant of industrial law, did not know how to exercise their rights as employees, and
as a result, became easy prey for greedy employers. Despite this,

many diarists asserted that in Westphalia workers were treated better than peasants working for a landlord. Some authors emphasized this factor very strongly: "There was one more thing in Westphalia that we didn't have at home. . . . [W]orkers were respected more highly than at home, there were no cases of ill-treatment."[70]

Those who came back from the Ruhr Basin refrained from entering the old system of social dependence and defied the traditional values; for example, "they no longer kissed the priest's hands."[71] Another migrant who came home from Westphalia observed that "he did not believe in [the existence of the] devil and argued with anyone who held otherwise."[72]

Some of the migrants to Westphalia were motivated by a desire to become independent of their family and escape the control of the rural community. These motives were far more frequent with migrants to the Ruhr Basin than with those to America because the journey to the heart of Germany was easier and less expensive, and involved fewer risks. As one priest put it:

> A desire to be free, to get to know the world, to have a good time and wear fashionable clothes, forces our youth to emigrate. . . . In the outside world, a girl or a boy thinks, there is no mother and no father—so they will not suppress extravagance and sinful desires. . . . [T]he young emigrate to enjoy themselves, to revel and dance, at least on Saturdays and Sundays.[73]

The fact that this opinion was expressed by a priest may be the reason for its bluntness and condemnatory tone. No matter who the author was, it is important to realize that many migrants' motives were far from being purely economic. First of all, they expected to find fewer prohibitions and to spend money in any way they wanted when they settled in a new place. It was commonly known that migrants in Westphalia drank a lot.[74] Many of them, especially the young ones, did not go to church regularly; others had Protestant spouses. Those who had observed prospective migrants were aware of changes awaiting them, but did not know what their exact nature would be: "When we were at a railway station, one of them kept saying: 'Now we are in Germany, there is no God here and no fast,' whereupon he started swearing at fasting on Friday, which surprised me greatly."[75]

The movement away from religion toward a new morality resulted in an avalanche of critical remarks addressed at those who had "betrayed the faith" and "spread corruption." This criticism, voiced by the clergy, the intelligentsia, and landowners, was supplemented by warnings against the Germanization of the migrants and against assisting the German colonization of the eastern provinces. While migrants reported no ethnic conflicts in their environment, we know that anti-Polish measures were taken by the Prussian authorities in the Ruhr District. The migrants had neither great expectations nor fears of living among Germans. What surprised people and met with disapproval were cases of Polish children speaking German to one another when they returned from Westphalia.[76] Opinions on migration to Germany, both oral and printed, were far less critical than those expressed about people migrating to the United States. Both the bad and the good sides of migration were considered, particularly if migration brought financial prosperity. Migration was still treated as an evil, but as a necessary evil that could not be completely eliminated.[77]

Conclusion

Despite the fact that they achieved most of their goals, Polish migrants working in the Ruhr Basin mines and steel works regarded the United States as a land of greater opportunity. They believed in an easier and a better life in America and in the possibility of getting rich there more quickly than in Westphalia. Indeed, some of those who had migrated to the Ruhr Basin decided later to go on to America. One of them cited the defense of national interests as a motive for leaving Westphalia. This motive was also mentioned by other emigrant diarists: "I had to go to Westphalia in search of bread. . . . I experienced contempt, ridicule and . . . other abuses of my nationality. . . . I managed to put away 500 marks but I did not want to stay there any longer. . . . I decided to go to America, to become rich and come back home to fight against Germanization."[78] He was, however, disappointed with his stay in America, too. He compared his American experiences with the German ones and concluded that the latter were better. In America he had not achieved the goals he had had set himself, and the high cost of travel had prevented him from a speedy return. This letter shows that there were many others like him: "Compatriots! You also live on foreign soil, but at least you are closer to your homes, so forget America, because life here is worse than in Germany."[79] This letter was published by *Wiarus Polski*, the Polish-language newspaper in Westphalia.

It can be said that Poles in Westphalia experienced fewer disappointments than those in America, as the Polish migration to Westphalia, unlike the migration to America, was not accompanied by many myths or legends. One can account for this with at least two reasons: the shorter distance and peasants' knowledge of basic German, which made communication in this language possible. The hopes and expectations of migrants to Germany had a more solid foundation and were more realistic. The migrants could easily return home in case of failure. All the hopes and expectations did not form a coherent system. They were simply a collection of images, many of which were incomplete and conflicting. Whenever knowledge of facts was insufficient, gaps were filled by the imagination, where oral accounts blended with peasants' ideals and dreams of farms, money, and good fortune. These original hopes could be completely fulfilled neither in Westphalia nor in America, but had to be modified in the course of the stay abroad.

Notes

We are grateful to Janusz Stygares, who translated the manuscript from the Polish.

1. For the background of Polish mass migration see Celina Bobinska and Andrzej Pilch, eds., *Employment-Seeking Emigrations of Poles World Wide in the Nineteenth and Twentieth Centuries* (Cracow, 1975); William I. Thomas and Florian Znaniecki, *The Polish Peasant in Europe and America* (New York: Alfred E. Knopf, 1927); Krzystof Groniowski, "The Socio-economic Base of Polish Emigration to North America, 1854–1939," in *The Polish Presence in Canada and America*, ed. Frank Renkiewicz (Toronto: The Multicultural History Society of Ontario, 1982); Christoph Klessmann, *Polnische Bergarbeiter im Ruhrgebiet, 1870–1945* (Göttingen, 1978).

2. See *Gazeta Górnośląska* (hereafter cited as *GG*), 10 Mar 1880; Ludwik Caro, "Nasi Wychodźcy Zamorscy," *Przegląd Powszechny* 296 (1908): 157–58.

3. See Andrzej Brożek, "Polityka Imigracyjna w Państwach Docelowych Emigracji Polskiej," in *Emigracja z Ziem Polskich w Czasach Nowożytnych i Najnowszych*, ed. Andrzej Pilch (Warsaw: Państwowe Wydawnictwo Naukowe, 1984), 123.

4. *Gazeta Polska w Chicago* (hereafter cited as *GPC*), 1 Mar 1877.

5. See Ryszard Kantor, "Tematyka Emigracyjna w Polskim Folklorze Ustnym w XIX i XX Wieku: Wprowadzenie do Problemu" (unpublished manuscript).

6. See Klaus J. Bade, "Massenwanderung und Arbeitsmarkt im deutschen Nordosten von 1880 bis zum Ersten Weltkrieg," *Archiv für Sozialgeschichte* 20 (1980): 309, n.102; see also letter from Jan Moczygemba,

13 May 1855, and from Leopold Moczygemba, 18 June 1855, to their parents, in Andrzej Brożek, *Ślązacy w Teksasie: Relacje o Najstarszych Polskich Osadach w Stanach Zjednoczonych* (Warsaw and Wrocław: Państowe Wydawnictwo Naukowe, 1972), 84, 86.

7. "Aus den Protokollbüchern der Auskunftsbüros im Bahnhof und im Schütting des Nachweisungsbüros für das Auswandererwesen," A III 9E, no. 20, Handelskammer Bremen, Archiv. See also *Gwiazdka Cieszyńska* (hereafter cited as *GC*), 10 July 1880.

8. *Wiarus Polski* (hereafter cited as *WP*), 17 June 1894.

9. See Stefan Ramult, *Statystyka Ludności Kaszubskiej* (Kraków: Akademia Umiejętności, 1899), 273.

10. *Gazeta Toruńska* (hereafter cited as *GT*), 14 Mar 1892.

11. See Ludwik Stomma, *Antropologia Kultury Wsi Polskiej XIXw.* (Warsaw: Instytut Wydawniczy Pax, 1986), 79.

12. See Tomasz Skorupka, *Kto przy Obrze Temu Dobrze* (Poznań: Wydawnictwo Poznańskie, 1974), 27.

13. Louis E. Van Norman, *Poland, the Knight among Nations* (New York, 1907), quoted in John J. Bukowczyk, *And My Children Did Not Know Me: A History of the Polish-Americans* (Bloomington, Ind.: Indiana University Press, 1987), 1.

14. See Brożek, *Ślązacy w Teksasie*, 13.

15. Letter from Jan Moczygemba, 13 May 1855, to his parents, ibid., 82.

16. Letter from Jan Gawlik, 7 Jan 1856, to his parents, in *Regiony* 3 (1976): 13.

17. Letter from Jan Gawlik, 20 Jan 1856, to his brother, ibid., 16.

18. *Zwiastun Górnośląski*, 14 Apr 1870.

19. Karolina Urbańczyk, "Grynoska w przedsionku raju," *Regiony* 3 (1976): 35.

20. Kazimierz Wajda, *Migracje Ludności Wiejskiej Pomorza Wschodniego w Latach 1850–1914* (Wrocław, Warsaw, and Cracow: Zakład Narodowy im. Ossolińskich, 1969), 99.

21. *GT*, 29 Mar 1884.

22. *GPC*, 25 May 1882.

23. [?] Jackowski, "O Emigracji pod Panowaniem Niemieckim," in *Pamiętnik Trzeciego Zjazdu Prawników i Ekonomistów Polskich w Poznaniu, 11–13 września 1893* (Poznań: Komitet III Zjazdu, 1894), 186.

24. *GG*, 2 Mar 1881.

25. Danuta Piątkowska, "Kontakty Polonii Amerykańskiej ze Starym Krajem w Świetle Polskiej Prasy na Śląsku (1870–1900)," *Zeszyty Naukowe Wyższej Szkoły Pedagogicznej im. Powstańców Śląskich w Opolu*, ser. A, (Opole, 1980), 91.

26. *Równość*, 29 June 1899.
27. *Katolik* (hereafter cited as *Ka*), 1 June 1886.
28. *GG*, 25 Feb 1882.
29. *Ka*, 16 Jan 1883.
30. *Ka*, 22 Jan 1884.
31. *GC*, 8 Feb 1868.
32. *Ka*, 22 Jan 1884.
33. *GPC*, 25 May 1882.
34. See *GG*, 25 Feb 1882.
35. *GG*, 29 Mar 1882.
36. Jackowski, "O Emigracji," 184.
37. See, for example, Klemens Kosicki, *Pojedynek Amerykański: Dziwne Przygody Chłopa Polskiego Urbana Długonosa* (Gniezno, 1912); Maria Julia Zaleska, *Wujaszek za Morza* (Warsaw, 1884); Stanisław Kozłowski, *Polska w Ameryce* (Warsaw, 1914); Władysław Anczyc, *Emigracja Chłopska* (Warsaw, 1907); Władysław Łembiński, *Amerykanie* (Poznań, 1885).
38. Anczyc, *Emigracja*, 27.
39. Ibid., 40–41.
40. Łembinski, *Amerykanie*, 21.
41. See Piątkowska, "Kontakty," 97.
42. See O.S.A., "List z Nowego Jorku," *Przegląd Emigracyjny* 22 (1893): 236–37.
43. "Die Werbung und Ansiedlung Polnischsprachiger Bergarbeiter mit der Bestellung von Seelsorgern aus der Heimat am Beispiel Bottrop (1871–1886)," in *Die Polen und die Kirche im Ruhrgebiet, 1871–1919: Ausgewählte Dokumente zur Pastoral- und kirchlichen Integration sprachlicher Minderheiten im Deutschen Kaiserreich*, ed. Hans Jürgen Brandt (Münster, 1987), 40–41.
44. See Kazimierz Wajda, *Wieś Pomorska na Przełomie XIX i XXw: Kwestia Rolna na Pomorzu Gdańskim* (Poznań: Wydawnitctwo Poznańskie, 1964), 276.
45. "Die Werbung und Ansiedlung," 41.
46. See Wajda, *Migracje*, 141.
47. See Christoph Klessmann, "Long-Distance Migration, Integration and Segregation of the Ethnic Minority in Industrial Germany; The Case of the Ruhr-Poles," in *Population, Labor and Migration*, ed. Klaus Bade (Leamington Spa: Berg, 1987), 103.
48. Skorupka, *Kto przy Obrze*, 132.
49. *Pamiętniki Emigrantów: Francja*, diary no. 6, (Warsaw: Instytut Gospodarstwa Społecznego, 1939), 66.
50. See Kazimierz Popiołek, *Historia Śląska* (Katowice: Wydawnictwo Śląsk, 1972), 320–25.

51. See Władysław Chojnacki, "Wychodźcy Mazurscy w Zachodnich Niemczech," *Przegląd Zachodni* 7–8 (1956): 338.
52. *Pamiętniki Emigrantów: Francja*, diary no. 34, 607.
53. See A. Podeszwa, "Ze Wspomnień Starego Westfaloka A. Podeszwy," *Studia Śląskie* n.s. 1 (1956): 261.
54. See Skorupka, *Kto przy Obrze*, 134–35.
55. *Pamiętniki Emigrantów: Francja*, diary no. 4, 19.
56. Jakub Wojciechowski, *Życiorys Własny Robotnika*, vol. 1 (Poznań: Wydawnictwo Poznańskie, 1971), 283.
57. H. Münz, 1909, quoted in Krystyna Murzynowska, "Polacy w Zagłębiu Ruhry w Latach 1890–1914," *Problemy Polonii Zagranicznej* 11 (1961): 115.
58. See Jerzy Kozłowski, *Rozwój Organizacji Społeczno-Narodowych Wychodźstwa Polskiego w Niemczech, 1870–1914* (Wrocław, Warsaw, Cracow, Łodź, and Gdańsk: Zakład Narodowy im. Ossolińskich, 1987), 44.
59. *Pamiętniki Chłopów*, 2d ser., diary no. 1 (Warsaw: Instytut Gospodarstwa Społecznego, 1936), 17.
60. *WP*, 4 Aug 1904.
61. See Chojnacki, "Wychodźcy Mazurscy," 338–39.
62. See Klessmann, "Long-Distance Migration," 109.
63. Stanisław Wachowiak, *Polacy w Nadrenii i Westfalii* (Poznań: Zjednoczenie Zawodowe Polskie, 1917), 10.
64. *Pamiętniki Emigrantów: Francja*, diary no. 6, 67.
65. See Wojciechowski, *Życiorys Własny*, 1: 288–89.
66. See *Gazeta Grudziądzska*, 9 Nov 1901.
67. Skorupka, *Kto przy Obrze*, 136.
68. Wojciechowski, *Życiorys Własny*, 1: 284.
69. *Pamiętniki Chłopów*, 2d ser., diary no. 1, 13
70. Podeszwa, "Ze Wspomnień," 257.
71. Leonora Strózecka, ed., *Pamiętniki Chłopów: Wybór*, diary no. 30 (Warsaw: Książka i Wiedza, 1955), 248.
72. Skorupka, *Kto przy Obrze*, 124.
73. *WP*, 28 June 1894.
74. See Skorupka, *Kto przy Obrze*, 130.
75. Wojciechowski, *Życiorys Własny*, 160.
76. Skorupka, *Kto przy Obrze*, 132.
77. See *Pamiętnik Trzeciego Zjazdu*, 191–203; Stefan Rosiński, "Emigracja Polska na Zachodzie w Świetle Cyfr," *Ekonomista* 3 (1919): 122.
78. *Pamiętniki Emigrantów: Stany Zjednoczone*, vol. 2, diary no. 41 (Warsaw: Książka i Wiedza, 1977), 393.
79. *WP*, 1 Nov 1894.

5

Across the Ocean or over the Border: Expectations and Experiences of Italians from Piedmont in New Jersey and Southern France

Franco Ramella

FROM the end of the 1870s, when migration from Italy to other European countries and to America began to worry the ruling classes, the most conservative groups attempted to oppose it by spreading the idea that migrants were victims of a hitherto unknown malady, the "fever of imagining these foreign countries as the Promised Land, which does not exist and has never existed on the face of the globe."[1] Many intellectuals heaped scorn on the "ingenuous credulity" that caused migrants to form a mythical vision of the countries they were bound for. A contemporary observer wrote that in the countryside rumor had it that in South America people employed "farming implements such as spades, hoes, and plows which were fashioned not of iron but of pure gold." He then added:

> Many believe these deceptions, even when they are patently obvious. Good advice, on the other hand, is regarded with suspicion. Emigrants think that their bosses, in league with the political authorities, want to prevent poor people from leaving in order to worsen their conditions and force them to work for breadline wages.[2]

Propaganda against emigration had no effect, however, neither

105

then nor later. In the forty years between 1876 and World War I, 14 million Italians applied for passports and crossed the country's frontiers. The majority returned after a more or less short period of working abroad. Others were seasonal workers who came and went every year; still others (about 4.2 million) settled abroad. Italian migration was a complex and heterogeneous phenomenon. It reflected profound economic, social, and cultural differences that the country's recent (1861) political unification had not obliterated. Albeit at different times and with different trends, farmers and rural laborers, factory workers and artisans, skilled and unskilled workers departed from all over Italy: from the North and the South, from the countryside and the mountain regions, from the underdeveloped areas and the industrialized ones. Forty-four percent migrated to other European countries (especially to France, Switzerland, and Germany); 30.5 percent chose North America (the great majority the United States); 23.5 percent directed their steps toward South America (particularly Argentina and Brazil); the remaining 2 percent went to other continents (principally Africa).[3]

It would hardly be credible that such an impressive movement of people could have developed if those involved had known nothing of what they were facing. Historical studies have revealed that the conservatives' condemnation of the decision to migrate was instrumental in their leaving. Conservatives feared the internal repercussions of such a massive exodus, and therefore it was fully in their interest to make it seem that the migrants were "poor naive people." However, the problem remained: Were their expectations really no more than myths? Studies on the subject by Italians have generally addressed the question only marginally.[4] In this paper I intend to contribute to the discussion, showing that the migrants were not without reliable information concerning their destinations, describing how they obtained such information and how in this way they shaped a realistic image of the host countries. I shall analyze two cases of migration from the Biella area, an important industrial district at the foot of the Alps in the northern Italian region of Piedmont. These migrants were skilled workers from two occupational groups that differed in their composition and in the nature of their migratory experience. One group, textile workers, crossed the ocean to work in the silk mills of Paterson and other New Jersey urban centers; they were mainly permanent migrants. The other group, building-workers, went to construction sites in southeast France, on the other side of the Alps; they were mainly temporary migrants.

Biellese Weavers to Paterson, New Jersey

When, around the mid-1880s, the first groups of textile workers began to leave the small industrial villages of the Piedmontese district for New Jersey, the expectations that they had of migration reflected their occupational status. They were for the most part skilled workers who for generations had lived principally from industrial work, albeit work supplemented by the subsistence farming that guaranteed part of their families' diet and constituted an important means of support during the long strikes. But their expectations were also an expression of the hopes and aspirations that had been dramatically frustrated in the years immediately preceding the start of emigration. The news circulating in the 1880s with regard to the new prospects of employment in the silk mills of New Jersey concerned, above all, wages: according to a newspaper run by the Biellese factory-owners, the local textile workers believed that wages were "very high."[5] From other sources we learn further that, at least among the more politically minded workers, the image of the United States was also that of a country in which the greatest freedom of organization and speech was guaranteed. In a letter sent in 1886 to a leader of the Left in the Biella area, a weaver who had migrated to West Hoboken—a town a few miles away from Paterson and, like it, a site of large silk mills—reflected this image very well. It was an image that was commonplace among intellectual Italian democrats in those years,[6] but evidently also present among workers in this Piedmontese area: "Writing to you for the first time from this great Republic," the letter writer stated,

> all I will say to you for the moment is that here we enjoy all the liberties. At present we weavers are on strike: we are asking for an eight-hour day and a pay raise of 25% and I can tell you in all truth that, if we were in Italy, by this time Italian injustice would have already interfered, passing judicial condemnations. But here, as you well know, there is an extensive freedom to strike and freedom of speech, and now, although the struggle has already been going on for four weeks, we have reached a point where the bosses have almost accepted that our union is strong enough to win and to obtain that which their bullying behavior has taken away from us.

The letter ended: "Soon I will write to you at greater length on the subject of the American liberties."[7]

The migration from the Biella area to New Jersey had been the consequence of a drastic change in the power-relationship between the weavers—who were the dominant nucleus of the textile working class in the local industry—and the employers. The Biella area was the location of an important wool industry: its development during the nineteenth century had been accompanied by strong social tensions, which had not prevented it from gaining a prominent position nationally but had made it an exemplary case of the weight of the "questione sociale" in Italy.[8] Social conflict erupted when the entrepreneurs began to bring into the factories the hand-weavers who had traditionally been out-workers.

The new situation did not involve a change in the instrument of production, which even in the factories remained the old hand-loom; but it aggravated the strong sense of social unease that in the preceding decades had accompanied the unpopular transition from a proto-industrial productive system to a factory system, a system that had begun with the mechanization of spinning in the 1820s and 1830s, and had caused the gradual decline of out-work. In the long conflict that for more than twenty years set determined industrialists, armed with strong political support at both the national and the local level, against the weavers, the latter exhibited an extraordinary capacity for resistance. Their strength was essentially based on limiting access to their trade. The job of weaver was reserved for the male members of the families. These families were tightly linked together by complex, solid systems of alliance, founded on kinship and neighborliness. In every little textile community in the area they traditionally earned their livelihood from the textile industry, and this knowledge of wool manufacturing was handed down from father to son.[9] Their monopoly of the trade was, moreover, strengthened by an important union that gained influence throughout the whole area. In this way the weavers took over the leadership of all the textile workers.

But at the end of the 1870s there was a radical change. After a long general strike that broke out in 1877 as a result of discipline problems at work, the owners introduced the power loom into the factories. The new machine, which spread slowly but irresistibly throughout the local wool industry, made it possible to break the hold of the weavers over the labor market. Unemployment spread among the workers: those who submitted to the humiliation of accepting work at the power loom saw their wages drastically reduced. The state played its part in supporting the owners: the old union of weavers was dissolved and outlawed; there were indiscriminate arrests among the workers, and threats of deportation.[10]

It was therefore in the context of this defeat of the hand-weavers and its repercussions on an entire social group of workers that the flow of migration from this area to the United States developed. And it is in this context that the image of America that began to take shape in the 1880s among the textile workers of the local wool industry is comprehensible. This image was strengthened in the following decade, when migration increased. In 1889 a local newspaper interviewed a young woman, who had recently returned from Paterson to her village "for health reasons," as she declared, "otherwise I would never have left America." She had gone back to working in a local textile factory and added: "Life over there is incomparably better than in Italy; you're paid more, you dress better, even the factory girls wear bonnets. In a word, life's good." Later, declaring that she "approved of the anarchy that will save the world," she described in enthusiastic tones her participation in the political life of the Italian working community in the American industrial center.[11]

America seemed to offer what these workers were looking for: jobs in abundance, good pay, and the freedom to express themselves politically. The new phase of intense development in the silk industry during the last fifteen years of the nineteenth century required a workforce capable of filling not only the jobs that were being newly created, but also those left vacant by the workers, chiefly of West European origin, who had made possible the setting-up of the industry and the launching of its first phase of expansion.[12] These West European workers had reacted to the introduction of new technologies and to the changes in the work process that characterized the new phase of growth either by abandoning an activity that now no longer matched their expectations or by claiming and obtaining the highest-paid jobs in the silk industry. For this reason the Italian workers—most of whom came from the northern part of the country, from the area of Biella and that of Como, in Lombardy, another important textile district—found plenty of job opportunities and, during the 1890s in Paterson and the nearby silk centers, replaced the previous wave of immigrants, mainly English- and German-speakers.[13]

The work they were offered was skilled: they were concentrated in the weaving departments. The wages were on average double those paid in Italy: the equivalent of seven lire as against the three-and-a-half lire that were paid in the Biella area for the same job.[14] Since the silk industry offered employment for both adults and children and for both males and females, and since, moreover, the wages paid to the women in the group—who were also assigned to the looms—were almost equal to those paid to men,[15] the more workers the head of the family was able to mobilize the more attractive migration became. There was thus a strong impulse on the part of the northern Italian group toward the employment of the entire family unit in the silk industry, and in particular toward the employment of wives.[16] Consequently, it was a characteristic of the northern Italian group right from the outset that it chiefly comprised families whose intention was to settle, and workers who were almost all employed in the silk industry.[17]

All this made these Italians a group that was not only very homogeneous from the occupational point of view but also very cohesive from the social point of view—a dense web of closely related individuals and families. Relationships differing in content were superimposed on one another: relatives, friends, neighbors, and workmates were often the same people. Interaction within the group was therefore intense and tended to cover almost the entire range of individual and social needs, in the economic as well as the emotional sphere, in the sphere of the exchange of services as well as that of leisure time—and also, within certain limitations, in the sphere of politics. The anarchists of Paterson were organized under the "Right to Existence Group," formed almost exclusively of northern Italian textile workers belonging to the political tendency of the "organizers," who maintained the need for worker unity through the formation of a militant union. Their activities had a large following and their newspaper, La Questione Sociale, had a wide circulation.[18] Their ability to achieve support from compatriots working in the silk factories was favored by the strong cohesion characterizing the northern Italian ethnic group. There also existed another political group composed of northern Italian textile workers; this one gave rise to the Italian branch of the Socialist Labor Party of Paterson.[19] Although it was considerably less influential than the anarchists, it is interesting to note that the ideological differences between the two did not prevent frequent collaboration—particularly in the case of raising money to send to Italy in order to support the strikes there. Such cooperation occurred on several occasions during the Biella-area strikes of the 1890s.[20] Here group solidarity based on a common area of origin prevailed over any ideological differences. And, in actual fact, the workers themselves were unable to draw any clear distinction between anarchists and socialists, save that the former were more active and offered an opportunity for political debate to immigrants with traditions of class struggle and unionization in their home country.

All this helped to give the members of the northern Italian

community a strong sense of group identity, which was a source of strength and security in the new society into which they had immigrated. Of course, this did not mean that exploitation in the factories of New Jersey was any less severe than that in the Italian factories. Nor did the naive vision of America as a "land of liberty" survive for long: here, as everywhere, it was power that counted, and it is unthinkable that the immigrant workers were unaware of this fact. The execution of the Chicago Haymarket anarchists in 1887 incited propaganda denouncing "the true face" of capitalism in the United States and the reality that lay behind the myth of "American liberties."[21] Nevertheless, during the 1890s Paterson was considered a safe refuge for radicals and was called "the holy city (the Mecca) of the anarchists."[22]

We can therefore say that among the northern Italian immigrant workers there prevailed a positive perception of their own position in the new environment. This view supported the positive image that, on the other side of the Atlantic, in Italy, had been growing in strength among their fellow workers. This image was not the only one that was circulating, for there were others that conflicted with it. For example, the late 1880s saw the conservative press in the Biella area launch a concerted drive to discourage textile-worker emigration to the United States, denouncing the "bewitching mirages flashed in front of the emigrants' eyes" with which they allowed themselves to be "seduced."[23] This was clearly a case of the propaganda of self-interest: in their own factories local employers had noticed that the concrete possibility of migrating increased the workers' opposition to any wage cuts or worsening of working conditions. In any event, it was felt at the time that the press campaign would have some effect since—as one left-wing newspaper remarked—the local textile workers had no previous traditions of emigration: a voyage to the United States was "a voyage into the unknown."[24]

In spite of this, a positive image of America remained the dominant one within the working-class group. This image represented the projection of hopes and expectations that had evolved through the bitter experience of the workers in the preceding period. It was confirmed by the information that had reached them from workmates who had migrated earlier.

In order to understand why this was the only information that they took to heart, and why they disregarded conflicting information that came through other channels, it is necessary to analyze the nature of the ties between those who had left and those who had stayed behind, and the role that people expected these ties to play in the event of a decision to emigrate. Mention has already been made of the social cohesion of the immigrant group in New Jersey. This cohesion came from the conditions that the migrants had found in the particular situation they had entered, and it created in a new social space a solid, compact web of relationships that had characterized the group in the industrial villages of the Biella area. From the point of view of those who had stayed behind, the departures of relatives and workmates represented a loss for their social network, but, at the same time—since migration did not necessarily mean the interruption of social ties—these networks were reproduced over a vastly larger geographical area. As a result, the functions of mutual assistance and active solidarity that the social networks had always performed were not destroyed; for anyone planning to emigrate, the presence on the other side of the Atlantic of migrants who were already settled and who formed part of the group meant an opportunity to make use of their support, which guaranteed protection and aid both of a material and of a psychological nature, and which facilitated the newcomer's adjustment to the new social environment. The information that arrived through the group's own internal channels did not pass on a generic image of the host country but gave specific assessments of employment opportunities and living conditions; at the same time the information made it possible for migration to take place with significantly reduced risk and uncertainty.

The migratory flow from the Biella area toward New Jersey reached its highest point in the 1890s. Very soon, during the first decade of the twentieth century, it began to decline and then abruptly slowed down.[25] This phenomenon was probably caused by a variety of factors, but one thing that certainly helped to discourage migration in that direction was the diffusion of a negative image of America among the workers in the textile villages of Italy. Since their former positive image came from information received through the migrant social network, this information must have taken on a negative hue. The question that must be asked, then, is how and why did the migrant group modify its perception of its own position in America, for as we know, during the first phase of migration expectations had not been disappointed.

Part of the answer undoubtedly lies in certain events that marked the beginning of the new century for the northern Italian working class in the silk industry: the attack on the anarchists of New Jersey in the wake of the assassination of the king of Italy and especially after the attempt on the life of the American president McKinley; the hostile campaign against the Italians in the silk industry that was started after the failure of a strike by the workers in the silk dyeing plants, a strike that had not directly involved the weaving departments where the northern Italians were concentrated, but whose effects had repercussions for them, too; and the temporary employment crisis caused by a fire that devastated Paterson.[26]

All these events had significant consequences: they probably damaged the group's cohesion, corroded its strong sense of security, aggravated its isolation. But other factors also played a role. Initially these immigrants considered the wages in Paterson to be high. They did so because their point of reference was the standard of living in their community of origin, that is, in the little industrial villages from which they came. But, significantly, the wage levels judged to be high by these recent immigrants were viewed as low by their workmates from other countries who had immigrated at an earlier stage and were already well established.[27] Indeed, it was for this very reason that the northern Italians were "not well thought of"—as was reported in Italy—by the other workers in the silk centers of New Jersey: the former accepted "meek wages" whereas the latter had "higher expectations."[28]

But the standard by which the northern Italian immigrants judged wage levels was to change as they and their families became more and more socially and culturally integrated into the new society and as, consequently, new expectations were awakened, modifying the earlier ones that they had brought with them from their home villages. The result was that wages no longer seemed as high as they had seemed before. The tensions in labor relations aroused by demands for higher wages made the silk industrialists, who had encouraged the weavers' immigration in the 1890s, look upon them in a new light. It now became more attractive for the employers to use cheap Jewish workers who had come over in a new wave of immigration from Central and Eastern Europe.[29]

These considerations—which would repay more thorough analysis—are of interest because they enable us to reformulate certain questions. Shall we say that the news that the immigrants sent to their fellow workers in the textile villages of the Biella area had become more "realistic?" It does not seem that the problem can be put in these terms; the case under discussion suggests that, in addition to the dynamics of the relationships with employers and with other worker groups, we should also consider the social and cultural change brought about by adjustment to the new society as one of the factors that influenced the workers' view of reality and hence the representation of this reality that they transmitted to Italy.

In 1913 the Industrial Workers of the World (IWW) organized

the famous strike of Paterson,[30] which aroused considerable interest in the left-wing press in Italy. The long, dramatic conflict was covered in particular by the Biella socialist newspaper. During the course of the strike, which lasted six months and ended in a crushing defeat for the workers, as many as a dozen detailed reports appeared.[31] The chief reason for the interest shown by the local socialist newspaper was that a significant proportion of the workers of Italian origin who had formed the vanguard of the Paterson strike were migrants, or sons of migrants, from this area. One of the reports sent from Paterson informed the local readers that, of the 16 women and 29 men arrested in the early months of the strike, no less than 13 and 22, respectively, were of Biellese origin.[32] Two months later, the same correspondent sent out an anguished, dramatic appeal:

> There is hunger in Paterson and the strikers are short of bread. We ask our good and generous comrades on the outside to assist us; their contributions will provide food for thousands of starving people, and help to weaken the stubborn arrogance of the police, the authorities, and the bourgeoisie in Paterson.[33]

The appeal went unanswered: there were no petitions among the workers of Biella in support of the strikers in the American city. Social conditions had become difficult in Italy too in 1913, but the absence of concrete manifestations of solidarity with the working classes of Paterson was probably also due to the fact that for several years now the ties between the Biellese migrants and the communities they had left behind had been much looser than they once were. The image of America among the textile workers of the Biella area that had been formed with the development of the migratory flow toward New Jersey had already greatly deteriorated by the time of the collapse of the big strike in Paterson. It was not, therefore, the dramatic outcome of this conflict that caused this image of America to fade; if anything, the defeat represented a further bitter confirmation of a disillusionment that had already gained a lot of ground.

Italian Building-Workers in Southern France

During the years in which the textile workers were departing for New Jersey, another migratory flow from the Biella area was at its height, one directed toward southeast France. The migrants in this case were skilled workers in the building industry who were present in great numbers in a large region bordering on Piedmont and lying between the cities of Lyon, Grenoble, and Chambéry. In this area, which contained the highest concentration of Italian migrants in France after the *départements* of the Mediterranean littoral, the building-workers, most of whom came from Piedmont and Lombardy, formed the largest occupational group in the composite Italian migrant community. And within this group workers from the Biella area were in turn a significant part.[34]

In the period during which this migratory flow was developing the general situation of Italian workers in France was markedly deteriorating.[35] From the beginning of the 1880s until the middle of the 1890s a climate of acute hostility toward the migrants from Italy had been forming in all sectors of French society. One of the reasons for this state of affairs was the fact that relations between the two countries were extremely bad, due to Italy's pro-German foreign policy.[36] When, in 1888, the Italian government modified the customs treaty with France to curtail the importation of products from that country, the government in Paris unleashed an out-and-out trade war, threatening to take revenge by closing its frontiers to Italian migrants. On top of all this there were recurrent tensions between the workers of the two countries because of the competition for jobs, and these tensions led to continual clashes.[37] In the same year, 1888, there were demonstrations in Grenoble "against the foreign builders," accompanied by the request that the Italian workers "be driven out of the municipal building-yard" and that "in future jobs should no longer be given to contractors who were not of French nationality."[38] The demonstrations in Grenoble had not given rise to bloodshed but elsewhere the periodic *chasses aux loups* (wolf-hunts—wolves being the name by which the Italians were commonly known) ended in tragedy.[39]

It is therefore not surprising that the general orientation of the authorities in Italy during this period was toward discouraging migration to France. Much attention was given in the press to anxious reports on the migrants' situation that the Italian consuls sent to the government in Rome, advising against workers crossing the Alps. For example, in 1892, in one of the reports printed in an authoritative publication of the Foreign Ministry on the subject of Italian emigration, the consul in Lyon wrote: "It would be a good thing if Italians abandoned the illusion that it is easy to find profitable employment in France."[40] Indeed, conditions became more and more difficult for the migrants, as was clear for all to see with, in 1893 and 1894, the two most serious outbreaks of xenophobia in the whole period. The bloody clashes between French and Italian workers in the salt-works of Aigues-Mortes, near Marseilles, led to numerous deaths among the Italians.[41] The intense emotions that were aroused still had not died down when, after the killing by an Italian anarchist of the president of the French republic who was on a visit to Lyon, anti-Italian riots shook the city with widespread lootings and beatings, and spread to numerous other centers in the region. In Grenoble demonstrators filed through the streets to the singing of the *Marseillaise* and the cry of "Italians out."[42] Throughout the region thousands of emigrants hurriedly fled toward the Italian and Swiss border.[43]

The image of France as an outlet for Italian migration was, then, decidedly negative during this period. Nevertheless, the migratory flow of building-workers from the Biella area toward this country tended to grow during those very years.[44] It should be added that France was not the only country to which they migrated, since they could choose from many other countries both in Europe and overseas.[45] Why then was France such a popular destination?

Conservative newspapers in the Biella area aligned themselves with the national press in passing severely negative judgments on Italy's neighbor. In the 1880s, the criticism went as far as branding France another Russia, with only one small difference: in Russia the pogroms were directed against the Jews, while in France their target was the Italian migrants.[46] This anti-French propaganda continued in the following years; it was not until the Aigues-Mortes massacre of 1893 that the local conservative press modified its extremist stance. That it did so was due to the fear that France would deport Italian workers as a counter-reaction to Italy's criticism. "If the throngs of our compatriots scattered abroad are ever sent back to Italy," stated a Biellese newspaper, "it will result in grave disorder among us and in great upheaval to our economy."[47] The newspaper's objective was to criticize the Italian government's stand on emigration, which it considered inadequate since expatriation, in its view, was to the country's benefit.

With regard to the local left-wing press, the prevalent attitude toward the situation was one of embarrassment.[48] This unease arose from the fact that the episodes of xenophobia called into question not only the socialist creed of universal proletarian brotherhood but also the myth (traditional in this area) of the French working class's revolutionary spirit. This myth was not completely unfounded, of course, and it had roots spreading through numerous sections of the working class due to the fact that many workers and artisans outside the textile field had spent periods of temporary migration in France during the 1800s. The famous song of the Lyon "canuts," the silk weavers of the 1834 revolt, was known and sung in the Biella area by local workers.[49]

The building-workers swelling the migratory flows of the 1880s and 1890s from this area to France had no need for information from the press to form their own autonomous image of the neighboring country. Their image was based on firsthand experience and was extremely realistic: faced with outbursts of xenophobia, for example, they did not delude themselves into thinking it possible to rely forever on the solidarity of the entire French working-class movement. When anti-Italian protests occurred in Grenoble in 1894, the glovers' union there supported a demand for the dismissal of Italian workers, even though all of these were union members and had never accepted wages inferior to those of local workers.[50] The Biella-area building-workers were well aware of the glovers' situation, since the two groups were in close contact and, in fact, later banded together to form the Italian Socialist Federation of Grenoble.[51]

However, these building-workers were also well aware that wages and working conditions in France were better than in Italy. "Here we are treated like gentlemen," wrote a young mason in 1889 to his old father back home in Biella:

> This week I am working [in a district in the *département* of Ain, near Lyon] with a fellow from Savoy. They give us 5 bottles of wine a day, so we're doing beautifully. My workmate is always insulting me because he says I work too hard, but to me it seems I'm doing nothing at all. I pay 2 lire a day for board and room, but they even give us coffee and a drink after every meal.[52]

It must be remembered that building work was in great demand in the area of France to which these migrants flocked. On the same days that Italian workers had to leave Grenoble in 1894, the mayor of the city had a notice "to the population" put up. It read:

> At this moment 40 building sites are closed. If this situation continues at length, it will mean great losses to all. It is well-known that the number of local building workers is insufficient to man the numerous sites; it is therefore indispensable to resort to foreign labor in order to continue the work in progress.[53]

However, it is necessary to add that the favored position enjoyed by Italian building-workers on the French labor market was also the result of other factors, and that these were probably the determining ones in influencing in a positive sense the image they formed of France as the most desirable destination for emigration. To understand these factors it is necessary to analyze the distinctive characteristics of building-workers from this particular area of Italy and the rapport that migrants had established over a period of time with the neighboring French community.

These workers differed from the textile workers bound for New Jersey during the same period in that migration was for them neither a recent experience—for it was already widespread, albeit chiefly along the borders of Italy, under the Ancien Régime[54]—nor the consequence of a dramatic break in a preexisting socioeconomic equilibrium. The origins of migration in the building trade from the Biella area—a phenomenon similar to that in many other localities in the foothills of the Italian Alps[55]—are the same as those that favored the establishment of proto-industrial wool manufacture: the poverty of the soil. It was because of the insufficiency of agricultural resources for such an extremely dense population that the inhabitants of the area sought work outside agriculture to supplement their income from the small farms they owned. In some villages these activities consisted, due to the presence of active merchants, of wool manufacture on the putting-out system; in others in building and public works, a specialty of the menfolk, who for eight or nine months of the year had thus to leave home while the women remained to run the small farms. In the villages where proto-industry evolved, it had a strong influence on stabilizing the population until, as we have seen, the processes of technological transformation led to the migration, in most cases permanent, of part of the population; in the villages where the building trades developed, migration—strictly seasonal—became the means by which the population was able to continue to survive at home.[56]

At the start of the nineteenth century, seasonal migrants began to extend their destinations to regions situated outside the Italian borders. Prominent among these regions were the French Alpine *départements* and the valley of the Rhône. This skilled workforce was used in the construction of the great roads across the Alps started by Napoleon,[57] and the numbers of these Italian migrants continued to expand throughout the entire area, with the development of investments in civil and military infrastructures, and with the growth of the towns and the spread of industrialization.[58] The penetration into these French regions of the group of building-workers from the Biella area was constant and continually increasing. Their high levels of skill certainly had something to do with this; but so also did the fact that some crafts in which they were expert, such as that of the stucco-workers, were not known at this time in France.[59] In the Alpine *départements*, moreover, their presence made up for the lack of local workers available for these activities: the inhabitants of the French mountain regions were, paradoxically, famous for being migrants themselves, and the development in the labor market for the building trade during the nineteenth century had not modified their habits, because the trades they practiced were different: they were waiters and domestics, street-sellers and chimney sweeps—to name only a few of the traditional activities for which they were known in many towns and cities throughout France and other countries.[60]

But what should be emphasized here is that the success of temporary migration by Italian building-workers and the repeated contacts with the French labor market enabled them to establish a very strong position in some sectors of construction work. These migrants had continued to be mainly seasonal and temporary, but a certain number of them, conforming to a pattern typical of migratory movements of this sort,[61] tended in time to settle in the immigration area, even though this did not involve severing their links with home. This happened especially in the case of those who had set themselves up as small contractors, so becoming the employers of those among their fellow countrymen who maintained the periodic nature of their migration. Social ties of various kinds beyond the worker-employer relationship can be traced to the fact that they came from the same groups of villages and these fostered a kind of solidarity, which was founded on a substantial convergence of interests, but which was not without conflict. As a result, the labor market in the building trade in the French area tended, for the Italian migrants, to take on a par-ticular configuration; it split into segments along lines based on one's belonging to the same, well-defined area of origin. But the relative ease with which employment was found in France also derived partly from the fact that the migrants were able to utilize a multiplicity of channels formed both by workmates who, like the small contractors mentioned above, had settled in the area, and by the temporary workers themselves, who each year dispersed into little groups in a myriad of localities, large and small, in the immigration area.[62]

It should be borne in mind that during the nineteenth century building and public works had not undergone changes comparable to those that affected all the other sectors of production. Despite a few significant innovations in the technology and in construction materials, production continued to leave considerable scope for the autonomy of the individual artisan. The sector was characterized not by large concerns using a stable workforce, but by a system of subcontracting.[63] This fact made it possible for small teams of skilled workers to take on small assignments of work for which they negotiated a flat fee. This was not always possible, and it was often necessary to accept jobs on a day-to-day basis. However, the skilled workers in the building trade aimed at winning these subcontracts, from which they derived greater profits and which above all safeguarded the artisan independence of which they were jealous. But the attainment of this goal imposed on them, since the subcontracts that they succeeded in getting were usually small, and therefore their work was of relatively short duration, the necessity of having access to a constant stream of information, which would reach them in good time and covered a vast territory.

The wider and more complex the network they were able to make use of, and the more deeply it was rooted in the local labor market, the greater were their chances of successfully obtaining and negotiating subcontracts. This network was the result of the handing-down of social ties from father to son and from one generation to another within the compact fabric of an occupational group that shared the same trade and lived on a pattern of migration well-established in the French region.[64] This explains why, despite all indications to the contrary, the migrants in the building trade from the Biella area continued to go to France during the "difficult" years of the late nineteenth century.

The flow of migrants continued into the new century, when certain changes occurred in the labor market of the building trade as a result of the growing proportion of unskilled workers.[65] The position of Italian migrants was adversely affected by this development: what happened as a consequence was not a slowing down of migration but a profound change in their social behavior. But that is another story, which concerns the radicalization of skilled workers for whom working far from home was not a matter of choice but a precondition for being able to carry on their own trade.

Conclusion

Migration of the two occupational groups did not develop blindly, nor on the basis of an ingenuous vision of the host countries. Migrants had at their disposal a large amount of information from various sources, some of which they accepted and some of which they discredited. In order to explain the selection that individuals and families made from a mass of sharply contradictory news and messages, it is necessary to examine the community to which these people belonged. Strong ties linking relatives, friends, and workmates in spite of the distance represented the channels through which information passed, and an image of the host country was shaped from the information provided. The greater the migratory flow in a certain direction, the more ample the information—and consequently the more realistic the expectations. My hypothesis is that an analysis of the migrants' social networks is essential to understanding the mechanisms by which they judged situations that were geographically and culturally far removed from their own, and how they chose their destination.

Both textile workers and building-workers were groups strongly characterized by a social cohesion founded on a combination of shared geographical origin and a common trade, but they did not represent the same type of migrant. The difference between them lay in the motivations that caused them to migrate. The weavers, who had achieved and long maintained a position of power and prestige in the small industrial communities of the Biella area, suffered a process of downward mobility. Aware of the irreversibility of the technological change that was the origin of their loss of social status, they migrated in order to build a new life in a new society. From the very beginning, therefore, they planned to settle permanently with their families in the New Jersey towns: silk mills offered steady employment not only to men but also to women and children, in exchange for the weavers' acceptance of the power-loom. The motives inducing the building-workers to migrate were different. Working in cities and returning home was part of their traditional way of life; they conceived of migration as a means to survive, maintain their own social status, and possibly improve it—but in their village of origin. It is for this very reason that they were seasonal and temporary migrants who migrated singly and had no interest in putting down roots abroad.

There was no correlation between the different migration patterns of the two groups and their destinations. It is well known that many Italian migrants to the United States were "birds of passage," while many Italian migrants to France settled there. The migrants' social networks influenced their choice of destination. Both groups consisted of skilled workers; consequently, they were interested not so much in the general conditions of the labor market in the host country as in the job opportunities corresponding to their professional experience. Thus migrants expected their social networks to perform not only the role of information channel but also of access channel to particular labor markets. All this accentuated the crucial importance of social networks in determining the direction of migratory flows, as well as influencing the migrants' expectations and shaping their image of their destination.

Notes

I wish to thank Horst Rössler, who read an earlier draft of this paper and made valuable comments.

Part of the data used here was collected during research sponsored by the Sella Foundation, Biella, Italy.

1. Pietro Biasutti, "Cause, effetti e rimedi dell'emigrazione transatlantica: Suo stato ed importanza attuale nella provincia di Udine," *Bollettino dell'Associazione agraria friulana* (22 July 1878), 46.

2. *Le condizioni dei contadini del Veneto: Parte prima della relazione del commendatore Emilio Morpurgo* (Rome, 1882), 109–10.

3. See *Un secolo di emigrazione italiana: 1876–1976*, ed. Gianfausto Rosoli (Rome: Centro studi emigrazione, 1978), 19.

4. See Emilio Franzina, "Le culture dell'emigrazione," *Mezzosecolo*, no. 5 (1985): 279–338.

5. *L'Eco dell'Industria* (hereafter quoted as *EI*) (Biella), 1 Aug 1889.

6. Rudolph J. Vecoli, "Free Country: The American Republic Viewed by the Italian Left, 1880–1920," in *In the Shadow of the Statue of Liberty: Immigrants, Workers and Citizens in the American Republic, 1880–1920*, ed. Marianne Debouzy (Paris: Presses Universitaires de Vincennes, 1988), 35–56.

7. Letter from Torello, West Hoboken, N.J., 19 Mar 1886 to Ubertini (Archivio Giuseppe Ubertini, Biella).

8. The first Parliamentary Commission of Inquiry into the workers' strike in Italy (1878) dedicated the central part of its final report to a long analysis of the "systematic war" that had characterized social life in this area from the late 1850s to the late 1870s. See Pietro Secchia, *Capitalismo e classe operaia nel centro laniero d'Italia* (Rome: Editori Riuniti, 1960), 116–25.

9. See Franco Ramella, *Terra e telai* (Turin: Einaudi, 1984).

10. See ibid.

11. *Biella cattolica* (Biella), 9 Sept 1900. The newspaper wrote, with evident horror, as it recorded the young girl's words: "Twice a week, in the evening, together with almost all her female comrades from Biella, she

would go to the lectures of Gori and Ciancabilla [two Italian anarchists active in Paterson] in a special hall, always crammed with people, and capable of holding up to two thousand. 'And there—the girl said—it's not like in Italy: there are no guards, and the speakers are not interrupted, even when they say that it would be a righteous and holy act to kill the kings and the people in authority.' " It is likely that, in reporting what the young woman had said, the newspaper deliberately exaggerated. The interview, besides, was not published until the following year, after the assassination of King Umberto I of Italy by an Italian anarchist who had migrated to New Jersey.

12. See U.S. Senate, Immigration Commission, *Immigrants in Industries, Pt. 5. Report,* vol. 11 (Washington, D.C.: Government Printing Office, 1911), 17–20.

13. See Carlo C. Altarelli, "History and Present Conditions of the Italian Colony of Paterson, N.J." (M.A. thesis, Columbia University, 1911), 3.

14. See *Tribuna Biellese* (hereafter quoted as *TB*) (Biella), 14 Sept 1900; Luigi Einaudi, "La psicologia di uno sciopero," *La Riforma Sociale* (October 1897), 201.

15. See U.S. Senate, Immigration Commission, *Immigrants in Industries. Pt. 5, Report,* 11: 37, 38.

16. See U.S. Senate, *Report on the Conditions of Women and Child Wage-Earners in the United States,* vol. 3 (Washington, D.C.: Government Printing Office, 1910), 60.

17. See U.S. Senate, Immigration Commission, *Immigrants in Industries. Pt. 5, Report,* 11: 48–51.

18. See George Carey, "La Questione Sociale," in *Italian Americans: New Perspectives in Italian Immigration and Ethnicity,* ed. Lydio F. Tomasi (New York: Center for Migration Studies, 1985), 289–97.

19. See *Corriere Biellese* (hereafter quoted as *CB*) (Biella), 21 Nov 1896.

20. See *CB,* 1896–1900, passim.

21. Vecoli, "Free Country."

22. Oreste Mombello, *Sessant'anni di vita socialista* (Biella: Industria et Labor, 1952), 7.

23. *EI,* 1 Aug 1889.

24. *La Sveglia* (Biella), 17 Feb 1883, and passim.

25. See Rinaldo Rigola, *Il movimento operaio nel Biellese: Autobiografia* (Bari: Laterza, 1930), 64–68.

26. See Carey, "La Questione Sociale," 294.

27. See U.S. Senate, Immigration Commission, *Immigrants in Industries, Pt. 5, Report,* 11: 17–20.

28. *TB,* 13 Sept 1900.

29. See U.S. Senate, Immigration Commission, *Immigrants in Industries, Pt. 5, Report,* 11: 17–20.

30. See Philip S. Foner, *History of the Labor Movement in the United States: The Industrial Workers of the World* (New York: International Publishers, 1973), 351–72.

31. See *CB*, 21 Mar 1913; 1 Apr 1913; 6 May 1913; 10 May 1913; 16 May 1913; 20 May 1913; 3 June 1913; 18 June 1913; 27 June 1913; 15 July 1913; 22 July 1913; 22 Aug 1913.

32. See *CB*, 6 May 1913.

33. *CB*, 15 July 1913.

34. See Franco Ramella, "Il Biellese nella grande emigrazione di fine Ottocento," in Franco Ramella, Chiara Ottaviano, and Marco Neiretti, *L'emigrazione biellese fra Ottocento e Novecento* (Milano: Electa, 1985), 311–61.

35. See Pierre Milza, *Français et Italiens à la fin du XIXe siècle* (Rome: Ecole Française de Rome, 1981), 144–49.

36. Ibid.

37. See Pierre Milza, "Un siècle d'immigration étrangère en France," *Vingtième siècle* (July–September 1985).

38. Archivio del Ministero degli Affari Esteri, Rome, *Serie Politica A*, busta 76, fasc. 3.

39. See ibid., *Serie Politica*, folder 622.

40. Ministero degli Esteri, *Emigrazione e colonie: Rapporti dei RR. Agenti diplomatici e consolari. Lione: Rapporto del regio Console comm. L. Basso* (Rome, 1893), 219.

41. See Teodosio Vertone, "Antecedentes et causes des evenements d'Aigues-Mortes," in *L'emigrazione italiana in Francia prima del 1914*, ed. Jean-Baptiste Duroselle and Enrico Serra (Milan: Angeli, 1978), 107–38.

42. Archives départementales du Rhône, Lyon, *Serie M;* Vital Chomel, "Les étrangers dans la ville: Travailleurs piemontais et société urbaine à Grenoble (fin du XIXe siècle)," *Le Monde Alpin et Rhodanien* (September 1984), 211–61.

43. See Chomel, "Les étrangers," 248–49.

44. See Ramella, "Il Biellese nella grande emigrazione."

45. Ibid.

46. See *EI*, 26 Feb 1882.

47. *EI*, 31 Aug 1893.

48. See Chiara Ottaviano, "L'immagine e le vicende dell'emigrante biellese nella stampa dell'epoca," in Ramella et al., *L'emigrazione biellese*, 427–28.

49. See Secchia, *Capitalismo e classe operaia*, 7.

50. See *Giornale delle Camere del Lavoro* (Milan) 6 July 1894.

51. See Ministero degli Esteri, *Emigrazione e colonie: Rapporti dei Regi Agenti diplomatici e consolari. Immigrazione e colonia italiana nel distretto consolare di Lione* (Rome, 1903), 124.

52. Letter from Felice Bosi, Crassier (France), 9 Aug 1889, to his father (Archivio Anna Maria Perotti, Curino [Biella]).

53. Archives municipales de Grenoble, Grenoble, F 7, 12152.

54. See Gio. Tommaso Mullatera, *Memorie cronologiche corografiche della citta' di Biella* (Biella, 1778).

55. See R. Foerster, *The Italian Emigration of Our Times* (Cambridge, Mass., 1919).

56. See Ramella, *Terra e telai.*

57. See Marcel Blanchard, *Les routes des Alpes occidentales à l'epoque napoléonienne (1796–1815).* (Grenoble, 1920).

58. See Abel Chatelain, *Les migrants temporaires en France de 1800 a 1914* (Lille: Presses Universitaires de Lille, 1976).

59. Ibid.

60. See Ministero degli Esteri, *Emigrazione e colonie: Lione;* idem, *Emigrazione e colonie: Chambéry;* Laurence Fontaine, *Le voyage et la memoire: Colporteurs de l'Oisans au XIXᵉ siècle* (Lyon: Presses Universitaires de Lyon, 1984).

61. See Charles Tilly, "Migration in Modern European History," in *Human Migration: Patterns and Politics,* ed. William H. McNeill and Ruth S. Adams (Bloomington, Ind.: Indiana University Press, 1978), 48–72.

62. See Ramella, "Il Biellese nella grande emigrazione."

63. See R. A. Goldtwhaite, *La costruzione della Firenze rinascimentale* (Bologna: Il Mulino, 1984); see Folhen and Bedarida, *Histoire du travail,* vol. 3 (Paris, 1969).

64. See Ramella, "Il Biellese nella grande emigrazione."

65. See Elisabetta Calderini, Rocco Curto, and Gemma Sirchia, *Hirondelles, 1860–1914: Storia e vicende dei lavoratori dell'edilizia in Piemonte* (Turin: Celid, 1985).

PART III
Images of America: Myths and Realities

6

The Dream of Independence: The "America" of England's North Staffordshire Potters

Horst Rössler

"I TELL you my friends, America is the place to live in."[1] This view of John Sutherland, who had migrated from North Staffordshire to the United States in 1844, was obviously shared by many British pottery-workers who had left their native country for America in the 1840s. Why did this trade group, which was said to be more deeply rooted in their native place than other working-class groups, decide to emigrate?[2] The following essay examines the economic and political reasons for the working potters' emigration; the role of trade unions, the press, and emigrant letters in promoting emigration and shaping the prospective migrants' image of America; the potters' hopes for economic, social, and political independence; as well as the immigrants' experience and achievements in the United States.

Background: The Situation of Pottery-Workers in Staffordshire

It was in the second half of the eighteenth century with the establishment of large manufactories—like that of Josiah Wedgwood for example, one of the most important and successful pottery entrepreneurs of that time—that there dawned a new era for this industry. Now the days when potmaking had been a widespread peasant industry were definitely gone, as were the days when potting was the affair of small master craftsmen.[3] Due to favorable geological and geographical conditions (rich coal and clay beds as basic raw materials; ready availability of water power for the grinding of raw materials and washing of clay), the rapid expansion of the British pottery industry from the late eighteenth century onward centered around the famous six towns of North Staffordshire, which came to be known as the "Potteries" (Stoke-on-Trent, Hanley, Burslem, Tunstall, Fenton, Longton). In 1841 the average number of persons employed in the 130 manufactories, which were mostly run as family businesses, was 250 to 300. Although the majority of the workers were employed in small workshops, the branch was dominated by the large establishments of the Wedgwoods, Mintons, or Davenports, which often employed more than 1,000 workers. From 1835 to 1850 the total number of employees in the North Staffordshire pottery industry increased from 20,000 to 25,000. According to the 1851 Census on Earthenware Manufacture in Staffordshire, 9,000 of these employees were female and 16,000 were male; of the latter, 6,100 were between 5 and 15 years of age. William Evans, the famous trade-union leader, talked of 7,000 operative potters in the mid-1840s, obviously excluding all boys, unskilled male assistants, girls and women (most of the latter were unskilled), and all ancillary occupations that were included in the census. Displaced agricultural laborers from the neighboring countryside provided the main reserve of labor. By the beginning of the nineteenth century, the pottery trade had already come to dominate not only the communities of the six towns but also the whole area, in which even mining was regarded as a mere ancillary industry to potting.[4]

Relatively unaffected by the Industrial Revolution, the pottery industry until the 1860s was organized as manufactory production, which nevertheless had "long since fallen as completely under capitalist exploitation as the factories themselves."[5] Yet, unlike the factory, the manufactory, which had grown out of handicrafts, was not based on the widespread application of machinery but, still, on the handicraft skill of the workforce. Eighteenth-century trade customs and work traditions therefore still played a role in the pottery industry well into the nineteenth century, indicating a certain influence of the skilled potters on work organization and work processes. However, under conditions of modern British pottery production, the most advanced of the time, these traditions became increasingly perverted or threatened. The custom of some categories of pottery craftsmen (e.g., throwers, flat pressers) to engage and pay their own "helpers" (usually women or children often related to them) had, by the 1840s, under the pressure to earn a decent family wage, turned into sometimes brutal child exploitation; and the irregularity of working hours (absenteeism on Mondays and Tuesdays and excessively long hours on weekends to catch up again),[6] so much cherished by many potters as an expression of a maintenance of control over their own working lives and as independence from modern industrial work control came increasingly under attack from the attempt of the masters—especially the big ones, such as Wedgwood—to discipline their workforce with authoritarian work rules and regulations, and with the heavy fines and penalties associated with this discipline.[7]

Modern manufactory production was characterized by a minute division of labor. The pottery-worker in a manufactory was no longer the widely skilled independent journeyman who had command of every process of the trade,[8] but a skilled detail worker who was specialized in one operation of the work process. Thus, in a pottery manufactory of the time, up to two dozen or more workers of different occupations (slip-makers, throwers, turners, hollowware pressers, flat-pressers, ovenmen, printers, painters, etc.) were employed in the various stages from the preparing of clay through the turning, throwing, and pressing to the glazing, firing, and decorating of the ware. This specialization went hand in hand with a hierarchical gradation of mostly skilled workers, and meant, above all, a general diminishing of the skills required of operative potters.[9] In order to be able to reduce the workers' wages, the employers tried to speed up this de-skilling process by various means: by an extensive employment of female labor; by a disproportionate employment of apprentices; and by an attempt to introduce machinery in the mid-1840s that would have affected above all hollowware and flat pressers.[10] Therefore, working in the Staffordshire manufactories of the time meant, for the great mass of skilled workers, that they "had little chance of becoming anything other than employed workmen."[11]

In times of economic crises the living standard of skilled pottery workers increasingly approached that of the other wage-earning classes. During the depression of 1837–42, and the no less severe depression of 1847–48, the pottery trade was almost constantly bad, hosts of potters were unemployed, and those who had work were thrown on short time. The crisis culminated in the winter of 1842: "Semi-starvation was the normal condition of thousands," as Charles Shaw remembered this period of his apprenticeship as a potter.[12] The same year brought the British working-class movement a defeat in a general strike for the People's Charter, in which something like 500,000 workers had participated. The strike had had its starting point among the North Staffordshire miners, and in August it reached its climax in the six towns in an outbreak in which the rank and file was predominantly pottery-workers. In early summer a second attempt of the Chartists after that of 1839 to push through, by means of mass petitioning, universal manhood suffrage, which would have given artisans, workers, and laborers a decisive influence on the exertion of state power, had failed. At the time, the Chartists had a strong and well-organized following among the Staffordshire potters. However, these struggles and defeats represented something of a watershed in the history of British and "Potteries" working-class radicalism, which declined thereafter and only recovered for a short time in 1848.[13]

In summary, one can say that the position of most working potters at the beginning of the 1840s was characterized by an increasing insecurity of employment, threats to their traditional skills and trade customs, and a severe loss of social status—that is, a drop from the former independent craftsman to the operative potter. Many potters no longer saw any chance of improving or even retaining their social position in Britain. As William Evans, leader of the United Branches of Operative Potters, and editor of its periodical, the *Potters' Examiner*, put it: the workers

> have no hope in *British* trade with its periodical stagnations and starvation-price for labour; they have no hope in *British* manufacturers, with their boundless lust of wealth, and their coreless, unfeeling hearts; they have no hope in *British* legislatures, with their inordinate love of power.[14]

Under circumstances such as these, many working men, like John Sutherland, preferred to migrate to North America expecting to realize there ideas of work and life that they were no longer able to realize in their native country. The hopes and expectations of prospective migrants were thus shaped by the workers' past experience in the "Potteries," which formed the background to a given image of America. Through migrating, as I will try to show, working potters wished to retain or achieve in America that independence in society they thought was denied them in Britain in the 1840s. This notion of independence was deeply embedded in the traditional artisan work experience and way of life. It was a very complex concept, and its various facets of meaning,[15] the most important of which were the independence, in workplace or economic terms, of journeymen potters, of master potters, and of potters-turned-farmers, as well as the notion of social and political independence, will be examined as decisive aspects of the potters' image of America.

Migration and the Trade Unions: The Press and Letters from Emigrants

In the 1840s mass migration from Britain to North America was already well underway, with figures rising from 2,600 at its lowest in 1840 to a peak of 55,000 in 1849. All in all in the years from 1840 to 1850 270,000 Britons (excluding the Irish) left for the United States. A novel feature in this migration movement was the high proportion of urban workers whose departures in periods of extreme economic crisis seemed to have nearly equaled the rural exodus. A heated and controversial discussion of pros and cons, which ran through all sections and classes of society, attended this migration: it was referred to in newspapers and pamphlets; discussed on lecture platforms and in philanthropic circles; debated in Parliament and by local authorities; argued about by industrial and land-owning interests; and opposed by some working-class organizations and approved by others.[16]

Before 1840 the "Potteries" were hardly afflicted by the emigration question, although in 1766 Josiah Wedgwood was already alarmed by the migration of a Staffordshire master potter to South Carolina, and in 1783 he sought to deter artisan potters from leaving England for America by warning them of the misery and poverty that might follow migration. His real concerns, of course, were the transfer of skill and know-how by migration and, as a result of this, the development of a pottery industry in America, which up to the 1850s was the greatest export market for Staffordshire pottery-ware. Wedgwood's fears were premature at the time, but came true in the 1840s when a first wave of working potters left for North America.[17]

The great majority of these working potters were labor migrants,[18] that is, migrants who intended to continue working in their craft after they had moved to North America. Their letters reveal that they usually sent for close relatives or tried to persuade friends and neighbors to follow them after the first few had settled in America, thus establishing their own informal migration network. Although we do not have any exact figures on how many working potters left Staffordshire in this way, it was obviously enough to alarm the pottery manufacturers. Some of these condemned migration in 1850 (as Wedgwood had done earlier) and accused potters' trade unions of having induced skilled potters to emigrate and having thereby transferred "our artisans in numbers to the enemy's camp," that is, to the developing American pottery industry. This was countered by one union that laid the blame for the process of labor migration on the employers, holding them responsible for unemployment and low wages, the real causes that had driven operative potters abroad. Anyway, the union boasted, insofar as working potters had emigrated with the aid of trade societies, they had gone to America to settle as farmers and abandon potting.[19]

Indeed, after the provisional defeat of the Chartists and the failure of the general strike, and in the aftermath of an appalling depression, which might return (as it did in 1847–48), as well as under the influence of widespread emigration already taking place in the early 1840s, potters' trade-union activity turned increasingly away from strike action, with emigration becoming the center of its policy. In 1844 the Potters' Emigration Society was established on the initiative of William Evans and the United Branches of Operative Potters as a means to relieve the local labor market of a surplus of working potters. The society pursued a double object: to create a demand for labor that would enable potters at home to get a fair day's wage for a fair day's work, and to enable migrant potters to leave for America and settle as farmers in Wisconsin. In spring 1847 the first fourteen families left the "Potteries" for Wisconsin to found a colony called Pottersville, a project that failed in 1850. Initially this rural settlement migration was seen by the union as a form of labor protest against the threatened introduction of machinery. But the project was also propagated as a deliberate alternative to British capitalist conditions and pushed as an opportunity to escape from modern industrial and urban society and to return to a traditional way of life.[20]

The fact that potting had been done on the land for centuries and that many pottery-workers had just migrated from the countryside into the "Potteries" may have been one reason for the strong interest on the part of one section of the potters in land settlement. Moreover, there was a general interest in land settlement among the working classes and labor organizations of the time, and the "Back-to-the-Land" call had a long tradition in Britain. This was not surprising at a time when Britain's transformation from a country dominated by agriculture to one dominated by industry was well underway, and neither was it surprising that ideas of agrarian reform played a prominent role in the writings of such influential and diverse political and social reformers as Thomas Paine, William Cobbett,

Robert Owen, or Thomas Spence.[21] At the end of the 1830s, Socialists launched home colonization schemes (whose activity centered on farming), and after the defeat of 1842 the Chartists concentrated on their own land scheme, both movements trying to resettle laborers and—above all—urban workers and artisans on British soil.[22] In addition, projects were called into being by the labor movement, which combined land settlement and emigration,[23] as did the Potters' Emigration Society.

From the very beginning the emigration policy of the United Branches of Operative Potters not only came under attack from other trade organizations and the Chartists, but also had to counter heavy criticism from sections of the potters themselves, all of whom preferred the struggle for shorter working hours and, above all, land settlement at home to emigration, which they denounced as transportation.[24] However, emigration dominated the politics of potters' trade unionism. After the Potters' Emigration Society had become a national society in 1848 and had opened up for the enrollment of members from other trades, and after the central union, the United Branches of Operative Potters, had disintegrated and collapsed, rival societies were established by some of the branch unions that were still functioning. The hollowware pressers' Mutual Assistance Society for the Removal of Surplus Labour and the respective Flat Pressers' and Turners' Surplus Labour Society, like the Potters' Emigration Society, organized the migration of working potters to America as a means of improving the conditions of skilled potters: at home, by creating a scarcity of workers on the labor market, and abroad, by giving them the opportunity to settle on the land. But all these societies restricted their operations to paying the expenses of the passage. No buying of land was intended, and each man was supposed to go out on his own and take his own land. In opposition to these societies a Miscellaneous Society of all branches advocated labor migration to the United States and disapproved of rural settlement migration.[25]

It was not only the potters' trade unions that directly organized migration; this movement was also encouraged by the *Potters' Examiner,* which thus played a vital role in the formation of an image of the United States among prospective migrants. Giving full support to land migration, this periodical published a great number of completely positive articles on the United States, describing in glowing terms the vastness, variety, and Eden-like beauty of nature, the fertility of the soil, and the natural resources, especially of Illinois and

Wisconsin,[26] thereby creating a rather mythical image of North America. By comparison, the Socialist press and the Chartist press were more critical. They closely followed the development of the social conditions of the laboring classes in the United States and used unemployment and trade struggles in the transatlantic republic to qualify this widespread, far-too-euphoric picture of America. But because this press dealt neither with the specific problems faced by British operative potters nor with the rise of an American pottery industry, its potential influence remained limited to a general image of America among prospective pottery migrants.[27]

Information about conditions in America provided by letters of previous migrants was of special importance and played the decisive role in shaping prospective migrants' expectations. For them, the great number of letters circulating among the neighborhoods of the pottery-workers' communities represented the most reliable and up-to-date internal sources of information suited, more than any other media, to their specific needs and interests. Moreover, a considerable number of these letters by labor as well as land migrants were usually published in full text, as it seems, by the *Potters' Examiner* and thus made available to a greater public. The reasons given by the trade periodical for the publication of emigrants' letters were a daily increasing "spirit of Emigration" in the district, which had induced the editor "to give insertion to a series of letters, sent by different individuals who have emigrated from this neighbourhood, and on whose veracity our readers may depend, for the better guidance of those who take the important step of leaving their fatherland." The editor emphasized that these letters had not been written for a public paper, but were "the domestic epistles of honest working men." However, not all of them were actually from migrant workers who had left the "Potteries."[28] These (printed) letters not only contain information that shaped the prospective migrant's image of America but are at the same time a source of an image of America themselves insofar as these letters from newly immigrated potters reveal a great deal about their ideas and preconceptions of America formed at home before they left for the New World.

But were these printed letters in any way representative? Or were those published not simply selected by Evans in order to further the migration movement? And was it not likely therefore that the editor was none too interested in publishing letters containing bad accounts of immigrant life? Such considerations certainly seem justified. However, it is important to note that, due to close informal relations within the community, the pottery-workers seem to have been able to exercise a considerable degree of control over the process of publishing emigrants' letters. For example, when the rumor spread in 1844 that the *Potters' Examiner* had declined to publish a letter from John Sutherland because it was said to contain disparaging accounts of North America, Sutherland's brother was forced openly to refute this libel. On the other hand, when in 1849–50 the trade periodical did try to suppress critical letters deploring the miserable conditions of some of the settlers in the Pottersville colony, relatives and friends at home used the pages of the local press and of other radical papers to have these emigrants' letters published, so that the *Potters' Examiner* was forced to do likewise.[29] What should be noted is that there were actually many possibilities for the publication of critical letters in various periodicals that were either hostile to emigration in general, or to emigration to America, or just to the potters' union's system of organized emigration.

The Independent Journeyman Potter in America

In the potters' image of America, various conceptions of independence played a dominant role. In its first essential aspect, independence meant the craftsman's opportunity to control the intensity and pace of work. This presupposed that the artisan's handicraft skill was sought for and required by the employer, because "for a working man to be independent, it is requisite, that the demand for his labour should be *certain*," as the *Potters' Examiner* stated.[30] In contrast to the manufactories of Staffordshire, where the potters' skills were increasingly threatened and partially devalued by a minute division of labor, the extensive employment of women and apprentices, and the attempted application of machinery, emigrants' letters pictured America as a country where the skilled potter was in a very powerful position, since the American pottery industry was still in its infancy. It lacked those basic requirements of any manufactory production that was not yet dependent on the use of large-scale machinery, that is, the skill and know-how that Staffordshire potters like Thomas Mountford disposed of.

In America Mountford had commenced work as a presser, but very soon it turned out that he mastered all the steps essential for potmaking. "I am pressing, glazing and firing now, and I suppose I shall have to go to throwing, for throwers are scarce." In circumstances such as these, the working potters, indeed, controlled the intensity and pace of work to such a degree that work was never rushed. In another letter it was reported that Thomas Biddulph "is very comfortably fixed; he can get twenty-five shillings a week without hurting himself. He can get more than that if he likes, there is no stint." This reminds one of eighteenth-century work habits where workmen tended to decrease their weekly amount of work when high wages meant that the usual living standard could be maintained by fewer hours' labor. Biddulph obviously cherished the absence of any modern (manu)factory routine and control for "a waggon and horses should not draw him back" to Britain, as he remarked; Mountford stressed that it was not the high earnings but, above all, the fact that you had no "tyrannical masters tyrannising you to death" (as in Staffordshire) that made work conditions in North America so attractive.[31]

An integral part of this conception of independence was the artisan's assertion that he ought to earn a real family wage so that he and his family would not be dependent on poor relief either in hard times or in old age. While in Staffordshire the low-paid potters "were placed on the coldhearted charity of parochial funds" in times of crisis, as the *Potters' Examiner* maintained,[32] letters from those potters who had migrated to the New World conveyed the impression that this could not happen to a potter and his family in America. Generally, the emigrants' letters pictured the United States as a country of high wages and a high living standard, although economic conditions there were not free from problems either. "Times are rather dull excepting in Potting," Bernard Howson wrote in 1844 from East Liverpool, Ohio, the center of the growing North American pottery industry. But even at that time these favorable conditions could already include the possibility of an overstocked labor market that would give the master "an opportunity of reducing wages," as George Garner observed. This, however, did not seem to be very likely, given the infant stage of development of the industry and the heavy demand for skilled labor, as was usually stressed in the emigrants' letters. Another problem might have been that of seasonal unemployment due to severe weather. But even in this case, too, heavy demand for skilled labor seemed to guarantee a better life in America than in Staffordshire. "I have never worked much in the winter since I came here," wrote Biddulph, but, nevertheless, he could cheerfully state: "I am better clothed and fed than I ever was in England."[33]

Potter migrants usually reported that in North America they could get higher wages than in the "Potteries." "I can as easily earn £2 here as I could £1 in England," wrote George Arblaster. The living standard in America seemed to be much higher anyway, as prices for foodstuffs were lower than in Britain. Compared with conditions in the New World, Staffordshire potters were worse off than negro slaves, as many potters who had migrated to America maintained; Thomas Gotham stated:

> There are hundreds of slaves in America better off than the poor potters [in Britain], the slaves have plenty to eat and drink. We have provisions very cheap—good beef at one penny a pound; we bought a QUARTER OF A COW *at three farthings a pound.* Potatoes at ten pence a bushel; good port at three farthings a pound; other provisions are proportionally low. We can get a good milking cow for one pound fifteen shillings.

On his way to East Liverpool John Henshall stopped at a little pottery in Philadelphia. The master as well as the four to five working potters had all immigrated from Staffordshire. Henshall added another facet to Gotham's image of America as a land where living conditions were excellent compared with those in Britain. "The lower orders are universally well dressed. Girls go to their work as fine as Squire's daughters, with green veils on their bonnets; and common day labourers can afford two or three clean shirts per week."[34]

Surely it was letters like these and the ones quoted below, more than any other information, that shaped the British potters' image of America. In a way, the favorable position of immigrated Staffordshire potters in the United States was summed up in two letters from the Poole brothers. These letters bear testimony to the pride of independent journeymen who had realized that their skills were needed to get an infant local industry going and who were determined to seize the opportunities that resulted from this situation. John Poole had met

> an American, who wanted a Turner. He lives about eighty miles from St. Louis. I engaged to go with him to see what could be done. When I got there I found a poorly constructed lathe, and throwing wheel, and everything in a rough state for Potting. He was a coarse ware manufacturer. Well, we [John and his brother] engaged to begin to make pots, he finding fixtures and everything for our use. He is also finding Board and Lodging till we have ware ready for the market; we are then to take half of the profits. We have built a slip Kiln, and a small Oven; and we have put the lathe and wheel in repair. We have fired a biscuit Oven, and very

well it looks. The Oven will hold one hundred dollars worth, or twenty pounds in your money. At the least calculation we shall make a Oven a week; but it is very likely that we shall make three a fortnight. . . . Ours is the only white ware Pottery in the State of Missouri. We get three shillings for a fours jug; two shillings for six cups and six saucers, and for other things accordingly. This is the place for Potting; if a Potter has a chance of making his fortune it is now.

And brother Elisha continued, revealing that the art of potting was indeed a mystery to the nonskilled and the basis for potential success to those who mastered it. "The man [American manufacturer] neither knows how to make a good glaze, nor does he know anything about the body. We do not intend to inform him, for we have a notion of commencing ourselves."[35]

From Journeyman to Master Potter

In a second essential and original meaning of the word, independence meant, of course, the rise from journeyman to master, from employed workman to the independent producer who owned the materials on which he worked, who marketed the produce of his own labor, and who himself employed other workmen.[36] While in Staffordshire in the 1840s, as a rule, the mass of the pottery-workers had no opportunity to achieve this kind of independence, America seemed to be the country where precisely this would be possible.

What the Poole brothers were still striving for, Samuel Walker had already succeeded in accomplishing: in 1844, he had built his own little pot works in Utica. "I have a potting room, kiln, and saggar-house, (kiln holds 7 bungs saggars,) wood-shed, (we burn wood here,) and a little house, which I live in, like Robinson Crusoe's." Walker, like others, had taken the chance that migration to America seemed to offer. The skilled craftsman potter had become an independent producer who appropriated the fruits of his own labor; who had no "tyrannical" master manufacturer above him; who controlled the whole work-cycle and decided what was to be produced. "My ware sells well, and at good prices, and, I think, I can do much better this way than doing journeyman's work. I am making Tea-Pots, Sugars, Milks, Pitchers, Flower-Pots, Bowls, Cups, Saucers, and some Toys." Letters like Walker's not only conveyed the image of an America where the self-confident and enterprising could get on. They also emphasized that basic qualifications, versatile occupational know-how (the art of potting), and diverse skills were the preconditions for the potential success of the "self-made man." "You will see what a perplexing job I have had," Walker wrote to the Staffordshire potter John Howson, who was to follow him to the United States in the summer of 1844,

> having every thing to do myself. I've been bricklayer, and car-penter, and smith; I've put up my shop, and built my kiln; been modeller and mould-maker, saggar-maker, brown-dipper, plain slip maker and presser; and have gone up and down the country for miles, seeking clay, &c. &c.

Walker was more than satisfied with the results of his efforts. The United States seemed to be the country where the skilled potter could fully develop his abilities and where he could produce a ware that was a match even for the products of a Wedgwood. Moreover, his letters made clear where the specific attraction for British potters to migrate to America lay, namely, in the absence of competition from large manufactories such as Wedgwood's or Minton's. "There is a comfortable business to be done here, preferable to anything you can do in England, with a small capital, against so powerful a competi-tion as there is in the British market."

Although conditions were portrayed favorably, problems were not at all withheld. Thus, lack of skilled labor and small capital impeded Walker (for the time being) from enlarging his one-man business.[37] Enoch Bullock deplored a frequent lack of materials, which even led him to take possible failure into consideration. "It is true I have often regretted commencing in business on account of the disappointments and uneasiness attending it; especially when you cannot obtain the materials you want for improvement." However, the social distinction between journeyman and master potter was obviously not yet felt as decisive. "I think [we] shall succeed," Bullock thought, "if not, I can earn as journeyman 7½ dollars per week, and not labour hard for it."[38] Other Staffordshire pottery-workers had become master potters in the United States, employing about half a dozen workmen and more. Their letters drew a picture of simple pottery production where any highly specialized mass production based on detailed division of labor, as in Staffordshire, was absent, and where master potter and journeymen still worked side by side in simple and transparent work processes. But their letters also sug-gested that there was such a heavy demand for pottery ware that success was beyond doubt and economic expansion only a matter of time:

> The first time we drew our kiln, I wish you had been here to have seen the sight. It was such a one that I never expected to see. There were potsellers, with their waggons, waiting for the ware, as it came out of the kiln. All the ware was drawn, packed and sold before dinner![39]

George Scott, a former pottery-worker, became one of these independent peddlers of pottery-ware. In a letter to the president of his trade union in Staffordshire, he confirmed the image of America as a country where "earthenware sells very high" and where one with a hundred pounds' worth of ware could make "an independent fortune, within four or five years' time."[40]

While some skilled potters dreamed of exploiting all opportunities of becoming a successful master potter that the expanding U.S. pottery industry provided, others dreamed of retaining a traditional way of life and work, as had been characteristic in Britain until 1750. As has been mentioned, that was a time when potting and farming had been one economic unit. "I know you would be the happiest man alive if you were here and had a piece of land and a small pot-shop upon it," Mountford wrote to his father. In 1844 an inquiry by a correspondent was answered in the *Potters' Examiner* by recommending migrants to go West and not to "the overcrowded cities of the Eastern States." Potters, however, "might migrate to almost any town, county or state of the American Union, without the least fear of bad results." The trade-union periodical drew a very rosy picture of work opportunities in the New World, which included the double perspective of the rise from the artisan potter to the independent producer referred to above. Whereas the letters hinted at problems (lack of or little capital, materials and skilled labor) the *Potters' Examiner* drew a euphoric picture of the American Union where any potter with skill and energy would be able to commence manufacturing for himself on the smallest amount of capital and on the smallest possible scale; it asserted that there would be a ready market as well as favorable deposits of raw materials and good conditions for transport, i.e., every possibility for water and land carriage. Furthermore, the *Potters' Examiner* stressed that "land too is cheap. A small farm might be united to a small works, and prospects opened for competency in after life." Various emigrants' letters replying to inquiries from people intending to migrate suggest that the latter had often not yet decided whether to migrate to America in order to go potting or to go farming.[41]

Back to the Land: The Potter Turns Farmer

America was not only the country where a combination of potting and farming seemed to be possible. From the point of view of many British workers, artisans, and laborers, it was above all the country where one had the opportunity of becoming a farmer, since land was cheap and one did not have to pay rent to useless landlords who had monopolized the soil, as in Britain. Farming in America was therefore praised by the *Potters' Examiner,* as well as in many emigrants' letters, as *the* opportunity to rise in the social scale from dependent operative potter to independent farmer.

Contrary to other working potters from Staffordshire, Thomas Filcher had no confidence in manufactory conditions in the United States. Obviously still under the impression of the bad experiences he had gone through in his native country, he felt himself confirmed in his rejection of industrial society by the monetary and commercial crisis prevailing in America in the early 1840s. In addition, he saw the threat of local labor markets perhaps being overstocked due to heavy immigration. From this he drew the following conclusion: *"There is, therefore, no certainty in anything else, but FARMING."* Unlike Samuel Walker, who had maintained that laboring on the soil would be very hard for a potter as he was not used to it, Filcher believed a change from working potter to farmer to be quite unproblematic. In the image he drew of America, a farmer could do without modern currency conditions completely and still lead a comfortable life:

> Do not be discouraged at the change of business; almost any body can farm in this country; and when you have gotten 20 acres of land of your own, fenced in and cultivated, you will be as independent as any of the great ones in England. It will not occupy half of your time; and it will produce for you all you need.[42]

Elijah Baddley conveyed an image of America as the "land of plenty" for all who lived on the land and were willing to work. Under the conditions he depicted reaping the fruits of one's labor seemed to be hardly any more difficult than reaping the bounties of nature that seemed to be available in abundance for everyone. "Grapes, plums, parsimony [*sic*] and other fruit grow in the woods, wild; and I can load a waggon an hour, just with grapes. There is plenty of apples,

peaches, pears &c. I raise plenty of hogs, cows and everything else."
For Baddley, who had migrated from Hanley to Tennessee, there was
only one message he could give his relatives in Staffordshire: "You
may tell my friends, that this is a country for poor men." Confidence
in a happy future but also in a kind of freedom and independence, a
self-determination of the rhythm of work and working hours that was
unknown to craftsmen and even to master potters, even in the United
States, seemed to be typical of the peasant's life in America. Thus
Thomas Goodwin wrote from his eighty-acre farm in Illinois:

> I am going on as well as I could wish, for I go where I please, and
> come when I please, and none say it is wrong. I have no masters
> here to come stamping and grumbling at me and threatening to
> turn me out of my place, if I miss a day! No, I can go for a week,
> and nothing said. But that is not all—I can go out with my gun,
> and shoot what I like, and no one says where are you going? No
> game laws here!—A man is at liberty to do as he pleases. . . . I am
> as independent, here, as some of the high ones in England;—I can
> get a living without labouring every day, and I am not afraid of
> going to the workhouse.[43]

How strongly this contrasted with the state of dependence the potters
were subjected to in the Staffordshire manufactories! But also: Was
this not, perhaps, a reflection of the hopes and expectations of many
prospective migrants?

It was not only Goodwin but other letter writers, too, who
cherished the free access to nature[44] and the absence of game laws in
America. For prospective migrants from Staffordshire, where poaching seemed to be the order of the day,[45] this was of special importance. Poaching was more than just trying to supplement the family
income in times of crisis, it was a semi-illegal defiance of the existing
order of things and an insistence on traditional popular rights. For
Staffordshire potters the absence of game laws in America, then, no
doubt meant more than the unlimited access to nature's bounty; it
was a symbol for America as a land of liberty.

In their propaganda the trade union and the Potters' Emigration Society stressed another, essential advantage of settling on the
land in Wisconsin. It was praised as an opportunity to escape from
working conditions in pottery manufacture that were among the
unhealthiest in Britain, as even official government reports had revealed. The *Potters' Examiner* pictured the working and living conditions on American soil as free from the many insidious and

malignant diseases so prevalent among potters due to the unhealthy workshop conditions in smoky Staffordshire. In romantic terms the change brought about by land migration was put as follows:

> O what a change would it be! to rush from the heated and poisonous workshops! from its Asthmas, Consumptions, Poisons, and Deaths!—to the fair fields of nature; to breathe for once, the pure breath of heaven; to gaze on the broad expanse of earth and sky; to feel that health and liberty is yours.[46]

Social and Political Independence in America

On a different level from economic expectations, another aspect of independence played a decisive role in the prospective migrants' image of the New World. It was the image of America as a country where more equal social relationships prevailed than in the "Potteries." In the United States it seemed possible to realize what could be called social independence.

For labor as well as rural settlement migrants, social relationships in America differed greatly and, evidently, in a positive way from those in the Old World. Whereas Shaw deplored social relations in North Staffordshire, which were characterized by a widespread deferential attitude of working potters toward their masters,[47] emigrant potters drew pictures of the United States in which masters and men were on the same footing and respected each other. "You see no distinctions of persons in this country that you do in England—there are no pulling off hats as they do in the old country," John Thomas maintained, and George Garner graphically pointed out the different experience of working potters in Staffordshire and North America:

> There is none of that lordlyship, as in England. Some of you are obliged to worship your masters, when meeting them on the road; I mean by almost ploughing the road up, with bowing and scraping to them; and perhaps just at the entrance of a place of worship. There is no such thing here. I have seen men, worth double the amount of those you idolize, working by the side of their men, during the week, and, on a Sunday, sitting by their side in a place of worship. The fine coat is thought of no more than the rough one.[48]

This image of America as a society where the working man was not socially dependent on what were called his "superiors" in the Old World can be found in many emigrants' letters. For Philip Pointon, one of the reasons for this independent attitude of working men lay in the better educational system in the United States, where children "don't go to school to learn only obedience to pastors and masters." As Pointon remarked, under relations where it did not seem to be common for workers and artisans to enter their employer's presence as socially inferior beings, they dared to openly express their convictions even if conscious that they differed from their masters': "You can speak your mind without fear of your employer discharging you."[49]

But what about the position of women in American society? The *Potters' Examiner* as well as most of the (usually male) letter writers tacitly took it for granted that in America, too, all the work associated with child-rearing and the home fell to the woman's lot, a self-evident fact that was therefore not worth mentioning. But some migrants depicted a social position of women in North America that was very different from the women's position in the Staffordshire "Potteries" and that should have particularly impressed female prospective migrants. Whereas some migrants intimated that women in America also worked in productive spheres, others, like Garner, pictured the life of women as one of complete freedom and independence, because "the women, here, never work at all; they consider it too mean; but walk up and down with a veil before their face; and are considered almost angels!" For John Howson, who, like Garner, was obviously formed by the patriarchal conditions in Staffordshire, social relations between men and women seemed to have been completely reversed. In America the men seemed to be dependent on the women. "This is the place for women! They make slaves of the men, who have to do marketing, fetch all water,—in fact the men have to do all that the women ask them to do." Altogether, women in America seemed much more respected and better protected legally than in the "Potteries." "There is no beating of women here! The man who would do so, would be sent to prison, if his wife made the least complaint."[50]

Arguing in favor of migration to America, the *Potters' Examiner* not only emphasized the opportunity of acquiring land very cheaply. The transatlantic republic was also depicted as a political model society, as a country where the "most liberal institutions of present man" existed, institutions that recognized the "natural equality and political independence" of all men.[51] This political independence, i.e., the possibility of participating in the political process free of all suffrage restrictions, was a decisive aspect of the expectations of prospective labor and rural settlement migrants from Staffordshire, where Chartism had played quite an important role in the early 1840s.

Thus it is not surprising that Thomas Filcher, who himself had presumably been involved in Staffordshire Chartism, was full of praise for American political institutions. According to his experience, every man "can breathe the pure and wholesome atmosphere of REPUBLICANISM. Since I have been here, I have had the pleasure of voting at a General, August Election, and I went in for *Pure Democracy*. . . . In fact this is a Democratic State." Only occasionally was the significance of democratic conditions generally called into question, and elections were criticized as a "regular office-seeking concern."[52] Potter migrants usually shared Filcher's sentiments. For Baddley, voting rights, the opportunity of unrestricted political discussions, and the fact that the political representatives of the people stemmed from the common people themselves were obviously very valuable features of the American political system as contrasted with the British:

> I know by experience, now, what is best, liberty or slavery. I vote for president!—did you vote for king?—I vote for members of congress, for legislators and all other officers! . . . I have seen the labouring man, disputing with the president on the politics of our country. Our legislators are common farmers, labourers, shoemakers, and any other trade.

Whereas in Staffordshire the local pottery manufacturers exercised political control over the whole community at various levels of authority—from member of parliament to chief constable and magistrate—migrant potters, like Garner, drew a picture of America where employers had no more political influence than working men:

> There is no canvasing of votes, through the medium of some influential manufacturers. No such thing! This would not be appreciated by them [i.e., by Americans]; they would tell you, that liberty, once fought for by Washington, is cherished by them, and cannot be violated.[53]

For prospective migrants, democratic political conditions in America were highly interesting in another respect, too. The transatlantic republic, unlike Britain, had no "tyrannical" bureaucratic and swollen state apparatus that was closely combined with a state church, both of which exploited the working population in England by means of an unjust system of taxation and other rates. This was just one reason why William Evans recommended that the "over-taxed operatives" of Britain migrate to America.[54] This consideration was equally important to those who aspired to become small pro-ducers, either in potting or in farming, and Samuel Walker was quite happy to be able to state: "I have not yet been called on for taxes, poor-rates, or any charges of any description whatever! This is a gloriously free country!" Thus political and economic expectations intertwined in a vision of American society where the existence of a representative, democratic political system seemed to guarantee its citizens the appropriation of the fruits of their own labor. "We pay no taxes, or tithe, but what we get is our own," as Baddley affirmed.[55]

American political institutions naturally met with the Char-tists' great approval, and, indeed, Chartism had done a good deal to promote among the working class the image of America as a land of political liberty, an image that had been held up by radical reformers in Britain ever since the late eighteenth century. Walker's assumption that America was the "home for all poor, distressed, or aristocrat-ridden-down of Europe"[56] was widespread among the British and European lower classes of the time. However, in contrast to the very positive image of America in the *Potters' Examiner* and the emigrants' letters, the Chartists pointed out various problems that the laboring classes in the United States had to cope with (unemployment due to mass immigration; wage reductions, etc.), problems that were not mentioned in the trade periodical's depiction of conditions in North America. An even more critical picture was outlined by the socialist press, which characterized America as a land where private property and competition ruled and where the condition of the working popu-lation, despite democratic political institutions, drew increasingly nearer to the miserable condition of the laboring classes in the Old World. Although in the mid-1840s the Chartists sometimes made a similar judgment, they continued nevertheless to propagate a positive image of America insofar as they continually emphasized how important republican institutions, like those in the United States, would be in establishing political and social conditions that would meet the needs and interests of artisans and workers.[57] So Evans's opinion, expressed at a lecture in support of the aims of the Potters' Emigration Society, that in the United States "the charter was in operation"[58] was certainly shared and cherished by many British artisans and working men who wished to migrate to America.

Conclusion

The potters' image of America was clearly influenced by the dream of America as a "land of liberty and plenty," a dream so widespread among the European common people of the time. But this dream, which concentrated, in the case of the potters, on various aspects of the idea of independence, blended with thoroughly realistic expectations. All men in the Great Western Republic had certainly neither equal political opportunities independent from their economic status, nor were all men and women on one footing (developing capitalist society in the United States knew class antagonisms and gender distinctions, too); and, certainly, not all the migrants could achieve independence and a comfortable life if they were merely industrious and worked hard. Contrasted with the Old World, however, more developed bourgeois-democratic conditions, political rights, and freedoms prevailed in the United States; and compared with the Old World, the United States was a more egalitarian society even though opportunities for upward social mobility were not that much greater than in Europe.

The rural settlement migrants seem to have gone to America with higher expectations than the labor migrants. The idea of America as a "land of plenty" was much more developed in the former group than in the latter. This image was supported by emigrants' letters and, above all, by the overtly positive and uncritical articles in the *Potters' Examiner*. As a result, the settlers were faced with great problems of acculturation: the change in the whole way of work and life that the working potter from the densely populated urban "Potteries" experienced in becoming an independent farmer in the backwoods of the West involved many difficulties. These were among the main causes that accounted for the ultimate failure of the Pottersville colony in 1850. However, when in 1849 a section of the settlers in Pottersville criticized the hardships and miserable conditions under which they had to live, this criticism from the ranks of the migrants was directed, significantly enough, against the emigration society, and not against migration to and land settlement in America generally. On the contrary, America was characterized by the migrants, then as ever, as a fine country in which one could succeed.[59] Indeed, only a few settlers returned to Britain; others remained where they were or migrated to the surrounding districts, where they tried farming independent from the emigration society. Up to the turn of the year 1849–50, around 300 to 350 working men and their families left for Wisconsin with the Potters' Emigration Society, among them thirty-five members of the hollowware pressers' union, one of the trade societies that numbered among the main supporters of the emigration scheme.[60] In addition, the Turners' Surplus Labour Society claimed, in 1850, to have helped forty turners move to America, but as their emigration scheme did not include the buying of land, we do not know how many of them actually tried to settle as farmers.[61] As Grant Foreman mentioned, according to an 1860 census around eighty of those migrants who came to North America with the Potters' Emigration Society, among them five former hollowware pressers, became heads of prosperous independent farming families in the area around the former Pottersville colony.[62] Yet, again, other settlers seemed to have returned to their former trade and became potters in America, as the Chartist Ernest Jones affirmed in 1851.[63] Whether there were migrants who had worked as potters in the United States and afterward abandoned that for farming we do not know.

The majority of those who had left England for America were labor migrants. In fact, in the emerging centers of the American pottery industry, working men from North Staffordshire constituted the great bulk of the labor force. Thus, for example, in 1850, in East Liverpool, Ohio, 74 percent of the potters (that is, 79 out of 107) were English-born, while in Trenton, New Jersey, in 1860, 40 percent of the pottery workers (that is, 39 out of 98) had been born in Britain. In the potteries of Bennington, Vermont, too, to a "large measure the working force was recruited from the Staffordshire potteries."[64] Thanks to a reliable informal network based on kinship relations and close contact through letters, the expectations of labor migrants seem to have been more realistic than those of the rural settlement migrants. Because the labor migration of skilled potters involved only geographical but not occupational change, these migrants had to cope with fewer difficulties of acculturation than did the land migrants. Such skilled workers were also real pioneers, because it was they who transplanted the pottery industry from Staffordshire to North America.

This migration of skilled working men coincided with the infant stage of the development of the North American pottery industry, a stage of development that at the same time was the result as well as the trigger for this migration. That the American pottery industry was still in its infancy also meant that it was still in a very experimental and mobile stage: one could fail to become an independent producer but then start anew. Conditions were still very different indeed from those in Staffordshire, where rigid occupational and class distinctions prevailed. The antagonism between journeyman and master potter was not nearly as developed in America as in Britain. Even though, in the end, only some could rise to the position of independent master potter and prosperous manufacturer, for the mass of the potter migrants the great demand for skilled labor meant a higher standard of living and better work conditions than at home.[65] For the working potters, as has been shown, this also meant independence.

The significance of migration as a means of trade-union policy at home is very difficult to evaluate. The emigration policy as a form of collective pressure certainly played a role in preventing the threatened introduction of labor-saving and skill-replacing machinery. But it should not be overlooked that the machinery of the time still had its faults, and, therefore, its application might not have been profitable for the manufacturers, anyway.[66] It is also debatable to what extent wages and conditions of employment for skilled Staffordshire potters had been positively influenced by migration, as Evans repeatedly asserted. In 1850 the Turners' Surplus Labour Society even claimed that the scarcity of workers in its branch at the time was due to the society's policy:

> We have entirely cleared our trade of its surplus hands; we have obtained large advances on the price of labour, we feel now, that we can command that just and equitable price for our daily toil, which every principle of justice and humanity decrees should be our due.[67]

But the question is whether these improved conditions for turners were not, above all, the result of a general improvement of the pottery trade in 1850. In this case, the emigration policy would have had a mere supporting function. But, in any case, the trade unions' mere threat of the removal of surplus labor to America seemed to have been a means to "make the Manufacturer respect the rights and privileges of his workmen."[68]

After 1850 the idea of land migration no longer seems to have played an important role among Staffordshire potters, whereas the idea of labor migration to America did. Working potters still expected to earn higher wages in North America, and it was this alone that seemed to matter at that time. In 1866, for example, Staffordshire potters again established a society for "the removal of surplus labour by emigration."[69] This scheme arose during a second wave of migration, which had begun after the end of the Civil War and came to an end with the beginning of the depression in 1873. However, potters continued to migrate to America, their numbers growing or slackening in relation to the state of the trade both in the United States and in Britain. But the application of machinery and the increasing employment of less skilled American-born workers in an expanding industry resulted in a significant decline of the skilled Staffordshire potters' share of the total labor force in the 1880s.[70]

Notes

I am very grateful to Robert Fyson for his helpful comments on an earlier draft of this essay and to William C. Gates for providing me with information about the doings of some Staffordshire potters in East Liverpool, Ohio.

1. Letter from John Sutherland, 25 Mar 1845, Gorstville, near Madison, Dane County, Wisconsin, in *Potters' Examiner and Workman's Advocate* (hereafter quoted as *PE*), 6 Sept 1845; the spelling of all quotations from letters was retained, as were all italics used by the newspapers and other originals.

2. For this view, see Harold Owen, *The Staffordshire Potter* (1901; rpt. Bath: Kingsmead Reprints, 1970), 75.

3. See John Thomas, *The Rise of the Staffordshire Potteries* (Bath: Adams and Dart, 1971), 3–9.

4. See Frank Burchill and Richard Ross, *A History of the Potters' Union* (Hanley, Stoke-on-Trent: Ceramic and Allied Trades Union, 1977), 23–25, 30, 6; *PE*, 3 Feb 1844; 17 Aug 1844.

5. Karl Marx, *Capital*, vol. 1 (London: Lawrence and Wishart, 1977), 282; for a penetrating analysis of manufactory as against factory production see ibid., 318–47.

6. See Charles Shaw, *When I Was a Child* (1903; rpt. Seaford, Sussex: Caliban Books, 1977), 12–16, 47–49, 54.

7. See Burchill and Ross, *The Potters' Union*, 42–43; Neil McKendrick, "Josiah Wedgwood and Factory Discipline," *Historical Journal* 4 (1961): 30–55; for the persistence of pre-industrial labor patterns before the coming of large-scale machinery production, see E. P. Thompson, "Time, Work-Discipline, and Industrial Capitalism," *Past and Present* 38 (1967): 56–97.

8. See William Henry Warburton, *The History of Trade Union Organisation in the North Staffordshire Potteries* (London, 1931), 24.

9. See ibid,; McKendrick, "Josiah Wedgwood," 33; Burchill and Ross, *The Potters' Union*, 47; for a detailed description of work processes see Burchill and Ross, *The Potters' Union*, 30–32.

10. See ibid., 29; Andrew Lamb, "The Press and Labour's Response to Pottery-Making Machinery in the North Staffordshire Pottery Industry," *Journal of Ceramic History*, no. 9 (1977): 1–6.

11. Warburton, *History of Trade Union Organisation*, 27. However, as has been mentioned, small-scale production prevailed in the "Potteries." There is also evidence that the majority of the manufacturers had been former working men (see A. Moyes, "Victorian Industrial Structure and Inter-Industry Relationships in the Potteries: A Framework and Exploratory Analysis," *North Staffordshire Journal of Field Studies* 19 [1979]: 42–46). This suggests that it was possible for workmen, if only a few, to set up for themselves. But in consideration of the crisis-ridden early and later years of the 1840s and the generally keen competition in the market, for many ambitious working potters it must have seemed more promising to try their luck in the United States.

12. Shaw, *When I Was a Child*, 94; see also Warburton, *History of Trade Union Organisation*, 104; Owen, *Staffordshire Potter*, 98–99.

13. See Robert Fyson, "The Crisis of 1842: Chartism, the Colliers' Strike and the Outbreak in the Potteries," in *The Chartist Experience: Studies in Working-Class Radicalism and Culture, 1830–1860*, ed. James Epstein and Dorothy Thompson (London and Basingstoke: Macmillan Press, 1982), 194–220; for a recent account of Chartism, see Dorothy Thompson, *The Chartists* (London: Temple Smith, 1984).

14. *PE*, 15 June 1844; the union was a federation of branch societies; for a characterization of its policy see Warburton, *History of Trade Union Organisation*, 111–14; the periodical appeared as the organ of the United Branches of Operative Potters from 1843 to 1848 under the title *Potters' Examiner and Workman's Advocate*, from 1849 to 1850 as the organ of the Potters' Emigration Society under the title *Potters' Examiner and Emigrants' Advocate;* its circulation was 2,000 copies.

15. For the notion of independence, see especially John Rule, "Artisan Attitudes: A Comparative Survey of Skilled Labour and Proletarianization before 1848," *Society for the Study of Labour History: Bulletin*, no. 50 (1985): 25–26; I. J. Prothero, *Artisans and Politics in Early Nineteenth Century London* (Folkstone: Dawson, 1979), 26–27; see also Charlotte Erickson, "Agrarian Myths of English Immigrants," in *In the Trek of the Immigrants*, ed. O. Fritiof Ander (Rock Island, Ill.: Augustana College Library, 1964), 75–78.

16. See U.S. Department of Commerce, *Historical Statistics of the United States: Colonial Times to 1970, Part 1* (Washington, D.C.: Government Printing Office, 1975), 106; W. S. Shepperson, *British Emigration to North America: Projects and Opinions in the Early Victorian Period* (Oxford: Basil Blackwell, 1957), 81, 7; for recent studies of early nineteenth-century migration to North America see Charlotte Erickson, "Emigration from the British

Isles to the U.S.A. in 1831," *Population Studies* 35 (1981): 175–97, and William E. Van Vugt, "Prosperity and Industrial Emigration from Britain during the Early 1850s," *Journal of Social History* 22 (1988): 339–54.

17. See Edwin Atlee Barber, *Pottery and Porcelain of the United States* (1893; rpt. Watkins Glen and New York: Century House Americana, 1971), 61–62; McKendrick, "Josiah Wedgwood," 47–50; Frank Thistlethwaite, "The Atlantic Migration of the Pottery Industry," *Economic History Review*, 2d ser. 11 (1958): 268–69, 270.

18. For a differentiated analysis of the notions of rural settlement and labor migration, see Dirk Hoerder, "An Introduction to Labor Migration in the Atlantic Economies, 1815–1914," in *Labor Migration in the Atlantic Economies: The European and North American Working Classes during the Period of Industrialization*, ed. Dirk Hoerder (Westport, Conn.: Greenwood, 1985), 3–31.

19. *Staffordshire Advertiser* (hereafter quoted as *SA*), 5 Oct 1850; see *SA*, 21 Sept 1850; 12 Oct 1850.

20. See, for example, *PE*, 3 Feb 1844; 2 Mar 1844; 4 May 1844; the best account of the history and failure of the Potters' Emigration Society and the role of its leader, Wiliam Evans, which, however, is still incomplete, is in Burchill and Ross, *The Potters' Union*, 85–98.

21. See E. P. Thompson, *The Making of the English Working Class* (1963; rpt. Harmondsworth: Penguin Books, 1974), 253–54.

22. See Dennis Hardy, *Alternative Communities in Nineteenth Century England* (London and New York: Longman, 1979), 49–58; Thompson, *The Chartists*, 301–6.

23. For socialist and communist emigration schemes, see Gregory Claeys, "John Adolphus Etzler, Technological Utopianism, and British Socialism: The Tropical Emigration Society's Venezuelan Mission and Its Social Context, 1833–1848," *English Historical Review* 101 (1986): 353–75; for discussions among trade unions and for trade-union support of emigration, see Robert A. Leeson, *Travelling Brothers: The Six Centuries Road from Craft Fellowship to Trade Unionism* (London: George Allen and Unwin, 1979), 183–92; until 1848 the Chartists usually rejected any form of organized emigration; only in 1843 was support given to the Chartist and Owenite Lawrence Pitkeithly's emigration scheme for settling workers on American soil, see *Norhern Star* (hereafter cited as *NS*), 1, 8 Apr and 15 July 1843.

24. See, for example, *PE*, 31 Aug 1844; 7, 14, 21 June and 5 July 1845; 5, 12 Dec 1846; *NS*, 28 June 1845; 25 Apr 1846; 5 Dec 1846; 21 Oct 1848.

25. See *PE*, 24 Mar 1848; *Potters' Examiner and Emigrants' Advocate* (hereafter quoted as *PEEA*) 9, nos. 95, 96 (1850); 9, no. 69 (1849).

26. See, for example, *PE*, 3 Feb 1844; 22 June 1844; 28 Sept 1844; 25 Jan and 8 Feb 1845.

27. For the widespread influence of the *Northern Star*, the main organ of Chartism, among Staffordshire potters in the early 1840s, see *Chartism in North Staffordshire*, ed. Robert Fyson (Stafford: Staffordshire County Council, 1981), 42; in 1842 the weekly sale of the *New Moral World*, organ of the Owenite Socialists, in Staffordshire, was fifty copies, see *New Moral World* (hereafter quoted as *NMW*), 4 June 1842; it should be noted that the influence of both movements declined after 1842, especially that of the socialists; the *New Moral World* ceased publication in 1845.

28. *PE*, 13 Jan 1844; Owen, *Staffordshire Potter*, 71, even argues that the printed letters formed the germ of the migration movement.

29. See *PE*, 28 Dec. 1844; *PEEA*, 1849–50, passim; for a critical discussion of (unpublished) emigrants' letters, see Charlotte Erickson, *Invisible Immigrants: The Adaptation of English and Scottish Immigrants in Nineteenth-Century America* (Coral Gables, Fla.: University of Miami Press, 1972), 1–9.

30. *PE*, 24 May 1845; see John Rule, *The Experience of Labour in Eighteenth-Century Industry* (London: Croom Helm, 1981), 52–55, 202.

31. Letter from Thomas Mountford, 1 Nov 1846, Whitewater, Wallworth County, Wisconsin, in *PE*, 12 Dec 1846; letter from Elijah and Charlotte Croxton, 30 Apr 1845, St. Louis, in *PE*, 8 Nov 1845; letter from Thomas Mountford, 19 Feb 1847, Whitewater, Wallworth County, Wisconsin, in *PE*, 19 June 1847.

32. *PE*, 13 Apr 1844; see Rule, *Experience of Labour*, 202; Prothero, *Artisans and Politics*, 27.

33. Letter from Bernard Howson, 12 Sept 1843, East Liverpool, Columbia City, Ohio, to John Howson, in *PE*, 16 Mar 1844; letter from George Garner, 25 Dec 1844, Birmingham, Allegheny County, Pennsylvania, in *PE*, 15 Feb 1845; letter from Thomas Biddulph, 4 Apr 1847, Schuyler County, Illinois, to Joseph Biddulph, in *PE*, 26 June 1847—George Garner, potter (thrower) was given a farewell supper by the Potters' Examiner Committee, see *PE*, 15 June 1844; in East Liverpool he was engaged by James Bennett with whom he afterward moved to Birmingham (Pittsburgh); Bennett was a potter from Derbyshire and became the founder of the East Liverpool pottery industry and a prosperous manufacturer, see Barber, *Pottery and Porcelain*, 192–99.

34. Letter from George Arblaster, 5 Feb 1844, East Liverpool, Ohio, in *PE*, 30 Mar 1844; letter from Thomas Gotham, 18 Dec 1842, St. Louis, to Michael Hill, Clayton, near Newcastle-under-Lyme, in *PE*, Oct 25, 1845; letter from John Henshall, 2 Nov 1846, Philadelphia, in *PE*, 30 Jan 1847; the little pottery where Henshall worked was that of R. Bagnall Beach, a potter from Hanley who became a prominent and prosperous pottery manufacturer; see Barber, *Pottery and Porcelain*, 176–77; Thistlethwaite, "Atlantic Migration," 275.

Due to a lack of concrete information in the emigrants' letters I cannot go into any detailed discussion of the comparative advantages of the pottery-workers' living standard in the United States at the time, as Peter Shergold has done in his study of relative standards of living in Birmingham and Pittsburgh, see *Working Class Life: The "American Standard" in Comparative Perspective* (Pittsburgh, Pa.: University of Pittsburgh Press, 1981).

35. Letter from John Poole, 17 July 1845, Washington County, Missouri, to John Mould, Cobridge, in *PE*, 29 Nov 1845; letter from Elisha Poole, December 1845, Caledonia, Belview Township, Missouri, to James Hammonds, Cobridge, in *PE*, 27 Dec 1845.

36. See Rule, *Experience of Labour*, 201.

37. Letter from Samuel Walker, 26 Apr 1844, Utica, State of New York, in *PE*, 22 June 1844; Letter from Samuel Walker, ? , Utica, State of New York, to John Howson, in *PE*, 17 Feb 1844; see also letter from Samuel Walker, 25 Mar 1844, Utica, State of New York, to G. Garner, in *PE*, 3 Aug 1844—Walker was a potter (painter) from Worcester who had probably migrated to America at the beginning of 1843; he established what he named "The Temperance Hill Pottery" at West Troy, New York, but died in poverty, see Barber, *Pottery and Porcelain*, 178; some of his letters were published in the *Potters' Examiner* (without his knowledge), and others circulated privately among (prospective) migrants; see letter from Leonard Brown, 11 Mar 1844, Paddock's Prairie, in *PE*, 11 May 1844.

38. Letter from Enoch and Sarah Bullock, 3 Aug 1846, Wellsville Pottery, in *PE*, 7 Nov 1846; in fact, the small Wellsville pottery, near East Liverpool, Ohio, was jointly owned by John Garner, George Garner (see note 33 above) and Enoch Bullock, who was brother-in-law to George Garner; established in 1846, the pottery was abandoned as unprofitable after only eighteen months. (Information kindly provided by William C. Gates.)

39. Letter from W- and S-, 1 Nov 1841, Alton, in *PE*, 20 Apr 1844; see also letter from W- and S-, 12 Sept 1843, Alton, in *PE*, 27 Apr 1844; in their first letter, W- and S- mentioned that they had engaged one Mr. Tams; James Tams was a Staffordshire potter from Longton and became a highly successful manufacturer in the United States; see Barber, *Pottery and Porcelain*, 226–28.

40. Letter from George Scott, 22 Aug 1846, Cincinnati, Ohio, to the President of the Printer's Branch, in *PE*, 24 Oct 1846; Scott in fact became a prosperous pottery manufacturer, see Barber, *Pottery and Porcelain*, 274.

41. Letter from Thomas Mountford, 1 Nov 1846; *PE*, 2 Mar 1844—it should be noted that this was written before the United Branches of Operative Potters and the trade periodical concentrated exclusively on the propagation of rural settlement migration; see, for example, letter from Thomas Filcher, 16 Apr 1843, Nauvoo, in *PE*, 3 Feb 1844; letter from Joseph

Walley, 29 June 1849, Portage Prairie, in *PEEA* 9, no. 63—Walley was a potter (hollowware presser) and trade unionist from Shelton who went to America with the Potters' Emigration Society and settled on the land at Pottersville.

42. Letter from Thomas Filcher, 17 Oct 1843, Nauvoo, to George Mart, in *PE*, 2 Mar 1844; see letter from Samuel Walker, 25 Mar 1844—Mart was a potter (china painter) in Stoke and a leading Chartist until 1842; Filcher was a potter from Staffordshire who migrated to America in 1842; from the letter quoted above it can be inferred that Filcher was very probably involved in Chartism himself. Filcher's rejection of industrial America and his simultaneous praise of agricultural America was shared by other migrants whose letters were published in the labor press of the time; see, for example, letter from Joseph Armitage, 27 Jan 1845, Woonsocket, Rhode Island, to Willis Knowles, Hyde, in *NMW*, 15 Mar 1845; letter from William Butterworth, 6 Apr 1843, New York, to the editor of the *Northern Star*, in *NS*, 29 Apr 1843.

43. Letter from Elijah Baddley, 1 Mar 1846, Lexington P.O., Henderson County, Tennessee, to Richard Baddley, Upper Hanley, in *PE*, 15 Aug 1846; letter from Thomas Goodwin, 26 Oct 1846, Paddock's Grove, Madison County, Illinois, to Charles Billington, in *PE*, 5 June 1847.

44. See, for example, letter from Benjamin Brunt, 21 Jan 1849, West Sterling, in *People: Their Rights and Liberties, Their Duties and Their Interests*, no. 42 (1849)—Brunt was a potter (hollowware presser) and trade unionist from Tunstall who, after a conflict with his master, had left for America with the aid of the Potters' Emigration Society.

45. I have checked the "Pottery Police Courts" column of the *Staffordshire Mercury* for the year 1845 and the "Potteries Police Intelligence" column of the *Staffordshire Advertiser* for the year 1847, both of which are full of cases against poachers; see also Shaw, *When I Was a Child*, 28–29.

46. *PE*, 2 Mar 1844; for health conditions in the pottery manufactories see Burchill and Ross, *The Potters' Union*, 37–40; see also William Evans, *The Life and Death of a Working Potter* (Newcastle-under-Lyme: T. Bayley, 1864).

47. See Shaw, *When I Was a Child*, 194–95.

48. Letter from John Thomas, 26 Aug 1849, Mercer, Mercer County, Pennsylvania, in *PEEA* 9, no. 66 (1849); letter from George Garner, 25 Dec 1844—Thomas was a potter (turner) from Staffordshire who had migrated to America with the aid of the Turners' Surplus Labour Society; although he intended to pay a visit to East Liverpool, his aim was to buy a fifty-acre farm.

49. Letter from Philip Pointon, 18 July 1850, Baraboo, in *SA*, 5 Oct 1850—Pointon was a Staffordshire potter who, aided by the Potters' Emigration Society, went to Wisconsin with his wife and six children; greatly dissatisfied, he left Pottersville after a few days and moved to Baraboo. The image of an America where more equal social relations between masters and men prevailed was confirmed by other emigrants' letters in the labor press;

see, for example, letter from Thomas Cooper, 9 Oct 1849, Albany, in *People*, no. 117 (1850); letter from James and Eliza Boothroyd, 15 Aug 1849, Six Miles West of Jacksonville, Illinois, in *People*, no. 97 (1850); letter from Richard Pilling, 12 Nov 1848, Stuyvesant Falls, Columbia County, State of New York, in *NS*, 16 Dec 1848; a critical picture, reflecting a different immigrant experience, can be found in a letter from Joseph Armitage, 27 Jan 1845.

50. Letter from George Garner, 25 Dec 1844; letter from John Howson, 8 Feb 1846, Zanesville, Muskingham County, Ohio, in *PE*, 16 May 1846; see also letter from John Henshall, 2 Nov 1846—Howson was a Staffordshire potter, brother of Bernard Howson; he was given a farewell supper by the Potters' Examiner Committee, together with Garner and two others; from the letter quoted above it can be inferred that he worked with Samuel Walker in Utica but left when he lost his work and ninety dollars after nine months. In the end, however, he and his brother succeeded in establishing their own manufactory in Zanesville; see John Ramsay, *American Potters and Pottery* (Clinton, Mass.: Colonial Press, 1939), 77, 234.

51. *PE*, 31 Aug 1844; *PE*, 3 Feb 1844.

52. Letter from Thomas Filcher, 17 Oct 1843; letter from William Maddock, 13 Sept 1844, New York, to Mary Maddock, Burslem, in *PE*, 7 Dec 1844—despite his critical remarks, Maddock thought that on the whole America was "far before England for the working man," and he supported the land plan of the Potters' Emigration Society.

53. Letter from Elijah Baddley, 1 Mar 1846; letter from George Garner, 25 Dec 1844; for the political influence of master potters in Staffordshire, see Burchill and Ross, *The Potters' Union*, 25–26.

54. *PEEA* 9, no. 63 (1849).

55. Letter from Samuel Walker, 26 Apr 1844; letter from Elijah Baddley, 1 Mar 1846; the idea that the working population's grievances were mainly due to exploitation by taxation played a crucial role in British artisan radicalism and can be traced back to the writings of Thomas Paine; see Prothero, *Artisans and Politics*, 83–84; for the spread of this idea in the "Potteries," see, for example, *NS*, 17 Nov 1838.

56. Letter from Samuel Walker, 26 Apr 1844.

57. See, for example, *NMW*, 1 Aug 1840; 4 June 1842; 15 June 1844; *MacDouall's Chartist and Republican Journal*, 14 Aug 1841; *NS*, 27 Apr 1844; 30 Nov 1844; 2 May 1846; 14 Dec 1850.

58. *Manchester Examiner and Times*, 30 Sept 1848.

59. See, for example, letter from Philip Pointon, 16 May 1850, Baraboo, in *NS* and *SA*, 29 June 1850; letter from Enoch Pickering, 16 Nov 1849, Fort Winnebago, in *People*, no. 89 (1849)—Pickering was a potter from Stoke and one of the pioneer settlers at Pottersville.

60. See *PEEA* 9, no. 68 (1849), where Evans talked of 300 working men,

and *SA*, 29 Sept 1849, where Evans talked of 350 families having emigrated; from 1848 on not only potters but workers and artisans of other trades also migrated with the Potters' Emigration Society; for example, emigrants' letters and lectures of the society suggest that quite a few migrants came from the Lancashire textile centers; for the hollowware pressers who migrated with the emigration society, see *PEEA* 9, no. 92 (1850).

    61. See *SA*, 30 June 1849; *PEEA* 9, no. 96 (1850); *PEEA* 10, no. 5 (1850); at least three, but probably many more, of the turners stuck to their trade: Joseph Tunnicliff became a respected workman at one of the Bennington, Vermont, potteries in the early 1850s; see John Spargo, *The Potters and Potteries of Bennington* (Southampton, N.Y.: Cracker Barrel Press, 1926), 237; two others became manufacturers themselves: Thomas Johnson was one of the owners of a pottery in Middlebury, Ohio, in 1852, and Samuel Alcock seems to have set up his own manufactory in Baltimore, Maryland; see John Spargo, *Early American Pottery and China* (New York: The Century Co., 1926), 337, 335.

    62. See Grant Foreman, "Settlement of English Potters in Wisconsin," *Wisconsin Magazine of History* 21 (1938): 395–96; for a sketch of the life of Henry Dooley, Staffordshire potter, trade unionist, and pioneer settler in Wisconsin, see *The Last of the Potters' Society* (mss., Wisconsin State Historical Society; copy in Horace Barks Reference Library, Stoke, City Central Library).

    63. See Jones, *Notes to the People*, vol. 1, 1851, 263; Jones did not prove his assertion, but William Hollins, for example, one of the hollowware pressers who had emigrated with the Potters' Emigration Society, turned up as a respected pottery-worker in Bennington; see Spargo, *Potters and Potteries*, 237; see also letter from Philip Pointon, 16 May 1850, where he stated that he intended to try potting after he and his family had got a little settled.

    64. Spargo, *Potters and Potteries*, 237; see William C. Gates, *The City of Hills and Kilns: Life and Work in East Liverpool, Ohio* (East Liverpool, Ohio: East Liverpool Historical Society, 1984), 88–89; Marc Jeffrey Stern, "The Potters of Trenton, New Jersey, 1850–1902: A Study in the Industrialization of Skilled Trades" (Ph.D. diss., State University of New York at Stony Brook, 1986), 260; see also Ohio Bureau of Labor Statistics, *Nineteenth Annual Report* (Columbus, Ohio, 1896), 11, 31.

    65. See ibid., 32; Thistlethwaite, "Atlantic Migration," 268, 272, 277.

    66. See Lamb "Pottery-Making Machinery," 4–6.

    67. *PEEA* 10, no. 5 (1850); see Foreman, "English Potters in Wisconsin," 382–83.

    68. *PEEA* 9, no. 95 (1850); see also *PEEA* 9, no. 96 (1850).

    69. *Bee Hive*, 13 Jan 1866—it was in fact a combined "Emigration and

Building Society"; one of its objects was to send fifty to a hundred journeymen and apprentices every year.

70. See Gates, *Hills and Kilns*, 89; Stern, "Potters of Trenton," 260–65; see also Ohio Bureau of Labor Statistics, *First Annual Report* (Columbus, Ohio, 1878), 231, 235–36; Rowland Tappan Berthoff, *British Immigrants in Industrial America*, 1790–1950 (New York: Russell and Russell, 1953), 76; Thistlethwaite, "Atlantic Migration," 274–75, 276–77.

7

Scandinavian Migrants' Images and the Americanization of the Work Process

Claudius H. Riegler

SCANDINAVIAN migration to America in the second half of the nineteenth and the first quarter of the twentieth centuries is one of the most thoroughly researched migration movements of this period.[1] According to Åkerman, its chronological development can be divided into an introductory phase (1850–69) and a growth phase (1870–83); and into a saturation phase (1884–92) and a regression phase (1893–1930).[2]

A comprehensive scholarly debate has emphasized the effect of general and special "push" and "pull" factors.[3] Extensive specialized studies have been devoted to the transatlantic information and transport system.[4] But there has been less research into the many-faceted, subjective image of America as a significant influence on migration decisions. Runeby's differentiated investigation of Swedish migrants' images of America during the early phase of overseas migration provides a starting point. But a similar study of the period of mass migration, emphasizing both objective factors and subjective perception, is missing.[5] Above all, an investigation of the images conveyed in the press, taking into account the reading habits of all sections of the population, is necessary.[6] Unfortunately, no comprehensive collection of "America letters" exists, although some have been published and others are available in many archives. Barton's study, with its unrepresentative social and historical selection, remains inadequate.[7]

The problem seems to be the same in other Scandinavian countries. In Denmark reliable data about the number of the Amer-

160

ican letters seem to be available,[8] but research into the press, especially the labor periodicals and their influence on migration, has not made much headway.[9] In Norway, historians of migration are aware of the influence of the press on the potential migrants' image of America, but this has not been investigated systematically.[10]

Because, in the case of Sweden, a comprehensive analysis of the contemporary press and migrants' letters is missing, this essay will attempt to provide a survey of the image of America and of the economic expectations held by labor migrants seeking industrial work there. We will rely on a limited number of primary sources and on the more important of the published studies. Characteristic aspects of the information provided by several Swedish and Danish daily newspapers about America and migration will be presented, with special importance given to the workers' press. Some examples of these newspapers are *Socialdemokraten* (The Social Democrat), published in Stockholm from 1885 on, and the paper of the same name published in Copenhagen from 1881 on. The two were closely linked and were the main organs of the developing socialist workers' movement in the two countries.[11] For Denmark this will be supplemented by a study of several specialized emigrant journals. While we can thus provide a survey of an important part of the information available to potential migrants, we cannot investigate the specific use made of it.

Second, we will deal with important elements of the image of America of a special group of migrants: skilled workers, technicians, and engineers. These went to the United States to explore new technologies, obtain additional training, and then return to Sweden. In this context we will describe the picture of the American economy, especially its technical and scientific aspects, as conveyed in the most important Swedish technicians' journal from 1870 to 1893.

Finally, the results of the 1907 oral survey of migrant opinions and of a questionnaire sent to Swedish settlers in America will be used to sketch both the typical expectations of the first-time migrant and their criticisms of conditions in their native country.

The Image of America in the Swedish and Danish Press

As Tedebrand has established, the majority of Swedish workers at the end of the nineteenth century read liberal and conservative newspapers.[12] Only in the 1880s did a social democratic press come into being. The first social democratic newspaper, *Folkviljan* (The People's

Will), was founded in Malmö in 1882. It was followed by *Socialdemokraten* in Stockholm in 1885 and *Arbetet* (Labor) in Malmö in 1887.

Taking a leading liberal provincial newspaper, *Karlstads Tidningen*, as an example, Tedebrand showed that working-class readers could get "a realistic picture of the situation in the American labor market" from nonlabor newspapers. The immigrants' opportunities were described regularly in "America letters," and "the readers were well informed about unemployment . . . , the struggle for the eight-hour-day, the strikes in the coal mines, the persecution of union members and the activities of the police force towards organised labor." Even the unequal distribution of wealth in the United States was emphasized in several articles.[13]

Nilsson undertook a detailed case study of information about America in *Socialdemokraten* in 1886–94. The newspaper was widely distributed among Swedish workers, despite an initial circulation of about only 5,000. For information about America, the paper relied especially on American newspapers and periodicals, and on letters from party members who had emigrated.[14] In 1886–87 the few articles dealing with America gave a negative picture of it—it was difficult to get a job and wages were low. This negative picture continued into the late 1880s. Unsuccessful strikes, wage cuts, and extensive unemployment were reported. A few successful strikes, however, were taken as signs that the American Republic seemed to guarantee to the working class the freedom to organize and stand up for its rights. During the 1890s, special attention was paid to trade-union activities and to strikes. According to Nilsson, extensive information about wages and working hours conveyed a favorable impression to Swedish workers. But, at a time when Swedish migration was rising again, reports about the American labor market turned pessimistic. The Homestead Strike in 1892 was considered by *Socialdemokraten* to be a prime "example of the powerlessness of the American labor organizations." With the onset of the depression of 1893, reports "of mass unemployment become more frequent," and in 1894 "the picture of America as a country of bankruptcies and shutdowns" predominated. In reaction to this, industrial and urban migration from Sweden sank to a low point. For Swedish observers, "the Pullman Strike in particular raised many important issues. At stake was the right of industrial workers to organize unions, to declare boycotts, and to strike."[15]

In Denmark, the pioneering work on emigration to America by Hvidt[16] deals with the picture of America conveyed by the press.

Since about 1866, the beginning of extensive emigration, numerous articles on migration and conditions in the United States appeared. One example, from the island of Langeland, shows a shift of editorial opinion from positive weekly reports about migrants and their motives in the late 1860s to a decidedly hostile view of emigration in the early 1880s. Danish newspapers often published letters from migrants that conveyed important to the Danish people general information as well as individual migrants' experiences.[17] Hvidt also looked at special emigrant magazines published since 1866: *Emigranten* (The Emigrant), 1866–72; *Udvandringstidende* (Emigrants' Newspaper), 1879–80; *Den nye verlden* (The New World), 1886–91, modeled on a Swedish emigrant magazine of the same name published from 1871 to 72; and *Kors og Stjerne* (Cross and Stars), 1889–? They were usually the mouthpieces of organizations that wished to facilitate migration. *Den nye verlden*, a well-produced publication, provided much factual information about working conditions in America.

General studies of the image of America in the contemporary Danish workers' press are not available. Callesen, studying *Socialdemokraten*'s reporting on the Haymarket affair in Chicago 1886 and the judicial murder of the accused anarchists in 1887, established that the readers generally received accurate information about the labor movement. This most important Danish workers' paper relied for information mostly on the German-language socialist newspapers *Vorbote* (Chicago) and the *New Yorker Volks-Zeitung*.[18]

With regard to Norwegian research, Semmingsen in her pioneering study barely looked at the image of the United States and the role of the press in its creation. In one provincial newspaper a contemporary opposition leader stated "that he regarded news from America as part of his struggle against the dominance of the official class in Norway." Some opposition papers published letters from Norwegian emigrants that gave information about American conditions in general. When commenting editorially, these newspapers made "comparisons which, as a rule, were not favorable to conditions in Norway." Semmingsen revealed that many predominant features of the Norwegian migrants' picture of America were idealistic. Even reports about modest success tended to confirm the image of America as a land of opportunity. Because of the institutional and cultural heavy-handedness of the Norwegian administration, America exercised a considerable attraction as a country to which men and women could escape.[19]

The Image of American Technology and Its Effect on Industrial Work in Sweden

In 1907, the Emigration Commission, which had been set up by the Swedish government, sent out investigators and questionnaires. One finding was that because of the lack of opportunities for technical training in Sweden, industrial workers went to America to learn new skills. The Swedish migrants repeatedly stressed the better possibilities for job training in the United States.[20] However, the most attractive country for artisans, industrial workers, technicians, and engineers was Germany. This was because of its geographical proximity and the good opportunities it offered for technical training. While this preference lasted into the 1890s and continued to some degree up to World War I, the increasing attractiveness of American firms for those wishing to acquire knowledge and practical skills is explained in part by the growing amount of available information.[21]

The World's Fairs in Philadelphia in 1876 and in Chicago in 1894 added to the impact of publications. Traveling "experts" visited both fairs, studied new developments in their particular fields, and spread the word back at home. Three examples will be used to illustrate this intense flow of information. First, we will discuss how the image of America held by Swedish migrants was, to a certain degree, influenced by the way in which the 1876 World's Fair in Philadelphia was received in Sweden. Next, the reports in the Swedish engineering journal *Teknisk Tidskrift* (Technical Journal) will be analyzed to show changes in information about American technology from 1870 to 1893. Third, the expectations of labor migrants will be sketched using the reports of the skilled workers and technicians[22] who participated in the state-sponsored migration to the United States for training purposes.

In the last quarter of the nineteenth century, international exhibitions provided demonstrations of the expanding industrial potential of America to the world. In contrast to the earlier, rather modest representations at the great European exhibitions in London, Moscow, Copenhagen, and Vienna, 1876 offered—on the hundredth anniversary of the Declaration of Independence—a unique opportunity "to give a more exact and true picture" of America: "The time had come for America to show her greatness to the outside world."[23] This exhibition may be considered the beginning of a broad American self-promotion campaign. Progress was most pronounced in iron, steel, transport (railroads), and engineering, and also in the electrotechnical, printing, and chemical industries. American training methods began to attract attention in Europe, and the rapid progress and growing significance of the American economy were also recognized in Sweden. Therefore, experts and representatives of the government were sent to the exposition. They were interested in the innovations in machine-tool building, since this was one of the most important and ambitious industries in Sweden. The investigators "came back with new impulses and ideas which were tested in Swedish factories, and American machines were even ordered."[24] As a result, a positive attitude toward American technology developed, which was supplemented by an awareness of the serious competition from American manufacturers in mechanical engineering. Swedish manufacturing processes had to be "revitalized and old and now unsuitable work methods had to be done away with."[25] By officially advocating a close acquaintance with American economic life, the government stressed the value of direct work experience. According to Bowallius, the contacts Swedish experts had established in Philadelphia definitely had "significance for the gradual change in the way of looking at American technology."[26]

Since 1870, the *Teknisk Tidskrift*, published especially for technicians and engineers, covered all technical areas and was an outlet for technical information from all over the world. From 1870 to 1875, the state of technology in German dominated its reports. News from the United States was rare: the first report merely mentioned that Americans were a practical and inventive people, as the sheer number of inventions showed; their innovations in iron and steel production were stressed, as was the remarkable quality of American railroad technology and the advantages of mass-production methods for producing agricultural machines. By the beginning of the 1880s, the *Teknisk Tidskrift* had established a solid image of America as a country of very inventive technicians and high-quality industrial products. The rapid development of American technology was regarded with a certain anxiety. Much could be learned from America "with regard to the favorable cost of railroad production as well as many other things"[27]; but training methods might have to be adapted from the United States, where the predominant tendency was to make science and technology independent of the old craft traditions—in other words, to separate engineering offices from the workshops. In *Teknisk Tidskrift* this tendency was eloquently promoted and promulgated.[28]

Several of the technicians and engineers who, with government grants, had gone for longer periods of work in the United States had their travelogues published in the journal between 1885 and 1890. The picture of America as "a country which leads the way in all areas"[29] was strengthened. "As the extent of information about America increased, so did the positive value judgments of American technology. . . . They now referred to the whole country. Earlier they had mostly referred to special areas of American technology."[30] This picture was consolidated through lectures from technicians' and engineers' associations. In the main, the image of America was that of those workers and public employees in industry who were interested in technology.

The fact that the government institutionalized a migration for training purposes to America substantially changed the general image of America and also had an effect on the expectations of labor migrants. As a result of the extensive and detailed reports on technological development in the United States, the interest of skilled workers, technicians, and engineers in gaining work experience in American factories grew. Since 1860 government grants had been given to workers, since 1873 to mining engineers, and since 1887 to all other technicians and engineers. At the beginning, the yearly total for workers amounted to 20,000 crowns, for mining engineers 6,000 crowns, and for the remaining technicians and engineers 5,000 crowns. In 1889, for example, these amounts were sufficient to send forty-five workers, seven mining engineers, and six other technicians abroad. In the 1890s the interest in migration to America for training increased above all among technicians. The amounts were therefore increased and a special fund was established for journeys to the Chicago World's Fair.[31]

However, little effort was made by the government or by captains of industry to evaluate the written reports of the migrants' experiences and to make them available to a larger public. It was unofficial dissemination and contacts that influenced the expectations of subsequent emigrants and labor migrants. After 1904 it was presumably this "training migration" that spread the still diffuse knowledge about American work methods, mechanization, specialization, mass production, and the beginning of the assembly-line system. Only after 1900 did the management of many Swedish enterprises see American industry and its organizational principles as a model. In sections of the artisan-minded new industrial workforce, the desire to copy the system of American work organization, management, and industrial relations increased. Those involved in working out trade-union strategies did not follow the American model. But the orientation toward it was strengthened by the Swedish technical intelligentsia's great receptivity to American "virtues": frankness, youthfulness, entrepreneurship, and openness to innovation. It was assumed that American manufacturers, in contrast to those in France and Germany, were proud of being able to hold their own, without any secrecy, against competition from foreign manufacturers. Therefore, American firms were also open to foreign workers. This encouraged the notion that jobs were easily available in American industry. The reportedly excellent opportunities, in contrast to Sweden, contributed to the idea that the migrants could choose whatever level of qualification and job they wanted.

On the other hand, from the few "America reports" that were published it was clear that in America work was harder and more strenuous than in Sweden, and that the organization of labor could no longer be influenced by the workers. Swedish observers noticed that "the workers knew little or nothing about what was happening in other parts of the factory."[32] This was one of the fundamental differences between methods of production in Sweden and in the United States, due to the very advanced division of labor in American mechanical engineering because of produce specialization.[33] By comparison, in 1908 in Sweden, at a time when employers were initiating an extensive campaign to intensify industrial work, special production, improvisation, and product variation with a resulting multiplicity of work functions still dominated the organization of labor in the factories. The predominant techno-culture in Swedish factories, with its manifold loyalties among workers who were still skilled craftsmen, was as yet immune to any control, whether in the form of the paternalism of the first-generation working owners or in the form of direct control by foremen. Against the endeavors of committed trade unionists to retain the control over work processes traditionally exercised by skilled industrial workers, employers tried to introduce "American" methods of work organization in order to counteract what began to be seen as a lower degree of work efficiency in Sweden in comparison to Taylorist-oriented work processes in the United States.[34]

Around 1910, the Swedish trade unions joined the American unions in their criticism of this strategy. The Swedish Metalworkers' Union warned of the consequences of division of labor: detailed control threatened to turn workers into robots, and the increase in the intensity of the work threatened to wear workers out prematurely.[35] But according to *Teknisk Tidskrift*, as a result of a more rational organization of labor and time, the industrial worker in America was better off than his counterpart in Sweden. He received higher wages and only occasionally had to work overtime. In appearance, he looked no different from the foreman. Physical working conditions and certain areas of industrial health and safety (ventilation, heating, hygiene facilities) were substantially better than in Sweden. But negative aspects also received attention. The widespread method of "hire and fire" was found to come from the deliberate exploitation of newcomers by new forms of production without legislative protection.

Because travel reports stressed the ease of transferring American labor methods, another barrier that could have prevented labor migration and permanent emigration disappeared. On the one hand an awareness spread among labor migrants from a genuine proletarian milieu that one's future lay within the constantly expanding labor market in Sweden and across the Atlantic. On the other hand, an internationalization not only of the working class but also of production methods became apparent from around 1910. From that time on, in Germany, in England, as well as in Sweden, first lessons were drawn from F. W. Taylor's scientific time-and-motion studies as the model for an optimum organization of work processes.[36]

The 1907 Survey of the Emigration Commission: A Study of Migrant Expectations

In April 1907, two public employees of the Emigration Commission, appointed in 1903 by Parliament, accompanied Swedish migrants on two different liners from Liverpool to the New World.[37] The intention of the head of the commission, the statistician Gustav Sundbärg, was to discuss the motives for the continuing migration and to propose effective remedies for it. But, in their questioning of 300 people, the two interviewers concentrated in great detail on migrants' economic expectations and their general image of America. In autumn of the same year, a female employee of the commission carried out a similar survey among female migrants. Although many of those interviewed were undertaking the trip for the second or third time, the answers produced a wealth of information about migrants "at that moment when they left their native land and when their ideas were exclusively based on the experience they had gathered at home." The commission also made an effort "to get an idea how conditions in Sweden were judged by those compatriots abroad who, over a lengthy period of time, had had the opportunity to experience a foreign land and to compare the opportunities in both the native and the new land." For this purpose, the Emigration Commission in May 1907 sent out a call to "the Swedes in America." Those "who could give worthwhile information about their fate and experiences" were asked to send responses.[38] The questionnaire contained a wealth of interesting questions about their lives, families, and property situation before migration, and about their present social conditions. It was distributed mainly through churches in America, and several Swedish-American magazines published it with editorial comments.

At times the commission was remarkably objective and even critical of the situation at home. From a comparison of the answers about living conditions in the country of origin and the receiving society it stated, "it should be possible to understand the economic reasons which created the desire or necessity to emigrate and to stay in America."[39] However, some parts of the questionnaire were worded in a way that seemed to imply criticism of emigration and caused offense; some American and Swedish-American newspapers considered the questionnaire a call to re-migration and a denunciation of the emigrants. Nevertheless, in 1907–8, some 400 letters from Swedish emigrants, some of whom had been in America for over forty years, arrived in Stockholm.[40] This, as Sundbärg stressed, was the first time that emigrants could make themselves heard by "presenting their experiences and reflections to the Swedish people."[41]

Thus, in 1907, the expectations and the image of America held by Swedish migrants, based on specific economic considerations, were revealed in their oral communications.[42] Although, as shown above, social democratic newspapers tried to look at America realistically and critically, the assumption of the basic superiority of the "American system" in practically all areas of life was widespread. With regard to the working conditions, security and continuity of employment were considered to be of particular importance. On the job, the legal position of workers in the face of employers misusing power (e.g., in case of a lockout) took on special significance. Linked to this was a very simplified picture of unlimited possibilities for earning a living. This, and the sense of kinship—based upon close family ties—felt toward the multinational American society, led to a view of emigration or temporary labor migration as a totally normal way of earning money. Crossing the Atlantic in search of work was considered preferable to internal migration to another area in Sweden:

> It is quite characteristic that they [the female migrants questioned in Liverpool] generally never thought of the possibility of looking for more favorable living conditions or a higher wage elsewhere in Sweden. America is the first alternative when there is no longer any means of earning a livelihood at home.[43]

Favorable living conditions took into account decent accommodation, minimum size and functionality of an apartment, and reasonable rent. Income tax was also important, and it was judged to be less of a burden in the United States, and to allow people to save some of their wages. Other aspects included gaining new work experience and better possibilities for training. These played a role in the expectations of both permanent emigrants and temporary labor migrants.[44] Finally, migrants hoped to raise their educational level and secure the future education of their children. This latter point was an important consideration for a large number of those emigrants who, from the beginning, had decided to stay permanently. An "anxiety, found everywhere, about the education and future of the children" almost exclusively shaped the image of America of those who left for good.[45]

However, a smaller group of seasonal or temporary agricultural migrants, men and women, needed money wages and savings for the establishment or maintenance of a farmstead in Sweden. For this group, neither expanded prospects in American society nor educational opportunities had any importance. What counted were higher wage levels in comparison with Swedish or other European areas because these migrants could have migrated seasonally to Denmark or Germany instead. These migrants were willing to forego higher living standards, work in shifts, and do overtime.[46]

In Sweden, where the rigorous work ethic concentrated on rules rather than on results,[47] a clear division between work and leisure time did not exist. Therefore, the question of "time autonomy"—that is, the independent use of leisure—was very important to all migrants. Especially those women who wanted to become domestic servants emphasized that they were entitled to a free afternoon each week in addition to the free Sunday: "During this time they themselves were in charge of their lives, could decide whether to go out or stay at home, just as they liked, without having to be on call." The fact that they could have their own living quarters contributed to their favorable impressions. Working-class women also pointed out the advantages of a more rational division of time in America. The heavy demands of working life, be it in the household or in the factory, would be balanced by a great amount of leisure time.[48]

Finally, according to the image given by the migrants, the individual had more personal freedom and privacy in the United States. A reporter from the Emigration Commission pointed out the immense trust that those migrants questioned by him had in "the democratic American social order" and in the "fairness of the republican system of government and its other great advantages." He stated that even though a certain disillusionment had spread with regard to personal earning possibilities, the economic, social, and also political advantages of America in contrast to Sweden were in a certain way still rated very high.[49]

The only negative aspect of the image of America was the widespread awareness that conditions of production contained considerable risks. Occupational diseases and accidents were common, safeguards for workers and their families in case of accidents or illness inadequate. Obviously, industrial health and safety standards were a basic concern for migrating workers. In their criticisms of the faults and weaknesses of protective legislation for workers, the role of the government in the workplace became a central issue.[50]

These general aspects of the image of America held by male and female migrants crossing the ocean for the first time struck the three investigators as particularly noticeable. In a more differentiated way, these aspects emerged also in the collection of individual life stories. Almost all of these migrants were in touch with relatives or acquaintances who had already been living in America, some of them for decades. This deeply influenced their image of America. New migrants had, for example, exact information about wage conditions. Matter-of-fact comparisons of industrial wages and expenses in Sweden and America resulted in the conviction that savings could be accumulated much more easily in America.[51] They were informed that they could acquire a greater degree of "experience and occupational knowledge." They believed in the "more secure position" of workers in America, as well as in the greater career opportunities there. "American work methods" became an often-used synonym for conspicuous innovations in the organization of work.[52]

Some of the male migrants combined their depiction of future prospects in America with an explicit criticism of social conditions in Sweden: at the workplace hierarchical structures, subordination, and coercion were the order of the day; permanent employment was rare, underemployment common. From this they derived the confident expectation that America would be a "country of greater freedom."[53]

Female migrants justified their decision to leave more confidently than men, and sometimes the women had euphoric expectations. After a hard life in Sweden, they had enthusiastically seized the opportunity to migrate. They often traveled in groups with girlfriends or female relatives of the same age. The experience of having been harshly exploited as female farmworkers or as domestic servants, of having had to submit to strict patriarchal rule in the family and to unremunerated use of their labor—all this explained the greater determination with which female migrants decided to leave. Like the migrating men, these women relied on both written and oral information, which they obtained from return migrants, about life and working conditions in America.[54] Prospective women migrants who suffered from particularly arbitrary pressures at work in Sweden expected to find very well regulated, steady jobs in America.

From this analysis of the pattern of individual attitudes toward the receiving country emerges a view of migrants who had gathered a remarkable level of information in forming their well-considered picture of life in America. Only occasionally—when personally experienced deprivations in Sweden had been overwhelming—were expectations unrealistic. Personal letters, reports in the press—above all, in the workers' press—and information supplied by returning migrants all contributed to this picture.

Criticisms of Swedish Society by Swedes Abroad

The letters in response to the Emigration Commission's questionnaire in 1907 time and again refer to the unfree working conditions in agriculture and lumbering, and the meager wages and other earnings that made providing for a family in Sweden very difficult. These were the recurring criticisms of emigrants looking back at their native country. They depicted an all-encompassing poverty culminating in the famine years of 1868–69, which had created apathy and had offered no prospects for the future. Family members capable of work often had had to go to Denmark or Northern Germany as seasonal agricultural workers or as laborers building canals, railways, and fortifications. Their hard-earned wages had helped the families to survive.[55] These seasonal labor migrations to neighboring European countries often provided the impulse for the final emigration to America. This was the case of P. A. J., who reported from Oklahoma that he had emigrated with his parents from Småland in 1870.[56]

Others, families as well as individual emigrants, had also left at that time, without waiting for the economic improvement that followed in the 1870s.

The letters that these emigrants sent home shortly after arrival dealt with spontaneous reactions to the new society, their negative experiences of the transatlantic crossing, and the different living conditions and customs they found in America.[57] However, in some of the 119 letters, which were published by the Emigration Commission in 1908, this period in Sweden and the significance of the move to America were discussed more thoroughly.[58] Reference was made to the harshness of Swedish property-owners and community officials, who, in spite of the famine, demanded normal rent and on occasion announced publicly: "It doesn't matter if the poor starve to death." The school system was described as inhuman, and its corporal punishment of pupils compared with that experienced by negro slaves.[59]

Those who emigrated after 1890 very strongly criticized the institutional link between church and state. They also frankly complained about the political system, especially the lack of voting rights. They suggested that "class barriers and snobbishness" in Sweden should "as far as possible be avoided and that the often disgusting titles should be discarded." Sweden was to rid itself of its "bureaucracy and pedantry" to permit the development of self-assured citizens. Compulsory military service, which in Sweden was sometimes welcomed by the oppressed lower agricultural workers as a rest from the excessive field work, was sharply criticized. "Do away with class barriers so that the working people can feel at home more easily. Give them the right to self-determination as in this country"—this was the concise demand of G. O., who had emigrated from Stockholm to Minnesota in 1906.[60]

The prosperity achieved by most through hard work was, on the request of the Emigration Commission, always described in figures as exact as possible. It seems that this effort to make material for comparison available was also an effort by the migrants to prove that they had made the right decision. An industrious life, better conditions for the acquisition of land, higher wages because of the greater effectiveness of the economic system, and also the benevolence of God, who "has opened up this country to us poor emigrants and has given us a sanctuary from oppression and poverty," were given as reasons for the better life in America.[61]

In their letters of 1907–8 many Swedish immigrants in America realistically assessed the economic improvements that, because of the modernization of the capitalist world market, had been achieved in their native land since their departure. But they remained sceptical. Only gradually, and in general only after World War I, did class-conscious workers remain in Sweden, even in difficult personal and economic circumstances, in order to struggle for better conditions and to build a socialist workers' movement. After the achievement of the franchise in 1918, the fight for workers' control and economic democracy brought about a Swedish way of social change.[62] The image of a humane society in America faded in the face of the compromises the American labor movement was making. By the 1930s, Swedish workers and small farmers had materially caught up with, and sociopolitically overtaken, their American counterparts.

Conclusion

The end of Swedish labor migration to America involved a significant change in collective behavior. Workers now made demands on the home government through their unions and through the political parties of the Left rather than putting the improvement of their competitive position at risk through migration. Capital—which for its part enforced American methods of production on Sweden[63]— made the image of America in Swedish working life a Trojan horse for Taylorism. However, whereas the latter had been strongly opposed, for example, by the metalworkers' union in 1910,[64] it was accepted in the 1930s when capital and labor came to a corporate consensus. Because of the very adoption of American methods by management and by labor organizations, Swedish industrial wages became the highest in Europe.[65] Mass migration, with its tendency to create a labor shortage and its simultaneous effect on the qualifications of the workers remaining at home, contributed to the Americanization of the work process in Sweden.[66]

Notes

1. For further bibliographical information, see *From Sweden to America: A History of the Migration,* Harald Runblom and Hans Norman, eds. (Uppsala and Minneapolis, Minn.: University of Minnesota Press, 1976); for a recently published work on the early Swedish migration to America, see Reinhold Wulff, *Die Anfangsphase der Emigration aus Schweden in die USA, 1820–1850* (Frankfurt a.M.: Lang, 1987); for a short presentation and discus-

sion from a theoretical labor history viewpoint, see Claudius H. Riegler, "Emigrationsphasen, Akkumulation and Widerstandsstrategien: Zu einigen Beziehungen der Arbeitsemigration von und nach Schweden, 1850–1930," in *Migration und Wirtschaftsentwicklung*, ed. Hartmut Elsenhans (Frankfurt a.M.: Campus, 1978), 31–69. For similar work on Denmark, see Kristian Hvidt, *Flight to America: The Social Background of 300,000 Danish Emigrants* (New York: Academic Press, 1975). On Norway, see Ingrid Semmingsen, *Norway to America: A History of the Migration* (Minneapolis, Minn.: University of Minnesota Press, 1978); Odd S. Lovoll, *The Promise of America: A History of the Norwegian-American People* (Minneapolis, Minn.: University of Minnesota Press, 1984).

2. See Sune Åkerman, *From Stockholm to San Francisco: The Development of the Historical Study of External Migrations* (Uppsala: Annales Academiae Regiae Scientiarum Upsalensis, 1975), 20.

3. For an overview of this debate, see Eva Hamberg, *Studier i internationell migration* (Stockholm: Almqvist & Wiksell, 1976).

4. See Kristian Hvidt, "Informationsspredning og emigration med saerligt henblik på det atlantiske transportsystem," in *Emigrationen fra Norden indtil 1 verdenskrig*. Rapporter til det nordiske historikermøde i Kobenhavn 1971, 9–12 augusti (Copenhagen, 1971), 129–58; Gösta Lext, *Studier rörande svensk emigration till Nordamerika, 1850–1880: Registrering propaganda, agenter, transporter och resvägar* (Gothenburg, 1977).

5. See Nils Runeby, *Den nya världen och den gamla: Amerikabild och emigrationsuppfattning i Sverige, 1820–1860* (Uppsala: Almqvist & Wiksell, 1969). For a later period, Wendelius has documented the image of America in Swedish fictional prose, 1890–1914: Lars Wendelius, *Bilden av Amerika i svensk prosafiktion, 1890–1914* (Uppsala: Lundequistska Bokhandeln, 1982).

6. See Fred Nilsson, *Emigrationen från Stockholm till Nordamerika 1880–1893* (Stockholm: Stockholms Kommunalförvaltning, 1970).

7. See H. Arnold Barton, *Letters from the Promised Land: Swedes in America, 1840–1914* (Minneapolis, Minn.: University of Minnesota Press, 1975).

8. See Kristian Hvidt, *Flugten til Amerika eller Drivkraefter i masseudvandringen fra Danmark, 1868–1914* (Aarhus: Universitetsforlaget, 1971), 339–43.

9. On the reciprocal effects of Danish and immigrant socialist newspapers, see Jens Bjerre Danielsen, "Ethnic Identity, Nationalism and Scandinavism in the Scandinavian Immigrant Socialist Press in the U.S.," in *The Press of Labor Migrants in Europe and North America 1880s to 1930s*, ed. Christiane Harzig and Dirk Hoerder (Bremen: Labor Newspaper Preservation Project, 1985), 181–204, especially 195f.

10. See Semmingsen, *Norway to America*, 125–29.

11. See, for example, Bo Blomkvist, *International i miniatyr: Studier i skånsk arbetarrörelse före 1880 och dess internationella kontakter* (Lund: Gleerups, 1979).

12. See Lars-Göran Tedebrand, "The Image of America among Swedish Labor Migrants," in Harzig and Hoerder, eds., *The Press of Labor Migrants*, 547–560. Information on the Swedish press is primarily based on this article.

13. Ibid., 557.

14. See Nilsson, *Emigrationen från Stockholm*.

15. Tedebrand, "The Image of America," 558.

16. See Hvidt, *Flugten til Amerika*, 447ff.

17. Hvidt names a series of four such letters from Chicago in *Berlingske Tidende* (April 1872) and 89 from Danish immigrants in America in *Politiken* (April–June 1885), see ibid., 448.

18. See Gerd Callesen, "Mellem klassesolidaritet og politisk kritik: Social-Demokraten og mordene i Chicago," *Arbejderbevaegelsens Bibliotek og Arkivs Årsskrift 1985* (Copenhagen, 1986), 15–21.

19. Semmingsen, *Norway to America*, 125–29.

20. *Emigrationsutredningen: Bilaga VII*. Utvandrarnes egna uppgifter (Stockholm: Norstedt, 1908), 9.

21. See Claudius H. Riegler, "Labor Migration of Skilled Workers, Artisans and Technicians and Technology Transfer between Sweden and Germany before World War One," in *Labor Migration in the Atlantic Economies: The European and North American Working Class during the Period of Industrialization*, ed. Dirk Hoerder (Westport, Conn.: Greenwood, 1985), 163–88.

22. Skilled workers traditionally hold a strong position in the Swedish workplaces. Regarding their influence on the politics of the labor movement, see Mats Johansson, "Arbetararistokrati och reformism," *Arkiv för studier i arbetarrörelsens historia* 34–35 (1986): 64–77. The technicians were a rather heterogeneous group of specially trained white-collar workers who entered modern engineering positions. See Rolf Torstendahl, "Vom Berufsstolz zum Angestelltenbewußtsein in Schweden, 1900–1940," in *Angestellte im europäischen Vergleich: Die Herausbildung angestellter Mittelschichten seit dem späten 19. Jahrhundert*, ed. Jürgen Kocka (Göttingen: Vandenhoeck, 1981), 142–68.

23. Ingrid Jansson, *Svensk rapportering av amerikansk teknologi på världsutställningen i Philadelphia 1876* (Stockholm: The Royal Institute of Technology, Stockholm Papers in History and Philosophy of Technology, 1980), 7.

24. Ibid., 16.

25. Redogörelser för Verldsutställningen i Filadelfia, afgifna till

Kongl. Svenska utställningskomiten (Stockholm, 1877), vol. 3, 398, here cited by Jansson, *Svensk rapportering*, 17.

26. See Marie-Louise Bowallius, *Den förändrade synen på amerikansk teknologi: Rapportering och värdering av amerikansk teknologi i Teknisk Tidskrift, 1870–1893* (Stockholm: The Royal Institute of Technology, Stockholm Papers in History and Philosophy of Technology, 1980), 16.

27. Ibid., 18.

28. See ibid., 8, and, for the United States, Daniel Nelson, *Managers and Workers: Origins of the New Factory System in the United States, 1880–1920* (Madison, Wis.: University of Wisconsin Press, 1975); David F. Noble, *America by Design: Science, Technology, and the Rise of Corporate Capitalism* (New York: Knopf, 1977), especially chap. 1.

29. *Teknisk Tidskrift* 20 (1890): 36, here cited by Bowallius, *Den förändrade synen*, 24.

30. Bowallius, *Den förändrade synen*, 24.

31. See Maja Hagerman, *Berättelser från utlandet: Svenska tekniker och arbetare på studieresor i Europa och Amerika under 1800-talets senare hälft* (Stockholm: The Royal Institute of Technology, Stockholm Papers in History and Philosophy of Technology, 1981), 7.

32. Travel report Lagerman (no. 256), here cited by Hagerman, *Berättelser från utlandet*, 22.

33. See Alf Johansson, *Den effektiva arbetstiden: Verkstäderna och arbetsintensitetens problem 1900–1920* (Uppsala: Almqvist & Wiksell, 1977), 106f. See also Kjell Jonsson, "Taylorismen och svensk arbetarrörelse, 1913–1928," *Arkiv för studier i arbetarrörelsens historia* 19–20 (1981): 3–30.

34. See Lars Magnusson, "Patriarkalism och social kontroll," *Arkiv för studier i arbetarrörelsens historia* 33 (1986): 46–61, here 56f. Lars Magnusson, *Arbetet vid en svensk verkstad: Munktells 1900–1920* (Stockholm: Arkiv, 1986); and, for the U.S., David Montgomery, *Workers' Control in America: Studies in the History of Work, Technology, and Labor Struggles* (Cambridge: Cambridge University Press, 1979), 113 ff.

35. See Christian Berggren and Sven-Åke Kjellström, *Verkstadsrationalisering och arbetsorganisation* (Malmö: Liber Läromedel, 1981), 21; see also Alf Johansson, "Taylorismen och arbetarrörelsen," *Arkiv för studier i arbetarrörelsens historia* 34–35 (1986): 3–30, here 22ff.

36. See Hans de Geer, *Rationaliseringsrörelsen i Sverige: Effektivitetsidéer och socialt ansvar under mellankrigstiden* (Stockholm, 1978); Nils Runeby, "Americanism, Taylorism and Social Integration: Action Programmes for Swedish Industry at the Beginning of the Twentieth Century," *Scandinavian Journal of History* 3 (1978): 21–46; Berggren and Kjellström, *Verkstadsrationalisering*, 14ff.; Christian Berggren, "Slog taylorismen aldrig igenom i Sverige?" *Arkiv för studier i arbetarrörelsens historia* 19–20 (1981):

31–50; Johansson, "Taylorismen och arbetarrörelsen."

37. For detailed information about the context of this first official inquiry into the causes of emigration from Sweden, see Ann-Sofie Kälvemark, *Reaktionen mot utvandringen: Emigrationsfrågan i svensk debatt och politik, 1901–1904* (Uppsala: Almqvist & Wiksell, 1972), 142ff.

38. *Emigrationsutredningen,* vol. 7 (hereafter quoted as *EU*), 27.

39. Ibid., 28.

40. One hundred nineteen of these letters were published in 1908, on the whole unabridged, in the twenty-volume series of commission publications; see ibid., 131–263.

41. Ibid., 29.

42. See ibid., 8–26, 33–128.

43. Ibid., 25.

44. See Riegler, "Labor Migration Of Skilled Workers," 176ff.

45. *EU,* 17.

46. Regarding labor migration to Denmark, see Richard Willerslev, *Den glemte indvandring: Den svenske indvandring til Danmark, 1850–1914* (Copenhagen: Gyldendal, 1983); for Germany, see Claudius H. Riegler, *Emigration und Arbeitswanderung aus Schweden nach Norddeutschland, 1868–1914* (Neumünster: Wachholtz, 1985); for the modesty of agrarian European immigrants and their impact on class organization in America, see David Brody, "Labor," in *Harvard Encyclopedia Of American Ethnic Groups* (Cambridge, Mass.: Harvard University Press, 1980), 609–18.

47. For a comparison, see Daniel T. Rodgers, *The Work Ethic in Industrial America, 1850–1920* (Chicago: University of Chicago Press, 1978), and Arthur Montgomery, *Industrialismens genombrott i Sverige* (Stockholm: Almqvist & Wiksell, 1947), 315ff.

48. *EU,* 24; see ibid., 26.

49. See ibid., 13.

50. A comparison on the occupational health aspect is given by Steven Kelman, *Regulating America, Regulating Sweden: A Comparative Study of Occupational Safety and Health Policy* (Cambridge, Mass.: Massachusetts Institute of Technology Press, 1981).

51. For Sweden, see, e.g., Ulf Beijbom, *Swedes In Chicago: A Demographic and Social Study of the 1846–1880 Immigration* (Stockholm: Scandinavian University Books, 1971); for Norway, see Semmingsen, *Norway to America,* 123–25.

52. *EU,* nos. 9, 54, 16, 39, 46, 48.

53. Ibid., no. 117; see also no. 121.

54. See ibid., nos. 130, 131, 126, 139, 135, 137, 160.

55. Despite higher wages, these possibilities were small, for people had to pay travel costs. Shipyard workers at Kiel in the 1870s regularly sent

money to their families in Sweden. See Riegler, *Emigration und Arbeitswanderung,* 109.

56. See *EU,* no. 175.

57. E.g., some letters of this kind are in Barton, *Letters from the Promised Land,* 143ff.; no details about the total number of "America letters" of the Swedes in this period are known. Hvidt, *Flugten til Amerika,* 343, calculates that 64,200 Danish immigrants wrote 238,000 letters in 1880, and that in 1910, 181,600 Danish immigrants wrote 1,283,000 letters back home.

58. See *EU,* 153ff.

59. See ibid., nos. 174, 187, 177.

60. Ibid., nos. 227, 231, 234.

61. Ibid., no. 188.

62. On the impact and restrictions, see Claes Fredelius, *Det socialdemokratiska försöket: Om arbetarkontroll och företagsdemokrati i svensk arbetarrörelse* (Göteborg: Barrikaden, 1977); Gunnar Olofsson, "Den svenska socialdemokratin—en rörelse mellan klass och stat," *Arkiv för studier i arbetarrörelsens historia* 27–28 (1984): 84–97.

63. See note 36.

64. See Berggren and Kjellström, *Verkstadsrationalisering,* 21. It is a hitherto unanswered question whether this resistance can be related, for example, to the findings of Piore, Sabel, and Zeitlin on the historical necessity of the type of mass production that dominated world capitalism from the 1920s. See Michael J. Piore and Charles F. Sabel, *The Second Industrial Divide: Possibilities for Prosperity* (New York: Basic Books, 1984); Charles Sabel and Jonathan Zeitlin, "Historical Alternatives to Mass Production: Politics, Markets and Technology in Nineteenth-Century Industrialization," *Past and Present* 108 (1985): 133–76.

65. See Lennart Jörberg, *100 Jahre schwedischer Wirtschaft* (Cologne, 1971), 32. Wages of industrial workers in Sweden as against other countries developed as follows between 1905 and 1930 (Indices: Sweden = 100):

Year	France	Germany	Great Britain	United States	Sweden
1905	77	89	119	213	100
1930	49	66	85	166	100

66. See Riegler, "Emigrationsphasen, Akkumulation und Widerstandsstrategien," especially 50ff.

8

Hungarian Images of America: The Sirens' Song of Tinkling Dollars

Julianna Puskás

SINCE the 1970s, the history of mass overseas migration has received considerable attention from East-Central European historians, with a number of studies and monographs tracing the process of migration and its causes, and even dealing with the American experiences of the immigrants. What has been less discussed, however, is the image of America that prevailed in the delivering communities, and how this image was shaped. Did the experience of the migrants bear out the hopes and expectations they had about America? What changes did this image of the United States undergo over the years?

The failure to deal with these issues has been due not so much to a lack of interest in them but rather to the difficulties involved in collecting the evidence on which to base a satisfactory answer. This is the type of difficulty to which Ingrid Semmingsen alludes in her study "Emigration and the Image of America in Europe." One of the chief impediments to an analysis of this image is "that impulses from without are assimilated by and within the human mind; such assimilation cannot be catalogued and only rarely leaves traces on documents."[1] For the most part we must rely on indirect sources for even approximate answers when dealing with questions of this kind. A further methodological difficulty is how to assemble our bits and pieces of information into a mosaic that gives a picture that is typical and yet colorful enough to do justice to the uniqueness of individual experience.

Our ability to reconstruct the picture is complicated by the limited availability of sources concerning certain countries and ethnic groups. In Hungary, for instance, very few "letters from America" are extant today. Neither traditions nor the vicissitudes of the political climate of the past century have been conducive to the village population's preserving their personal letters and documents, and it was from the villages that the majority of the migrant masses hailed. What is available to us is the "letters from America" published in the contemporary press. A great many of these have been preserved in libraries, and they are vivid sources of information on the chief features of the contemporary image of America, although the editors were hardly impartial in their choice of the letters printed. The hopes and dreams the migrants cherished with regard to America and the bitterness of their awakening to reality were also salient themes of Hungarian-American literature and folklore, and will be among the sources we shall be relying on.

The problem of migration to America was a highly controversial issue in Hungarian politics at the time. Thus a great many documents are available on the subject, documents originating from local government bodies all the way up to the central government, as well as from a great variety of social organizations. Analyzing these documents for the reasons for emigration, one gets information not only on the image of America that putatively served to lure migrants overseas but also on the propaganda designed to discourage them from making the move. Thus, in reconstructing the image of America in Hungary, we can rely on official reports, the minutes of parliamentary debates, the records of congresses held on the problem of emigration, and contemporary press reports, as well as on the propaganda publications, but always, of course, with due reservation. Last, but by no means least, we can turn to oral testimony in our attempt to reconstruct the contemporary image of America. The fact that mass migration took place in the not-so-distant past has enabled us to interview migrants and their direct descendants in the past twenty years both in their communities of origin and in the communities where they finally settled.[2] Although time may have tarnished the value of such information, its usefulness is unquestionable when collated with the other sources.

In this study, then, I shall attempt to answer the questions I have posed on the basis of the comparative analysis of all of the above sources.

The Antecedents

The image of America that developed in Hungary in the last decades of the nineteenth century had roots dating back to the 1830s.[3] It was an upper- and middle-class picture, however, one that had little to do with the social groups that were to emigrate in masses some fifty years later, for it was the liberal nobility of the reform generation, anxious to set the country on the road to bourgeois transformation, that turned avidly to the American example of independence and subsequent unparalleled economic prosperity and social progress. These liberals saw the United States as the model to follow in their own attempts to achieve national sovereignty. Hungarian visitors to America had no end of praise for the burgeoning nation in their published diaries and travelogues. The overall positive picture was but little marred by the disapproval always expressed of the institution of slavery, which was accepted as the shortcoming of American democracy. Those who went to America specifically to study some branch of agriculture or industry returned with reports that were no less glowing. The positive image of America spread from a small elite through various progressive professionals, and, by the 1870s, regular press reports were beginning to make it a basic attitude of the literate public.

It was this image of America as "the land of liberty" that impelled Hungarian political émigrés to seek refuge there after the defeat of the 1848 Revolution and War of Independence against Austrian absolutism. In the two or three decades following, however, it was but seldom that a Hungarian immigrant turned up in America: adventurers in search of a fortune, some déclassé elements trying to regain their middle-class lifestyle, a few intellectuals, and yet fewer merchants and tradesmen. From the 1880s on, however, it was a radically new class of people—rural artisans and peasants—who set out to discover America for themselves. It was the emigration of this group that marks the beginning of mass emigration.

The Social and Economic Background of Migration

Hungary started on the road to bourgeois transformation only in the second half of the nineteenth century.[4] Society there was predominantly agrarian, and characterized by appalling inequalities in land distribution: a few thousand families owned about 50 percent of all the land. Compared to other European countries, the percentage of the dwarf-holders and of the landless within the peasant population was extraordinarily high.

The struggle for bourgeois transformation was part of the

struggle for independence from the Habsburgs in 1849. Serfdom was abolished, but the War of Independence was defeated. Then, in 1867, after two decades of absolute rule, the Habsburgs came to a compromise with the Hungarian ruling classes. It was in this period of political consolidation that industrialization really started in Hungary.

Those employed in the pre-industrial sectors of the economy—the peasants, rural craftsmen, and the miners—experienced the process of modernization as the gradual deterioration of their lifestyle. The demographic boom accelerated the rate at which the smallholdings had to be divided up into ever more minuscule plots of land, and although the industrial sector was expanding, it was hardly diversified enough to absorb the growing surplus agricultural population. Young people were having more and more difficulty finding jobs. Land was mortgaged in the attempt to pay local and state taxes, and, as the creditors closed in, the impoverished peasantry often had no choice but to sell all they owned. Competition from industry and the end of the guild system put artisans in dire straits. And the development of the transportation network cut deeply into the earning opportunities of those who had made their living in the hauling trade.

The process of modernization had other consequences as well. As the changes in the economic structure brought attitudinal changes in their wake, traditional social ties started to disintegrate. A more mobile rural population inevitably got to know quite a bit about the world outside the village boundaries. The results of compulsory primary education were also beginning to be felt at this time: literacy broadened horizons and raised new expectations.

Up to the mid-1850s, the rural migrants' chief routes were within Hungary or were directed toward the neighboring countries. From then on, however, most of them headed for the United States.

In Hungary it was the hilly northern countries that were the first regions of migration to America, with the pioneers coming mostly from among the Slovaks and Germans of the area. It was a region where the population had never been able to rely just on farming and animal husbandry for its livelihood, and there was a tradition of engaging in auxiliary occupations as well. Some worked in cottage industries, others were itinerant traders, still others worked on the construction of roads or in the mines. A great many of them undertook seasonal agricultural work and migrated to the more fertile central plains, particularly at harvest time. This tradition of great mobility served to make people more open to the idea of emigration.

The first reports sent to the authorities on the rural population's migration to American came from the districts immediately adjoining Austrian Galicia. It was mostly the Hungarian miners working in the salt mines of Galicia who brought back word of the work opportunities to be had in the United States. They told of how America was looking for workers, and that anyone who went to work in a mine or factory there would make wages he could not imagine, in his wildest dreams, making in any part of the Habsburg Monarchy. It was money enough not only to support himself and his family, but also to buy a house and land on his return. Such and similar stories were spread by the agents of the shipping companies as well, who, by the 1890s, were practically all over Galicia. Their "enticement," however, stood a chance of success only if they were supported by the testimony of trustworthy acquaintances of the prospective migrants. Knowing this, the shipping companies were eager to enlist as their agents men who had been to America.

Creating a Negative Image of America

Hungary's ruling political and economic elite, primarily the landowners, reacted strongly to the news of migration to America from its very inception, rightly feeling that migration threatened to deplete their pool of cheap agricultural labor. From the 1880s on, we find a number of calls being made for laws to restrict the would-be emigrants. The various Hungarian governments, however, all of which professed liberal principles, could not call into question the freedom of the individual to emigrate. The concession they made to the landowner lobby was to pass laws to control the process of emigration, and to encourage anti-emigration propaganda.

"Heartless agents are luring the gullible people to America with false promises," we read in the reports of county authorities time and again.[5] Thus it was primarily the activities of the emigration agents that were brought under control. The 1881 bill "On Emigration Agents" was introduced by the minister of the interior as follows: "Having studied the matter of emigration I have become convinced that the decision to emigrate is not one brought on by reflection of the individuals themselves, but the result of the persuasion and heartless promises of various agents and profiteers."[6] The law passed permitted only officially licensed agents to operate; those operating without a permit were liable to prosecution. For quite some time the authorities issued absolutely no permits of this sort; for all that, the wave of emigration, far from abating, only grew.

Using the press as a propaganda organ to discourage emigration was tried as a more promising tack. From the early 1880s on, papers carried sensational stories of the bitter experiences of Hungarian migrants working in the foundries and mines of America. The titles themselves were designed to intimidate: "Emigrant family sick of living,"[7] "Hapless emigrants,"[8] "Flight back home,"[9] and so on. Although the *Népszava* (The People's Voice), the paper of the Hungarian Social Democrats, refused to go in for anti-emigration propaganda of this sort, it, too, gave a none-too-optimistic picture of the situation in which Hungarian emigrants often found themselves, "making their daily wages of $1.20 working 12.5 hours a day."[10]

But the press defamation campaign had little success. For one thing, its effectiveness was undermined—especially in the migration regions—by a number of county papers carrying stories (primarily letters) of success in America, as well as hardship. But the main reason for the failure of the press campaign was that the rural population most affected seldom got hold of a newspaper, let alone a national paper. Villagers were simply not in the habit of reading papers. The most they were likely to read besides the Bible and little booklets of the lives of the saints were almanacs, or penny dreadfuls recounting some historical event or legend. It was for this reason that a member of Parliament suggested to Parliament that

> the people be given popular booklets so they might get to know of the lives and lifestyles of those who have emigrated to America. [Let them find out that] the amount of energy that here, in our dear homeland, is sufficient to make a living for a lifetime is soon exhausted in America; and even if the emigrant should return to the land of his fathers, he will do so a physical wreck with his energies depleted, and will no longer be able to earn his bread here again.[11]

As a result, a number of such cheap, short booklets appeared in the first decade of the twentieth century, "true stories" telling of "experiences in America." By way of illustration, the following is a summary of one entitled "The Happy Land as It Really Is."[12]

The hero is Michael, a young peasant lad; his letter to his friend tells his distressing tale. On returning to his village after doing his stint of military service, he was met by poverty and the news that his sweetheart had been forced by her parents to wed "a well-off man." In his sorrow, he "longed for that distant land across the seas, where there is no misery and no poverty." He had heard emigration agents speaking of it: "They promised an El Dorado far across the ocean. You'll never be poor again, for the boat takes you to a country where poverty is unknown."

Michael's tribulations started already in Hamburg. The agent, who had promised him wonderful wages in America, informed him that the price they had agreed on would not get him that far. He made him sign a contract to work on the boat for the duration of the passage. The story of the crossing is calculated to inspire dread. There is a storm: "We were in constant fear of our lives. There's nothing like a stormy ocean to teach a man to pray." It was only when he finally reached shore that Michael discovered that the contract which the agent had had him sign obliged him not only to work on the boat, but to work six months on a farm in Dakota. "I've been deceived, frightfully deceived. Müller, who misled us all, is a heartless villain, who lives like a king on bamboozling unsuspecting simpletons to come to this strange land. He lures you to America, saying that here, everyone can get rich. It was only when I set foot on this land of liberty that I realized that I was a slave"—so wrote Michael from Dakota to his friend, and set out post-haste for home.

From New York he wrote: "There is no real air here; it sits heavy upon a Hungarian used to the open air of the plains. I set out for the coast toward America's largest city with the purpose of setting sail with the first available boat for the homeland I so faithlessly deserted." "What a lot of stupid stories they tell folks at home of how here one can get rich without hardship or toil. I've never seen the least sign of it. If anything, I've seen that everyone works much harder for their daily bread."

In New York, Michael met some Slovak compatriots, "who were seeking The Happy Land just like I was. What an air of misery, of poverty they had!" He invited the "hungry troupe" to eat at a saloon, and was robbed while there. The stamp for the letter he earned helping the street-sweeper out for half an hour. The last station of Michael's calvary was a charity hospital. "It was charity that took me off the pavement where I had collapsed." After recovering in the hospital, he wrote to the Hungarian consul to arrange for his trip home.

The construction of the stories and the morals to be drawn from them were pretty well the same in the case of all the popular pamphlets: the naive and gullible poor were lured to America "by perfidious agents making false promises and painting pictures of an

El Dorado," who, after taking their last pennies, left them to fend for themselves. Then came the history of their miseries and exploitation in the New World (they were the "white slaves"). In the end, they either perished, or there appeared the Hungarian consul as the last resort, who helped the disillusioned and contrite fortune-seekers to return to their homeland.

Preachers and teachers, too, were called upon to help spread the negative image of America, as, for instance, we find in this address to Parliament by Kálmán Török:

> It is particularly priests and teachers who have the task—since the poor industrial and agricultural workers are lured by the sirens' song of tinkling dollars—to call the attention of the [potential] migrants also to that terrible, heart-rending death-rattle that breaks forth from the lead mines of America.[13]

"Indeed, this is an issue that we must take up in the pulpits," added another member of Parliament, Bishop János Hock, "for that is the priest's best opportunity to enlighten his flock as to the uncertain future and ceaseless toil that await them in America today, where there is economic recession, and where, as here, they will be able to make only a subsistence living."[14]

For all that, not all priests, teachers, and professionals in the villages came to propagate a negative image of America. On the contrary: some of them operated as emigration agents, and thus had a financial interest in speaking no evil of America. Others were reluctant to make anti-America propaganda precisely because they had first-hand knowledge of the hardships the potential emigrants were faced with at home, and because they had seen the salutary effects that the money sent from America was already beginning to have in the villages.

Even among the contemporary landowners, not everyone supported the campaign "to paint so dark a picture" of the fortunes of the emigrants. As Count József Majláth noted, "the fact that there are many people who do indeed improve their lot cannot be ignored, and this being so, we can hardly hope to impede emigration with paltry methods."[15]

Negative propaganda of the type described above did not, in fact, keep people from migrating to America. Statistics show that one-and-a-half million people coming from Hungary landed in the United States in the four decades preceding World War I. The majority of them were young men, but, after 1907, more and more of the arrivals were women. By 1913, women predominated among the immigrants hailing from Hungary.[16]

The Positive Image of America

There were regions of Hungary from which conspicuously large numbers of migrants sailed overseas, and then there were others from which hardly anyone left. These very great regional differences in the intensity of migration indicate that the image that a village population cherished of America was essentially not influenced by the views of the other social strata. It was not only that the rural population got their information from other sources, it was also information with a very different message. The rural image of America came from relatives, personal acquaintances, and friends, and was confirmed by chain-migrations starting in communities located along the country's northern borders. It was from here that the flow of information spread south, carried by Slovaks and Germans to the neighboring Magyars and other ethnic groups. The source and direction of the information flow give us a better pictures of the centers of migration and of its spread than could any map based on purely economic parameters.[17]

The greatest attraction the rural population saw in America was the money that could be earned in American industry, the dollars that could be sent or brought home. "With a very few exceptions, the emigrants left determined to return home after having accumulated certain savings."[18]

The village population of most regions of Hungary at the end of the nineteenth century, and especially the peasantry, could not very well reconcile themselves to the idea of ameliorating their lot through conclusively breaking with the community, and even less could they imagine settling in another country. The hopes and plans they had in setting out at all centered on their community of origin: it was life there that they wanted to improve with the money earned somewhere else. Migration to America was considered to be a temporary measure, much like going off to find work in other regions within or just outside Hungary. The only difference they saw was that America was farther off, and they would have to count on a longer stay.

The temporary character of the migration to America was repeatedly emphasized by all the counties affected by the exodus.[19] Based on such reports, as late as 1913, the minister of the interior noted in a circular: "The majority of our emigrants are motivated not by the desire to settle permanently in some foreign land, but by the prospect of higher wages, and the greater possibility of striking it rich."[20] That there was a great deal of truth in this is borne out by the statistics: the ratio of those who returned to their original communities remained high throughout the entire migration period.[21]

The salient feature of the image of America was therefore that the earning opportunities there were much superior to what they were anywhere else. Nothing served to confirm this impression of the stay-at-homes as conclusively as the money sent back.

"There are known cases of substantial sums of money—and of purchases made using them—circulating among the people";[22] and "the emigrants send money to their relatives, and urge them to join them overseas in jobs they have secured for them beforehand."[23] Land cleared of debts, "new houses with tiled roofs, . . . the money regularly arriving from America and [the] savings accounts are all mute but eloquent emigration agents, ones that no earthly power can eradicate."[24] The entire face of the village was altered by the money sent home: the new "American houses" were the largest and most modern in the community.[25] In Mezőkövesd village *Pénzgödör* (Money Pit) and *Dollárhegy* (Dollar Mountain) are the names of the areas where the re-migrants from America bought fields and built houses.[26]

In the rural world of want, where a day-laborer's wages—if he was lucky enough to get hired—were hardly enough for his family to subsist on, the wages paid in America appeared nothing short of fabulous. The dollars sent home, as we read in the minutes of a meeting of the Szabolcs County Council, "created a blind faith in America's being an El Dorado easily accessible to all, a place where everyone can achieve not only a comfortable livelihood but also, without too much difficulty, riches with the work of one's own hands."[27] Many of the official contemporary documents and reports opposing emigration blamed the popular picture of America, that of "getting rich quickly," and castigated the putative belief "that America was an El Dorado."

Realities of the American Experience

We can get a more realistic picture of what it was that was really expected of America from those directly involved, the migrants themselves, "Americans'" who either returned to their native communities or settled in the United States for good. Let us, then, listen for a moment to what they had to say:

"A number of people had already emigrated from Rozvágy," recalled József B.

> Some of them had already returned, others were still in America. All of them agreed that though in America they didn't give you dollars as a present, anyone who worked hard and diligently, and didn't squander his earnings, was able to set aside enough in a couple of years to make an independent existence for himself here back home.[28]

István O., from Almáska, gave the following reason for emigrating: "We were expecting a baby, and decided we could not base the family's future on two *holds* [1.5 acres] of land. . . . I would have to go to America to earn enough money to buy the necessary land."[29] Mrs. János M. recalled her impressions from her very earliest years: "Even as a little girl I often heard the grown-ups speaking of life abroad in the evenings." What she gathered was that "there, whoever is willing to work enjoys respect, and if someone lives economically, he is able to set aside quite a fine sum in just a few years."[30]

America was a place where there was employment; although the work was hard, the wages were high, and the savings that could be set aside would guarantee the returnee an independent peasant livelihood. These were the hopes that had moved all those interviewed who had been to America, and clearly, they were no exception.

Those who ended up staying remembered in much the same terms what their motivation had been. As they told it, "We didn't come to America to stay here, but to make a few dollars; we'd buy a few *holds* of land, and be able to live better at home."[31] The first impression almost all of them had of America was one of disappointment; many of them wouldn't have minded turning back. "The women didn't like it here; no one did. But how could they have left? they had no means of leaving."[32]

The Hungarian-American songs tell of the disappointment, of the lost illusions:

> Of America I heard such fine things said
> That I set out to make my fortune and my bread.
> Nothing good, only bad luck came my way
> Surely I'm the most unhappy stray.
>
> . . . .
>
> Here's America, better yet, misery-ca
> To think that I will never get home again!

None here will encourage the poor wanderer
No pity for me, only sorrow, only pain.

. . .

Hey America! with hills and valleys to the sea,
If Hungarians' curses worked, damned you'd be!
Be damned forever, doomed for all eternity!
To leave it all behind me, how happy I would be.[33]

There were those who finally settled in America because they couldn't save enough, and were ashamed to return to their communities of origin. Others made the trip home and back a number of times before making up their minds to stay for good. As the immigrants got better acquainted with life in America, the social and political shortcomings of life in the old country became increasingly evident. "It was a very difficult start for me here," wrote one of them,

it was so difficult that I didn't plan to stay even as much as a year. But in time I got used to it; and when I went back to the old country, three times in all, I couldn't help seeing the conditions of the workers with different eyes, and I couldn't have stayed there for anything. And so I took my family and came back here again. If only I'd done it twenty years earlier.[34]

We find a fine collection of reasons for staying away from Hungary in the hundreds of letters sent in reply to a question put by the Hungarian-American paper *Szabadság* (Liberty) in January 1909.[35] The letters are most informative of the conditions they had left behind them. "We came not to amass a fortune, but to make a decent living,"[36] was a sentiment echoed time and time again in as many words:

For if we had been able to make a living in Hungary with diligent work, as indeed we can here, I hardly think so many poor people would have taken the wayfarer's staff in hand and headed for America. No one lured us here; it was want that drove us.[37]

The Hungarian immigrants' picture of America grew more diversified with the process of their acculturation: "Even at home the eyes of the village people are opening up; and here in America, one's eyes are not only open, but twinkle brightly on comparing conditions at home with the way things are here."[38] The fact that people treated each other in a more equal manner than in the old country was also not lost on the Hungarian immigrants: "Everyone here is simply 'Mister'; there are no titles of the kind there are in Hungary"; "There's no looking down on one another; everyone's equal; people don't take their hats off either to one another, or to the authorities."[39] It was attractive features of this sort that confirmed them in their decision to stay for good:

> Why we changed homelands can be told here on these pages, for we are in America, where though we cannot say everything, we have much more right and freedom to speak up than at home: the rewards for diligent work are at least a decent living. What will always be a source of sorrow, is that [in Hungary] this is still not to be had, for if it were, then I myself would still be there.[40]

Illusions in the Images of America

It can hardly be said that the migrants themselves painted a realistic picture of their American experiences to friends and relatives left behind in the old country. A number of complex factors operated to make their accounts—whether in the form of letters, or of personal spoken reports on trips home—a mixture of truth and wishful thinking.

Those who stayed at home were, for obvious reasons, interested mainly in the amount of money that could be earned, and in the job opportunities available. Both questions and answers centered on these two issues. Those contemplating emigration, especially in the early phases of the emigration wave, had ears for little else, and so were largely unaware of the numerous negative aspects of immigrant life. Or, if they did hear stories of this nature, they could attach no meaning to them within the old environment.

Nor were the letters sent home calculated to dispel illusions. For one thing, those who were successful in their new lives were more inclined to write home than those who encountered only failure.[41] This was one reason why the American experience looked brighter to those watching it from back home. Another fact to keep in mind is that the social groups most involved in mass migration were not in the habit of communicating in the form of letters. Although only a minority were illiterate, even those who could write had no practice in writing about their experiences. The letters sent home were often written by proxy—for instance, by saloon-keepers, shipping-line agents, justices of the peace, or parish priests, all people with a personal interest in the arrival of more and more migrants, and thus people inclined to enhance the picture of America that was sent to the folks at home.

The desire to give an honest, unembellished report was also at times frustrated by the expectations of the delivering community itself, for before the migrant left home, plans had been laid; his work had been cut out for him, so to speak, and those waiting at home wanted to hear how far he had got toward realizing these plans. In this way, those in America were forced into a kind of role-playing: to keep up the positive "American" image, they often preferred to say nothing of the often intolerable hardships of their day-to-day lives. Some were motivated to engage in this kind of deception by default, for fear that they would discourage their much-missed family members from joining them, particularly their wives. This is how A. Margit summed up this process of deception and disillusionment:

> My dear wife: Come to America; here you'll be a lady; you needn't work here, there's everything here. And then by the time the poor little greenhorn woman got there, all that everything had evaporated, and her husband had nothing but a great pile of debts. . . . How gladly she would have worked, had she been able to get a job; but there's no place she can work, for she can't even speak the language.[42]

That painting "life in America" in rosy colors was pretty much the order of the day is reflected also by the fact that making fun of this propensity is one of the major themes of Hungarian-American humor and satire.[43]:

> If he writes home
> What does he tell his wife?
> Boastful and self-satisfied
> He tells of his good life.
>
> If he picks turnips for a farmer
> He'll write he's bought a farm
> Hundred and sixty acres' yield
> Will soon fill his barn.
>
> Or if he is a laborer
> He's sure to be in foreman's rank

> He gives his orders . . . in the bar
> But neither at work nor at the bank.[44]

There is absolutely no question that the photographs sent from America confirmed the illusion of its being the land of boundless opportunity. The pictures show elegant gentlemen dressed in dark suits and leather shoes, many of them behatted and immodestly sporting what appear to be gold watch chains; the women and girls are in their Sunday best, with handbags to match. The people left behind in the village gazed at these photos with wonder and incredulity:

> The wife stared and stared at the picture, and then ran to me, asking if that really were her husband. She even asked him in a letter "Is that really you, Istók? For you look like a veritable gentleman; even your cheeks are as round as if you ate meat every day and had a beer after."[45]

The pictures were indicative of more than just prosperity to those looking at them in the village back home. In Hungary at the time, rural people still wore mostly homespun and home-sewn clothes. The closed social structure was reflected in the clothing typical of the various social classes. The pictures showed the migrants in clothes that only "gentlefolk" wore in Hungary: "Even the constable has no clothes like that!"[46] The migrants sending the photos were very well aware of the impression they would make. "If only the priest at home could see me, or the schoolteacher, when I get all dressed up, he'd sooner doff his hat to me than I to him,"[47] was the way one of them put it. But those with an interest in the growth of immigration were no less clear about the impact of such photos, and so urged the migrants to have themselves photographed in all their American finery and to send the pictures home.

Any letter from abroad was bound to cause a great sensation throughout the entire village,[48] to say nothing of a visit by someone "from America." The most conspicuous effect of migration and return to the community was the change in the migrants' personalities.[49] The villagers assembled to admire them and listen to them. Gone was the terseness of the written communications; there was plenty of time to tell a long story in all its details, and the listeners' attention never flagged. The importance of the returnees in forming the image of America was underlined by the fact that face-to-face verbal communication was the most credited source of information in the closed world of the peasantry. The degree of credence a story was given depended a great deal on whether it was first-hand experience that was being recounted or just something the person had heard. The personal experiences of mutual acquaintances were later passed on at occasions such as spinning together on a winter's night, corn-husking, or visits with friends, neighbors and family. The fact that the migrant was the center of attention inspired quite a few of the returnees to color and exaggerate their accounts of what they had seen and experienced:

> If a man like that comes home dressed like a gentleman and speaking English, in his hard black hat, he is a more marvelous and more effective advocate of America than any agent. When he speaks, especially when he enjoys the attention he is getting and wants to make the best of it, he will exaggerate to those standing about him in awe. They will believe everything he says, and I have almost always found that following the return to the village by one or two emigrants who have made good, the incidence of migration from that particular village always grows considerably.[50]

Thus the migrants, with their essentially antithetical experiences, contributed willy-nilly to the development and conservation of an idealized image of America. When writing home, they were always at pains to show the positive side of the picture, and reinforced it with the photographs and money sent. The difficulties they faced in adjusting to a radically different working-class life, their loneliness in an inhospitable environment, their longing for home were, at most, given expression to others in America. For those who stayed in the old country, the implicit contradictions of the experience of emigration never became really evident.

The determination of the donor community to cling to a positive image—as the only hope of escape from a bad situation—was a further filter on the incoming information. The donor community simply did not tolerate the tarnishing of its America-image with information on what it was like to be an outcast "Hunky," nor with taking real notice of the relatively large number of tragic accidents.

> The example of the unfortunates who'd perished abroad had no real impact. They spoke about them for a while, but then soon forgot them. Most people felt that they'd been misfits from the start. Those who came home empty-handed likewise went un-

noticed, for they'd been no better off before; that was why they'd left.[51]

It was an image of America where good luck, success, and happiness were the just rewards of hard, diligent work. It was a picture that made no concession to individuals; if someone failed, was unhappy, or suffered an accident on the job, his own personal shortcomings were to blame. It was an image of America that— experience notwithstanding—permitted migrants to set out optimistically for the great unknown.

With the passage of time, the image of America not only became more diversified, but gave rise to yet more powerful illusions. The few negative elements that the experience of mass migration could not quite cover up were all forgotten. It was the myth of a land of boundless opportunity that endured in the delivering communities, and continued to live on even when the chance of migration was taken away from them for good.

Notes

1. Ingrid Semmingsen, "Emigration and the Image of America in Europe," in *Immigration and American History,* ed. Henry Steele Commager (Minnesota, Minn.: University of Minnesota Press, 1961), 30.

2. See Julianna Puskás, "Magyarok az Egyesült Allamokban és Kanadában—interjúk" (Hungarians in the United States and Canada—interviews); on tape in the archives of MTA (Hungarian Academy of Sciences), Institute of History, Budapest.

3. See Károly Vörös, "The Image of America in Hungarian Mass Culture in the Nineteenth Century," in *Etudes Historiques Hongroises,* ed. F. Glatz (Budapest: Akadémia Kiadó, 1985), 647–66.

4. See Julianna Puskás, *From Hungary to the USA (1880–1914)* (Budapest: Akadémia Kiadó, 1982), 44–64.

5. Report from the subprefect of Szepes county to the minister of the interior, 6 Nov 1914, in František Bielik and Elo Rákos, *Slovenské vyst'ahovalectvo: Vydavatel'stvo Slovenské* (Bratislava: Akadémia Vied, 1969).

6. Preamble to the bill "On Emigration Agents" (1881), OKI (Parliament, Documents of the House of Representatives) vol. 24, 242.

7. *Pesti Napló* (hereafter quoted as *PN*) (Budapest), 5 Aug 1880.

8. *PN*, 29 Nov 1895.

9. *PN*, 28 Mar 1901.

10. *Népszava* (Budapest), 1 Sept 1903. The Social Democrats took the

following stand: "We're no friends of emigration, although we feel that the miserable economic and social conditions are enough to account for it." *Népszava*, 4 Sept 1900.

11. From the speech of Kálmán Török, MP, OKN (Parliament, Minutes of the House of Representatives), vol. 21, 71, 73—13 Nov 1908.

12. László Vetési, *Boldogország a maga valóságában: Egy magyar munkás amerikai levelei* (The Happy Land as It Really Is: A Hungarian Worker's Letter from America) (Budapest: Lampel, 1902).

13. Speech of Kálmán Török, MP, OKN, vol. 21, 13 Nov 1908.

14. From the speech of János Hock, MP, OKN, vol. 21, 13 Nov 1908.

15. Count J. Majláth, "A kivándorlásról" (On Emigration), in *Szabadság 10. éves jubileumi sz.* (Tenth Anniversary Issue of *Szabadság*), ed. T. Koháni (Cleveland, 1901).

16. See Table 7, in Puskás, *From Hungary*, 40.

17. See ibid., 59.

18. Report from Szepes County's subprefect to the minister of the interior, 8 Sept 1882, OL, BM, III-17-8361/1883 (National Archives, Ministry of the Interior, Document, Budapest).

19. See also reports from Abauj-Torna, Borsod, Bereg, Gömör, Szepes, Szatmár, Zemplén, and other counties' subprefects to the prime minister. OL-K 16 (National Archives: The Centrally Registered and Filed Documents of the Prime Minister's Office, Budapest), 1905-XVI-1450.

20. Decree no. 205578/1913 sz. of the minister of the interior in Bielik and Rákos, *Slovenské vyst'akovalectvo*, 349.

21. Of the 585,344 migrants who went to the Untied States between 1908 and 1913, 221,596 returned. See Puskás, *From Hungary*, 27.

22. Report from the prefect of Borsod County to the prime minister, 29 Feb 1904. OL-K-26.

23. Report from the subprefect of Trencsén County to the prime minister, ibid.

24. József I. Gerényi, *Az amerikai kivándorlás oka és hatása* (The Causes and Effects of Emigration to America) (Bártfa: Salgó, 1913), 125.

25. Zoltán Fejós, *A kivándorlás Amerikába a Zemplén középsö vidékeiről* (Emigration to the USA from the Central Part of the Zemplén Mountains (Miskolc: A Herman Ottó Muzeum évkönyve, 1980), 316–17. Even today, houses with tin roofs are called "American" houses in many places, although the original dwellers are long gone.

26. See. B. Gunda, "America in Hungarian Folk Tradition," *Journal of American Folklore* 83 (1970): 415.

27. Minutes of the Szabolcs County Assembly, 7 Nov 1901.

28. Puskás, "Magyarok az Egyesült Allamokban és Kanadában," interview with József B., 1968.

29. Ibid., interview with István O., 1968.
30. Ibid., interview with Mrs. János M., 1968.
31. Ibid., interview with Piroska P., New Brunswick, N.J., 1983.
32. Ibid., interview with G. Kovács, Detroit, 1983.
33. "Amerikás dalok" (American Songs) in *Magyar Népdalok*, vol. 2, ed. Gyula Ortutay (Budapest: Szépirodalmi Könyvkiadó, 1970), 635–47.
34. Letter from András Molitorisz, Allegheny, Pa., in *Szabadság* (hereafter cited as *Sza*), 29 Jan 1909.
35. In January 1909, *Szabadság* published in Cleveland as the Hungarian-language paper in America with the largest circulation, asked its readers for letters telling why they came to America. One thousand nine hundred letters were sent in by way of reply. Most of these were published by the paper in its Sunday issues.
36. Letter from Mrs. Farkas, in *Sza*, 22 Jan 1909.
37. Letter from A. Margit, in *Sza*, 15 Jan 1909.
38. Letter from Mrs. L. Joós, Wilkes Barre, Pa., in *Sza*, 5 Feb 1909.
39. Quoted in Fejös, *A kivándorlás Amerikába*, 322.
40. Letter from J. Neuman, Passaic, N.J., in *Sza*, 5 Feb 1909.
41. A summary of my research in the village of Szamosszeg.
42. Letter from A. Margit, in *Sza*, 5 Feb 1909.
43. The richest source in this respect is the comic paper *Dongó* (Gadfly), edited by György Kemény, which appeared from 1903 to 1933, first in Cleveland, and later in Detroit.
44. István Jovicza, "Amerika," quoted in G. Hoffmann, *Csonka Munkásosztály az Amerikai Magyarság* (The Hungarian Americans Are a Truncated Working Class) (Budapest: Pesti Könyvnyomda Rt., 1911), 230–31.
45. Letter from Mrs. L. Joós, in *Sza*, 5 Feb. 1909.
46. Letter from Mrs. Ferenc Tóth, New Philadelphia, Pa., in *Sza*, 22 Jan 1909.
47. Quoted in Fejós, *A kivándorlás Amerikába*, 304.
48. See *Eperjesi Lapok* (Esperjes Papers) (1882), quoted in István Rácz, "A parasztok elvándorlása a faluról" (The migration of peasants from the villages), in *A parasztság története Magyarországon a kapitalizmus korában, 1848–1914* (The History of the Peasantry in Hungary under Capitalism, 1848–1914), 2 vols., ed. I Szabó (Budapest: Akadémiai Kiadó, 1965), 463.
49. See U.S. Senate, Immigration Commission, *Emigration Conditions in Europe, Report*, vol. 4 (Washington, D.C.: Government Printing Office, 1911), 388.
50. *Sza, 10 jub. sz.* (*Szabadság* Tenth Anniversary Issue), 38.
51. Ibid.

9

Images of America among Slovene and Other Yugoslav Migrants

Matjaž Klemenčič

PRIOR to World War I, the territory of post–World War II Yugoslavia, where the majority of the Yugoslav peoples lived, was divided among the Austro-Hungarian Monarchy to the north and west, and Serbia, Montenegro, and, to some extent, the Ottoman Empire to the south.[1] Their different levels of economic development explain the varying possibilities for, and the intensity of, migration.[2] According to U.S. records, between the turn of the century and World War I, about 460,000 Slovenes and Croats, 140,000 Bulgarians, Serbs, and Montenegrins, and 50,000 Dalmatians, Bosnians, and Herzegovinians emigrated from the Yugoslav territory. No statistics were available concerning the ethnic affiliation of the migrants to the United States until the census of 1910, when about 210,000 Slovenes, 140,000 Croats, and 52,000 Serbs (first- and second-generation) were registered as living in the United States.[3] These data reveal that the greatest proportion of Yugoslav migrants came from the economically more developed areas in the north, Slovenia and Croatia.

Who Came to America?

The Yugoslav-born geographer Branko Mita Čolaković has emphasized the importance of the socioeconomic and cultural background of the people in specific regions, and their awareness of the possibility of emigration, as two of the factors important to an understanding of emigration. A third reason facilitating emigration was the close vicinity of the ports of Trieste (Trst) and Fiume (Rijeka), and the early development of a railroad network that made other European ports accessible.[4]

Although the Slovenian and Croatian territories were economically far ahead of the Yugoslav areas further south, the Habsburg Monarchy's policy of hindering the economic development of Slovenian and Croatian territories and of independent Serbia was also a major cause of emigration. A statistical analysis of the Slovene Styria (Štajerska) and Carinthia (Koroška) regions confirms that their economic development was deliberately neglected, causing the emigration of much of the Slovene population that was not qualified for those industrial jobs available; at the same time, German-speaking Austrians were settling in the depopulated regions.[5] Slovenia's population of 1,140,000 in 1880 increased by almost 10 percent up to 1900; during the first decade of the twentieth century, however, the growth rate dropped to little more than 1 percent. Between 1880 and 1914 the balance of migration for the Yugoslav ethnic territories was negative: the Slovenian-settled territories suffered a net loss of 147,000, Croatia-Slavonia of 176,000 people.[6] Only in those areas where industrialization had improved job opportunities (for example, in Upper Carniola) were the rates of emigration low.

The migrants' age structure, divided in U.S. statistics into three groups, reveals that the U.S. labor market received mainly young males. Among the Croatian and Slovene migrants, 91.1 percent were between 14 and 45 years of age, only 5.5 percent were less than 14 years old, and 3.4 percent were older than 45 years. Only 18.4 percent of the migrants were women. Accordingly, the age structure of the Old World Slovene ethnic territories shows a disproportionately low number of men aged between 14 and 45.[7] We may therefore hypothesize that expectations and information about America resulted in a screening process. The United States, in the mind of the prospective migrants, was a nation where the very young, the aged, and women had little chance of supporting themselves. America was not seen as a haven for the poor, tired, and oppressed peoples of Europe, as Emma Lazarus has put it, but as a labor market for healthy males.

The U.S. statistics on the work qualifications of the Slovene and Croat migrants at the time of arrival contain information about their social status before migration and confirm the data on both retarded economic development and the selective character of migration. American statisticians discerned four groups: experts, skilled workers, unskilled workers, and, finally, those with no trade or profession—women and children. Only a number of clergymen, a few writers, politicians, engineers, and technicians are listed. The third category included field hands, workers, farmers, and domestic servants: 29.1 percent of the Croatian and Slovene migrants between 1898 and 1914 were field hands, both male and female, or farmer's sons who had not inherited the family farm; industrial workers and apprentices amounted to 44 percent. Thus, almost three-quarters of all the migrants were industrial workers and field hands. To these have to be added the domestic servants, who made up 7.8 percent. There were relatively few independent farmers, 1.6 percent, who, in most cases, came to earn money in order to pay off debts at home. The fourth group, the so-called supported persons—that is, women and children without any occupation—amounted to 13.1 percent.[8] This occupational structure explains in part the strong workers' movement that Slovene and Croatian migrants developed in the United States, or, in other words, American social and economic conditions were different from what the migrants had imagined: a labor movement was necessary to improve working and living conditions.

Between 1908 and 1914, expectations induced the families or friends of 34,000 migrants to pay the fare for them. In the same period, 174,313 migrants joined friends and families in the United States, suggesting that reports about working conditions were favorable or at least not sufficiently negative to stop migration. Between 1898 and 1914, 3.2 million people emigrated from the Austro-Hungarian Monarchy. While Slovenes and Croats constituted 14 percent of the emigrants, they made up only 10 percent of the monarchy's population in the period. Among the independent South Slav countries of Bulgaria, Serbia, and Montenegro, emigration activities began to dwindle after 1900.[9]

Means of Communication

Prospective migrants among the Slovenes and other Yugoslavs received their images, or clichés, about America from a variety of sources—ranging from newspaper articles and immigrants' letters published in periodicals to debates in the Austrian Reichsrat (Diet) and the parliaments of other Yugoslav territories. The debates on issues of migration in the Reichsrat and in the Croatian Sabor (Parliament) were reported by the press.

In the northern regions of Yugoslav settlement, the literacy rate was quite high. In 1890, 48.6 percent of the population of the Slovene ethnic territories were literate, 8.3 percent were semi-literate, and 43.1 were illiterate. About two-thirds of the Croats could read. Naturally, the level of literacy was higher in the towns and lower in the rural areas. But the newspapers did reach every Slovene and Croatian village, and they were sometimes read in public. In the southern regions of the Yugoslav ethnic territories literacy was lower.[10]

In the 1920s and 1930s, that is, after the end of mass migration but at a time when close contacts between migrants and their kin and friends at home were still maintained, the image of America and of the Yugoslav experience in America came from a different source, the influential memoirs of renowned Slovene, Croatian, and Serbian immigrants to the United States, dating from the period after the mass migrations. They include those of Louis Adamic (Slovene-American writer), Ivan Molek (editor of the Slovene-American newspaper *Prosveta* [Enlightenment], official organ of the Slovene National Benefit Society), Michael Idvorski Pupin (inventor and professor at Columbia University), and Stjepan Lojen (the leader of the socialist movement among the Yugoslav-American workers).

The Origin of the Image of America, 1840–1880s

The first known migrants to the United States were Slovene missionaries in the 1830s, who then attracted "economic" migrants by descriptions of America in the Slovene press of the Old World since 1844.[11] These early migrants settled in America with the intention of becoming successful farmers and had to face all the hazards of the American West.[12]

During the 1850s, the Slovene periodical *Novice* (News) published letters written by immigrants. One man complained: "America is no longer that promised land to which Europeans once migrated and soon became rich, and to which many still come but deeply regret having done so if they don't have enough money to buy land." He described his living conditions, how he had to chop wood all day to keep his hut warm; that he could hardly call it a house because the wind blew through every nook and cranny; that snakes came to warm themselves and had to be killed. On the positive side, food was better since in the United States hunting was a very profitable venture and there were lots of ducks, geese, pigeons, partridges, pheasants, and rabbits, as well as deer and roebuck, wolves and bears. However, food and beverages were also different: no "wine or beer anywhere," only whiskey, from which people easily got drunk, became wild, and committed murders. "They drink an awful lot of coffee and tea here—

at each meal," and—in an important note to subsistence peasants—
"they eat three times a day, and always more meat dishes, too."
Saloon-keepers were a different breed from Slovenian innkeepers:
"[You can't] expect anyone to bring something for the horse. . . . If the
owner doesn't feel like giving the horse any feed, you have to take it to
him yourself." There was less of a work ethic and more independence.
In this case, our traveler did not like the end result.

He reported about economic prospects by implicit comparison
with the Old World: "Animals have lots of pastureland on the huge
meadows here, which no one ever mows. How many hundredweight
of hay remain on the fields here and are wasted!" This confers an
image of space and wealth. But initial capital was necessary: "A man
could get on fine in America, if only he had the money to buy lots of
livestock, since livestock's expensive here." He gave the prices and
translated them into Old World currency:

> Unless a man's got his own property, life's not very pleasant.
> Americans well know that the majority of those who immigrate
> here don't have any money, and that's why they don't like for-
> eigners—"Detchmen" [Dutchmen] or "Chermans" [Germans]—as
> they call them.

The author of the letter then pointed out differences between the
cities and the countryside. To him, American "towns and houses are
almost all alike; if you've seen one, you've seen them all. In the towns
the houses are made of stone or brick, and in the country they are
made of wood." He then described scenes of life that conformed to
many people's clichés about Old World villages rather than cities of
the new:

> The roads are very bad. It would not be an exaggeration to say
> that any cart-way at home is better. It is very common to overturn
> on such roads. Even if you live in a town, you don't live as nobly
> as in the big towns of Europe; here the streets are so ugly that it is
> terrible. Every ten feet some pig rams into you, and you have to
> get out of its way. It is easy to understand why the streets can't be
> clean, when you know that they throw everything out onto the
> streets: leftover food, dead cats, etc.

His conclusions were that work depended on what religion you
were, but that there was more religious liberty (or confusion?), and

that it was a country where only money counted but that land was available:

> Here they really hate Catholics, and especially the Catholic priests. Last year in Hamilton, they needed over 300 workers to build a community hall and there were lots of laborers of our faith there, but they didn't want to take any of them. On the other hand, there are so many religions here I haven't even heard of before.

> No one should advise anyone to come here with the idea that he's coming to a promised land. Only those who come with a big purse and who can buy themselves enough land do all right here. Here there's lots of fallow land which no one has cultivated, especially in the state of Minnesota, where we are now.[13]

The majority of the Slovenes and Croats who left before the period of mass migration during the 1880s took up work on farms. Hardly any of the news in the Slovene periodicals and papers was about city life. The only people who brought to Austria and Slovenia first-hand news regarding city life were the refugees of 1848, who began returning to Austria during the 1870s. Among them was Anton Füster.[14] However, his biography was not widely distributed. In fact, in the 1880s, people read more about the American countryside and wilderness, or about the Indians, in the popular biography of the Slovene bishop and missionary Frederik Baraga. Slovene priests even kept their parishioners informed of the American Indians' troubles and needs, and collected funds for Baraga's missionary work.[15] This was the ground onto which an image of industrial America had to be superimposed.

The Image of America at the Turn of the Century

The image of the exaggerated bounty of America inspired by immigrant letters was skillfully enhanced by the pamphlets and posters disseminated by agents of private companies, railroads, and steamship lines in European ports, towns, and villages. Designed to sell land, ocean passages, or seats on American trains, such advertisements picturesquely illustrated the scenic beauty of America and described the comforts and low costs of the transportation and accommodation offered. As Alan M. Kraut has pointed out, the information in these advertisements was often outdated, and new emigrants departing from Western European ports read about opportunities that no longer existed. By the turn of the century there was little land being distributed by railroad companies in the American West at prices immigrants could afford. Moreover, because many Americans considered Northern and Western Europeans to be more desirable settlers than Southern and Eastern Europeans, such propaganda was circulated primarily throughout Northern and Western Europe— especially in England and the German states—even after the shift in migration patterns in the late nineteenth century.

Nevertheless, such advertising eventually also reached Southern and Eastern Europe, as is evident from the colorful posters that hung in travel agencies, coffeehouses, and other public places in these regions.[16] For instance, only recently in Ljubljana, the capital of present-day Slovenia, a building was demolished that contained a lovely picture of an American metropolis covering an entire wall. This building, in Kolodvorska Ulica, i.e., Railway Street, had once been the headquarters of one of the many agencies for emigration. Even though literacy was not widespread in Southern and Eastern Europe, every community had some inhabitants who could read, and although newspapers were expensive, often an educated individual— a priest, doctor, merchant, or teacher—subscribed, or several townsmen shared a subscription.[17]

In newspaper articles, the image of the United States that is presented is very much linked to the particular political orientation of a publication. Two newspapers were in circulation in Slovenia in the 1880s: *Slovenec* (The Slovene), which was the Slovene People's Party's newspaper, and *Slovenski narod* (The Slovene Nation), the Liberal Party's paper. In addition, the Yugoslav Socialist Workers' Party's paper, *Delavec* (Worker), was founded during the 1890s. People also read Austrian and German newspapers, as the use of the German language was quite acceptable and widespread in educated society and government offices. In every village in Slovenia in those days, the sources of learning, the priest, the schoolmaster, and the well-situated farmers, regularly received and read newspapers. People also read light literature to a considerable extent. Local editors often reprinted articles from the above-mentioned most popular papers, ensuring the circulation of news throughout the remotest regions. Numerous return migrants also subscribed to these newspapers.

Among the factors that accelerated migration by propagating a challenging image of America were the large steamship companies, as well as letters sent to relatives back home. Stories about America, both positive and negative, were then spread further during corn-husking and other chores on the farm, or in the evening, when all the members of the family were gathered around the big ceramic stove in the living room.

In both of the major newspapers, one can find articles that present America in a rosy light as well as others that describe it quite unfavorably. The Catholic-oriented *Slovenec* stressed its own concern for religious morale among Slovenes in America, while the Liberal-oriented *Slovenski narod* expressed concern chiefly for the material well-being of the Slovene immigrants.

For instance, *Slovenski narod* published a letter about the 2,000 Slovene immigrants living in Calumet, Michigan. Apparently they lived under good conditions, and there were some rich businessmen among them, some of whom had already become "Americanized." Some even had their own houses. The Slovenes were employed in the mines, steel mills, and lumbering.[18] According to *Slovenski narod* the Slovenes in Leadville, Colorado, were earning from $2 to $5 a day, which was five to ten times more than what they would have earned at home for the same type of work.[19] A comparison of the weekly wages of the American-born and of the "new immigrant" workers shows that on average, the former earned $14.37 per week and the latter only $11.92.[20] After a period of adjustment, migrant workers no longer simply compared their wages with the old country but also to those of native-born workers. Experience changed their image of America.

Slovenski narod also reported on successful Slovenes, like the mine-owner Josip Golob of Sevnica, who was worth "more than a million florins [$100,000] in property," or the founder of banks in Cleveland, Ohio, Maxham, Pennsylvania, and Lorain, Ohio.[21] The Catholic *Slovenec* published similar success stories: a Slovene named Lakner became the co-owner of a big mine 60 to 100 feet wide and 6,000 feet deep. Lakner was reported to have said that he was training 400 workers and that, over the next few years, he planned to raise their number to 2,000. The newspaper gave special emphasis to his promise that in his company Slovenes would not be last in line.[22] The general public's conceptions of America were also influenced by articles on the successes of intellectuals or famous artists, such as the inventor Nikola Tesla or the vocalist Milka Trnina.

The expectations of potential migrants were further heightened by speeches such as that of the Slovene deputy Šuklje, delivered before the Austrian parliament in the 1890s and published in *Slovenec*. In 1905 Šuklje claimed that if a Slovene worked diligently and hard in America, he can under favorable conditions, save up to 1,000–1,500 [$200–$300] perhaps even 2,000 crowns [$400] a year. Thus, if he returns after three or four years of working there, he can bring 3,000 to 4,000 [$600–$800] at the most 8,000 crowns [$1600] back with him. This amount of money is a fortune to our peasant,

since, for example, a schoolteacher's wages in the 1890s were approximately 104 gulden ($400) a year. An average worker earned 8 gulden monthly, which was approximately $10 in 1918.[23] Furthermore, Šuklje cited the fact that Slovenes sent at least 2 million crowns ($400,000) per year from America to lower Carniola alone, and that with this money the people of lower Carniola repaired buildings, repaid debts, or deposited money in their savings accounts. But, among all returnees from the United States in the whole of lower Carniola, only two had fortunes exceeding 30,000 crowns ($6,000), and one of them had made his fortune as the owner of a brothel.

On the other hand, Šuklje pointed out that the final financial balance of emigration was negative, and that it would be better for the nation's economy in the long run if people would not emigrate: work would have been done in Slovenia that would have increased the national income, governmental revenues, and capital accumulation.[24]

Returning migrants who had not been successful, who had failed, or who came back in broken health discouraged emigration only marginally because successful persons were more conspicuous.

A large number of persons were completely misled about life across the Atlantic. After coming to the United States, many saw the real nature of American opportunities. Čolaković cites the story of a group of Slovenes who were informed by friends about good jobs in Minnesota, and who, upon arrival, found that there were no good jobs left, except in mining: "The salary was 12.5 cents per hour and the work was several hundreds of feet underground."[25]

The letters written from America by the Croatian journalist Ivan Lupis-Vukić, which from 1896 to 1897 were published in the Zadar periodical *Narodni list* (The National Journal), also contributed to the awareness and image of America in Croatia. In 1896, for example, Lupis-Vukić reported on the presidential elections and argued that the Mckinley would win against Bryan because the Democrats had completely lost the trust of the people. Not only had Grover Cleveland's 1892 promises of economic welfare remained unfulfilled, the country was in one of its worst depressions. As to world politics,

Lupis-Vukić noted in March 1896: "Our old Europe, which up to recent times has been accustomed to tailor the fate of the whole world, cannot believe that peaceful and good America could become a world factor overnight." Lupis tended to idealize America. He explained that working habits, occupational flexibility, and social customs were different from those in Europe, where "people are ashamed to learn to be tailors, shoemakers, blacksmiths, and machinists. But people come to America and learn what business is!" In New York, "you will see how John Rockefeller—the richest man in America, who's worth 140,000,000 dollars—is at his office every morning at 7:00 a.m." Was this a tongue-in-cheek remark directed at Austrian bureaucrats or at the complacent bourgeoisie?

> [He] will pick a paper off the floor if it can be used. Come and you will see the president of a giant steel corporation, in his shirt-sleeves, no vest, and rolled-up sleeves, talking to and managing the workers and, if necessary, getting messed up, too. This is America, this is business. . . . There is no need for playing the gentleman here.[26]

In fact, according to the custom in those days in Europe and in the Balkans, those who had achieved wealth hardly did any physical work themselves. It was considered beneath the dignity of a factory-owner or an intellectual to work, so that the Slavic immigrants could hardly believe their eyes when, in America, they saw wealthy men in working clothes, actually doing work.

Negative reports about the United States were published mostly in the Catholic paper *Slovenec*. In 1893 it paraphrased an article from *Ameriški Slovenec* (The American Slovene): "In many places mines and factories have been closed down and . . . thousands are without work and pay." This was corroborated by private letters, "which now come quite often and complain about the bad times." The author of the article, critical of his "hedonistic countrymen," felt that they deserved a lesson on "how good and necessary it is in days of plenty to think about days of poverty and want." Also: "How many of them would now wish to come back to the old country," but lack the means for "such an expensive and long journey. The intelligent ones saved their money and sent it home to be deposited in our banks." The newspaper continued with a story of a worker who used to be a farmer back in the old country and who had now lost his job in a factory. After two months without work his savings were gone and his only choice was to return home. Friends or relatives had to send the money for the trip. The same article mentioned two young Slovene villagers who had died in work accidents. One fell into a furnace in Steeltown and died of terrible burns. The other, a railroad brakeman, was run over by a train, had his legs cut off, and died. He was buried "in that far-off American soil" on St. Mary Magdalene's day. The company payed 1,000 florins ($10) compensation to his relatives for him.[27]

In the same period, *Slovenec* published a report from the Austrian Consul in Philadelphia: "Working conditions have drastically worsened. Many coal-miners have lost their jobs." He presented the staggering figures: in "Chicago 50,000 workers and their families are without work. In Philadelphia, 6,000 to 8,000 Austrian immigrants were unemployed during the winter." In 1896 most of the 5,130 Austro-Hungarian migrants arriving in the United States were unable to find employment anywhere.[28]

As early as 1891, *Slovenski narod* published a letter written by Jože Zalokar to a friend. In this letter, he mockingly describes America and the lives of the Slovenes there: about a hundred Slovenes already have "lucrative jobs," with nothing to do but lie in the sun and chew on grass during the day and lie under the pine trees counting the stars at night. In the mornings they fill their empty stomachs with saliva, for lunch they eat ants, and for dinner mosquitoes. They pay no taxes. Every night their stomachs court their backs. Each carries his belongings with him. They walk on the soles they were born with and the clothes they wear don't look much newer, either.[29]

Newspaper reports did not improve after the long depression ended. More than a decade later, the Catholic *Slovenec*, as well as the liberal *Slovenski narod*, published negative evaluations of emigration. *Slovenec* complained in 1908 that America was of no use to the majority of Slovene emigrants and that some good could be wrested from it only by those deemed

> fit enough to slave for American millionaires. Here and there, someone becomes rich, but the majority degenerate, both spiritually and physically, and lose themselves in America like drops in an ocean, with no benefit either to themselves or to anyone else.[30]

In 1909 a letter published in *Slovenski narod* described the prevailing conditions of migrant workers in America as being much worse than four years earlier: "Those who come to this promised land now, and do not have a relative, friend or acquaintance here, will wish that they were dead, rather than alive." Many people who had good land or a good salary back home had come, but could not "even get the worst kind of job." If they had no means of returning, in a short while they became what in Slovenia is called a "baraba," a scoundrel, and what the Americans simply called "tramps."[31] *Slovenec* in the same year reprinted a note from America:

> The idea that America is a gold mine, from which one can dig up golden dollars and return to one's homeland as a rich man, should be forgotten. Here, work is hard to find and one must work hard for one's pay. . . . We appeal to the Slovene newspapers to warn people against often rushing to their misfortune.[32]

As we have pointed out, the bulk of the migrants were farmers and field hands, who had to weigh the originally positive but now increasingly negative reports about the United States and compare them with their actual living conditions. There were few industrial workers, as the working class was still weak in Slovenia. Because, toward the end of the nineteenth century, the bourgeoisie were not yet numerous, there were also relatively few businessmen among the Slovenes, although later, in the United States, Slovene immigrants proved to be very enterprising.[33]

Somewhat less was written about America in Croatia and much less in the press accessible to the masses in Serbia and Montenegro, although similar articles did appear in these parts of the South Slav ethnic territories. Because the rate of return was very high among the South Slav migrants, information also came from returnees.[34] People in the cities were, in general, better informed on political matters than those living in the country—as well as on the working conditions in the United States. Their knowledge of German enabled them to read all the major Viennese newspapers.

According to the Catholic *Slovenec*, many women migrated to America to find a husband or to flee with a lover from the moral condemnation of parents. In many articles, women were warned to stay at home and, if married, to wait there for their husbands' return. Yet, if their going to America was unavoidable, they were advised to report to the nearest Catholic priest soon after their arrival.[35]

Letters from migrant women describing America arrived in every Croat, Slovene, and Serb village. The effect of these letters on Slovene villagers, for instance, is described by the priest Jurij Trunk:

From a Slovene village in Carinthia, where emigration was not yet well known and not at all necessary, a young girl . . . emigrated to America. A few months later, she sent her girlfriends a photograph. The girl had changed into a fine young lady, all decked out in a white blouse and—what to many a peasant girl represented true fortune (!)—a wide-brimmed hat. All of a sudden, the village was overwhelmed with excitement. Even the daughters of well-off peasants were taken by the "American plague," and severe opposition was necessary to prevent large numbers from emigrating. Some did nevertheless needlessly leave their homes—all because of a hat![36]

To counteract out-migration, newspaper articles and information from people already living in America warned women of the dangers lurking there, such as pimps and brothels. The liberal press, on the other hand, preferred to emphasize points such as the equality of women in America.

The "America" of the Labor Press

The proletarian press primarily pointed to social conditions as the major cause of emigration. It published reports on the American workers' way of life, working conditions, and unemployment. It emphasized the depletion of the ranks of the Serbian, Slovene, and Croatian working class through migration and the increasing class consciousness of migrant workers in America. *Radničke novine* (Workers' News) noted:

Today North and South America are filled with the most skilled Serbian workers. There are as many organized Serbs here, as there are now in Serbia! They can be found in every American town. This is evident from correspondence, the subscriptions to the *Radničke novine*, to *Borba* [Struggle] and orders for Yugoslav books.

Migration was not "adventure or curiosity or habit—as the [local] authorities have explained" it. Under existing conditions in southern Serbia, "no one returns from America, and, recently, whole families have been moving there.[37] The Zagreb periodical *Slobodna riječ* (The Free Word) bitterly denounced the treatment of immigrants at the New York entry facilities. In the immigrant hospital on Hoffman Island "everything is possible. . . . The treatment of patients, particularly of children and their mothers, . . . makes the barbarous actions which take place at Ellis Island look mild." Wards were overcrowded, beds were without mattresses, there was no separation of sexes, meals were bad, the tin dishes were rusty. On Ellis Island the doctors of the Immigrant Department found the most healthy to be "sick":

> For women whose children are in the hospital on Hoffman Island, and who are waiting for them to get well again, life is bitter and full of sadness. . . . [T]hey are not only exposed to all kinds of ill treatment, but are also forced to do the hardest kinds of jobs.[38]

Once inside the new country the life of the migrants, according to *Slobodna riječ*, remained a treadmill of hurrying and being hurried: before dawn people get up,

> heat up coffee prepared the night before; they drink this up very quickly, and then everyone puts his lunch prepared the night before under his arm; the first member of the family to leave shouts "good-bye" . . . and one by one they disappear; one goes to the factory, one to work on the streets, the women and daughters to the factory or to the stores, and the children to school.

People are trying to beat each other to the trams, in order to arrive at their workplace on the dot. Each carries a small bag under his or her arm and many also a tin container of coffee. Since the time allowed for lunch is very short, usually half an hour, everybody is forced to carry their lunch with them. In numerous factories, where the shifts are twelve hours long, breaks last only twenty and sometimes only fifteen minutes.[39] However, unemployment was worse, concurred *Slobodna riječ* and the above-quoted Austrian consul. In February 1914, 270,000 miners were looking for work; automobile factories had dismissed 50,000 workers in Cleveland, 75,000 in Detroit:

> Therefore, my fellow workers have come to the conclusion that it is best to help themselves! . . . They are struggling against a mighty enemy who has all the weapons on his side, like nice, sweet journalist lies, insidious slander and provocations, and the courts, police and army.[40]

The image of America presented in the labor press thus differed little from that of the Catholic and liberal press in its overall assessment. The labor press decried the drain of class-conscious workers; the other publications emphasized the loss to the Slovene nationality. The labor press pointed to growing militancy among immigrant workers; the Catholic paper suggested that it had been a mistake to migrate and that the result was a return with no savings. To the Austrian government the labor issue was as important as the military one. Emigration was to be reduced to prevent too drastic a reduction both of available recruits and of farmworkers.[41]

Cultural Persistence and the Image of America

Although to Yugoslav immigrants America was attractive primarily because of its purported economic opportunities, other motives played a large role in their decision to emigrate. For a significant number of economically and politically oppressed South Slavs in the Habsburg Monarchy, America was the land of freedom, where they would be allowed to maintain their ethnic heritage. The famous Serbian inventor Michael Idvorski Pupin, for example, explained why he left his native village as follows:

> The rulers in the country wanted to make me a Magyar; I left Prague, because Austrian "Germanism" was distasteful to me, and I will leave Delaware City if you expect me to renounce my Serbian nationality and become an American. My mother, my village and my Serbian language and nation are my Serbian identity, and you can expect me to stop breathing before I will stop being a Serb.[42]

To Pupin, America was first and foremost the land of Benjamin Franklin, a man interested in technology and one of the signers of the Declaration of Independence, as well as that of Abraham Lincoln, emancipator of the slaves—an achievement comparable to the emancipation of serfs in Eastern Europe.

Fleeing military service in the Austrian army was another cause of emigration from the Slovene ethnic territories, and the absence of the draft system in America was one of the country's attractions. Numerous articles published in the Austrian press reported activities of Austrian security authorities in apprehending persons who attempted to avoid the seven years of military service. Although a great number of migrants succeeded, dozens of young men were arrested each year for attempting to leave the country without permission. A black market for passports existed: many drafted Slovene youths bought passports from Croats, because, as citizens of the Hungarian part of the monarchy, Croats, they reasoned, would not be subject to Austrian martial law.[43]

Evasion of military service by migration could mean loss of national heritage. In 1912 Jurij Trunk wrote that people compelled by circumstances to emigrate should do so as whole families with the intention of making America their new home. This, in his opinion, was how the English, French, Germans, and Swedes had migrated. They should become American citizens and remain in the United States. But, nevertheless, they should stick together and form ethnic communities:

> He who clings to his countrymen and remains in close spiritual contact with his homeland will also eventually triumph over [the homesickness of] his soft, Slovene heart. Every family in free America can remain Slovene if it wants to, for to settle in America and become an American citizen does not and should not mean a renunciation of one's Slovene homeland or one's native tongue. The homeland must remain the mother and America must become the bride. Only he who does not forget his God in his new homeland, can remain true to his ancestral homeland, to his mother, and to the Catholic Church, thus preserving his most precious treasure—his faith.[44]

These ideas stem from a clergyman who, in his native land, was one of the foremost fighters against the pressures for Germanization. He also struggled for the preservation of Slovene culture and the Slovene nation in southern Carinthia. To him, and to other contemporary observers, the pressure of Germanization in Carinthia and Styria, as well as the pressure of Magyarization in the eastern territories of the monarchy were far stronger than any influences exerted by America on the Slovene immigrants, because in America Slovenes could keep their cultural identity. In Trunk's opinion, America posed problems only in connection with the preservation of the Catholic faith, since the American Slovenes were far less dependent on the clergy's guidance than their countrymen and -women in the villages back home.

Reflecting on Emigration after 1920 and New Developments

After the 1920s a number of books by Slovene-American authors began to reflect on their experience, and developed a more differentiated image of the country. Ivan Molek wrote naturalistic novels, printed both in America and back home, that affected the Slovenes' image of America while at the same time giving an interesting picture of Slovene migrants in America. In *Dva svetova* (Two Worlds), published in 1932, Molek presented a complex picture of America. His accurate descriptions take on a historical dimension. Although his own opinion of America was negative, he did approve of the political freedom there. Some of his characters, return migrants, reflect the more elusive image of America. It was a

> magic country, where there was no dark, only white bread—and daily, not only at Christmas and on festival days: roast on the table; a country where coins of silver lie in the streets and sensible people do not pick them up, for they know that "only a bit farther, just around the corner, lies gold in plenty."

According to one of these returnees, " 'in the far West, where everything is still wild . . . there are mountains of gold. There are no nights there, because the gold shines as the sun does during the daytime.' " By 1932 "there were many former Americans" in Slovenia:

> Almost every other farmer's house, the huts of the workers living on "day's payment" excepted, boasted an "American uncle" or had someone on the other side of the ocean. All those "uncles" . . . were far wealthier in praise about the land of dollars than in dollars in their pocket.[45]

The images of America portrayed in the writings of the best-selling Slovene-American writer of the 1930s and 1940s, Louis Adamic, show what lured him to America as a young boy. In his semi-autobiographical *Laughing in the Jungle*, Adamic describes his notion of the United States:

> It was a grand, amazing, somewhat fantastic place—the Golden Country—a sort of Paradise—the Land of Promise in more ways than one—huge beyond conception, thousands of miles across the ocean, inutterably exciting, explosive and quite incomparable to the tiny, quiet, lovely Carniola. A place full of movement and turmoil, where things that were unimaginable and impossible in Blato [Adamic's village] happened every day as a matter of course.

He imagined how in America one could

make pots of money in a short time, acquire immense holdings, wear a white collar and have polished boots like a *gospod*—one of the gentry—and eat white bread, soup and meat on weekdays as well as on Sundays, even if one was but an ordinary workman to begin with.

In Blato, very few could afford this even on Sundays, whereas in America, one did not even have to remain an ordinary workman. The "Amerikanec," the returned migrant, sometimes bragged about ranches larger than the whole of Carniola.[46]

Upon arrival in the United States in 1913, and particularly after reading Upton Sinclair's *The Jungle*, Adamic was to find that America was "more a jungle than a civilization." All of a sudden he realized "that America was a veritable battleground of tremendous and savage forces. So *this* was America!" People were shot dead in fights, which helped him begin to understand events such as the Ludlow massacre near Colorado in 1913, and the much written about dynamite assassinations in Los Angeles that took place a few years earlier. His new perception made him hate the country intensely for a while.[47]

After World War I, cooperation among the Yugoslav organizations and cultural groups of America and Yugoslavia, both the "progressive" and the Catholic, continued to contribute significantly to enhancing the image of America in Slovenia. Books by Ivan Molek and other socialist writers living in the United States, published in Chicago by the "Prosvetna Matica Jugoslovanski Socialistične zveze" (Educational Center of the Yugoslav Socialist Federation), were sold in Slovenia, and Slovenes also had access to books by American authors.[48] The image of America was also enhanced by material and financial support from Slovene-Americans: packages of presents for war victims, aid to the newly founded Yugoslav "Matica," a donation of $150 for the monument of the great Slovene author Ivan Cankar at Vrhnika.[49] While new American laws restricted immigration, a positive image of America was kept alive by the reports of Slovene-American cultural activities, such as the opening of the Slovene school for the graphic arts in Cleveland, founded by the renowned Slovene-born "Cleveland painter," Harvey G. Prusheck.[50]

The returnees exerted a strong influence on the image of America in the Kingdom of the Serbs, Croats, and Slovenes that was founded in 1918. Between 1919 and 1924, 16,433 people of Croatian and Slovene origin returned; at the same time, 24,309 persons migrated, often for the second time, to the United States. A large number of the returnees found that the new monarchy could not offer them jobs. In addition, the political situation was none too promising. The newly established state of Serbs, Croatians, and Slovenes was already at that time on the brink of economic collapse and did not offer any economic perspectives for the future. Immigrants who returned to their old country had no chance of finding employment and thus they simply went back to the United States again. The Yugoslav authorities did not impede their migration, and the newspapers intensely debated the restrictive American immigration laws.[51] Some of the Slovene migrants came from among the half million Slovenes and Croats who were living in Italy at the time.[52] American democracy must have appealed strongly to these people, living as they did, in a land where the Fascists were already in power.

In 1927 it was proposed that a socialist and "free-thinking" literary and scientific monthly be founded, which was to be published in Chicago and Ljubljana.[53] However, this idea, which was put forward by Slovene-American socialists associated with the *Proletarec* (Proletarian) newspaper, was not welcome in Yugoslavia in the period between the wars, and the free flow of information about America was restricted by the monarchy, much in the same way that it would be restricted, after World War II, by the Yugoslav Communist authorities.[54]

At the Emigrant Congresses organized in 1931 in Ljubljana, Zagreb, and Belgrade, the representatives of the American Slovenes, Croats, and Serbs informed the political and cultural representatives of Yugoslavia about the position of the immigrants in the United States, and about their way of life there as well as the problems they faced, at the height of the Depression in the United States. The picture existing in Yugoslavia about emigrants and their lives was rather inaccurate, and the exaggerations of the returnees contributed much to it. The prevailing view in the homeland was that the emigrants were "lost" and that any effort to "save" them was in vain. Because, even after long stays abroad, migrants still felt close to their homeland, it became the main task of the Congress to create favorable conditions for exchanges between the immigrants and institutions in the homeland.[55] While some Yugoslav-American delegates made inquiries about the possibility of returning to the homeland, many of the papers at the Congress dealt with the problems of the second generation, with those who were born in America. Ivan Mladinec presented the tensions between family pressure on the young and the influence of the educational system, society, and the streets.[56]

By this time, reports on the economic depression in the United States had become frequent in Yugoslavia. Seven million American workers were homeless and starving in this merciless country.[57] This experience is summed up by a character in one of Adamic's novels, an exhausted migrant returning to his native Carniola (Slovenia):

They go, because each thinks that he will get the better of America and not America the better of him. . . . America needs their hands even more than they need her dollars, and makes use of them. Once upon a time the immigrants were called "dung" in America. . . . They are still "dung." The roots of America's greatness still feed on them. . . . More people are swept under than rise to riches.[58]

But the depression had reached Yugoslavia, too, and return to the homeland might bring the support of a family network, but not economic security.

Notes

1. See Janko Pleterski, *Narodi, Jugoslavija, revolucija* (Ljubljana: Časopisna založniška delovna organizacija Komunist, 1986), 11.

2. See Vladimir Klemenčič, "Karakter, uzroci, i posledice iseljavanja iz Jugoslavije," in *Iseljeništvo naroda i narodnosti Jugoslavije i njegove uzajamne veze s domovinom, Zbornik,* ed. Ivan Čizmič, Radoslav Rotkovič, Tihomir Telisman, Koča Jončič, and Vladimir Klemenčič (Zagreb: Zavod za migracije i narodnosti, 1978), 105–110.

3. See Matjaž Klemenčič, *Ameriški Slovenci in narodnoosvobodilna borba v Jugoslaviji* (Maribor: Založba Obzorja, 1987), 39, 52.

4. See Branko M. Čolakovič, *Yugoslav Migrations to America* (San Francisco: R & E Research Associates, 1973), 27.

5. See Matjaž Klemenčič, "Germanizacijski procesi na Štajerskem od srede 19. stoletja do prve svetovne vojne," *Časopis za zgodovino in narodopisje* 50 (Maribor, 1979): 351.

6. See Klemenčič, *Ameriški Slovenci,* 41.

7. See ibid., 42.

8. See ibid.

9. See ibid., 43.

10. See Matjaž Klemenčič in cooperation with Igor Žiberna, *Stanje pismenosti in šolskega obiska na slovenskem etničnem ozemlju v letih 1865–*

1910 (Maribor: Research Project for the Research Council of Slovenia, 1985).

11. See "Pismo iz Amerike," *Novice*, 23 May 1844.

12. See Alešovec Jakob, *Ne v Ameriko: Povest Slovencem v pouk* (Ljubljana: Katoliška tiskarna, 1912), 239.

13. *Novice*, 22 Oct 1854, quoted in Jože Zavertnik, *Ameriški Slovenci* (Chicago: Slovenian National Benefit Society, 1925), 251.

14. See Janez Stanonik, "Ameriška leta slovenskega izboraženca Antona Fistra," *Slovenski koledar* (Ljubljana: Slovenska izseljenska matica, 1980), 167–204.

15. See Leon Vončina, *Friderik Baraga, prvi slovenski apostolski misijonar in škof med indijanci v Ameriki* (Celovec and Klagenfurt: Družba Sv. Mohorja, 1986), 167.

16. See Alan M. Kraut, *The Huddled Masses: The Immigrant in American Society, 1880–1921* (Arlington Heights, Va.: Harlan Davidson, Inc., 1982, 15–16.

17. See ibid., 13–14.

18. See *Slovenski Narod* (hereafter quoted as *SN*), 15 June 1900, quoted in Danilo Zadravec, "Poročila Slovenca in Slovenskega Naroda o izseljevanju Slovencev" (B.A. thesis, University of Maribor, 1984), 9.

19. See *SN*, 4 Sept 1900, quoted in Zadravec, "Poročila," 28. See Gerald Rosenblum, *Immigrant Workers: Their Impact on American Labor Radicalism* (New York: Basic Books, 1973), 71, quoted in Igor Žiberna, 'Proletarec'—socialistični časopis ameriških Slovencev in stavkovno gibanje v ZDA med leti 1913 in 1929 (B.A. thesis, University of Maribor, 1986), 3.

21. *SN*, 16 Mar 1920, quoted in Darko Kožič, "Poročila Slovenskega Naroda o izseljevanju Slovencev v letih 1920–1930" (B.A. thesis, University of Maribor, 1986), 7.

22. *Slovenec*, "Politični list za slovenski narod," 2 July 1908, quoted in Alenka Nežmah, "Poročila Slovenca in Slovenskega Naroda o izseljevanju iz Avstroogrske monarhije v letih 1906–1910" (B.A. thesis, University of Maribor, 1984), 21.

23. See Janez Šumrada, "Gospodarjenje neke slovenske družine konec 19. in v začetku 20 stoletja," *Zgodovinski časopis* 38 (Ljubljana, 1984): 3–174.

24. See *Slovenec*, 13 Oct 1905, quoted in Zadravec, "Poročila," 17.

25. Čolakovič, *Yugoslav Migrations to America*, 27.

26. Nenad Gol, "Lupisovi 'Listovi iz Amerike,'" *Matica: List iseljenika Hrvatske* (Zagreb, 1975), 5–21.

27. *Slovenec*, 9 Aug 1893.

28. *Slovenec*, 29 May 1897, quoted in Carmen Potnik, "Poročila Slovenca in Slovenskega Naroda o izseljevanju Slovencev v letih 1895–1899" (B.A. thesis, University of Maribor, 1985), 15.

29. See *SN*, 12 May 1891, quoted in Lidija Janžekovič, "Izseljevanje

Slovencev iz slovenskega etničnega ozemlja v letih 1890–1895 na podlagi poročil Slovenca in Slovenskega Naroda" (B.A. thesis, University of Maribor, 1984), 30.

30. *Slovenec*, 27 Nov 1908, quoted in Nežmah, "Poročila," 14.

31. *SN*, 28 Aug 1909, quoted in Nežmah, "Poročila," 20.

32. *Slovenec*, 12 June 1909, quoted in Nežmah, "Poročila," 33.

33. See Ferdo Gestrin and Vasilij Melik, *Zgodovina Slovencev od konca osemnajstega stoletja do leta 1918* (Ljubljana: Državna zalozba Slovenije, 1966), 155.

34. Some of the returnees played an important role in contemporary events. See Mary Prisland, *From Slovenia to America* (Chicago: Slovenian Women Union of America, 1968), 39.

35. See *Slovenec*, 9 Aug 1893.

36. Jurij Trunk, *Amerika in Amerikanci* (Celovec and Klagenfurt: Trunk Inc., 1912), 402.

37. Jovan Dubovac, "Prilog pojavi iseljavanja iz Srbije u SAD pred prvi svetski rat, in Čizmič et al., *Iseljeništvo naroda i narodnosti Jugoslavije*, 165.

38. *Slobodna riječ* (hereafter cited as *Sr*), 29 July 1911.

39. *Sr*, 9 Feb 1914.

40. *Sr*, 7 Feb 1914.

41. See A. Fischel, *Die schädlichen Seiten der Auswanderung und deren Bekämpfung* (Vienna, 1914), 6.

42. Michael Pupin, *From Immigrant to Inventor* (New York, 1923), 48.

43. See *SN*, 15 June 1900, quoted in Zadravec, "Poročila," 9. Marjan Drnovšek, *Pot Slovenskih izseljencev ma tuje, od Ljubljane do Ellis Islanda— otoka solza v New Yorku 1880–1924* (Ljubljana: Založba Mladika, 1991), 123.

44. Trunk, *Amerika in Amerikanci*, 407.

45. Ivan Molek, *Dva svetova* (Chicago: Prosvetna Matica Jugoslovanske Socialistične zveze, 1932), 18. Molek also summarized a letter sent by a newly arrived immigrant to his friend in the old country, who read it "at least ten times in succession and knew its contents from memory within an hour": "Things are fine with him. . . . He lives with homefolk; has a job—Frank had written "job" not "work"—good pay. Plenty of entertainment and pretty girls, too. In brief, America is a fine country. Made-to-order, especially for a liberal. . . . Plenty of freedom; you can be fully active and say what you think. At the first opportunity Frank will send Slovene newspapers from America so that Tony can see how fully active people can be there. . . . And so forth: nothing but milk and honey," ibid. But see also his accounts of moral corruption, *Zajedalci* (Chicago: Slovene National Benefit Society, 1920), 56–59.

46. Louis Adamic, *Laughing in the Jungle* (New York and London: Harper Brothers, 1932), 32–33.

47. Ibid., 42–43.

48. Letter from I. Molek, 22 Sept 1927, to Jugoslovanska socialistična zveza (Immigration History Research Center, Yugoslav Socialist Federation Papers, box 40, folder 320, St. Paul, Minnesota).

49. See *Slovenec*, 9 Sept 1920, quoted in Franc Kregar, "Poročila Slovenca o izseljevanju v letih 1920–1930" (B.A. thesis, University of Maribor, 1984), 17. The Matica was an association of intellectuals and cultural workers who worked to maintain and promote Slovene culture.

50. See *Slovenec*, 26 Jan 1933.

51. See *Slovenec*, July 1924, quoted in Kregar, "Poročila," 20.

52. See Klemenčič, *Ameriški Slovenci*, 56.

53. See letter from I. Vuk, 6 June 1930, to Charles Pogorelec (Yugoslav Socialist Federation Papers, box 41, folder 324).

54. See Matjaž Klemenčič, "Proletarec and the Acculturation of Slovene Workers in the United States," in *The Press of Labor Migrants in Europe and North America, 1880s to 1930s*, ed. Christiane Harzig and Dirk Hoerder (Bremen: Publications of the Labor Newspaper Preservation Project, 1985), 475–86.

55. See *1. slovenski izseljenski kongres v Ljubljani dne 1. julija 1935* (Ljubljana: Družba Sv. Rafaela, 1936).

56. See "Izveštaj članovima američkog izletničkog odbora za iseljenički kongres," March 1931 (Yugoslav Socialist Federation Papers, box 41, folder 324).

57. See *Slovenec*, 6 Feb 1932.

58. Adamic, *Laughing in the Jungle*, 5–6.

10

From "Promised Land" to "Bitter Land": Italian Migrants and the Transformation of a Myth

Gianfausto Rosoli

MANY economic, demographic, and political factors give rise to emigration—overpopulation, the spread of poverty, the yearning for freedom. Cultural factors, however, have not as a rule received the attention they deserve, despite their fundamental role in shaping the elementary perception of rights and unsatisfied needs, the promise of a better future, and the messages and images that regulate "push" and "pull" mechanisms.

In general we identify elements of acculturation by studying integration in the adopted country. Cultural factors in the pre-departure or pre-arrival stage are seldom considered, as if the problems encountered in the country of origin automatically disappear in the new country.[1] It is clear that cultural factors were at work at every step of the migration experience. They must be regarded not only as effects creating new expectations and values, but also as causes of migration responsible for the final choice of migrants.

The real protagonists in the migration experience are generally silent actors from the viewpoint of historians on account of the insurmountable difficulties in documenting and analyzing their reactions and attitudes. In the Italian case, these difficulties are magnified because of the high percentage of illiterate Italians. Virtually the entire Italian population was illiterate in 1861, about half the population of the south was illiterate in 1900, and 53 percent were still illiterate in Calabria in 1921.[2] Personal accounts by migrants are essential, although not available in sufficient numbers, for understanding migrant culture and avoiding the misunderstandings that denied the lower classes having a culture of their own.

Cultural Factors Influencing Migration

The purpose of this essay is to study the migrants' image of America before leaving Italy, to examine the relative importance and role of the "New World" myth. From the time of Columbus the idea of the New World, which in Italy always comprised North as well as South America, existed as a composite image in the eyes of Europeans. It acquired new meaning and significance in the popular ideas that spread throughout the nineteenth century.[3] Our analysis is limited to the country of origin and is of necessity oversimplified. The image continued to exist and was modified in America, the image held on one side of the ocean influencing that held on the other. It did not remain unchanged over time, for America evolved economically and politically, became a dominant power in international relations, and introduced new immigration policies.

The image of America is therefore a complex nonlinear outcome of migrants' individual experiences, their intended length of stay in the new society, the collective elaboration of the myths about America, the spread of "American fever," and the institutional organization and political ambivalence of the sender countries with respect to migration. It is obvious that the United States in the early nineteenth century, needing settlers and offering great riches and opportunities, was completely different from the country a century later, when restrictionism had become the dominant philosophy (first in the United States and later in other nations on the American continent). Restrictionism overturned the axiom *gobernar es poblar* (to govern is to populate), substituting for it a nativist model that upheld the privileged position of the early settlers. Emigration is a function of the spread and circulation of those quasi-mythical and matter-of-fact images of the New World. In the collective imagination, the image of America as the ideal country of promise and liberty underwent a gradual decline from the nineteenth to the twentieth century. Its monolithic and positive image was undermined by contradictions and ambiguities. Latin American countries were the first to lose status in the eyes of the migrants because of their economic crises of the late nineteenth century, the conflicts among Latin American countries, and manipulation through propaganda in Italy.

Immigration provoked different attitudes in the countries of destination and in the countries of origin. In the latter, anti-emigrationists and supporters of emigration were guided by opposing interests as well as by conflicting images. Supporters of emigration were generally responsible for creating the positive and messianic images of America. They were usually members of the new Italian commercial middle class, on the one hand, and members of the political establishment that held to an "escape valve" theory of migration, on the other; the former profited from the business of transporting migrants, the latter hoped to avoid social unrest. Supporters of emigration included those who favored liberal ideas connected with the Italian *Risorgimento* and those who were optimistic about the New World.

Anti-emigrationists made up a broad and diversified coalition, which included groups with conflicting aims: landowners who feared losing cheap labor; the traditional middle class, which considered notions of a better world to be irrational; protectionists who preferred settlement in Italy's African colonies to the free countries in the New World; socialists who feared a weakening of the labor movement; and Catholics who were afraid of loss of faith and a degradation of morals.[4]

The popular images of the New World were spread by oral and written means within the family and village. Of particular importance are letters, autobiographies, and diaries of migrants, popular travel literature, and emigrant guides printed by emigrant agents, which all contributed to the myths about America.

The literature of the educated classes, interacting with popular ideas, developed an image of an expansionist Italy and a peaceful penetration of the Americas by Italian labor, as in the case of a liberal like Einaudi.[5] The liberal myth of a "new great Italy" that was to rise on the banks of the Rio de la Plata was closely linked with spontaneous emigration, to be followed by the movement of Italian capital. This model of peaceful expansion stood in sharp contrast to "Africanist" military colonies, but also to Macola's idea of an aggressive Italian presence in Latin America.[6] Economists initially assumed that migration was merely a natural and spontaneous occurrence, but later came to recognize it as a form of indirect colonialism effected through emigrants' remittances and merchant shipping.[7] As a result of cultural and political factors, the preservation of the national character of the Italian communities abroad became a nationalistic vision.[8] Comparison of the opportunities for Italian workers in North and South America further sharpened the differences between, and the economic and political consequences of migration to, these two areas.

The United States was portrayed as an imperialist and aggressive power by Italian nationalists in the early twentieth century.[9] As far as Latin America was concerned, by this time the image of a promised land (if it ever existed) had collapsed. Praising Argentina, as Angelo Trento points out, was a way of speaking badly about Brazil, while encouraging emigration to Brazil was a way of criticizing structural flaws in the Republic of Argentina.[10] The myth of America had lost much of its positive aura in that period, so that as early as 1915 Tropeano could speak of the "end of America."[11]

As Massara points out, referring to the United States, Italy's established political forces always exploited the image of America in order to fulfill their aims. They created a double image—"one a mythological image for the dissatisfied rural masses whose exodus encouraged the mobilization of agrarian capital, and a second, more realistic image for a culturally backward middle class in which the United States served as a model for a late industrial takeoff."[12] These ideas ultimately came to have an influence at a popular level (and can be found in many socialist arguments). By the beginning of the twentieth century, America had become for some groups the anti-myth, an enormously enlarged projection of an ambiguous European reality.

The Americas in the Collective Memory of Migrants

The study of popular culture is fundamental to an understanding of the images that guide migration, especially for the spread of both the mythical and the concrete images of the New World. Emigrant letters, diaries, and autobiographies contain a great deal of direct and indirect evidence on the transformation and evolution of European peasant cultures, and on internal mechanisms of group solidarity, providing valuable reference points that help us to understand these countries and their social relations. The letters of migrants, which are now more easily available, even in published form, are a promising but as yet little used research source. A few Italian scholars have collected and analyzed this primary source material,[13] and in southern Brazil there is a growing interest in preserving the written testimony of Italian peasants.[14]

The old and the new intertwine in the images of the new countries, based on a new popular culture and supported by new mass media and growing literacy. However accurate they may have been, whether written only to serve the aims of emigration agents or as private family communication, these letters were the direct expression of individuals. Some wrote both public letters and personal ones; some even copied the letters of others. The myth of America was then created by a myriad of factors that influenced public opinion— in the traditional ways through meetings in taverns, fairs, and markets, and outside churches after services, or in more modern ways through the circulation of ideas in newspapers and magazines.[15]

The letters of migrants were a leading factor stimulating exodus. For this reason they were destroyed by landowners and conservatives, who often succeeded in preventing them from being read in public or published in periodicals. They were in great demand from persons seeking reliable (or presumably reliable) information,[16] and were also used by emigration agents to reach people who distrusted other forms of information.

Public authorities were forced to recognize that government decrees were powerless against the information that was received in a "lettera Americana."[17] As Franzina points out, letters containing information about America or other destinations were spread by family and village networks. Emigrant letters were read in public before attentive audiences who listened in "religious silence." The listeners gave greater value to letters that contained a realistic picture of conditions in America. Sometimes the letters were circulated as leaflets or booklets, as happened in Bassano, in 1887, when a printer sold a letter from America extolling the success of the people who settled in America,[18] which was but a facsimile copy of one printed in Mantua, with a different date. The myth of the New World grew in a rural and artisan setting during an age in which internal communications were rapidly developing and in which there was a growing demand for popular information from newspapers and publications. Emigrant letters published in newspapers confirmed, with the benefit of personal experience, an already existing popular image that would otherwise have seemed too abstract and remote.[19]

Emigrant letters, booklets, and the propagandistic message put out by emigration agents spread commonplace impressions about the "Promised Land" awaiting hungry and unhappy people across the ocean. New publicists, such as Bossi in 1886, were not afraid to say that Brazil was "the promised land of the Bible and more. It will be the refuge for millions of persons who will be driven out of the old European lands by poverty."[20] The religious and millenarian meaning of the Promised Land, deeply rooted as it was in rural culture, was also an expression of the yearning for land ownership. It was no accident, then, that the image of the New World was extraordinarily popular with Italian (and not only Italian) rural people in both North and South, although only occasionally did ownership of a small farm confirm the success of the migratory process. Anti-emigrationists and landowners fought long and hard against the arguments peasants used to justify their emigration to America, arguments that the middle class identified, conveniently, as an "irrational convulsive fever that encourages peasants to imagine that there exists elsewhere that promised land which does not exist and has never existed on earth."[21]

Anti-emigrationists, especially landowners and provincial conservatives in Veneto and Calabria, attacked emigrants' letters and the illusions they generated.[22] Peasant credulity did indeed give rise to myths and chimeras, but also to realistic hopes for improvement. Morpurgo pointed out in the famous *Inquiry* into peasant conditions conducted by the assembly deputy Jacini in 1886 that "people who suffer have such a tendency to want to improve their lot" that they become gullible, while "good" advice from the landlord was "distrusted." "They rely on the unknown," one of Jacini's collaborators explained, "and they believe that their lives will improve even if it involves great sacrifices." A mayor questioned by them replied somewhat indignantly:

> It was not lack of work . . . which made the rural class emigrate. . . . It was rather that peasants left because of the emigration agents who promised heaven and earth in America and who often spoke about the great wealth in the overseas countries, where farm tools—spades, hoes and plows—were made of solid gold, instead of iron.[23]

As in other countries, the blame was laid on the emigrant agents, also called swindlers and slave dealers (which in fact they often were). But this fails to explain why they exercised such power over the poverty-stricken lower classes.

Certain agencies and organizations tried to use or even censor migrants' letters in order to exercise control over the flow of private information, which was increasing because of the spread of literacy. In 1875, the Society for the Protection of Emigrants, under the patronage of Senator Torelli, made extensive use of such letters to discourage unpremeditated migration.[24] In 1892 the Società Geografica Italiana collected hundreds of emigrants' letters from Latin American countries where economic crisis was about to set in. Unlike the landowners, who were interested only in disseminating bad news to discourage departures, the Società tried instead to direct migrants to safe destinations and to establish institutions that could guarantee jobs and protect Italians abroad.[25]

From the first emigration act in 1888, which permitted agents to practice their questionable activities, to 1901, when pressure from both Catholics and Socialists led to a new law outlawing their activities, the controversy over emigration was conducted in terms of the contrast between positive and negative images, between instant wealth and failure and marginalization. In addition, some leading church personalities came out against "artificial" emigration with the argument that it was trade in human flesh.[26]

But the image of the New World was no longer an abstract and remote one. The real condition of Italian emigrants began to emerge from the communications received. The notion of a Golden Age started to decline after the first waves of migration to America. This was not due to anti-emigration propaganda, but rather to the collective experience and suffering of Italian migrants and to their slow and painful acculturation in American society, a process obstructed by native structural and cultural factors. From Mazzei to Mazzini, the Italian Enlightenment and Risorgimento tradition had extolled the United States as a model of freedom and liberty, and, in particular, as an advanced middle-class society. This static and idealized image of the New World was now superseded by a more troubled and realistic picture, often rendered in somewhat impressionistic tones and overdrawn black-and-white contrasts. This turning point occurs perhaps at the moment when out-migration begins to bring about an analysis of social structures and to create strains and tensions within labor, religion, ideology, and local loyalties. Massara has pointed out that while the traditional image of America was related emotionally to the period of the discoveries, the new heterogeneous and for the most part "scientific" literature aimed to "redeem America," which was justified more than ever in view of the new wave of mass emigration.[27]

To capture the historical memory of migration, we need, in addition to the letters, the migrants' personal continuous testimonies. Diaries portray the reactions and attitudes of the period without literary elaboration or historical reinterpretation.[28] Even the name "America" implied a liberating force in many diaries and writings.[29] In the earliest diaries—for instance, that of Andrea Guagliardo, who went to America in the mid-nineteenth century—the entire story is intertwined with the myth of America.[30] Although the world of emotion and remembrance is intimately linked to the village of origin, the liberating experience of emancipation is at the heart of the confession of Carmine Biagio Jannace from Benevento.[31]

Even though the exotic, the surprising, and the unsurpassable are sometimes overemphasized, the diaries dwell on the possibilities of success in America, on pride in one's occupation, and on the moral and intellectual skills that allowed these migrants to overcome unforeseen difficulties. It emerges in the *Memories* of Veltri, the entrepreneur for the Canadian Pacific Railroad who brought many fellow townsmen from Grimaldi to work in railway construction.[32] Occupational skill is the outstanding trait of migrants from Biella, who distinguished themselves as weavers and masons in America and Europe.[33] This is the case with Giardi's diary, and with many others as well.[34]

Rural settlements are remembered somewhat differently. The incredible difficulties encountered during the journey, and the dramatic fluctuations in the fortunes of the rural pioneers in Dall'Acqua's diary, for example, are described on an equal footing with hard work.[35] The reward is an opportunity to create *ex novo* an American settlement that is given the same name as the village of origin and taken as if it were the fulfillment of a Biblical promise.[36]

But it is above all the industrial workers' diaries that are critical of the new society and the unwelcome emphasis on productivity in the new economic structure.[37] The story of their struggles is dramatized by their heroic resistance against repression by their employers and the persecution suffered by union members, strikers, ethnic politicians, and libertarians, particularly but not exclusively in the United States. The criticism is even stronger in the memoirs of socialists and in the gloomy pages about the Red Scare in the 1920s, anticipating several themes of the "America Amara" image, bitter America.[38]

Transforming the Image: Travel Literature, Commercial Images, and Migration Experiences

During the last decades of the nineteenth century, the need for practical information was evidenced by the growing number of travel guides and books examining the less positive aspects of America as well as its ideals of freedom, which latter aspect was particularly emphasized by the socialists and by the anarchists.[39] Travel literature was an effective medium for popularizing America among the lower classes; illustrated periodicals acted as an important means of spreading information to the emigrant world. In fact, in certain periodicals travel literature was considered "a duty when it treated great Italian colonies in which brothers distinguish themselves for their activity and honor the mother country."[40]

The readers were offered a picture of life and work in the new Italian emigrant colonies that, if not idyllic, was at least intriguing. The long-standing dream of land-ownership seemed at last to come true there. These descriptions enchanted readers interested in American destinations and offered a version less manipulative than the one given by the emigration agents. Through the pages of the illustrated magazines, workers and peasants learned about the fertile plains of Argentina, about slavery in Brazil, and about the great advances in industrial civilization in the United States. "Engravings and illustrations were no less eloquent than texts in documenting the adventurous and the exotic (including by the end of the century, the huge industrial and urban agglomerations of North America)."[41] They suggested the prospect of a rapid improvement in the moral and material standards of living in comparison with the mother country.

For most working-class readers this New World could not be achieved at home: the future could be reached only by emigration. This explains the interest in almanacs, encyclopedias, immigrant guides, and illustrated periodicals that focused on American society. It also explains why there was more information available on America than on other European destinations, which by 1880–1900 were still absorbing about one-half of the Italian migration flow.

Yet there was also popular literature that warned migrants about the moral and material dangers of the New World, and religious literature that underlined the great dangers in very moralistic terms. But the "alarmist" tendency, found particularly among Salesians and other orders, did not prevent their missionaries from working with and helping migrants. As a result, information about the New World was also spread through religious bulletins. As an example of popular religiosity, the ex-voto tablets sent to Italian sanctuaries and churches by migrants in thankfulness for God's grace pictured them in the most diverse landscapes in the New World—no loss of faith, but God's help everywhere.[42]

In the second half of the nineteenth century, a dreamlike, escapist style of description was superseded by more matter-of-fact reporting. There were the special correspondents, with links to Genoese shipping companies, who wrote for *L'Italia all'estero, Il Corriere Mercantile*, and *Il Commercio-Gazzetta di Genova;* for *La Borsa*, a mouthpiece for Ligurian and Italian shipping companies between

1865 and 1884; and, with regard to Brazil, for *L'Amazzonia*.[43] Some first-hand accounts warned against the risks and uncertainties of migration.[44]

Emigrant guides provide a means for understanding the attitude of the philanthropists, middle classes, and the common people vis-à-vis the new countries. They offered detailed descriptions about geography and politics, and information on salaries, food prices, and laws regulating rural settlement. They listed important addresses and sometimes even contained an elementary foreign-language dictionary. The guides were also a way of transmitting a broad variety of messages, from advertising to ideological articles. The authors were ingenious personalities and included well-known names in the immigration debates: Jacopo Virgilio, the liberal Genoese economist; Bernardino Frescura, a geographer and traveler, who alone published nine emigrant guides; Camillo Manfroni, a university professor; and numerous intellectuals and supporters of the shipping companies' interests, as well as spokesmen for free emigration.[45] Some emigrant guides had a strongly propagandistic message: one guide to Peru, for example, was aimed at capitalists and immigrants, encouraging Italian merchants and speculators to invest in Peruvian mines and rubber plantations.[46]

Traditional descriptive guides were replaced by semi-handbooks. The *Italian Emigrant's Yearbook*, edited by a bookseller in Genoa with branches in Argentina, offered standard information on Argentina in the 1905 edition, which was sponsored by an olive oil firm. The second part offered illustrated advertisements, lists of organizations and institutions, and the names of all the successful Italian businessmen in Argentina.[47] Thus the image of the new country tended to change from that of an exotic and strange land into a more familiar place, as the network of fellow settlers became known. Emigration thus began to reveal its nature as a mass movement toward familiar colonies, created by the sacrifices of earlier colonizers.

After a few decades the guides began to report on the negative aspects, too. The opportunities offered by the La Plata region and the success stories of Brazil or the United States were followed by more responsible and paternalistic advice. The guides stressed the unfavorable climatic conditions (as in Brazil, for example) and institutional drawbacks such as the loss of personal freedom (the recent history of slave labor in Brazil, the frequent cases of peonage and even lynching in the United States), the severity of foreign laws, or the unpredictability of economic fortune.[48]

Travel books also changed. The critical curiosity of many accounts published in the *Nuova Antologia*, for instance, which was still influenced by the optimistic vision of Adolfo Rossi (once an anonymous emigrant and later an emigration commissioner), made way for somber evaluations of the future of Italian emigrants by Amy Bernardy, Angelo Mosso, Ausonio Franzoni, and Guglielmo Ferrero.[49] This version of Italian emigrant culture ceased to create a myth about the Americas, in the eyes of informed Italians, but created something closer to its opposite. "The image of the United States turns of necessity from the stereotypical to the nightmarish experiences of emigrants."[50] Opportunities appeared more and more circumscribed and limited. The new reality was the city with its growing masses of the poor, and not the frontier. Many observers at the end of the nineteenth century pointed out that the old "America = freedom + future" equation no longer held true. Critical reports by emigrants influenced the works of socialists, Catholics, and liberals who analyzed the contradictions within American societies that often did not respect the freedom that they proclaimed. Within the immigrant communities, which were ruled by new immigrant elites, real prospects and hopes were replaced by nationalistic values and symbols.[51]

From Promised Land to Bitter Land

The turning point in the transformation of the image was the emergence of restrictionism, which became America's dominant philosophy after World War I. From 1917 onward, the United States refused entry to illiterate immigrants and, especially after the Russian Revolution, to radicals of all sorts: the door to the New World was closed. Restrictionist ideology became official policy and added to the economic difficulties of the sending countries. Travel guides were no longer needed. Letters and diaries of first-generation immigrants were less important. A new genre of literature, with a new group of authors, began to influence the image. The experience of the immigrant colonies in the Americas found its reflection in the work of ethnic writers. Novels written by representatives of the Italian communities directed attention to the ambiguous relationship with the new country and the tensions resulting from new citizenship, on the one hand, and allegiance to the country of origin, on the other.[52]

In the 1920s, the double image formed in the villages of origin and in the Americas, particularly in the United States, was transformed. For those who remained in the Old World, in the isolated villages of southern Italy, the myth of America, once the "myth of the future," received a new lease on life during the Fascist era, for political reasons. The old emigrant who returned to Italy realized, after an absence of a few decades, that instead of finding the familiar faces he could remember, he had become instead a foreigner in a strange land. But for those Italians who had settled in the New World and who could no longer return, there was the opposite myth, the "myth of the past," of a paradise lost, the dream of a happy arcadia reinforced by Italian nationalism.[53] The wheel had turned full circle. The immigrant who remained in America and tried to change his personal reality or the system had become an outcast. Sacco and Vanzetti were emblematic of this; they represented the end of the myth of freedom.[54] The core of the contradiction lay in emigration itself, which can be considered as a kind of metaphor for the relations between Italy and America.

The popular myth of the *Terra Promessa*, the Promised Land, underwent a gradual decline through the elaboration of the vision of *Terra Amara*, the Bitter Land.[55] If it was no longer possible to create new lands where immigrants could place their hopes, expressed symbolically by re-creating the Italian home villages in rural or urban villages in America and giving them the names of the villages of origin, racist restrictionism changed the metaphor of the "ungrateful land." This metaphor, which used to refer to places of origin, where life was dismal, was turned upside down: America was now the ungrateful land, with its Golden Door seemingly forever closed to the disinherited, the starving, for those without hope: to all those whom—and by whom—the myth of America had been created.

Notes

Translated by Stefano Luconi and Ira Glazier.

1. See Oscar Handlin, *Gli sradicati* (Italian translation, Milan: 1958), 248. For ideologies and myths surrounding the most important countries of destination, see Selim Abou, *L'identité culturelle: Relations interethniques et problèmes d'acculturation* (Paris: Anthropos, 1981), in particular, 147–235.

2. See, also for other aspects, the fundamental work by Ercole Sori, *L'emigrazione italiana dall'unità alla seconda guerra mondiale* (Bologna: Il Mulino, 1979), 205–11; Commissariato Generale dell'Emigrazione, *Annuario statistico dell'emigrazione italiana dal 1876 al 1925* (Rome, 1926); Gino Arias,

La questione meridionale (Bologna: Zanichelli, 1921); Francesco Coletti, "Dell'emigrazione italiana," in *Cinquanta anni di storia italiana*, vol. 3 (Rome, 1911).

3. See *Le Americhe* (Milan: Electa Ed., 1986); see also the essay by Emilio Franzina, "Ricchi e poveri attraverso l'Atlantico," 194–206. See also the special issue of *Movimento operaio e socialista*, "Dall'Italia alle Americhe: Storie di emigranti e immagini dell'emigrazione," *Movimento operaio e socialista* 1–2 (1981): 3–191.

4. The popular saying "In America you lose your faith," which was spread both in Italy and in other Catholic countries, was propagated also by ecclesiastic hierarchies that, when the migration movement started, tried to deter it because of the moral dangers that were usually ascribed to it and the lack of places of worship in the receiving countries. See the first pontifical documents collected in *Chiesa e mobilità umana: Documenti della Santa Sede dal 1883 al 1983*, ed. Graziano Tassello and Luigi Favero (Rome: Centro Studi Emigrazione-Roma [hereafter, CSER], 1985).

5. See Luigi Einaudi, *Un principe mercante* (Turin: Bocca, 1900).

6. See Ferruccio Macola, *L'Europa alla conquista dell'America Latina* (Venice: Ongania, 1894).

7. See Attilio Brunialti, *Le colonie degli italiani all'estero* (Turin: UTET, 1897); Gigliola Dinucci, "Il modello della colonia libera nell'ideologia espansionista italiana: Dagli anni '80 alla fine del secolo," *Storia Contemporanea* 10, no. 3 (1979): 427–79; Gerolamo Boccardo, *L'emigrazione e le colonie* (Florence: Le Monnier, 1871); Leone Carpi, *Delle colonie e dell'emigrazione d'Italiani all'estero sotto l'aspetto dell'industria, commercio ed agricoltura*, 4 vols. (Milan: Ed. Lombarda, 1874).

8. See Antonio Annino, "La politica migratoria dello stato unitario," *Il Ponte* 30, nos. 11–12 (1974): 1229–68; *Italia e America dal Settecento all'età dell'imperialismo* (Venice: Marsilio, 1976); Emilio Franzina, *La grande emigrazione: L'esodo dei rurali dal Veneto durante il secolo XX* (Venice: Marsilio, 1976).

9. See Luigi Villari, *Gli Stati Uniti d'America e l'emigrazione italiana* (Milan: Treves, 1912). Critical reports on the United States can be found in the magazine edited by Giovanni Preziosi, *L'Italia all'estero*. Francesco S. Nitti argued that only in Latin America could the Italian emigrants meet with success, in Francesco S. Nitti, *Scritti sulla questione meridionale*, vol. 1 (Bari: Laterza, 1958), 395–401. Enrico Ferri, first socialist and then nationalist, went to extremes and called for a "big stick" policy to defend Italian workers abroad: Luigi Crovetto, "Enrico Ferri in Argentina," in *L'Italia nella società argentina: Contributi sull'emigrazione italiana in Argentina*, ed. Fernando Devoto and Gianfausto Rosoli (Rome: CSER, 1988), 63–70. For the political debate, see the groundbreaking work by Fernando Manzotti,

La polemica sull'emigrazione nell'Italia unita (Milan: Dante Alighieri, 1969).

10. See Angelo Trento, "Argentina e Brasile come paesi di immigrazione nella pubblicistica italiana (1860–1920)," in Devoto and Rosoli, eds. *L'Italia nella società argentina*, 211–40. See also Chiara Vangelista, "Vita d'emigrante: Il colono nella piantagione di caffé paulista secondo l'interpretazione dei viaggiatori italiani (1880–1930)," *Miscellanea di storia delle esplorazioni* 7 (Genoa: Bozzi, 1982): 247–310; and especially Teresa Isenburg, "Nois não tem direito de terras, tudo e para a gente da Oropa: L'immagine del Brasile nell'Italia di fine secolo," in *Migrazioni europee e popolo brasiliano*, ed. Gianfausto Rosoli (Rome: CSER, 1987), 206–28.

11. Giuseppe Tropeano, *La fine dell' "America": L'ultimo aspetto della emigrazione* (Naples: Ed. Partenopea, 1915), 146.

12. See Giuseppe Massara's discerning introduction to the bibliographical work *L'immagine degli Stati Uniti attraverso le testimonianze dell'esperienza italiana in America, 1850–1914* (Rome, 1983), iv. See also his *Viaggiatori italiani in America (1860–1970)* (Rome: Ed. di Storia e Letteratura, 1976).

13. Emilio Franzina, "La lettera dell'emigrante tra 'genere' e mercato del lavoro," *Società e Storia*, no. 39 (1988): 101–25, contains many bibliographical references for further research. See also his "Le culture dell'emigrazione," in *La cultura operaia nella società industrializzata* (Milan: F. Angeli-Maison des Sciences de l'homme, 1985), 279–338; Samuel L. Baily and Franco Ramella, eds., *One Family, Two Worlds: An Italian Family's Correspondence across the Atlantic, 1910–1911* (New Brunswick, N.J.: Rutgers University Press, 1988); Paolo Cresci and Luciano Guidobaldi, *Partono i bastimenti* (Milan: Mondadori, 1980); P. Via and G. Sterlocchi, *"Vengo caramente a salutarvi": Lettere di emigranti valchiavennaschi in America, 1853–1946* (Chiavenna, 1983); G. Boselli, *Lettere di emigranti della Val di Taro* (Parma, 1979).

14. See Rovilio Costa, *Imigraçã italiana no Rio Grande do Sul: Fontes historicas* (Porto Alegre: Escola Superior de Teologia, 1988); see also the numerous transcriptions of first emigrants' oral recollections (concerning the journey, ties with the country of origin, first settlement) in Rovilio Costa and Arlindo Battistel, eds., *Assim vivem os italianos*, 3 vols. (Porto Alegre, 1982–83); Luis A. De Boni, *La Merica: Escritos dos primeros imigrantes italianos* (Porto Alegre, 1977).

15. See Franzina, "Le culture dell'emigrazione," 285–88. Many emigrants' letters were published in Italian newspapers with conflicting aims in mind: for a collection of those sent to local administrations and a discussion of their content, see Emilio Franzina, *Merica! Merica! Emigrazione e colonizzazione nelle lettere dei contadini veneti in America latina, 1876–1902* (Milan: Feltrinelli, 1979), especially 11–72.

16. E. Lussana, *Lettere d'illetterati: Note di psicologia sociale* (Bologna, 1913), had already pointed out the solemn importance of letters in the peasant world; see ibid., 19–20. For a more recent period, see Emiliano Giancristofaro, *Cara moglia: Lettere a casa di emigranti abruzzesi* (Lanciano: Carabba, 1984); Angela Rositani, "L'emigrazione calabrese come strumento di rivalsa sociale, 1950–1980: Un'analisi dell'epistolario delle famiglie," in *L'emigrazione calabrese dall'unità ad oggi,* ed. Pietro Borzomati (Rome: CSER, 1982), 241–56; Aurora Campus, *Il mito del ritorno: L'emigrazione dalla Sardegna in Europa attraverso le lettere degli emigranti alle loro famiglie, anni 1950–1971* (Sassari: Edes, 1985); Arrigo Bongiorno and Aldo Barbina, eds., *Il pane degli altri* (Udine, 1970).

17. Ministero dell'Agricoltura Industria e Commercio, *Statistica dell'emigrazione italiana all'estero nel 1878 confrontata con quella degli anni precedenti* (Rome, 1880), ix–xiv; see the reports for Veneto quoted in Franzina, "La lettera dell'emigrante," 115.

18. See "Emigrazione," *La Gazzetta di Mantova,* 22–23 Mar 1888; *Gazzetta di Venezia,* 1 Mar 1887, quoted in Franzina, "Le culture dell'emigrazione," 287.

19. Some "optimistic" letters gave detailed information about the profitable choices migrants had made and practical directions about the journey and the tools and other necessities that had to be brought along; see Franzina, "La lettera dell'emigrante," 117.

20. B. Bossi, *Il Brasile: Il giornalismo e l'emigrazione* (Genoa, 1886).

21. P. Biasutti, "Cause, effetti e rimedi dell'emigrazione transatlantica: Suo stato ed importanza attuale nella provincia di Udine," *Bollettino dell'Associazione Agraria Friulana,* no. 4 (22 July 1878): 46, quoted by Franzina, "Le culture dell'emigrazione," 288.

22. In Calabria, one local newspaper stated: "Emigration is increasing and threatens to depopulate the whole village. All the workers are seized with the fever to leave for the United States of America, which they see as a sort of Eldorado. . . . The reason for this [leaving their country] can be found in the desire to earn money and move up to the same level as those in a better economic condition." "Cose di Platì," *Cronaca di Calabria* 7, no. 15 (11 Apr 1901); see Mirella Mafrici, "La polemica sull'emigrazione nella provincia reggina in età giolittiana attraverso la stampa periodica locale," in Borzomati, *L'emigrazione calabrese dall'unità,* 89–113.

23. *Le condizioni dei contadini nel Veneto.* Parte prima della relazione di Emilio Morpurgo sulla XI circoscrizione (Inchiesta Jacini) (Rome, 1882), 109.

24. See Nunzia Messina, "Considerazioni sull'emigrazione italiana dopo l'Unità, 1876–1879," in *Il movimento migratorio italiano dall'Unità nazionale ai giorni nostri,* ed. Franca Assante, 2 vols. (Naples and Geneva:

Droz, 1978), vol. 2, 247–348.

25. See the quotations in Franzina, "La lettera dell'emigrante," 122; Egisto Rossi, *Del patronato degli emigranti in Italia e all'estero: Relazione al primo Congresso Geografico Italiano (Genova, 1892)* (Rome: Società Geografica Italiana, 1893).

26. The attitude of the church in Italy (bishops, clergymen, and Catholic laity) is now largely documented in the papers presented at the international historical meeting, Piacenza, 3–5 Dec 1987: *Scalabrini tra vecchio e nuovo mondo*, ed. Gianfausto Rosoli (Roma: CSER, 1989): see in particular Luigi De Rosa, "Stato e Chiesa nell'assistenza agli emigranti italiani," 237–52; Francesco Malgeri, "La tutela legislativa dell'emigrante e l'apporto dei cattolici," 253–68.

27. Massara, *L'immagine*, iv; see also Joseph Rossi, *The Image of America in Mazzini's Writings* (Madison, Wis., 1954).

28. Nevertheless, see the important literacy contributions "L'America degli italiani." *Letterature d'America* 9–10 (1981); William Boelhower, *Immigrant Autobiography in the United States* (Venice: Foscarina, 1982); Vanni Blengino, *Oltre l'Oceano. Un processo di identità: gli immigrati italiani in Argentina (1837–1930)* (Rome: Ed. Associate, 1987); Pasquino Crupi, *Letteratura ed emigrazione* (Reggio Calabria, 1979); Pasquino Crupi, *Un popolo in fuga* (Cosenza, 1982).

29. See Antonio Margariti, *America! America!* (Casalvelino: Galzerano, 1979).

30. See Adele Maiello, "Il diario di Andrea Guagliardo, contadino in Fontanabuona," *Indice per i beni culturali del territorio ligure* 8 (1983): 14–20. See also the important material collected by Marco Porcella, *La fatica e la Merica* (Genoa: Sagep, 1986).

31. See Carmine B. Jannace, *La scoperta dell'America* (Padua: Rebellato, 1971). For a similar case, see Mary Halls Ets, *Rosa: the Life of an Italian Immigrant* (Minneapolis, Minn.: University of Minnesota Press, 1970).

32. See John Potestio, "Le memorie di Giovanni Veltri: da contadino a impresario di ferrovie," *Studi Emigrazione*, no. 77 (1985): 129–40.

33. See Fondazione Sella, *L'emigrazione biellese fra Ottocento e Novecento*, ed. Valerio Castronovo, 2 vols. (Milan: Electa, 1986); *L'emigrazione biellese nel Novecento*, (Milan: Electa, 1988); Corrado Grassi and Mariella Pautasso, *"Prima roba il parlare . . .": Lingue e dialetti dell'emigrazione biellese* (Milan: Electa, 1989).

34. See *Il diario di Salvatore Giardi: Ricordi d'Australia* (Tirano, 1913); Romano Panozzo, *Vita dura e avventurosa di un emigrante dell'Alto Vicentino (1922–1942)* (Thiene, 1983).

35. See G. Dall'Acqua, "Gli emigranti: Appunti di viaggio," in Battistel and Costa, eds., *Assim vivem os italianos*, 2: 1109–79.

36. Among the many examples, see Luis De Boni and Rovilio Costa, *Os italianos do Rio Grande do Sul* (Porto Alegre, 1979), and the extensive documentation on the Italians in Argentina, Brazil, and the United States in *Euroamericani: La popolazione di origine italiana nel mondo* (Turin: Fondazione Giovanni Agnelli, 1987).

37. See Elisabetta Vezzosi, "La Federazione Socialista Italiana del Nord America tra autonomia e scioglimento nel sindacato industriale, 1911–1921," *Studi Emigrazione*, no. 73 (1984): 81–110; Susanna Garroni and Elisabetta Vezzosi, "Gli emigranti dell'ideale," in *May Day Celebration*, ed. Andrea Panaccione (Venice: Marsilio, 1988), 85–107. Recollections and suggestions can be found in the testimony of Joseph Tusiani, *La parola difficile: Autobiografia di un italo-americano* (Fasano: Schena, 1988); and that of Vanni B. Montana, *Amarostico: Testimonianze euro-americane* (Livorno: Bastogi, 1975).

38. See Peppino Ortoleva, "Testimonianze proletarie e storia negli USA," *Primo Maggio*, no. 5 (1975): 51–62; Peppino Ortoleva, "Una voce dal coro: Angelo Rocco e lo sciopero di Lawrence del 1912," *Movimento operaio e socialista*, nos. 1–2 (1981): 5–32; Gisela Bock, Paolo Carpignano, and Bruno Ramirez, *La formazione dell'operaio massa negli USA, 1886–1922* (Milan: Feltrinelli, 1976); Leonardo Bettini, *Bibliografia dell'anarchismo* vol. 1, pt. 2; *Periodici e numeri unici anarchici in lingua italiana publicati all'estero (1872–1971)* (Florence, 1976); Errico Malatesta, *Scritti scelti*, introduction by Gino Cerrito (Rome: Savelli, 1970); Anna Rosada, *Giacinto Menotti Serrati nell'emigrazione (1899–1911)*, (Rome: Ed. Riuniti, 1972).

39. See Ulisse Barbieri, "Emigrate! . . . Emigrate! . . . qui si muore," *La Favilla*, 13 May 1885.

40. *L'illustrazione popolare*, no. 42, 16 Oct 1887, 658.

41. Franzina, "Le culture dell'emigrazione," 299.

42. For the efforts of the Salesian order to help Italians in America, see Gianfausto Rosoli, "Impegno missionario e assistenza religiosa agli emigranti nella visione e nell'opera di don Bosco e dei Salesiani," in *Don Bosco nella storia della cultura popolare*, ed. Francesco Traniello (Turin: Società Editrice Internazionale, 1987), 289–329. For the activity of the Scalabrinian order in America, see *Scalabrini tra vecchio e nuovo mondo*, edited by Gianfausto Rosoli (Rome: CSER, 1989).

43. See Mario Enrico Ferrari, *Emigrazione e colonie: Il giornale genovese "La Borsa" (1865–1894)* (Genoa, 1983); Mario Enrico Ferrari, "L'Amazzonia: Una rivista per l'emigrazione nel Brasile settentrionale," *Miscellanea di storia delle esplorazioni* 9 (Genoa, 1984): 244–300; D. Furfaro, "Il contributo di Vincenzo Grossi al dibattito sul problema della colonizzazione," *Miscellanea di storia delle esplorazioni* 7 (Genoa, 1982): 203–46; Francesco Surdich, "L'emigrazione di massa e la Società Geografica Ital-

iana," in *Un altro Veneto*, ed. Emilio Franzina (Abano Terme: Francisci, 1983), 234–56.

44. In 1876 Nicola Marcone, a former deputy from Abruzzo, led a group of poor emigrants from Abruzzo to Paranaguà, in Paranà, Brazil, where Savino Tripoti, an unscrupulous adventurer from Teramo, had established a colony. Marcone's writings were used by the local administration to deter peasants from emigrating. Nicola Marcone, *Gli italiani al Brasile* (Rome: Tip. Romana, 1877). See the true story by A. Marazzi, *Emigrati*, 3 vols. (Milan: Dumolard, 1890), which is the source of the better-known and more accurate tale by Edmondo De Amicis, *Sull'oceano* (Milan: Treves, 1890).

45. See Cecilia Lupi, "Qualche consiglio per chi parte: Le guide degli emigranti (1855–1927)," *Movimento operaio e socialista*, nos. 1–2 (1981): 77–89. Both governmental and private institutions used these guides. From 1901 on, the Commissariato Generale dell'Emigrazione directly or indirectly fostered the publication of practical guides with a particular political message.

46. See *Guida del Perù per capitalisti e immigrati* (Lima: Tip. Fabbri, 1902).

47. See Edoardo Spiotti, *La Repubblica Argentina: Annuario dell'emigrante italiano* (Genoa, 1905 and 1906).

48. See Giacomo Moroni, "Il peonage nel Sud degli Stati Uniti," *Bollettino dell'emigrazione*, no. 5 (1910): 3–20; Luigi Villari, "Gli italiani nel distretto consolare di New Orleans," *Bollettino dell'emigrazione*, no. 20 (1910): 3–46; Camillo Cianfarra, *Diario di un emigrante* (New York, 1900); Giusto Calvi, *I senzapatria: Note dal vero da New York a Napoli* (Valenza, 1901); Alberto Pecorini, *Gli Americani nella vita moderna osservati da un italiano* (Milan: Treves, 1909).

49. See Adolfo Rossi, *Un italiano in America* (Milan: Treves, 1891); Adolfo Rossi, *Nel paese dei dollari* (Milan, 1893), and *Impressioni italo-americane* (Rome, 1907); Giuseppe Giacosa, *Impressioni d'America* (Milan: Cogliati, 1898); Gherardo Ferreri, *Gli italiani d'America: Impressioni di un viaggio agli Stati Uniti* (Rome, 1907); Guglielmo Ferrero, *Fra i due mondi* (Milan: Treves, 1913); Amy Bernardy, *America vissuta* (Turin: Bocca, 1911); Amy Bernardy, *Italia randagia attraverso gli Stati Uniti* (Turin: Bocca, 1913); Giovanni Preziosi, *Gli italiani negli Stati Uniti del Nord* (Milan: Lib. Ed. Milanese, 1909); Ausonio Franzoni, *Pel decoro del nome italiano in America* (Milan, 1901); Angelo Mosso, *Vita moderna degli italiani* (Milan: Treves, 1906).

50. Massara, *L'immagine*, vi; see in particular Rudolph Vecoli, "Free Country: The American Republic Viewed by the Italian Left, 1880–1920," in *In the Shadow of the Statue of Liberty: Immigrants, Workers and Citizens in the American Republic*, ed. Marianne Debouzy (Paris: Presses Universitaires de Vincennes, 1988), 35–56.

51. See the still valid remarks by Grazia Dore, *La democrazia italiana e*

l'emigrazione in America (Brescia: Morcelliana, 1964); Fernando Devoto, "La primera élite italiana de Buenos Aires," *Studi Emigrazione,* no. 94 (1989): 168–94; Romolo Gandolfo, "Notas sobre la élite de una comunidad emigrada en cadena: El caso de los agnoneses," in Devoto and Rosoli, eds., *L'Italia nella società argentina,* 160–77.

52. See Constantine Panunzio, *The Soul of an Immigrant* (New York: Macmillan, 1922); Constantine Panunzio, *Immigration Crossroads* (New York: Macmillan, 1927); Paschal D'Angelo, *Son of Italy* (New York: Macmillan, 1924); Jerre Mangione, *Mount Allegro: A Memoir of Italian American Life* (New York, 1942).

53. Massara, *L'immagine,* vii.

54. See Bartolomeo Vanzetti, *Autobiografia e lettere inedite* (Florence: Vallecchi, 1977); R. S. Fuerlicht, *The Story of Sacco and Vanzetti: Justice Crucified* (New York: McGraw-Hill, 1977); L. Joughin and E. Morgan, *The Legacy of Sacco and Vanzetti* (Princeton, N.J.: Princeton University Press, 1984); *Sacco-Vanzetti: Developments and Reconsiderations* (Boston: The Public Library of the City of Boston, 1982).

55. See Emilio Cecchi, *America amara* (Florence: Sansoni, 1940).

11

From Myth to Reality: America in the Eyes of East European Peasant Migrant Laborers

Ewa Morawska

In Europe: The Myth of the "Golden Land"

Between 1880 and 1914 about 7.5 million people from Russia and Austria-Hungary arrived in America. Nearly two-thirds of them were peasant labor migrants. Most of the remaining third—2 million—were Jews, and a small number came from the other classes within the Christian population. This transoceanic movement in search of work was part of the intense multidirectional labor migrations that had been sweeping through East Europe since the 1860s, reflecting the region's progressive incorporation into the larger, Western-centered capitalist system.

It was only in the second half of the nineteenth century, and specifically during the five decades preceding World War I, that Eastern Europe entered the process of accelerated urbanization and industrialization. Even then, however, it was a drawn-out and incomplete transformation, fraught with contradictions: initiated and executed "from above" by the old ruling class, encumbered by the ubiquituous remnants of the feudal past in social forms and political institutions, hampered by the dependent character of the region's economic advance, which lacked internal impetus and was subordinated to the much more developed Western economies.[1]

Between 1870 and 1910, the urban population of Eastern Europe increased by 125 percent and the transportation network (in railway kilometers) expanded by over 150 percent. The number of factories and industrial workers increased by 75 percent in Austro-Hungary and 67 percent in Russia, and the value of industrial output in these two empires grew by impressive factors of four and eight, respectively.[2] Largely promoted and sustained by West European investments, these transformations plugged the East European economies into the orbit of the expanding capitalist system, without, however, creating a sufficient base for the diversification and independent growth of autonomous local industries. On the eve of World War I, foodstuffs, primary goods, and raw materials remained the dominant exports of both Russia and Austria-Hungary, accounting for about three-quarters of their international trade, and the proportion of the population employed in agriculture in these two countries was still a high 65 percent in Austria-Hungary and 78 percent in Russia, almost double the average of the most developed Western societies.[3]

The belated abolition of serfdom and the abolition of feudal manorial estates (1848 in the Austrian monarchy and 1861–64 in Russia) had cumulative long-term effects on East European economies. Executed without rearrangement of the old sociopolitical order, the land reforms provided millions of formally enfranchised peasants with neither sufficient land nor the means to acquire it. Coupled with a demographic boom—between 1860 and 1910 the population of the region increased by more than 100 percent—the consequences of these partial solutions were to influence greatly the course of East European economic development during the five decades preceding World War I. One effect was the rapid fragmentation of peasant landholdings as they were divided and subdivided among their progeny; at the beginning of this century, 50 to 70 percent of the landowning peasantry, depending on the province, were owners of dwarf- and small-holdings of less than five hectares. The second consequence was the creation of a huge agrarian proletariat. On the eve of World War I the number of "superfluous" people—landless and wage-dependent descendants of the serfs—averaged almost one-fourth of the total rural population of Eastern Europe.[4]

The profound economic and social imbalances in the region accompanying its urbanization and industrialization and its "dependent pull" into world capitalism, were "pushing out" domestic labor to become part of this larger system. The enormous rise in the numbers of the landless rural population, and of dwarf-holders incapable of maintaining themselves from the soil, forced thousands of peasants every year out of their villages in search of employment and

income. For instance, at the turn of the century in Galicia, Subcar-
pathian Rus', Slovakia, and Greater Poland, over one-half of the
dwarf-holding families regularly earned outside income (in some
districts of these provinces the proportion reached 70 percent).[5] The
colossal dimensions of these migratory movements, evidenced in
contemporary reports from virtually all quarters of the region, indicate that at the beginning of the twentieth century no less than one-
third of the adult agrarian population of the vast territories covering
Hungary, Slovakia, Poland, the western part of the Ukraine, Subcar-
pathian Rus', Transylvania, Croatia-Slavonia, and northern Serbia
had lived or worked in places different from those of their birth.[6] The
gross estimates of the size of these labor migrations (covering both
seasonal and permanent movements) conducted outside of the region
between 1860 and 1910 show that the combined migrations from all
Polish territories affected about 9 million people; in Hungary in the
same period, an estimated total of about 6 million people migrated
from their permanent residences in search of wages. In only six years,
from 1906 to 1911, nearly 3 million people migrated from Austrian
territories.[7] The paths of these labor migrants crisscrossed in all
directions: in short- and middle-distance harvest migrations within
the provinces of Eastern Europe, across provincial boundaries to the
cities for seasonal work in the factories, and—in increasing volume
toward the end of the century—outside of the region to the Lower
Austrian and east German farmlands and farther west to the industrialized regions of Germany and France, and, farther still, across the
Atlantic. This long-distance movement was greatly facilitated by the
linking of Eastern Europe to western parts of the continent by railway networks, and to the United States by improved and relatively
cheap ocean transportation.

Contrary to the customary representations in American ethnic
literature of America's uniqueness in attracting the largest proportions of turn-of-the-century migrants from Europe, in terms of volume alone, the back-and-forth labor migrations of East European
peasantry on the continent were considerably greater than their
movement across the Atlantic. For instance, of the estimated total of
all kinds of migrations by Poles between 1880 and 1914, the United
States received no more than 20 percent. If we compare only the two
destinations that attracted the largest proportions of wage-seeking
migrants from Polish territories during the three-and-a-half decades
preceding World I—Germany and the United States—it turns out
that Polish migrations to the United States were only one-third the
size of those to Germany.[8] However, even though migrations across

the Atlantic from Eastern Europe between 1880 and 1914 involved all in all no more than about 7 to 8 percent of the rural population of the region, of all places that peasant laborers could and did go, it was only America that had a "Great Legend" of unmatched riches awaiting the emigrants.

News about the "golden land" was first spread through the East European countryside by agents of American employers (before contracting labor became officially outlawed by the U.S. government in 1885), who came seeking low-skilled workers for rapidly expanding heavy industries, which were suffering a labor shortage as the number of immigrants from Western Europe dwindled. Representatives of steamship companies in Hamburg, Antwerp, and Bremen likewise solicited potential migrants with promises of fast and easy earnings on the other side of the Atlantic. This advertising and solicitation by outside agencies performed the function, in the words of one contemporary observer, of "opening up new regions which are ripe for emigration [due to the local conditions] and setting the ball rolling. [They hasten] the starting and make smooth the avalanche."[9] Once initiated by the interaction of "pull" and "push" impulses, travels from Eastern Europe to America soon became self-sustaining: the more people had gone before, the larger the flow grew, with relatives and friends following the pioneers in a pattern of chain-migration.

Indeed, calculated in rubles and *Kronen*, the wages that could be obtained in America appeared to be dream pay to the impoverished peasants, incredibly more than anything they could ever earn at home, or even from work in remote Western Europe. Although about 50 percent higher than income from local agricultural labor, industrial wages in East European cities were 33 to 40 percent lower than those in German factories, and 65 to 70 percent lower than in the United States.[10] At the turn of the century, an industrial laborer in Hungary made approximately $3.50 a week; of this, he spent, on the average, $2.00 a week, which left him with monthly savings of about $6.00. From their whole season's earnings in Germany and Lower Austria at the same time, labor migrants from the village of Maszkienice in Galicia saved about $50 per "migrant capita"—not an insignificant sum of money, sufficient to carry the family through the winter, or to purchase new clothing or an animal for the farm, but not enough to buy an additional acre of land or build a new house or farm building. In America, a single man could save at least $15 to $20 a month, and a hardworking young woman could save up to $10. The economic calculation was obvious: it meant, in Austrian *Kronen*, the unheard-of ability to afford a full hectare of land out of a single year's savings, or to earn the price of four cows in six months or of a large new brick farm building in nine. "For these minds," noted a contemporary observer, himself of peasant origin, "accustomed to the poor local wages [and living conditions], it was like a fantasy."[11]

"American fever" was further increased by letters (between 1900 and 1906 alone over 3 million letters arrived in Eastern Europe from the United States) comparing emigrant laborers' earnings with those obtained at home, by photographs of well-fed and urbanely dressed "Amerikanci"—Americans—by remittances sent to the villages, and not least by the returning migrants themselves, who told colorful sagas, often exaggerated, about America's wonders and their own accomplishments there.

In the county of Ropczyce, in the central part of Austrian Poland, the average sum sent from America by money orders to seven villages between 1902 and 1907 was $140 per household, and in Maszkienice the combined postal remittances and personal savings of U.S. returnees averaged $850 per capita (the average number of years spent in America was 3.5). In 1901 alone, seven thousand Croatian migrants from one Zagreb county sent home $291,869, and in 1903 Hungarian migrant laborers from the county of Veszprem sent back home no less than $621,856. In one year, 1906, the little village of Cetinje in Montenegro received $30,000 from America—"more money than passed through the hands of its postmasters in the twenty preceding years." All in all, during the six years from 1900 to 1906, the total amount of American money received in Russia and Austria-Hungary from peasant labor migrants was a staggering $69 million.[12] The enormous amount of dollars that had come into the possession of peasant households as the result of American labor migrations—plainly visible to all as it was turned into land, cattle, brick houses, barns, and better food and dress—augmented the hopes of those who had not yet gone themselves, and fortified their belief that America was the peasant El Dorado. "The talk is all about America," wrote a Croatian from Lika-Krbava at the beginning of the century,[13] and the talk was the same in many corners of Eastern Europe. The American success story spread through the region. Louis Adamic recalled:

> I experienced a thrill every time a man returned from the United States. Four or five years before he had quietly left for America, a poor peasant clad in homespun, with a bundle on his back. Now, an *Amerikanec*, he usually sported a blue serge suit,

buttoned shoes with India rubber heels, a derby, a celluloid collar and a long necktie made even louder by a dazzling horseshoe pin, while his two suitcases of imitation leather bulged with gifts from America for his relatives in the community. Thus, the ambition to go the United States was kindled in boys by men who had been there.[14]

Similar images appear time and again in peasants' reminiscences:

America became the subject of endless and feverish conversations and longings, and going there appeared to incarnate a happiness simply beyond words. When, after a few years spent in America, Walenty Podlasek returned to Wierzchoslawice [a village in Galicia], such processions of people visited him every day that he was forced to hide so that they could not torment him with their questions. . . . [And when] with the dollars he brought with him [he] purchased a dozen or so hectares and started to build one house in Wierzchoslawice and one in Tarnow, the people went wild with envy and desire.[15]

It was, then, first and foremost, the image of "that incredible land of gold," as went the popular song about America, where within two weeks people made as much money as a peasant would earn working the whole year at home, that emigrants setting off to cross the Atlantic held in their minds. For some, it was accompanied by a more vague but also appealing vision of America as "the land of freedom." Peasants understood "freedom" in terms of their own experience in an Eastern Europe that was still sunk waist-deep in feudal remnants, as a freedom from *poddanstwo* (serfdom): from subordination in social demeanor and cultural mores of the class of toilers to the class of the *pany*—the genteel possessors of means and status. "The life in America is such as at home even *Jasnie Pan* [i.e., the noble] does not have"; "[One eats and drinks in America] and is not subordinate to anyone"; "America is a free country. . . . [Y]ou don't have to be *poddanem* [a serf] to anyone"; "In the office and in the bank, everywhere they treat a man with respect, whether he is dressed up [in a genteel fashion] or dirty [from work]"—such stories about America, although much less widespread than those about the "golden land," were also repeated in East European villages as peasants gathered to discuss this strange country and to ponder whether and how to go try their luck there.[16]

In America: "Work Like a Horse," "Good Times, Bad Times"

For the majority of those who crossed the Atlantic, the sojourn in America was to be temporary: although longer than the customary six to eight months of seasonal labor in Western Europe, it was, however, not to exceed a few years. Over two-thirds of the peasant laborers arriving in the United States at the turn of the century were from the landless stratum, and the remaining were owners of small- and medium-size holdings. A few years of work in America, they calculated, should be sufficient to earn enough money to secure an independent existence at home in the village. "I thought this," wrote a contemporary peasant emigrant, "[in America I will] work a few years, save money, [then] will return [to Europe] and will marry into a good *gospodarstwo* [farm], and I will be a *kmiec* [yeoman]." And another: "I lived with this single thought: to earn money and to return home and to buy a farm even better than my father's"; and one more: "I wanted to earn a lot of money, to make my life [in the village] easy."[17] And, indeed, a large number of emigrants—at least 30 to 35 percent, according to recent estimates—returned to Europe.[18] The majority stayed on, extending their sojourn from one year to the next amid prolonged uncertainty and indecision. A Slovenian recorded his feelings in a diary as he traveled in 1903 from Pennsylvania to Michigan in search of a better job:

> During the journey I remembered the promise I had given Mother upon my departure for America: "We shall see one another in two years." I felt ashamed. It was absurd! [Time passed and] instead of returning home, I was traveling in the opposite direction, more than a thousand miles away at the other end of America![19]

And from a husband in Glasport, Pennsylvania, to his wife waiting in Poland:

> I received your two letters, and in both of them I heard nothing else but if I would come back. You see, my dear treasure, although you write to me that I love money better than you, nevertheless you see that I love you and the money . . . because when we have a great deal of money then we fill ourselves up by eating and drinking and when we dress up, then it will be pleasant to look at each other. . . . So you see, I want to work [here] for some time yet.[20]

As the migrants stayed on, kept on working, and established families and ethnic communities in American cities, their picture of America changed: the image of an easy "poor man's El Dorado" gave way to a complex, ambivalent evaluation, with the costs and gains of their transplantation and a new life cautiously weighed against each other. "Nikde nebolo Slovakom tak dobre ako v Amerike. Ale nikde netrpeli tol'ko ako v Amerike"—"Nowhere did the Slovaks have it so good as in America. But nowhere did they suffer as much as in America."[21] This equivocal message from an account of the Slovaks' history in America also mirrors the experience of Polish, Ukrainian, Rusyn, Hungarian, and Yugoslav peasant migrants who came to live in this country.

Soon after arrival, as they moved into the crowded foreign colonies and found employment in nearby factories, they realized that the America awaiting them there was not what they imagined at home. "My disappointment was unspeakable," recalled a Galician peasant,

> when after a twelve-day journey I saw the city of Johnstown [a mill town in Western Pennsylvania]: squalid and ugly, with those congested shabby houses [in the immigrant section of town], blackened with soot from the factory chimneys. This was the America I saw.[22]

And another one, from Chicago:

> The neighborhood [where we lived] was near the mills. . . . [E]veryone wanted to live as close to them as possible, so as to save some money on transportation. In addition, many of us were afraid lest we get lost or meet [the Americans] with whom it would be difficult to communicate. . . . Practically every house had so-called bortniki—peasants on board, often fifteen of them in one small apartment. . . . It resembled more a hospital when you looked at the men sleeping on the floors and everywhere around. I thought this America did not look so inviting as I imagined [at home] from the stories told there.[23]

And from Detroit, another center of East European settlement at the beginning of the century:

> Immediately after coming [here] I noticed that America was not so beautiful and ideal as I dreamed about it. . . . The

streets in working-class neighborhoods, [dirty], unpaved, made a very unpleasant impression. Oil and gasoline smelled everywhere beyond endurance. Comparing it I realized what air we had in Europe in the countryside, and what [air there was] in America in the city.[24]

In such surroundings, the lush greenery of the European villages appeared even greener and the fields more aromatic, intensifying the nostalgia and bewilderment peasants felt in the alien, urban-industrial environment. Throughout the mill- and coal-towns of Pennsylvania, where thousands of East European laborers settled, Magyar immigrants sang:

> Coal-dust soaks up our tears,
> Our laughter is drowned in smoke,
> We yearn to return to our little village,
> Where every blade [of grass] understood Hungarian.[25]

And, most of all, as the migrants were quickly to realize, contrary to the stories circulating in the East European countryside—the very stories that mobilized them to undertake the journey to America in the exciting hope of altering their lives by quickly amassing "gold"—there was no money "lying on the streets." "Dear wife," wrote a Polish peasant from Passaic, New Jersey,

> it is not true what people said that in America gold lies on the streets; it is not true, because for money [here] one has to work hard. . . . [D]ear wife, if you think that money in America is easy to come by, one has to work oh, so hard for it.[26]

Although unavoidably disappointed from the start by the confrontation of old-country dreams with American reality, having already taken a significant step by leaving the village and crossing the ocean, the immigrants were stubborn and determined to confront the new situation: "I came [to Johnstown], so dirty, awful . . . but I was already here, so whether it pleased me or not, I had to go at it, and make the best of it," recalled a Polish woman who had joined her brother in America in 1906 in the hope of earning a substantial dowry for herself and her younger sisters at home.[27] As they stayed on, America as it actually was in their daily experience still appeared a promise, perhaps, but one to be redeemed at the price of terribly hard work and deteriorating health, dismal living conditions, and recurrent insecurity—a price much steeper than what they had ever imagined in Europe. "Ameryka dla byka, Europa dla chłopa"—America for the ox, Europe for the man, went a popular saying among peasant-immigrant laborers, implying that only those with unusual stamina and strength could meet the challenge of work demands in American industries, whereas men of average physique and endurance should stay at home.

Not surprisingly, because it absorbed most of their time and energy, peasant migrant laborers associated "their" America primarily with the drudgery of industrial work. It was not that they were not accustomed to arduous manual labor; in Europe toiling was also part of their daily existence. But even for the landless who worked for others, the pace and character of labor on the soil was not experienced as so profoundly alienating as was their industrial employment. "Dear brother," wrote a migrant steelworker from Braddock, Pennsylvania, to his home village,

> If you want to, you can come to the same city where I live. Here you will find work right away as long as you are willing to work. But I tell you . . . that here work is not the same as in the old country. In the old country, you can work the way you like and every Sunday and holiday you can rest. But here in America, it is not like that, because here, as soon as you start a job, you have to work day and night and holidays and non-holidays. . . . Because even if you want to have a day of rest, they will not give it to you; but rather you have to work straight through just like the horses or oxen back home. Yet not even like that because horses and oxen are idle every Sunday and holiday there. Here you don't have any free time. You can make money fast, but you have to work hard for it.[28]

And from an autobiographical novel by Thomas Bell about the life of Rusyn peasant-immigrant workers in nearby Homestead, Pennsylvania:

> Here work never stops. The furnaces are going day and night, seven days a week, all the year round. I work, eat, sleep, work, eat, sleep until there are times when I couldn't tell my own name. And every other Sunday the long turn, twenty-four hours straight in the mill. . . . The long turn was bad but the first night turn

coming on its heels was worse. Tempers flared easily, men fought over a shovel or a look and it was fatally easy to be careless, to blunder. . . . *Jezus*, what a life![29]

Inexperienced with factory machinery, unaccustomed to the pace of industrial labor, and physically exhausted, immigrant workers suffered from frequent industrial accidents and various physical ailments. And these, if serious and long-lasting, were a disaster, annihilating the hopes for accumulating capital that had brought them to America and that sustained them in their arduous labor, as well as wiping out whatever savings they had managed to put aside. "As long as a man is healthy and can work, then it is good [here], but if he is not well, he cannot work and then there is only misery for that man."[30] And a husband wrote from Pittsburgh to his wife in the village:

So, dear wife, it depends on you whether you want to come to America or you prefer that I come back home. If you think you want to come here, consider it well that it is not like at home. Here as long as you have good health you have food. [At home] one planted potatoes and food was ready. But here it is worse—misery when the husand and father gets ill—then what will his woman do? So, dear wife, write me what you want, I can always send you a [steamship] ticket but [do not want] you [to] regret later these American delights.[31]

And another immigrant worker wrote:

Because I was very ill, I lost my job. . . . Those beautiful dollars of gold and silver, which I earned with hardship and with my blood, disappeared all too soon because my illness was serious and unfortunate. I tried to save myself with all my resources and so almost 190 rubles [$95; the average daily pay of unskilled immigrant laborers in American factories at the beginning of the century was $1.50] were spent and wasted on doctors and very costly medicine. And now I have plenty of debts to pay off. My illness resulted from the heavy work [I was doing]. I was all swollen like a log, but especially I suffered with my head. It was swollen like a pail. So let nobody think that it [is] so good in America because everyone has to work hard, as hard as a horse. . . . But it is true, that [when there's work] one can make a ruble here much faster than one can make a half ruble in an entire summer there [at home].[32]

But one more unpleasant and unexpected fact about America that the immigrants discovered soon after their arrival was that even for those strong, healthy, and willing to meet the challenge of "horse-like" labor, steady employment could not be relied on. In Europe, peasants' work also had a seasonal character, but the periods of work and idleness were predictable and could be planned for, and the effects of their labor on the soil counted in the annual scale. In America, they had to save now in order to survive next month, in addition to putting aside extra money to take or send back home. The frequent slumps and layoffs that characterized industrial production in American factories at the beginning of the century particularly affected unskilled foreigners employed in large floating labor gangs that were easy to assemble and disband, repeatedly reduced or even entirely annihilated whatever capital the immigrants had accumulated by thrift and deliberate deprivation, and deeply cut into their subsistence wages. "In America, it is good for someone who has a job, but if he does not have a steady job then he can hardly make enough for a living," wrote an emigrant from Philadelphia to his friend in the village in reply to his request that he advise him about coming there.[33] "Bad times, good times, bad times, one after another"[34]— this theme appeared over and again in the immigrants' recollections of their encounter with the United States.

"Work like a horse" and the insecurity arising from the rotation of "good times, bad times" in the factories were two recurrent motifs in the peasant-immigrants' accounts of their experience as industrial workers in America. They felt America found them useful only for their labor, and useless if they were not working—just like farm animals back in Europe. "Here in America in the working class, man exists only to work and to support his family if he has [the means]. A man who does not work has no value"; "Here they select workers just as they pick out beasts at the market in the old country or as they do for the army, just as long as they are strong and healthy, that is how they deal with people."[35]

"They" was another common reference as the migrant laborers reflected on the America they came to know. The old-country dreams about no more *poddanstwo*, for those who had harbored such ideas, evaporated, too, as immigrants found themselves segregated in foreign colonies in American cities, isolated from mainstream political and cultural life, unprotected by American labor unions that barred their participation, and bossed around in the factories and coal mines as a second-rate "Hunky" workforce—hired, fired, and moved around at will as their managers desired. Thomas Bell narrated the experience of Slovak immigrants in the steel mill in Braddock, Pennsylvania:

> Working under [an American] boss was less a matter of doing one's work well than of pleasing him, of allowing for his prejudices, flattering him, noting whether he was in good humor, laughing at his insults . . . and at all times building up his self-esteem by fearing him. He didn't like Mike [hero of Bell's story]. He told him: "You're a smart Hunky and I don't like smart Hunkies. Furshtay?"[36]

To many immigrant laborers, the exploitation, contempt, and degrading treatment they encountered as lower-class "Hunkies" in America from the industrial and political bosses did not appear so fundamentally different from their situation in Europe. "In the old country," wrote Thomas Bell,

> the Slovaks had been . . . a nation of peasants and shepherds whom the centuries had taught patience and humility. In America [thrust into the blast furnaces and rolling mills] they were all this and more, foreigners in a strange land, ignorant of its language and customs.[37]

All in all, their American experience led a number of peasant-immigrants to the same conclusion, pointedly expressed by Kracha, another of Thomas Bell's heroes:

> I've been in America long enough to learn that it's run just like any other country. In Europe your emperors and grand dukes own everything, and over here it's your millionaires and your trusts. They run the country to suit themselves.[38]

They had come to America to earn money, to make a living, and when

> they realized that bosses were the same everywhere, and when the epithet Hunky was hurled at them, they shrugged. It was hardly pleasant, but there was nothing one could do about it. . . . They kept to themselves, speaking their own tongue, retaining their old customs.[39]

This inner social and cultural world of their own—which extended between the old-country village and the new homes and ethnic communities they founded in America, and which to a significant extent separated them, within and without, from the mainstream American world—served as the primary counter-reference peasant-immigrants used in measuring their achievements and in evaluating American life. Seen from inside this inner world and evaluated by its value standards, "the foreigners' America," for all its costliness and fickleness, nevertheless appeared to peasant-immigrants to possess undeniable advantages over the villages they had left behind. It was, on the whole, a better place for them. "My parents," recalled a second-generation Slovenian-American, "they saw all the bad things in this country, they were not blind, but . . . they still preferred it here than to go back to Europe." In the repeated musings of Kracha, Thomas Bell's immigrant hero, we find: "Braddock is no paradise, I admit, but have you forgotten how we had to live in the old country?"[40] This comparative reference to their existence in Eastern Europe was a natural, common evaluative standard used by the immigrants, especially during that prolonged period when they still thought of going back home, and, even later, after they had for all practical purposes settled permanently in America.

Low as earnings were—the lowest rates paid to any American laborers—and obtained at the cost of terribly hard work, these earnings of peasant-immigrants, which they continued to translate into the old-country currency as well as calculating them in dollars, still appeared as "dream pay" to them when evaluated against the opportunities in the home village. "For a forty-eight-hour week, after a week I received $12 and right away translated it into *Kronen;* it was 60 *Kronen* a week [in Eastern Europe a farm laborer at the beginning of the century received $1.70–$3.00 a week plus board]," an immigrant wrote in his diary. And from another immigrant memoir: "When I would get my *pejda* [pay] . . . I thought myself a rich man because in two weeks here I made more than in the old country in one year." Like Szabo Janos, an emigrant from Baranya county in Hungary, they "kept on working and thinking. . . . Every ten minutes he had made a nickel. What could he buy with that? Lots. [Then he made] a dollar and that was a landmark. . . . And if you have been a farmhand in Baranya County, a dollar is not merely a piece of money, it is also power, prestige, command over the universe."[41]

In the comparisons they made with their old-country existence, the improved material standard of living the immigrants enjoyed in America was the dominant criterion. A Slovenian noted in his diary something one finds over and again in immigrant accounts of their American experience: "Although my standard of living . . . was at its lowest compared with American standards, it was splendid compared with that in the old country."[42] Remembering well the subsistence diet consisting of a monotonous rotation of cabbage, bread, and noodles, East European peasant-immigrants evaluated their accomplishments in America by the amount and quality of food on their tables—the American Dream for the poor—but these were the categories in which they genuinely experienced both improvement in their life situations and America's blessings. A Polish immigrant miner from Johnstown, Pennsylvania, recalled: "We had very little, but there was more of this bread here than there, and something on this bread, too." And again: "It was terribly hard work, and we lived poorly. . . . But we ate good broth with meat . . . while at home [in Europe] only borsht and potatoes, borsht and potatoes." And another one from New Bedford, Massachusetts: "When in the old country I saw meat only at Christmas and Easter, and from time to time when they killed a rabbit at home, now I have sausage every day for dinner."[43] Achievement was also measured by the "city dress" they could afford to wear and display on the photographs sent home to the village: "Now I am telling you dear *kum* [relative] . . . that I was going to send you our photographs for Christmas . . . so that you could see how we look in this new country. It seems to me, dear *kum*, that if you'd see my wife and your sister in town, you wouldn't dare to approach her with greetings."[44] Among the criteria used by the peasant-immigrants to evaluate their improved position in America, the "gentility" of their new style of living was also important. A reference group in their comparisons and self-evaluations was that of the old-country noblemen, the *pan* or baron. "I have a good job and make two dollars a day which is four Russian rubles. . . . Life I have such [here] that even a *pan* at home does not have," wrote an immigrant to his family in Russia. And others: "I am a great *pan* [in America]. . . . I make a ruble here faster than six *Groschen* there"; "In America . . . a pound of the fattest meat costs $.03 and $.04, the leaner the more expensive, a pound of sausage $.03. I am a *pan* here." And a Hungarian: "I finish my work, get dressed, and I too am a gentleman," unlike in Hungary.[45]

As time passed, peasant-immigrants gradually abandoned their expectations of returning to Europe and came to perceive their stay in America as permanent. Although the old country and their former life there became an increasingly blurred and remote memory, it remained an important point of reference as they evaluated their position in this country. More and more, however, their family and ethnic communal life in American cities became both the primary focus of their interest and activities, and the immediate context in which they defined and pursued their goals, as well as the comparative framework within which they evaluated their current situation, achievements, and failures.

The immigrants' notion of accomplishment differed from the mainstream American standard of individual ability and performance realized through formal education and occupational mobility. The ideal of a good life as defined by the cultural system of East European ethnic communities in the first decades of this century had several components, including the steady industrial employment of the head of the household; the optimum possible combination of wages and working conditions within the occupational segment of American industries reserved for foreigners; some savings; plentiful food on the table; American dress; a home with a garden in a better immigrant neighborhood away from the factories and away from the original "Hunky rows" without basic facilities; and, not least, a good reputation among one's fellow immigrants in the ethnic colony, established through regular, visible participation in communal activities, events, and organizations.

For the peasant labor migrants leaving for America at the turn of the century, the undertaking had concrete and pragmatic purposes: to earn within a few years the maximum amount of money to be invested in material possessions at home, which, in turn, would result in the elevation of their family's social status in the village. As their sojourn turned into permanent settlement, the immigrants transferred this basic orientation to their new situation: their goal was now to accumulate as many material possessions as possible, first as a safety net against economic insecurity, then in order to achieve the closest approximation of what their ethnic communities defined as success. Since recurrent industrial slumps made their incomes unsteady, in pursuit of these goals immigrant families relied on various strategies, such as adding up the contributions of several family members—including housewives who took in boarders and children employed at odd jobs, reducing household expenditures by making clothing at home, and keeping gardens with small animals, or, in small towns, larger plots of ground on which they planted beets and potatoes.[46]

It was on the basis of the amount of material possessions accumulated and displayed in public that the immigrants were accorded prestige in their ethnic colony and ranked in its internal social status hierarchy:

> The showmanship [was important], the front you put on for others. It included [all or at least some combination of the following]: Home ownership, nice furniture that is "advanced," more modern and "American" than was usually possessed by the immigrant households . . . dress that yourself, your wife and children wore; food, that is eating better; the style of family celebrations like throwing big weddings and baptisms.[47]

The second important component of a good life, and, by the same token, a way to gain status in the immigrant communities, was active participation in ethnic life:

> People who were officers of [the Slovak] *Jednota* who mingled, and went to [ethnic] conventions, they were looked up to. If you had [wealth] but did not come outside, kept to yourself, then you were not so respected.[48]

Despite the insecurity of their economic status, and for all the tensions, repeated setbacks, and bitter disappointments the immigrant working-class families experienced in the realization of all these goals, slow improvement of living conditions was possible.[49] In Europe, accumulation above the subsistence level was inconceivable for most peasants, unless they migrated every year for an extended period of time, leaving their families behind. Although at a very steep price, America offered this opportunity, even for the working-class "Hunkies." The accomplishments of their fellow immigrants and the progressive socioeconomic differentiation within the ethnic communities were evidence enough.[50] Furthermore, compared with their initial years as newcomer "greenhorns"—another perspective the immigrants used to evaluate their current American life—they perceived their later existence in the East European communities as easier, more affluent, and more comfortable: "I worked hard and poured a lot of sweat," recalled a Galician peasant fifteen years after his arrival in America in 1912,—"My hands [are] hardened from labor like leathery shoe soles and all my fingers contorted . . . but I have gained some money to secure further existence."[51] In a letter to his relatives in Europe, another immigrant evaluated his American experience after a similar length of time spent in this country: "In

America . . . [it is] better than at home, but at the beginning always hard. But the one who endures will have it easier later."[52] And another wrote:

> Well, if your wife was thrifty, she baked at home, kept chickens in the garden, sewed for the children—you did not spend too much, then, because everything was so cheap. If you had other people working in the family and if you did not drink in bars and saved your money . . . [you] could get things here and make good, better than in the beginning.[53]

The superimposed reference frameworks of the village in the old country, where prospects were uniformly bleak, and of the years spent in America, which, although alternating between "bad times and good times," had nevertheless permitted a slow, step-by-step elevation of their living standard, gave even the poor immigrant families a sense of motion and accomplishment.

Conclusion

The immigrants' encounter with American reality quickly demolished the unrealistic dreams they had harbored in the old country about "the incredible El Dorado-land." Their lives in America, as they were soon to discover, were to be hard and insecure. But, compared with the alternative they had known in Europe, peasant-immigrants perceived this country as a *lesser evil*. "America is not perfect, [it is] true, but elsewhere these failings are even more numerous and more pronounced," concluded an editorial in the Chicago Polish-language newspaper *Zgoda* in 1910.[54] As they came to know America, the immigrants' perception of the country, and of their own circumstances in this new environment, formed a many-sided and ambivalent picture, composed of several attitudinal components reflecting their multiple roles as peasant migrant-sojourners still attached to their rural homeland, as unskilled industrial laborers in American factories, as "Hunkies" at the lowest echelons of the American sociopolitical structure, and as members of their own ethnic communities with a distinct cultural value system and internal social hierarchy. This perception was informed by a profound sense of the complexity and relativity of things: good and bad, hope and disappointment handed out simultaneously, gains and losses coming from the same bag. "I am not praising it excessively, but I am not negative about it either"; "I do not praise it here . . . nor do I put it down," wrote the immigrants about America and their lives here at the beginning of the century.[55] And a similar equivocal evaluation, in which satisfaction and sorrow were inextricably mingled, was expressed in a poem about America published at the same time in an immigrant foreign-language newspaper, each stanza ending with the same refrain: "Avoid too much praise, do not criticize too much, wherever roses grow, you will also find thorns."[56]

Notes

1. On the dependent or peripheral character of Eastern Europe's economic capitalist transformation at the turn of the century, see Ivan Berend and Gyorgi Ranki, *Economic Development of East Central Europe in the Nineteenth and Twentieth Centuries* (New York, 1974), and, by the same authors, *The European Periphery and Industrialization, 1780–1914* (New York, 1982). See also Alexander Gerschenkron, *Economic Backwardness in Historical Perspective* (New York, 1965); Immanuel Wallerstein, *The Modern World-System* (New York, 1980), vol. 2, chaps. 5 and 6; and Daniel Chirot, *Social Change in the Modern Era* (New York, 1986).

2. See Berend and Ranki, *Economic Development of East Central Europe*, 118–20, 128–36; *The European Periphery and Industrialization*, 25, 144–57; Chirot, *Social Change in the Modern Era*, 87; C. Trebilcock, *The Industrialization of Continental Powers, 1878–1914* (New York, 1981), 233–35, 351–59; Vladimir Dedijer et al., *History of Yugoslavia* (New York, 1974), 358–63; Ivan Berend and Gyorgi Ranki, *Hungary: A Century of Economic Development* (New York, 1974), 62–63; Jerzy Topolski, ed., *Dzieje Polski* (Warsaw, 1978), 160–61; Zanna Kormanowa and Irena Pietrzak-Pawłowska, eds., *Historia Polski*, vol. 3, pt. 1 (Warsaw, 1963), 217–21, 406, 641–52; Jan Sveton, *Obyvateľstvo Slovenska za Kapitalizmu* (Bratislava, 1958), 185–87.

3. See Berend and Ranki, *Economic Development of East Central Europe*, 135–37; *The European Periphery and Industrializatoin*, 25, 159; Chirot, *Social Change in the Modern Era*, 102–3.

4. The data on demographic growth are from Jerome Blum, *The End of the Old Order in Rural Europe* (Princeton, N.J., 1978), 418; on the segmentation of peasant landholdings and the rural proletariat, data are from Ewa Morawska, *For Bread with Butter: Life-Worlds of East Central Europeans in Johnstown, Pennsylvania, 1890–1940* (Cambridge and New York, 1985), 26–27, Table 1.1: "Distribution of Gainfully Occupied Population and Peasant Landownership in East Central Europe around 1900."

5. Compiled from Sveton, *Obyvateľstvo Slovenska*, 72–73; B. Il'ko,

Zakarpatske Selo na Pochatku XXst, 1900–1919 (Lvov, 1973), 120–21; *Polish Encyclopaedia,* vol. 3 (Geneva, 1922), "Economic Life of Poland," 216–18, 344–45, 413–14; Wladyslaw Rusinski, "The Role of Peasantry of Poznan (Wielkopolska) in the Formation of the Agricultural Labor Market," *East European Quarterly* 4 (January 1970): 515; Ryszard Turski, *Miedzy Miastem a Wsia: Struktura Spoleczno-Zawodowa Chłopów-Robotników w Polsce* (Warsaw, 1965), 75–85.

6. Compiled from Elzbieta Kaczynska, *Społeczenstwo i Gospodarka Północno-Wschodnich Ziem Królestwa Polskiego w Okresie Rozkwitu Kapitalizmu* (Warsaw, 1974); 31–33; Ion Aluas, "Industrialization and Migration of the Transylvanian Peasantry at the End of the Nineteenth Century and the Beginning of the Twentieth Century," *East European Quarterly* 4 (January 1970): 502; Ladislav Tajtak, "Slovak Emigration and Migration in the Years of 1910–1914," *Studia Historica Slovaca* 10 (1978): 55–64; I. Szabo, ed., *A Magyar Parasztsag a Kapitalizmus Koraban, 1848–1914* (Budapest, 1965), vol. 2, 321–71; Julianna Puskás, "Emigration from Hungary to the United States before 1914," *Studia Historica Academiae Scientiarum Hungariae* 113 (1975): 10–17; Berend and Ranki, *Hungary: A Century of Economic Development,* 24–26; Ireneusz Ihnatowicz et al., *Społeczenstwo Polskie od X do XX Wieku* (Warsaw, 1979), 459–66.

7. Compiled from Ihnatowicz et al., *Społeczenstwo Polskie,* 459–66; Benjamin Murdzek, *Emigration in Polish Social-Political Thought, 1870–1914* (New York, 1975), 314–89; Leopold Caro, *Emigracja i Polityka Emigracyjna ze Szczególnum Uwzględnieniem Stosunków Polskich* (Poznań, 1914), 20–31; Kormanowa and Pietrzak-Pawlowska, eds., *Historia Polski,* vol. 2, pt. 1, 216–19; Imre Ferenczi and Walter Willcox, *International Migrations* (New York, 1929), vol. 1, 225–26, 233, 416–20, 588–91, 727, 786–90, 878–81, and vol. 2 (1931), 349–52, 377–89, 401–3, 413–14, 429–32; Celina Bobińska and Andrzej Pilch, eds., *Employment-Seeking Emigrations of the Poles World-Wide in the Nineteenth and Twentieth Centuries* (Cracow, 1975), 37–48, 63–75, 78–88, 93–97; Berend and Ranki, *Hungary: A Century of Economic Development,* 26; Julianna Puskás, *From Hungary to the United States, 1880–1914* (Budapest, 1982), 14–28; C. A. Macartney, *The Habsburg Empire, 1790–1918* (London, 1968), 7–55; Richard Pfaunder, "Die Grundlagen der nationalen Bevölkerungsentwicklung Steiermarks," *Statistische Monatschrift* (1907): 557–92; Wilhelm Hecke, "Binnenwanderung und Umgangssprache in den Oesterreichischen Alpenländern und Südländern," *Statistische Monatschrift* 2 (1913): 393–92, and "Binnenwanderung und Umgangssprache in den nördlichen Ländern Oesterreichs," *Statistische Monatschrift* (1914): 653–723.

8. See Ewa Morawska, "Labor Migrations of Poles in the Atlantic World Economy, 1880–1914," *Comparative Studies in Society and History* 31 (1989): 237–72.

9. Quoted in Emily Balch, *Our Slavic Fellow Citizens* (1910; rpt. New York: Arno Press, 1969), 52–53.

10. See Morawska, *For Bread with Butter*, 46–47, Table 1.4: "Average Wages of Farm Laborers and Industrial Workers in Selected East Central European Countries and in the West at the Beginning of the Century."

11. Macartney, *The Habsburg Empire, 1790–1918*, 717; Emil Lengyel, *Americans from Hungary* (Philadelphia, 1948), 113–15; Franciszek Bujak, *Maszkienice. Wieś Powiatu Brzeskiego: Stosunki Gospodarcze i Spoleczne* (Cracow, 1901), 49–50; Władysław Orkan, *Listy ze Wsi*, vol. 1 (Warsaw, 1925), 120.

12. Compiled from Stanisław Hupka, *Ueber die Entwicklung der westgalizischen Dorfzustände in der 2. Hälfte des XIX Jahrhunderts* (Teschen, 1911), 210; Franciszek Bujak, *Maszkienice. Wies Powiatu Brzeskiego: Rozwój od R. 1900 do R. 1911* (Kraków, 1914), 101–5; Frances Krajlić, "Croatian Migration to and from the United States between 1900 and 1914" (Ph.D. dissertation, New York University, 1975), 115–16, 133; Paula Benkart, "Religion, Family and Community among Hungarians Migrating to American Cities, 1880–1930" (Ph.D. dissertation, John Hopkins University, 1975), 12–16; Edward Steiner, *The Immigrant Tide: Its Ebb and Flow* (New York, 1908), 163; Frank Sheridan, "Italian, Slavic and Hungarian Unskilled Immigrant Laborers in the United States," *Bulletin of the Bureau of Labor* 72 (September 1907): 408; Balch, *Our Slavic Fellow Citizens*, 140, 183, 471–73.

13. "Notes from My Village," by a Croatian schoolteacher, quoted in Balch, *Our Slavic Fellow Citizens*, 189.

14. Louis Adamic, "The Land of Promise," *Harper's Magazine* 17 (October 1931): 618–19.

15. Wincenty Witos, *Moje Wspomnienia*, vol. 1 (Paris, 1964), 188.

16. See Witold Kula, Nina Assorodobraj-Kula, and Marcin Kula, eds., *Listy Emigrantów z Brazylii i Stanów Zjednoczonych* (Warsaw, 1973), Introduction, 85, 87; Josephine Wtulich, ed., *Writing Home: Immigrants in Brazil and the United States, 1890–1891* (New York, 1986), letter #146; Marek M. Drozdowski, ed., *Pamiętniki Emigrantów: Stany Zjednoczone*, vol. 2 (Warsaw, 1977), 470.

17. On intentions of East European peasant labor-migrants to return home, see Ewa Morawska, "Return Migrations: Theoretical and Research Agenda," in *A Century of European Migrations, 1830 to 1930: Comparative Perspectives*, ed. Rudolph Vecoli (University of Illinois Press, 1991). On the social composition of the turn-of-the-century East European migrants to the United States, see U.S. Senate, Immigration Commission, *Abstracts of the Reports of the Immigration Commission*, vol. 1 (Washington, D.C.: Government Printing Office, 1911), 358, and U.S. Senate, Immigration Commission, *Emigration Conditions in Europe, Report*, vol. 4, 377. Quotations from Droz-

dowski, ed., *Pamiętniki Emigrantów*, 1:205, 499; 2:299.

18. Estimates of the proportions of returnees in J. D. Gould, "European Inter-Continental Emigration: The Road Home: Return Migration from the U.S.A.," *Journal of European Economic History* 9 (1980): 41–113; Morawska, "Return Migrations."

19. Ivan Molek, *Slovene Immigrant History, 1900–1950: Autobiographical Sketches by Ivan (John) Molek*, ed. Mary Molek (Dover, Del., 1979), 52.

20. W. I. Thomas and Florian Znaniecki, *The Polish Peasant in Europe and America* (Boston, 1918–20), vol. 2, 338.

21. Konstantin Čulen, *Dejiny Slovakov v Amerike* (Bratislava, 1941), vol. 1, 121.

22. Ethnic Oral History Collection (1979–82), interviews with immigrant and second-generation East Europeans in Johnstown and vicinity in western Pennsylvania (in the possession of Ewa Morawska).

23. Drozdowski, ed., *Pamiętniki Emigrantów*, 2: 299–300.

24. Ibid., 2:431.

25. Quoted from Lengyel, *Americans from Hungary*, 129.

26. Kula et al., eds., *Listy Emigrantów*, Introduction, 78.

27. Ethnic Oral History Collection, interview.

28. Wtulich, ed., *Writing Home*, letter #259.

29. Thomas Bell, *Out of This Furnace* (Pittsburgh, Pa., 1976), 32, 47.

30. Wtulich, ed., *Writing Home*, Letter #110.

31. Kula et al., eds., *Listy Emigrantów*, introduction, 83.

32. Wtulich, ed., *Writing Home*, letter #177.

33. Ibid., letter #98.

34. Bell, *Out of This Furnace*, 60.

35. Drozdowski, ed., *Pamiętniki Emigrantów*, 1:366; Wtulich, ed., *Writing Home*, letter #177.

36. Bell, *Out of This Furnace*, 160.

37. Ibid., 123.

38. Ibid., 66.

39. Ibid., 124.

40. Ethnic Oral History Collection, interview; Bell, *Out of This Furnace*, 59.

41. Drozdowski, ed., *Pamiętniki Emigrantów*, 2: 259, 302; Lengyel, *Americans from Hungary*, 143.

42. Molek, *Slovene Immigrant History, 1900–1950*, 28.

43. Ethnic Oral History Collection, interview; Drozdowski, ed., *Pamiętniki Emigrantów*, 1:233.

44. Kula et al., eds., *Listy Emigrantów*, Introduction, 92.

45. Ibid., 85–87, 90–91; Puskás, *From Hungary to the United States*,

1880–1914, 137.

46. On the economic strategies of East European immigrant families, see Ewa Morawska, "The Modernity of Tradition: East European Peasant-Immigrants in an American Steel Town, 1890–1940," *Peasant Studies* 10 (Summer 1985): 257–78; and *For Bread with Butter*, chaps. 4 and 6.

47. Ethnic Oral History Collection, interview.

48. Ibid.

49. On the conflicts and tensions involved in the immigrant families' attempts at the realization of goals valued in their ethnic communities, see Ewa Morawska, "Sociological Ambivalence: The Case of East European Peasant-Immigrant Workers in America, 1880s–1930s," *Qualitative Sociology* 10 (Fall 1987): 225–51.

50. On the internal social stratification in the East European immigrant communities, see Ewa Morawska, "The Internal Status Hierarchy in the East Central European Immigrant Communities, 1890–1930," *Journal of Social History* 16 (September 1982): 75–107; and idem, *For Bread with Butter*, chap. 7.

51. Drozdowski, ed., *Pamietniki Emigrantów*, 1: 155.

52. Kula et al., eds., *Listy Emigrantów*, Introduction, 86.

53. Ethnic Oral History Collection, interview.

54. *Zgoda* (Chicago), 30 June 1910.

55. Wtulich, ed., *Writing Home*, letters 167, 172.

56. *Zgoda*, 30 June 1910.

12

Paddy's Paradox: Emigration to America in Irish Imagination and Rhetoric

Kerby A. Miller

THE title of this essay, "Paddy's Paradox" (or, if you prefer, "Caitlin's Conundrum," since half the post-Famine migrants were women), reflects the remarkable discrepancies between the objective realities of Irish migration to the United States (especially in the post-Famine period, 1856–1921, when most departures occurred) and the popular interpretations of the exodus and the perceptions of America that prevailed in rural Ireland, especially—but by no means exclusively—among Irish-speakers in the western counties.[1]

On one hand, for example, the vast majority of Irish Catholic migrants left home for essentially mundane reasons similar or identical to those that produced mass migration from other European countries: crop failures, falling agricultural prices, and, most important, the increasing redundancy of petty farmers, farmers' children, and agricultural laborers that had been brought about by the dynamics of agrarian and industrial capitalism—more specifically, by the decline in cottage industries and by the shift from subsistence to commercial agriculture, which, in Ireland, entailed the consolidation of holdings, the conversion of tillage to pasture, the introduction of labor-saving farm machinery, and the adoption of impartible inheritance and the dowry system by farmers and peasants alike. Thus, although Irish Catholics often blamed landlordism or the British government for migration and its causes, many of the most compelling, immediate reasons for migration (especially during the post-

Famine era) were generated *within* the Irish Catholic community, and it is uncertain how much hardship and migration among the rural lower classes (laborers, small-holders, farmers' non-inheriting children) were really attributable more to profit maximization among Catholic graziers, strong farmers, and rural parents, generally, than to the machinations of Protestant proprietors or British officials.[2] Likewise, although at mid-century many Irish immigrants—often impoverished and malnourished Famine refugees—experienced severe deprivation and discrimination in American cities and on public works sites, post-Famine immigrants generally fared much better, and, by 1900, despite frequently recurring economic depressions, Irish Americans (the emigrants and their American-born children) had amassed considerable property, achieved what the historian David N. Doyle has called "occupational parity" with native-born Protestant Americans, and acquired unusually great influence within the Democratic party, the Catholic Church, and the American Federation of Labor.[3]

Realistically, then, we could expect that the Irish at home would respond "rationally" both to the socioeconomic trends and exigencies of Irish life and to the superior occupational and social advantages available overseas; consequently, that they would interpret migration from Ireland as "opportunity" or even as "escape"; and that they would perceive the United States as a land where enhanced socioeconomic security or status could be attained through individual industry and/or assistance from the Irish-American community. To be sure, many contemporaries noted (or lamented) that post-Famine migrants regarded migration in increasingly positive, instrumental terms, and the letters that such migrants sent back to Ireland certainly provided those at home with a wealth of objective information concerning American conditions and opportunities. Moreover, the fact that relatively few migrants ever returned to Ireland (perhaps 10 percent), compared to the sizable return migrations among other groups (between 40 and 50 percent for Poles and Italians, for example), suggests that Irish migrants found relative affluence and contentment overseas.[4]

Nevertheless, Irish perceptions of the United States and of migration remained extremely contradictory and, in a sense, "irrational." For instance, Irish countryfolk—especially in the far West—commonly held two, diametrically opposed images of America, neither of which comported with the objective realities of Irish-American experience. The United States was seen either as a land of incredible and easily attainable wealth—as "sort of a halfway stage to heaven"—or else as an awful, forbidding place where many, if not most, Irish emigrants pined and starved their way to early graves.[5] The Irish at home often interpreted migration itself in terms of individual obligation and sacrifice, rather than ambition and opportunity. Moreover, the interpretation that enjoyed the greatest popular currency and legitimacy was that of emigration as exile, as involuntary expatriation, which was obliged by forces beyond individual choice or control, sometimes by fate or destiny, but usually by the operations or consequences of "British misgovernment," "Protestant Ascendancy," or "landlord tyranny." As we have seen, this interpretation was not literally credible, but whereas the Irish at home and abroad *individually* employed the exile motif (as in their personal letters and memoirs) only sporadically and situationally, they expressed it *collectively* with almost monotonous regularity in their songs, poems, speeches, sermons, and newspapers. Most especially, emigration as exile was a regular theme in the appeals for public loyalty and largesse of Irish and Irish-American nationalists and clerics, and their great success suggests that the hearts and wallets of ordinary Irishmen and -women, in the Old and the New World alike, were almost instinctively receptive to the imagery of political banishment.[6]

The Origins of Popular Imagery

How, then, can we account for "Paddy's Paradox"?—for the vast disparities between the realities of migration and of the Irish-American experience and many of the popular perceptions or interpretations of those phenomena? Likewise, how can we account for the profound contradictions between many of those seemingly "irrational" perceptions themselves—for instance, between the fabulously favorable and the fantastically negative images of the United States?

During the nineteenth century, many Irishmen claimed that at least some of these false images or perceptions were disseminated by Irish emigrants' letters and remittances from America or by those migrants who returned to Ireland for visits or to settle down. Supposedly, this was true especially of the notion that America was a veritable paradise. Thus, in 1836 one migrant warned that "nine-tenths of the letters sent home to Ireland contain exaggerated statements" that deluded naive, would-be migrants such as the poor Kerrywoman who, after arriving in New York much later in the century, lamented bitterly that "she was like many other fools [in Ireland] who were led to believe they would pick up money in the streets of America."[7] Similarly, many contemporaries believed that Irish-American remittances (averaging £1 million annually after mid-century) "raised a furor" for migration among impoverished peasants, who responded to such unheard-of wealth by crying " 'Hurrah for Amerikey!' " while they stampeded to the nearest embarkation ports.[8] Likewise, it was commonly believed that "returned Yanks," sporting stylish clothes and their proverbial gold watches, "always g[a]ve a grand account of themselves" and of the land where they had amassed their reputed fortunes.[9]

However, although the letters sent home prior to 1820 by Irish migrants (mostly Ulster Presbyterians) often described the New World as an arcadian "promised land," and although some later letters written by refugees from the Great Famine of 1845–50 or the near-famine of 1879–80 glowingly contrasted American bounty with Irish poverty, it is still extremely doubtful whether emigrants' letters, returned Yanks' boastings, or even Irish-American remittances were primarily responsible for propagating that image of the United States.[10] My own research into over 5,000 Irish emigrants' letters and into the folklore collections at University College, Dublin, indicates instead that the overwhelming majority of such letters and returned migrants—especially in the post-Famine era—imparted objective and carefully balanced information concerning the United States and its comparative advantages and disadvantages for potential migrants. Indeed, many Irishmen and -women in America not only gave cautious or even derogatory information about the United States (especially during the depression-ridden 1870s, 1880s, and 1890s), but also made conscious attempts to shatter the naïve illusions and expectations that prevailed at home, warning the recipients of their letters that the remittances sent home were usually the result of great effort, hardship, and sacrifice by the donors themselves.[11] Thus, in 1853 an Irishwoman in New York City wrote of a friend back in County Donegal, remembering that the latter "used to think money was got on the streets here, but if ever she arrives in this country she will find it quite different, as there is nothing got here by idleness."[12]

Nor is it likely that Irish emigrants' letters played a major role in propagating the other "irrational" perceptions of America or of emigration. With respect to the fantastically negative image of the United States, for example, although many migrants admonished their relatives not to leave home during American economic depressions, and although a few Irish Americans (such as the transplanted Corkman, Pádraig Cúndún, who described native Americans as "a malicious host—treacherous, lying vicious, [and] lewd") were savagely critical of their adopted country, most letters—as noted above—balanced warnings of specific, avoidable dangers with favorable information concerning America's generally superior economic advantages. (This was true even for Cúndún, whose venomously anti-American poems contrasted strangely with his letters' idyllic descriptions of the comfort and plenty he enjoyed on his "snug farm" in upstate New York.[13]) Likewise, although many emigrants' letters (usually written to aged parents) were often couched in dutiful, familial terms, the letters, by themselves, could not support the notion that migration itself resulted from personal sacrifice rather than economic calculations; indeed, many letters made clear that their authors' individual ambitions (if not their alienation from Irish society or even from their own families) had inspired their departures, sometimes in the face of parental or communal opposition. Finally, although many migrants expressed homesickness in their letters, and although some clearly regretted leaving Ireland and longed to return, only a minority (although perhaps a significant one) openly described themselves as exiles or specifically blamed their departures on "British oppression" or "landlord tyranny." Instead, most migrants tempered homesickness with reason, as was the case, for instance, with J. F. Costello, a farm laborer from County Limerick. Now a ranch-hand in the Pacific Northwest, Costello admitted that he considered Ireland to be "the dearest spot in the world," but he rationalized that "home sickness is something that's natural": "I often get a relapse of it," he acknowledged, "but somehow there seems to be no cure only to stand it. . . . [W]hen you cannot have what you like, you must learn to like what you have," and, after all, he concluded, "I still think I am in as good a country as there is in the world today for a poor man."[14]

It would seem, then, that the Irish at home made highly selective use of the information conveyed by the "America letters" and by returned Yanks, for only such usage—ignoring contradictory or objective evidence—could corroborate the images and perceptions that persisted in post-Famine Ireland regardless of such evidence. Thus, with respect to the popular illusion that America was an earthly paradise, one migrant despaired that his Irish correspondents did not *want* to read letters that "never contained anything of the marvellous, and [which were] not calculated to make [them] believe that riches grow like grass" in the United States.[15] Similarly, the notion that all Irish migration was tantamount to political banishment flourished in speeches, sermons, and popular music and literature regardless of a wealth of mundane and contrary evidence. One can only conclude that, for the most part, the Irish at home were not being deluded by the Irish overseas; rather, the Irish in Ireland were deluding themselves.

It is arguable that these images of the New World and interpretations of migration were rooted in the most archaic aspects of popular Irish culture. For example, in the sixth and seventh centuries the Irish missionaries who left home to spread Christianity through northern Europe described themselves as self-sacrificing "exiles for Christ," enduring what was called "white martyrdom for a man, when for God's sake he parts from everything that he loves."[16] Indeed, long before the Norman conquest of Ireland in the twelfth century, Gaelic poets commonly employed the Irish word *deoraí* (literally, exile) to describe anyone who left Ireland for any reason. Given the traumatic impact of the later, more thorough English-Protestant conquests, it was natural that seventeenth- and eighteenth-century Irish bards would apply *deoraí* and similar terms to the fates of banished Catholic chieftains and their expatriated adherents—thus providing seemingly apposite models for subsequent, ordinary migrants raised on traditions of defeat, despoliation, and deportation.[17] Similarly, the notion that the New World was a "promised land" or an earthly paradise might be traced to biblical prophecies and millennial visions, as expressed by the bards of a beaten people—"Like the Children of Israel," one poet claimed—or to embellished stories of Golconda, the fabulous riches of the Spanish Indies, as told in the sixteenth century by, say, Iberian merchants in Connaught or Elizabethan soldiers in Munster.[18] Finally, the contradictory but equally fantastic negative image of the New World might be rooted in ancient voyage tales and other traditions that associated the West or traveling westward with death or banishment, with legends that later seemed to be corroborated by the wretched treatment and appallingly high mortality rates endured by Irish indentured servants and prisoners transported to the American colonies in the 1600s and 1700s and by the earliest travel accounts penned by Irish bards, such as Donnchadh Ruadh Mac Conmara, who in the mid-eighteenth century returned to describe the New World as a howling wilderness.[19]

During the earliest years of Catholic migration, such images—especially the negative ones—were common in the Irish countryside, particularly among impoverished peasants whose parochialism was so great that they could barely conceive of life beyond their native parishes.[20] Even in the late nineteenth and early twentieth centuries, these perceptions of America and of migration, generally, prevailed most widely among the most culturally traditional and least-literate Irish-speaking communities along the west Atlantic coast. In these districts, *deorai* (exile) remained the only term for *emigrant*, and—in contrast to eastern Ireland, where Anglicized countrymen assessed America more "rationally"—western Irishmen commonly still believed that the United States was either a "land of gold" or, conversely, a "land of sweat" and "snakes." Perhaps one reason these images endured in the face of contradictory evidence was that, for pre- or semi-literate Irish-speakers, steeped in archaic legends, there was no sharp distinction between what their more modern, urbanized countrymen called "mythology" and the "real world"; thus, for Irish-speaking peasants, the unseen, "rationally" unprovable world of the fairies was just as authentic as the physical objects they could see and touch. Furthermore, the users of Irish—a language elaborate in its vocabulary and nuance—seemed to delight in extravagant superlatives and fantastic analogies. Hence, for such people migration could appear as either a descent into hell or an ascent to heaven, and America could become more than just a barely imaginable place—it could become a "wonder"—and so the stories told around western Irish hearths about *An tOilean Úr* (literally, The New Island: America) took on the same fabulous dimensions as the ancient tales of *Tír nAn Óge* and other mythical lands across the western ocean.[21]

However, by 1900 only 14 percent of Ireland's inhabitants still spoke Irish, and by then even the peasants on the western coasts had experienced at least several decades of mass migration, its mundane causes, and its practical (and generally beneficial) consequences.[22] How and why, then, did these archaic and objectively anachronistic perceptions still prevail and even flourish (as in the case of emigration as exile), not only in the western counties, but throughout a Catholic Irish society that was now overwhelmingly literate, English-speaking, and virtually inundated by letters and other information from or about America? These notions must have been deeply rooted in an Irish Catholic culture that transcended linguistic, regional, and social differences, and they must have performed crucial functions in modern Irish society or they would not have survived so pervasively.

I would contend that these traditional, communal perceptions of migration and of the New World were more than literary affectations or quaint fragments of folklore, Rather, they were logical and integral expressions of a still-pervasive cultural system or worldview that tended to devalue and even discourage individual action, ambition, and the assumption of personal responsibility—especially when actions, such as migration, seemed innovative and contrary to the customary patterns of behavior and thought that enjoined, by example and precept, passive, communal, and pre-capitalist values such as continuity, conformity, and duty. This belief system was incorporated in the secular, religious, and linguistic expressions of traditional Gaelic society, and although conquests and confiscations largely destroyed the classes that had dominated that society, substantial social and economic continuities between pre- and post-conquest ways of life still validated many elements of that system, especially among the masses of poor Catholics who remained enmeshed in subsistence-oriented and often—until after the Great Famine—Irish-speaking communities.[23]

In terms of the secular aspects of pre- and post-conquest Catholic society, both practically and ideally that society was and remained hierarchical, communal, familial, and customary—and each emphasis, as expressed through land-tenure systems, farming practices, traditional proverbs, for example, diminished the individual's responsibility in relation to the society and its governing processes and institutions, whether native or imposed by conquest. Likewise, the religious expressions of Irish society reinforced the temporal constraints and sacralized their emphases on obedience to collective and seemingly timeless authority; this was true of both pre-modern or "peasant" religion, with its fairy-belief and "predictive celebrations," and the more formal, hermetically sealed religious system imposed through the Catholic Church's nineteenth-century "devotional revolution." Finally, the Irish language in its semantic structure makes sharp distinctions between active and passive states of being, and, in comparison to English, classifies a much broader range of phenomena into an area in which action and self-assertion are inappropriate. For example, whereas an English-speaker says "I met him on the road," signifying that "I" was in control of the event, the Irish-speaker says *do casadh orm ar an mbóthar é* (literally, "He was twisted on me on the road"), indicating his passive reception of a fated or chance encounter.[24]

Within the parochial context and the ideological framework of this pre-capitalist worldview, with its overriding emphases on communal obligations and the authority of tradition, it was perfectly "natural" that the New World, so alien to received wisdom, would be conceptualized in customary, magical, and Manichaean terms, and that migration itself would be perceived as an act of self-sacrifice or even as exile. Indeed, the most common way for an Irish-speaker to describe migration has been *dob éigan dom imeacht go Meirice:* "I had to go to America," or, more precisely, "going to America was a necessity for me"—an impersonal interpretation entirely consistent with the use of *deoraí* (exile) to designate *emigrant,* as one subject to imposed pressures, and likewise consistent with historical traditions of Irish rebellion and banishment.[25]

But how could such notions, and the traditional worldview that sustained them, survive in a post-Famine Ireland characterized by what some scholars have called "modernization": that is, by the processes of agrarian capitalism and urbanization, and, in cultural terms, by what contemporaries called "Anglicization"? In a rapidly commercializing society, dominated by an affluent Catholic *bourgeoisie* composed of rich graziers, merchants, and professionals, in which even the poorest farmers and laborers were tied to the imperatives of an international market for goods and labor, it would appear logical that new situations and activities would discredit pre-capitalist norms and archaic beliefs, and give rise instead to values and perceptions more compatible with novel realities and exigencies.

On one level of analysis, it is arguable that both the "irrational" interpretations of migration and the New World, and the pre-capitalist outlooks that supported those interpretations, could remain central in Irish popular consciousness because of the structural contradictions and psychological tensions that marked a society in swift but uneven transition. Although it is broadly and retrospectively accurate to describe post-Famine Ireland in terms of *overall* "progress" or modernization, in some crucial respects the rates of contemporary change were remarkably slow, allowing substantial continuities in social structures and attitudes. For example, despite increasing urbanization and market pressures for consolidation of farms, as late as 1911 Ireland remained an overwhelmingly agrarian society where almost 70 percent of all farms were still under thirty acres in size, and nearly 46 percent under fifteen acres. Thus, although graziers and "strong farmers" (those holding thirty acres or more) had engrossed some 60 percent of all Irish *farmland,* their poorer brethren—who occupied holdings valued at less than £15—constituted over two-thirds of all *farm families.*[26] These "family farms" conformed to what the Irish sociologist Damian Hannan has called the "peasant model": characterized by "a subsistence economy, where production for the market is not the dominating purpose of production," where "use values rather than exchange values are dominant," and where the perpetuation of the family holding itself, rather than profit, is the overriding goal.[27] Indeed, according to the contemporary economist Moritz Bonn, in the early twentieth century over half these family farms were "deficit holdings" incapable of generating profits.[28]

Thus, although contemporaries sometimes decried the rationalization (or "Anglicization") of rural values that accompanied agrarian-capitalist development, and complained that some culturally deracinated Irish youths no longer viewed migration in traditional, sorrowing terms, the old images and many aspects of their corroboratory worldview still seemed applicable to many social realities and processes that remained eminently "explainable" in premodern categories. As a result of the uneven distribution and impact of commercialization, many traditional institutions, task orientations, and even linguistic patterns (in Hiberno-English as well as the vanishing Irish language) lasted well into the twentieth century. Moreover, not only did the influence of externally imposed authorities (Protestant landlords, British officials) long remain potent, but within Catholic Ireland itself the disappearance of secret agrarian societies, increased clerical authority, the social marginalization of farm laborers and farmers' non-inheriting children, and the enmeshing of small-holders in webs of debt to local shopkeepers and usurers—all these "modern" developments may have reduced, rather than widened, the scope of responsible choice enjoyed by most rural dwellers in the new, post-Famine social order. In other words, some aspects of Irish "progress" may not have promoted more individualistic or assertive outlooks, but instead enjoined continued or even increased dependence on and deference to familial obligations, patron-client ties, and communal authority figures in order to ensure survival and status.[29]

However, although mitigated, socioeconomic and cultural changes in post-Famine Ireland were great and, in some respects, rapid and traumatic. Nevertheless, those very innovations, so pregnant with social disruption and demoralization, themselves encouraged greater popular reliance on traditional values and "explanations" that could relieve the tensions consequent on rapid transition. In order to ensure social and psychological equilibrium—especially among subordinate and relatively powerless social groups, the "losers" in the lottery of agrarian capitalism—changes had to be interpreted in customary and comforting ways. Thus, whereas most post-Famine Irish responded "rationally" to new economic exigencies or opportunities (for example, by adopting impartible inheritance or by migrating), they often fell back on traditional cultural categories ("it was a necessity . . .") to justify, exculpate, or obscure causation and accountability—sometimes, as in the case of migration, by projecting responsibility for change on uncontrollable and/or "alien" forces, or by conceptualizing America in terms of traditional images that, whether fabulously favorable or fantastically awful, seemingly *compelled* certain responses and actions regardless of personal volition. In these ways, Irishmen and -women could assimilate traditional values and customary, communal sanctions to the actual practice (or nonpractice) of the new, supposedly "freer" actions (for example, migration) demanded or made available by Ireland's role in transatlantic capitalism—in the process, cloaking the rising tide of individual calculation in the assumed anonymity and fatalism of explanatory strategies that assuaged psychological and social tensions.[30]

Reality and Imagery in Western Ireland

Such unconscious strategies were most necessary and prevalent in Ireland's western counties, from west Munster north to Connaught and County Donegal, where socioeconomic and cultural changes came so swiftly after 1878 that they threatened to create a social and moral collapse. Prior to 1878, the West was still dominated by petty farmers—many of them Irish-speakers—who depended heavily on potatoes for subsistence, who practiced partible inheritance and, often, various forms of co-tillage, and who still exhibited a marked cultural insularity and a comparatively great aversion to emigration—"cling[ing] to their inhospitable mountains as a woman clings to a deformed or idiot child," as one critic remarked. However, in the late 1870s and early 1880s a combination of potato-crop failures, the collapse of farm prices, widespread evictions, and other factors destroyed the fragile economic props of the West's semi-traditional society and unleashed a flood tide of desperate emigrants from the region. Although the immediate crisis subsided by 1882, it institutionalized permanently high rates of western migration, because those who survived the depressed 1880s and 1890s did so largely through increased dependence on commercial agriculture, primarily grazing, and on village traders, shopkeepers, and usurers. In turn, this commercialization entailed the abandonment of communal farming patterns and farm subdivision, and the adoption of consolidated farmsteads and, most important, impartible inheritance.[31] Consequently, in western as in eastern Ireland (where these patterns had long prevailed), social relationships became more instrumental and migration became a societal imperative: "One son will stay at home and keep on the farm," as a west Kerryman declared, "and the others will go away because they must go."[32] Simultaneously, rapid Anglicization accompanied commercialization, eroding western peasants' cultural ties to their homeland and thereby facilitating departures mandated by structural changes. Moreover, migration itself promoted cultural discontinuities that in turn encouraged more departures, for letters and gifts from relatives overseas invited obvious comparisons between American bounty and western Irish poverty, inspiring intense dissatisfaction with customary and now purportedly "inferior" lifestyles at home.[33]

In great measure this commercialization and Anglicization had profound and logically predictable effects on the ways western peasants viewed emigration. Thus, visitors to western hearths reported that adolescents in west Kerry "talked of nothing else" but emigration, that their peers in west Connaught were "delighted when their passage arrived," and that westerners who were too old to migrate bitterly envied the good fortune of the departed.[34] However, while traditional western society and culture seemed "like a sea on ebb," many customary features remained despite or even because of the contradictory effects of rapid change.[35] In turn, these residual relationships and outlooks continued to generate or reinforce traditional interpretations of migration.

For example, although increased dependence on grazing, retail, and credit networks entailed the *ultimate* destruction of peasant agriculture, in the short run such involvement shored up the semi-subsistence family farms that still dominated the western landscape. Likewise, government policies designed to relieve the West's distress gave family farmers time to adjust to market conditions in ways designed to realize traditional, "peasant" goals. Many of these adjustments, particularly impartible inheritance and obligatory emigration for the disinherited, were radical innovations in western contexts, but the goals themselves were decidedly conservative: generational continuity, relative self-sufficiency, and security on the family holding. Thus, emigration, like the earlier seasonal migration, served highly conservative functions in western Ireland, because the departures and remittances of "superfluous" youngsters precluded felt necessities for even greater changes among those who remained at home. Similarly, despite Anglicization, in many districts cultural and linguistic continuities remained remarkably strong, and while some visitors to the West lamented what they perceived as the region's social fragmentation and cultural decline, other observers complained of the seemingly intransigent conservatism of its inhabitants—"held down by the weight of old custom and prejudices." Consequently, although western Ireland *as a whole* exhibited the island's highest migration rates after 1880, popular aversion and resistance to migration remained equally marked. This was especially true in isolated districts along the coast (where the population actually increased in some decades), but, throughout the West, farmers' sons who *inherited* land were much more likely to stay at home and marry than were their counterparts elsewhere in Ireland, despite the fact that the holdings that westerners inherited were generally much smaller and poorer than those in the eastern counties. Moreover, even among non-inheriting children *preferences* to remain at home seemed unusually strong, for on the average western farm families supported much larger numbers of dependent relatives—postponing or avoiding emigration—than did eastern families. Finally, the western Irish who did migrate seem to have had much higher rates of return than their eastern peers, and in many western communities *all* the migrants' eventual returns seem to have been commonly, if erroneously, anticipated.[36]

In part, cultural conservatism alone—the continued strength of the Irish language and its associated folklore in many districts—can help explain the persistence of old images, rooted in Gaelic culture, concerning migration and America. Thus, the belief that emigration was exile *(deoraí)* and the notions that the United States was either "the Land of the Snakes" or a place where "gold and silver [lay] out on the ditches, and nothing to do but to gather it," as one west Kerryman fantasized, could persist among parochial peasants who only understood that the New World was the antithesis, positive or negative, of western Ireland.[37] However, considering the flood of objective information about migration that reached the West after 1880, these archaic perceptions could not have survived and flourished had they not performed crucial social and psychological functions—had they not relieved, as well as reflected, the contradictions and tensions of western Irish society, especially with regard to migration.

In the late nineteenth and early twentieth centuries, western Ireland was an almost schizophrenic society, where strikingly novel social processes and outlooks coexisted with others that remained obdurately conservative. In turn, these inconsistencies inspired widespread demoralization, alienation, and insecurity: change was too rapid, exposure to radically different and purportedly superior lifestyles too sudden, and the discrepancies between tradition and innovation, ideals and realities, were too profound to be assimilated easily or explained "rationally." Thus, for example, a growing sense that western Ireland was doomed, coupled with traditional prophetic visions, could strengthen the belief that America, and particularly its cities—the sources of most of the remittances that now poured into the West—were what the Donegal novelist Séamus Ó Grianna called *caisleáin óir* (castles of gold); in turn, this image of a paradise overseas helped overcome traditional resistance to and fear of migration and so encouraged or facilitated the mass departures of the disinherited, departures demanded by the new social order. Conversely, the equally popular and traditional negative image of the New World not only reflected the fact that many western Irish, poor and unskilled for the most part, encountered great hardship and homesickness overseas, but, more important, its discouraging effects may have helped prevent the total depopulation of a region whose inhabitants evinced growing contempt for their native parishes and folk ways.[38]

However, in another sense these mythical notions were so irreconcilable that they only further exposed and exacerbated the demoralizing contradictions of western society, for while the lure of the *caisleáin óir* threatened the West with demographic and cultural deracination, the fears inspired or intensified by the opposing image threatened to discourage the wholesale migration necessary to secure the region's relative stability. In the last analysis, these conflicting perceptions, like the tensions they reflected, could only be "resolved" (or ignored) by the maintenance of the archaic fiction that emigration was exile, a departure for which the emigrant was not responsible, one attributable neither to the migrants themselves nor to the new dynamics of western Irish society. Only that "explanation" could mitigate popular enthusiasm for the "land of gold," reconcile popular fears of the "land of sweat," and so assimilate mass migration to the traditional categories of western thought. Thus, migration was sanctioned, but as the "fated" result of uncontrollable forces rather than as the consequence either of individual ambitions or of nontraditional and inequitable social arrangements. Instead, according to accepted wisdom, the migrants just "had to go," for it was "the way of the world." Such fatalism was customary and comforting—both to the emigrants and to those left behind—for the exile motif absolved community members of responsibility for actions that violated every inherited notion of community, and it helped those who feared leaving home to endure stoically a supposedly predetermined present and an uncertain future that they were unable or unwilling to conceptualize realistically. Moreover, since in the Irish-speaking West the image of involuntary expatriation was inextricably linked to a centuries-old folklore of protest against the hated *Sasanaigh* (literally, Saxons: that is, British and Irish Protestants), the fervent nationalist agitation that characterized much of the region from 1879 to 1921 could both draw upon and reinforce, in modern political terms, the archaic perception that exile was caused by British oppression—a perception that further externalized causation and obscured the socioeconomic conflicts within western Irish society.[39]

Hegemony, the Family, and Post-Famine Emigration

Although these compromises between innovation and tradition may have been psychological necessities, and although these images may have been rooted in legends and folklore, nevertheless the force and precision of such ideological adjustments—such as the fiction that all migration was basically political exile—were themselves largely determined by Catholic Ireland's governing classes and institutions. If we apply the theory of cultural hegemony, as articulated by Antonio Gramsci and Raymond Williams, for example, it is arguable that in nineteenth-century Ireland (especially the post-Famine period) the Catholic middle classes (urban merchants and professionals, graziers and strong farmers), in alliance with the Catholic Church, generated a new, dominant Catholic/nationalist culture that assimilated the traditional, pre-capitalist values and images of the Irish peasantry to the hegemonic imperatives of the bourgeoisie—that is, to the latter's need to exercise effective political and moral leadership over the Catholic lower classes so as to mitigate internecine conflict within the Catholic community and to mobilize the lower classes' traditional longings and practical grievances against the Protestant Ascendancy and the British government. This dominant or hegemonic culture was incorporated primarily through three key social media: first, the Catholic Church, which not only dominated religious life as a result of the "devotional revolution" but which also assumed pervasive influence over Catholic education; second, Irish nationalist movements, which shaped the political consciousness of an increasingly literate and mobilized people; and, third and most intimately, the strong-farmer *type* of rural family (the "stem family")—characterized by impartible inheritance, the dowry system, postponed marriage, and (circumstances permitting) capital accumulation—that became ubiquitous, even among the poorest peasants, in the late nineteenth century. By disseminating its norms and goals through these three media (as well as others), the Catholic bourgeoisie succeeded in creating a politically actionable ideological bloc: a transcendant political alliance that found expression and ultimate triumph in the Home Rule party of 1882–1916 and the Sinn Féin movement of 1916–21.[40]

However, bourgeois leadership and Catholic unity were always threatened by tensions and, sometimes, open conflict between the Catholic middle classes and their erstwhile followers among the peasantry and rural and urban laborers. Specifically, the task of the Catholic bourgeoisie was complicated by the fact that the rural middle classes (graziers and strong farmers) and, to a lesser degree, the Catholic Church, shared major responsibility for mass, lower-class migration: the former through the processes of agrarian capitalism, which made peasants, farm laborers, and farmers' non-inheriting children economically superfluous; and the latter, some critics charged, through the church's deadening and stifling impact on social life and personal expression. On the one hand, middle-class politicians and clerics had to oppose migration publicly, both because wholesale departures vitiated nationalist movements and Catholic congregations, and, more important, because migration and its economic causes were the issues that most concerned the disadvantaged sectors of Irish society whose mass support the nationalists needed. On the other hand, however, the Catholic bourgeoisie had no inclination to adopt the really radical measures (such as the nationalization of the land, advocated by Michael Davitt and James Connolly) necessary to halt migration by restructuring an Irish Catholic society whose very shape, stability, and class system mandated and depended on migration's continuance. Consequently, since middle-class nationalists could not justify migration in "rational," secular terms, they had to generate obscurantist "explanations" that would draw upon popular, residual notions—the most important of which was the old belief that emigration was political exile. Furthermore, they conceptualized contemporary Irish society in terms of a purportedly traditional and timeless "holy Ireland": an idealized, organic rural community whose benign institutions and spiritual values could nurture all of Ireland's children *at home* were it not for British misgovernment and the corroding effects of Anglicization. Indeed, in that ideological context, emigration for reasons other than political duress could not be sanctioned but was rather stigmatized as "selfishness" or even communal "treason," since "holy Ireland's" faithful sons and daughters were allegedly too selfless and unworldly to desert voluntarily "the holy peace of home" for the fleshpots of America or other Protestant, secular societies.[41]

Of course, "holy Ireland" did not really exist, and, in the sense that the concept ignored or obscured the real and often ruthless aspects of Irish capitalism, it was at best an appealing illusion, at worst a pious fraud. However, its force lay not only in the fact that the values and notions it embodied were incorporated "from above," through bourgeois-dominated political and religious institutions, but also in the fact that those values and notions were drawn from and reinforced the traditional norms and images that were still current among the rural lower classes themselves. Moreover, as we have seen with respect to western Ireland, the consequent "explanations" of Ireland's social discontinuities and inequities not only served the hegemonic imperatives of the Catholic bourgeoisie, but also performed crucial functions in mitigating tension and conflict among the poorest sectors and on the most intimate levels of Irish society. Ironically, just as the idealized peasant family was the purported microcosm of "holy Ireland"—static, corporate, and paternalistic—so post-Famine society's *real* farm families, in the Anglicized East as well as in the Gaelic West, both demanded and generated such notions and images in order to "explain" their members' migrations in traditional, nonresponsible terms. Thus, the dynamics and needs of the stem family in general—and of rural parents in particular—replicated the larger processes of agrarian capitalism and coincided with the hegemonic imperatives of Catholic Ireland's governing classes.[42]

Despite the commercialization of post-Famine society, a persistent lack of scope for individual enterprise within Ireland confirmed the Irish farm family's position as the dominant socioeconomic and cultural unit. Family bonds took precedence over all other associational ties, and religious teachings sacralized authoritarian parent-child relationships and the cooperative ethos mandated by the exigencies of small-farm agriculture. Most farmers depended heavily on their children's unpaid labor and their willingness to support parents in old age. In general, children were trained to be dutiful, submissive, and self-effacing—to subordinate individual motives and desires to customary notions of family welfare and status. Although the relationships between fathers and children were often distant and domineering, emotional bonds between mothers and sons were proverbially close, at times smotheringly so, as frustrated farmers' wives—often trapped by the dowry system in loveless marriages to men much older than themselves—lavished compensatory affection on male offspring.[43]

The family's importance, its close-knit relationships and socialization patterns, produced highly ambivalent attitudes toward emigration among parents and offspring alike. On one hand, migration threatened family integrity, physically sundered ties to birthplace and kin, and violated customary notions of proper behavior. "The Irish are distinguished for love of their kindred," wrote the American consul at Londonderry in 1883, "and that love has hitherto acted as a check to the obvious motives that induce them to leave their homes." Consequently, parents—especially mothers—often reacted to their children's impending migration with opposition or desperate grief, and they feared that the latter's departure would condemn them to a comfortless old age and a lonely death. Sometimes parental protests prevented or at least postponed their children's migrations, and although in most instances ambition or financial imperatives overcame parental objections, most migrants felt genuine sorrow at leaving childhood homes and kinsmen. Moreover, many letters and memoirs indicate that both parents and emigrants often mourned their separation for many years, sometimes until death.[44]

On the other hand, there is no doubt that many migrants were eager to leave home, both to fulfill ambitions and to escape parental repression. It is equally certain that many, perhaps most, parents either explicitly or implicitly urged their children's departure as a vital necessity to preserve social stability and improve the material welfare of those who remained at home. Given the dearth of non-farm employment, farmers' near-universal adoption of impartible inheritance made migration mandatory for the great majority of sons and daughters who would receive neither land nor dowries and whose continued presence threatened intrafamilial and social strife. In addition, many parents wanted money from the children sent abroad, both to finance further migration and to bolster Ireland's small-farm economy. Money from America not only purchased most passage tickets but also was used by farmers to pay rents and shop bills, to enlarge acreage and livestock herds, and to improve farmhouses and general living standards.[45] For example, in 1907 a witness before a parliamentary commission testified that rural savings accounts were "largely earned abroad," and one year later a French traveler noted that "throughout the West of Ireland" "the landlord's rents are often merely a tax levied on the filial piety of child emigrants."[46]

Thus, "holy Ireland's" basic social unit, the family farm, both mandated migration and fed vampirelike upon the meager resources its victims earned abroad: a contradiction that outraged the urban socialist James Connolly, who urged, "Those who prate glibly about the 'sacredness of the home' and the 'sanctity of the family circle' would do well to consider what home in Ireland to-day is sacred from the influence of the greedy mercenary spirit . . . ; what family circle is unbroken by the emigration of its most gentle and loving ones."[47] Indeed, migration at once reflected and reinforced an increasing instrumentalism in family relationships that defied traditional norms and prescribed emotions. For instance, although family bonds were probably closest in the one- and two-room cabins of western Ireland, even there economic considerations predominated. Thus, when Paddy Gallagher's family in west Donegal received an offer from a cousin in Philadelphia to pay his sisters' fares to America, his parents at first wept loudly at the prospect of "breaking up . . . the family." However, a neighbor, hearing the commotion, consoled them: "You may thank God," he admonished, "that the door is going to be opened for your children going to America. Look at our children that sent us twenty pounds at Christmas. Thank God, we were able to pay our debt and raise our heads."[48] In these circumstances, even the most devoted parents soon became reconciled to their children's migration.

However, Irish parents' calculating attitudes toward their sons' and daughters' departure had potential dangers that threatened the very interests that their migration was designed to promote. Impartible inheritance, the fathers' arbitrary selection of male heirs and dowried daughters, postponed marriage even for the fortunate, leaving emigration or social sterility for the rest: all exacerbated the intergenerational tensions normally expected in periods of rapid social and cultural change. Moreover, for various reasons at least some farmers' children did not want to migrate: in part because of their extreme youth, inexperience, and attachment to relatives and familiar scenes; in part because of child-rearing practices that encouraged dependence and portrayed the outside world as "dangerous and hostile." Thus, whereas the old notion of America as the "land of the snakes" could serve the interests of those few parents who wanted to *prevent* their children's migration, the fears of the New World which that image reflected and reinforced could make the offspring of other farm families reluctant to obey social imperatives and parental injunctions that mandated their departures. The point is that, whether migrants left home eagerly or reluctantly, *if* they perceived and resented the explicit or implicit compulsion that parents and neighbors had exerted upon them, then they might refuse to render either the emotional or the financial homage that parents demanded.[49]

Those dangers were real: some popular ballads blamed migration on the capricious decisions of "cruel parents"; and the fact that a typical migrant such as Julia Lough felt obliged to assure her mother, in a letter from Connecticut, that "you need not ever be afraid . . . we will ever say you were the cause of sending us away," indicated parents' awareness of their children's potential resentment.[50] Indeed, although contemporary eulogists and Irish countrymen themselves claimed that nearly all migrants dutifully remitted money home, other testimony suggests that a large number rarely or never did so. Thus, one elderly informant from County Mayo admitted that although "there were many requests for financial assistance from home, . . . it can be truthfully said, that not even half these importunate letters were answered, much less complied with."[51] Of course, failure to write and send remittances could stem from many causes, including illiteracy, poverty, and consequent shame exacerbated by the emigrants' awareness that "american letters is no use in ireland without money in them."[52] Nevertheless, many "neglected" parents could justly blame themselves for their children's alleged "ingratitude": for at worst they had compelled migration, at best they had helped rationalize family relationships. In the first case they often inspired lasting resentments, while in the latter they undermined the traditional and emotional bases of their own authority and implicitly encouraged their children to demonstrate a similar degree of pragmatism.

In these circumstances, it was necessary for Irish parents—indeed, for rural society as a whole—to generate perceptions of migration that would obscure causation and responsibility, that would encourage or at least sanction migration yet, at the same time, neither inspire their children's indignation nor allow them to feel so self-motivated or ambitious that they would forswear or forget filial obligations. The discrepancies between customary expectations and mass migration—and the consequent fear, grief, and bitterness—were most blatant in districts where agrarian capitalism, impartible inheritance, and large-scale migration were relatively recent innovations. However, migration itself quickly generated its own, corroboratory folk ways—one of the most important of which was the already described belief that the New World was an earthly paradise, whereas by contrast Ireland was "a Purgatory, where the Irish must suffer in patience before going to America."[53] In general, the fabulous image of the United States reflected Irish countrymen's diminishing faith in their own society: their attempt to compensate for Irish poverty and insecurity by projecting archaic legends and traditional aspirations for comfortable self-sufficiency onto a barely comprehended urban-industrial society. Since, after 1840, the great majority of Irish migrants no longer settled on American farms, the peasants' old arcadian vision was translated into an equally mythical urban setting where, in the words of one ballad, "The houses were all jasper / And the streets were paved in gold. . . ."[54]

The fact that this vision survived the impact of mass public education, much information to the contrary, and the Irish countryman's proverbial skepticism indicates that the belief in the *caisleáin óir* served practical functions vital to the families that composed rural society. For example, in many parts of Ireland interfamilial relationships were characterized by a jealous and secretive competitiveness. Migration played a role in this rivalry, because in order to maintain its own petty status each family that sent children to America carefully guarded the news that came home and always pretended that its offspring were doing well. Many families burned their children's letters as soon as they read them, and the receipt of an "empty American letter" (that is, one that contained no remittances) was rarely admitted. Thus, given endemic rural jealousy, every family's pretense that its own children were prospering overseas naturally encouraged the common notion that America was so rich that *anyone* could prosper there: in every household, the feeling was that "if such lazy, worthless creatures as the neighbor's children could afford to send home £10 every month, then America must truly be a land where gold can be picked up off the streets." Furthermore, since all young migrants would be expected at least to equal this spurious standard of achievement, it was only natural that parents would ignore letters that described America realistically or that pleaded poverty as an excuse for not sending remittances. "They might not have bothered sending their pictures," exclaimed the angry father of emigrants from County Roscommon, "for we know well what they look like. The pictures I would like to see are a few of Abraham Lincoln's."[55]

However, the most important function of America's alluring mythical image was in assuaging the bitterness of departure for potentially reluctant young migrants. Given the abundance of contradictory information, Irish child-rearing practices must have been crucial in transmitting that image from generation to generation. Parents who knew that their own decisions concerning inheritances would inevitably consign most of their children to the United States could try to forestall any resentment by holding the fabulous vision of the New World before their youthful imaginations. As a French visitor to Ireland remarked, "Children are brought up with the idea of probably becoming emigrants"—"trained to regard life 'in the country' as a transitory matter, merely a period of waiting until the time shall come for them to begin life 'over there.' "[56] Indeed, even Canon Michael O'Riordan, one of the staunchest defenders of "holy Ireland," admitted parental culpability when he wrote, "Children learn from their childhood that their destiny is America; and as they grow up, the thought is set before them as a thing to hope for."[57] Thus, whereas traditional proverbs—vital instruments of socialization—formerly enjoined loyalty to birthplace, new aphorisms suited to new social realities stigmatized Irish life as hopelessly impoverished, and condemned stay-at-homes as lazy or weak. Given such an upbringing, reinforced by Irish youngsters' own perceptions of Ireland's real inadequacies and America's real attractions, it was no wonder that travelers in the Irish countryside reported that "the lads of fourteen and fifteen are all growing up with the determination to bid adieu for ever to their native land."[58]

The vision of the *caisleáin óir* must have struck a responsive chord in many Irish youths. Among those who feared or resented the "necessity" to leave home, the prospect of a promised land, with "gold and silver out on the ditches," surely made that imperative much easier to fulfill. Moreover, the image was also useful for would-be migrants who faced parental opposition to their departures, for if the United States was the paradise it was reputed to be, then they would be fools not to go there—and, once abroad, they could send back enough of that proverbial gold to stem their parents' tears. However, before the migrants left Ireland, the lure of America had to be carefully balanced by parental and communal sanctions against individualism and materialism. Otherwise, there was the danger that migrants who eagerly rejected Ireland for the land of gold might also reject Irish associations (familial, especially, but also religious and political) in their lust for wealth and excitement. In 1978 the anthropologist Robin Fox noted the consequent paradox still extant on Ireland's remote Tory Island: although a child who does not migrate is "lazy," one who does is "disloyal."[59] In other words, although Irish parents encouraged migration, they demanded that departures take place not from hedonistic ambition but only out of familial obligations to relatives at home or already abroad. Thus, on the one hand, parents criticized migrating children as "selfish," "ungrateful," and "disloyal" for "abandoning" them and yet, on the other hand, made clear that migration for the family's sake was a duty that could not be ignored or avoided. Eager emigrants, enraptured by their vision of the *caisleáin óir*, were cautioned that "it's not wealth and riches that make a person satisfied," constantly reminded of the lonely misery their "deserted" parents would endure, yet also admonished to depart in order to relieve pressure at home and to remit money: "Confound you," people would say, "what's the use of spending your life here—Would it not be better for you to go to America and earn something for your father and mother?" Such conflicting messages placed would-be migrants in an extremely difficult position: it was "a shame" to migrate, but also "a shame" to remain at home. However, while "selfish" migration threatened family welfare and psychic peace—and violated both traditional norms and the "holy Ireland" ideal—migration undertaken in a proper, "dutiful" spirit promised to mitigate all conflicts and resolve all contradictions. In short, sufficient expressions of sorrow (often truly felt) and, most important, steady and ample remittances (often willingly sent) constituted the "price" that many migrants paid to relieve the tensions between desire and duty.[60]

Clerical and nationalist strictures against "selfish" migration and materialism in general served to reinforce parental injunctions— persuading, for example, the migrant Thomas Garry not to "delay in Relieving [his family in Ireland] as it is a duty Encumbered on [him] by the laws of Church."[61] Again, however, traditional child-rearing practices were probably crucial insofar as they stigmatized "boldness," enjoined conformity to authority and communal opinion, and inspired the felt need to avoid individual responsibility. Moreover, the very process of chain-migration both reflected and corroborated such tendencies. One's ability to migrate usually depended on family ties stretching across the Atlantic in the forms of letters and remittances, and the fact that most post-Famine migrants at least initially joined relatives overseas made departures seem much less acts of *self*-assertion than of conformity to established custom—much less as disruptions of all family bonds than as a process of reunion whose continuance depended on the new migrants' persistent loyalty. In addition, if youthful socialization was not sufficient to instill grief and guilt, highly ritualized leave-taking ceremonies known as "American wakes" seemed almost purposely designed to obscure migration's secular causes, wring the last drops of sorrow and self-recrimination from the intending emigrant, and impress upon him or her a sense of eternal obligation to those left at home. And, once the migrants were overseas, parents and other relatives often deluged them with letters, either pitifully entreating or imperiously demanding that their children or siblings remit some of that reputedly plentiful gold to their personal "mother Irelands."[62]

Finally, the key notion that resolved both familial tensions and the contradictions between America's opposing images was the perception that emigration was exile—an enforced process for which neither parents nor their children were ultimately responsible. Even if departure was desirable because of the supposedly enormous gulf between Irish poverty and American prosperity, even if it was obligatory to preserve the stem family and the smooth functioning of Irish agrarian capitalism, in the last analysis the migrants simply "had to go" because past oppression and contemporary misgovernment by England had ruined Ireland and, as one priest put it, made migration an "artificial" necessity.[63] In a sense, this politicization of emigration was natural, given historical and literary traditions—corroborated and formalized by pervasive nationalist agitation—that "explained" all discontinuities and offered such an appealing resolution of the conflicts and inequities within Irish Catholic society. Thus, as a nationalist politician testified before Parliament in 1908, although rural parents' real attitude toward emigration was "the more children in America the better," those children themselves obligingly "attribute[d] their being in exile to landlordism and the support given it in the past by the [British] Government."[64] Such a perception helped to ensure that the departed remained emotionally tied to a beloved and beleaguered "holy Ireland" whose families and farms, parish churches and patriotic cause, fully deserved the self-perceived exile's eternal devotion and dollars. And through such fidelity, as one popular ballad put it, Ireland's "banished children" would fulfill their duty and "prove their worth wheresoever they roam / True to their country, their God, and their home."[65]

Of course, some migrants refused to conform to the prescribed perceptions of emigration as political exile, for whether they left home bitterly or joyfully they clearly recognized the gross discrepancies between the harsh realities and the "idolatrous self-image" of "holy Ireland"—the actual sources of socioeconomic or personal repression that made life at home untenable or unbearable.[66] For instance, Irish farm laborers and women, generally, seemed the most consciously self-motivated migrants: realistic about America's material advantages and openly eager to escape from exploitative situations. However, most post-Famine migrants were neither alienated nor self-assertive enough to defy openly or consistently communal demands that they de-emphasize individual motivation and conceptualize migration in dutiful or compulsory terms—especially when such attitudes and perceptions had been internalized from birth and reinforced by every institution shaping rural life. For the migrants themselves, as well as for their parents, the interpretations of migration as obligation or as exile were both customary and expedient. Fortunately for eager migrants, the process of chain-migration enabled independent volition to be "explained" as passive acquiescence. As a result, it was common for post-Famine migrants to make the highly dubious claim that they never had the slightest notion of leaving Ireland until the purportedly unexpected arrival of supposedly unsolicited passage tickets from America confronted them with an inescapable "duty" or "fate." Thus, while Irish clerics and nationalists might denounce migrants as "traitors" to "holy Ireland" and its "sacred cause," the very process of migration enabled young Irishmen and -women to circumvent such injunctions in terms that seemingly validated traditional, dependent outlooks. For example, when interviewed decades later, an elderly man in County Westmeath mistakenly "remembered" that in the early 1880s, during the Land War, "*except* when pre-paid sailing tickets came, emigration was over, [for] all were wanted at home to carry on the fight" against Protestant landlords and "English tyranny"; however, "when pre-paid sailing tickets came," eager young migrants could then argue that they simply "*had* to go," while nationalists, priests, and parents could claim that such excused and supposedly exceptional departures implied no renunciation of communal loyalties.[67]

In conclusion, we must remember that "Paddy's Paradox" or "Caitlin's Conundrum" was internalized, and so the conflicts that migrants found most difficult and painful to resolve were often those in their own minds. In his short story significantly entitled "Going into Exile," the Irish novelist Líam O'Flaherty convincingly and movingly portrayed a young girl's contradictory emotions on the night before her departure for America: at one moment she was filled with "thoughts of love and of foreign men and of clothes and of houses where there were more than three rooms and where people ate meat every day," yet in the next instant "she was stricken with horror at the thought of leaving her mother and at the selfishness of her thoughts . . . that made her hate herself as a cruel, heartless, lazy, selfish wretch."[68] Even the obligatory grief and promises expressed at the "American wakes" did not fully erase or alleviate such tensions between desire and duty. For instance, in a letter from New York the migrant Anne Flood oscillated between self-assertion and self-destruction as her internalized conflicts threatened her psychic well-being. She began her letter boldly, telling her mother—who wanted her to return to County Meath—that she was "happy and contented

. . . and never enjoyed better health" in her life. "I never once thought of going home," she admitted, and "you know when I was home I often wished myself in this Country and now to return I think would be quite a folly." However, she faltered, "I would say more on this subject but I feel so nerv[ou]s I do not know from what effect," and so terminated the letter rather abruptly, in handwriting whose increasing unsteadiness showed the effects of growing strain.[69]

In fact, few recently arrived migrants dared to be as "bold" as Anne Flood, and whether sincerely or calculatingly it was thus much easier—and, perhaps, kinder to all concerned—to obscure motivation by claiming or implying that migration was either fated and unwilling exile or informed solely by filial piety and self-sacrifice. "For God's sake and for ours," begged one harassed migrant of his parents at home, "endeavor to shake off your sorrow and do not leave us to accuse ourselves of bringing down your grey hairs with sorrow to the grave by leaving you when we should have stayed by you. Our intentions were good and still continue—and, if God prosper our endeavors, we will soon be able to assist and cheer you."[70] As that plaintive plea indicates, although its practical resolutions financially sustained "holy Ireland's" family farms and nationalist movements, in personal, psychological terms "Paddy's Paradox" could be a painful and an oppressive burden.

Notes

This paper was presented to the conference "Ireland and the United States: The Transatlantic Connection, 1800–1980," held at the University of Notre Dame, Notre Dame, Indiana, 10–11 Apr 1987.

Although argued and presented here in novel ways, the information on, and analysis of, Irish history, society, and culture contained in this essay reflects some fifteen years of research and writing that culminated in the publication of Kerby A. Miller, *Emigrants and Exiles: Ireland and the Irish Exodus to North America* (New York: Oxford University Press, 1985). Consequently, to economize on time and space, many of the following citations merely refer to the relevant pages of that work (and their accompanying notes). However, direct quotations are fully cited.

1. At least 4 million Irish people emigrated between 1856 and 1921, compared with 2.1 million during the period of the Great Famine (1845–55), approximately one million in 1815–44, and less than one million during the two centuries preceding 1815. See Miller, *Emigrants and Exiles*, 137, 169, 193–201, 291–93, and 346–53.

290 KERBY A. MILLER

2. See ibid., 361–412.

3. See David N. Doyle, *Irish Americans, Native Rights, and National Empires: The Structure, Divisions and Attitudes of the Catholic Minority in the Decade of Expansion, 1890–1901* (New York: Anno Press, 1976), 48–49, 59–63; Miller, *Emigrants and Exiles*, 492–534 passim.

4. On returned migrants, see Marjolein 't Hart, " 'Heading for Paddy's Green Shamrock Shore': The Returned Emigrants in Nineteenth-Century Ireland," *Irish Economic and Social History* 10 (1983): 96–97; and John Bodnar, *The Transplanted: A History of Immigrants in Urban America* (Bloomington, Ind.: Indiana University Press, 1987 ed.), 53–54.

5. Quotation from *North American Review* 52 (1837): 202.

6. See Miller, *Emigrants and Exiles*, 270–79, 334–44, 535–68.

7. Letter from W. Simpson, 6 June 1836 (ms. 20,340, National Library of Ireland, Dublin); G. R. C. Keep, "Some Irish Opinions on Population and Emigration, 1851–1901," *Irish Ecclesiastical Record* 85, no. 6 (1955): 385–86.

8. See *Cork Examiner*, 20 Apr 1859.

9. See *Kilkenny Journal*, 25 Sept 1901. On "returned Yanks" generally, see Arnold Schrier, *Ireland and the American Emigration, 1850–1900* (New York: Russell and Russell, 1970 ed.), 129–43, 152.

10. E.g., Miller, *Emigrants and Exiles*, 160–61, 203, 312–13, 472, 507.

11. E.g., ibid., 357–59, 506–20.

12. Letter from Jane Fleming, 3 May 1853 (D.1047/1, Public Record Office of Northern Ireland, Belfast; hereafter cited as PRONI).

13. See Risteárd Ó Foghludha, ed., *Pádraig Phiarais Cúndún* (Dublin: Foilseacháin Realtais, 1932), 40–44 and passim (trans. Dr. Bruce D. Boling, University of New Mexico).

14. Letter from J. F. Costello, 11 Jan 1883 (courtesy of Professor Arnold Schrier, University of Cincinnati).

15. Letter from Brian Garahan, 19 Dec 1817 (ms. 9.1:098, O'Conor Don Papers, Clonalis House, Castlerea, Co. Roscommon).

16. Seán de Fréine, *The Great Silence: The Study of a Relationship between Language and Nationality* (Dublin: Foilseacháin Náisiunta Teoranta, 1965), 25.

17. See Miller, *Emigrants and Exiles*, 105.

18. See T. F. O'Rahilly, ed., *Measgra Dánta* (Cork, 1927), vol. 2, 146 (trans. Dr. Bruce D. Boling, University of New Mexico); Miller, *Emigrants and Exiles*, 485.

19. See Miller, *Emigrants and Exiles*, 557–58, 142–49.

20. Ibid., 235.

21. Ibid., 477–78. Ms. 1408, 148, 188, 319–28 and passim; ms. 1409, 240–43; ms. 1410, 132; and ms. 1411, 338–39, 356 (Department of Irish Folklore, University College, Dublin; hereafter cited as DIF/UCD).

22. Statistics *re* Irish-speaking and literacy, 1851–1901, tabulated in Donald H. Akenson, *The Irish Education Experiment: The National System of Education in the Nineteenth Century* (London: Routledge and Kegan Paul, 1970), 379–80.

23. See Miller, *Emigrants and Exiles*, 107–30.

24. Ibid., 114–21.

25. Ibid., 121.

26. Ibid., 380–83, 429–30.

27. See Damian F. Hannan, "Peasant Models and the Understanding of Social and Cultural Change in Rural Ireland," *Irish Studies 2. Ireland: Land, Politics and People*, ed. Patrick J. Drudy (Cambridge: Cambridge University Press, 1982), 142–44, 146.

28. See Moritz Bonn, *Modern Ireland and Her Agrarian Problem* (Dublin: Hodges, Figgis, 1906), 48–50.

29. See Miller, *Emigrants and Exiles*, 121–24, 412–13, 428–35.

30. Ibid., 121–24, 428–35.

31. Ibid., 397–402, 469–73.

32. John M. Synge, "In West Kerry," *The Aran Islands and Other Writings by John M. Synge*, ed. Robert Tracy (New York: Vintage Books, 1962), 218.

33. See Miller, *Emigrants and Exiles*, 424–26, 472–73.

34. See Pádraig Ua Duinnín, *Muinntear Chiarraidhe Roimh an Drochsaoghal* (Dublin: M. H. Gill and Son, 1905), 54–61 (trans. Dr. Bruce D. Boling, University of New Mexico); Tracy, *The Aran Islands*, 291; ms. 1407, 45–46, and ms. 1409, 4–5, 11–32 (DIF/UCD).

35. Robin Flower, *The Western Island, Or the Great Blasket* (New York: Oxford University Press, 1945), 18.

36. See Miller, *Emigrants and Exiles*, 473–76; Congested Districts Board, Inspectors' Confidential Reports, 1891–95 (Trinity College, Dublin), 106–7, 459, 500.

37. Maurice O'Sullivan, *Twenty Years A-Growing* (New York: Viking, 1933), 239.

38. See Miller, *Emigrants and Exiles*, 478–79; "Maíre" [Séamus Ó Grianna], *Caisleáin Oir* (Dundalk, 1924).

39. Miller, *Emigrants and Exiles*, 478–81.

40. On cultural hegemony, see Antonio Gramsci, *The Modern Prince and Other Writings* (New York: International Publishers, 1957), 67, 118–24, and passim; Raymond Williams, "Base and Superstructure in Marxist Cultural Theory," *New Left Review* 82 (November–December 1983): 3–16; Joseph V. Femia, *Gramsci's Political Thought: Hegemony, Consciousness, and the Revolutionary Process* (Oxford: Clarendon Press, 1981); and T. J. Jackson Lears, "The Concept of Cultural Hegemony: Problems and Possibilities," *American Historical Review* 90 (June 1985): 567–93.

As applied to Ireland, see Miller, *Emigrants and Exiles*, 124–30, 435–69; and, more specifically, idem, "Emigration as Exile: Cultural Hegemony in Post-Famine Ireland," conference paper, in *A Century of European Migration, 1830–1930*, ed. Rudolph J. Vecoli (Urbana: University of Illinois Press, 1991).

41. See Miller, *Emigrants and Exiles*, 458–66; Rev. Joseph Guinan, *Scenes and Sketches in an Irish Parish, Or Priest and People in Doon* (Dublin: M. H. Gill, 1906), 43.

42. Miller, *Emigrants and Exiles*, 465–69, 481.

43. Ibid., 54–60, 115, 481–82.

44. Ibid., 482–83; quotation from Arthur Livermore, 31 July 1883 (U.S. Consular Reports, Ireland, microfilm T-368, National Archives, Washington, D.C.).

45. See Miller, *Emigrants and Exiles*, 483.

46. Royal Commission on Congestion in Ireland, *British Parliamentary Papers—House of Commons, Reports*, vol. 5 (3630), 1907, 466; L. Paul-Dubois, *Contemporary Ireland* (Dublin: Maunsel and Co., 1908), 305.

47. James Connolly, *Labour in Ireland* (Dublin: Three Candles Press, n.d.), 226.

48. Patrick Gallagher, *Paddy the Cope: An Autobiography* (New York: Devin-Adair, 1942), 62–63.

49. See Miller, *Emigrants and Exiles*, 484.

50. Robert L. Wright, ed., *Irish Emigrant Ballads and Songs* (Bowling Green: Bowling Green University Press, 1975), 12–13; letter from Julia Lough, 20 Oct 1891 (courtesy of Professor Arnold Schrier, University of Cincinnati).

51. Ms. 1410, 129 (DIF/UCD).

52. Letter from A. B. McMillan, 4 May 1895 (D. 1195/5/41, PRONI); letter from J. Kells, 18 Nov 1883 (M. 7075, Irish National Archives, Dublin); ms. 1407, 281 (DIF/UCD).

53. See Miller, *Emigrants and Exiles*, 485; Paul-Dubois, *Contemporary Ireland*, 359.

54. See Miller, *Emigrants and Exiles*, 485–86; C. Mac Mathuna, "Song of the Exile," *Irish Times* (Dublin), 16 Dec 1976.

55. Miller, *Emigrants and Exiles*, 486–87; ms. 1407, 36–37, and ms. 1409, 297 (DIF/UCD).

56. Miller, *Emigrants and Exiles*, 487; Paul-Dubois, *Contemporary Ireland*, 359.

57. Rev. Michael O'Riordan, *Catholicity and Progress in Ireland* (London: Kegan Paul, 1906), 292.

58. See Miller, *Emigrants and Exiles*, 487; ms. 1407, 45–46; Henry Coulter, *The West of Ireland* (London: Saunders Newsletter, 1862), 287–88.

59. Miller, *Emigrants and Exiles*, 487–88; Robin Fox, *The Tory Is-*

landers: A People of the Celtic Fringe (Cambridge: Cambridge University Press, 1978), 29.

60. Miller, *Emigrants and Exiles*, 488–89; Micheál Ó Gaoithín, *Beatha Peig Sayers* (Dublin, 1970), 89–90 (trans. Dr. Bruce D. Boling, University of New Mexico); ms. 1409, 45–46, 60 (DIF/UCD); Hugh Brody, *Inishkillane: Change and Decline in the West of Ireland* (London: Allan Lane, 1973), 165–66.

61. Appendix, Minutes of Evidence, Select Committee on Colonization from Ireland, *Irish University Press Series of the British Parliamentary Papers, Emigration*, vol. 5 (Shannon: Irish University Press, 1968), 129.

62. Miller, *Emigrants and Exiles*, 489–90, 556–68.

63. Ibid., 490; O'Riordan, *Catholicity and Progress*, 292.

64. Reports, Royal Commission on Congestion in Ireland, *British Parliamentary Papers* 7 (3748), 1908, 811.

65. Schrier, *Ireland and American Emigration*, 100.

66. See Miller, *Emigrants and Exiles*, 490–91; Joseph J. Lee, "Women and the Church since the Famine," *Women in Irish Society: The Historical Dimension*, ed. Margaret MacCurtain and Donncha Ó Corrain (Dublin: Arlen House, 1978), 43.

67. See Miller, *Emigrants and Exiles*, 490–92; ms. 1408, 130 (DIF/UCD).

68. Liam O'Flaherty, "Going into Exile," *1000 Years of Irish Prose*, ed. Vivian Mercier and David H. Greene (New York: Grosset and Dunlap, 1952), 369–78.

69. Letter from Anne Flood, 5 Feb 1853 (courtesy of Pádraig Ó Droighneain, Navan, Co. Meath).

70. Letter from F. D., 12 Aug 1835 (Box 45, Richard J. Purcell Papers, Catholic University of America, Washington, D.C.).

About the Contributors

Laura Levine Frader is Associate Professor of History at Northeastern University, Boston, Mass., USA, where she teaches European social and labor history and women's history. She is author of a recently completed book manuscript, *Peasants and Protest: Agricultural Workers, Politics, and Unions in the Aude, 1850–1914*, and has published articles on French agricultural workers and revolutionary syndicalism.

Nancy L. Green is Chef de travaux (assistant professor) at the École des Hautes Études en Sciences Sociales in Paris, where she teaches Jewish studies and comparative migration studies. She is the author of *The Pletzl of Paris: Jewish Immigrant Workers in the Belle Époque* (1985) and numerous articles on French Jewish history, the Jewish labor movement, and migration to France.

Dirk Hoerder (Dr.Phil., Free University of West Berlin, 1971) teaches North American social history at the University of Bremen, Germany. He is the head of the Labor Migration Project and in recent years has been working on a concept of migration in the Atlantic economies.

Michael John (Dr. phil., University of Vienna, 1980), economic and social historian, specializes in the areas of housing research and migration research. He teaches at the Department for Social and Economic History, Johannes Kepler University of Linz, Austria.

Matjaž Klemenčič (Ph.D., Edvard Kardelj University of Ljubljana, 1983) teaches at the Department of History, University of Maribor, Slovenia. He specializes in the history of Slovenes in the United States and is author of the book *Ameriški Slovenci in NOB v Jugoslaviji* (Slovene Americans and the People's Liberation Struggle in Yugoslavia) (Maribor: Založba Obzorja, 1987).

Albert Lichtblau (Dr. phil., University of Vienna, 1980) has specialized in migration research and now researches primarily in the field of anti-Semitism. He is a social historian, and currently works as scholar at the Center for Anti-Semitic Research, Berlin, Germany.

Kerby A. Miller is Associate Professor of History at the College of Arts and Science, University of Missouri-Columbia. He specializes in Irish migration history and has recently published *Emigrants and Exiles: Ireland and the Irish Exodus to North America* (1985).

Pierre Milza is Director of the Centre d'Histoire de l'Europe du Vingtième Siècle and Professor at the Institut d'Etudes Politiques in Paris. He is the author of numerous books and articles on fascism, Italian history, and contemporary international relations, particularly *Français et Italiens à la fin du XIXe siècle* (1981) and, most recently, *Fascisme français, passé et présent* (1987).

Ewa Morawska (Ph.D., University of Warsaw; Boston University) teaches at the Department of Sociology, University of Pennsylvania. Her areas of specialization are social change and modernization; American ethnic and migration studies; East European societies (historical and contemporary). She is author of the book *For Bread with Butter: Life-Worlds of East Central Europeans in Johnstown, Pennsylvania, 1890–1940* (1985).

Julianna Puskás is a senior researcher at the Institute of History at the Hungarian Academy of Sciences, Budapest. Since the 1970s she has specialized in migration research. She is author of the book *From Hungary to the United States, 1880–1914,* (1982).

Franco Ramella (laurea, Turin, 1974) is Associate Professor of History at the University of Turin, Italy. He has published on the Italian working class and Italian emigration. He is author of the book *Terra e telai* (Land and Looms) (1984), and has recently coedited (with Samuel L. Baily) *One Family, Two Worlds: An Italian Family's Correspondence across the Atlantic, 1901–1922* (1988).

Anna Reczyńska (Ph.D., Jagiellonian University, Cracow, 1975) teaches at the Instytut Badán Polonijnych, Jagiellonian University of Cracow, Poland. She specializes in the history of Polish migration to Canada and is author of the book *Emigracja z Polski do Kanady w okresie miedzywojennym* (Emigration from Poland to Canada between the Two World Wars) (1987).

Claudius H. Riegler (Dr. phil., University of Erlangen-Nürnberg, 1982) teaches language and organizes education programs at Öja Course Center, Ystad, Sweden, and is a research associate at the Science Center for Social Research, Berlin, Germany. He took international labor migration and Scandinavian social history and labor policy as his main subjects and is author of *Emigration und Arbeitswanderung aus Schweden nach Norddeutschland, 1868–1914* (Emigration and Labor Migration from Sweden to Northern Germany, 1868–1914) (1985).

Gianfausto Rosoli is director of the quarterly *Studi Emigrazione* and member of the Centro Studi Emigrazione-Roma (CSER). He is author of many essays and research projects on Italian migration for national and international institutions, including the Italian Foreign Ministry, the National Council for Research, UNESCO, and ILO. He has recently edited *Emigrazioni europee e popolo brasiliano* (Rome: CSER, 1987) and *Scalabrini tra vecchio e nuovo mondo* (1989). He coauthored, with Philip V. Cannistraro, *Emigrazione Chiesa e fascismo* (1979) and edited, with Fernando Devoto, *L'Italia nella società argentina* (1988).

Horst Rössler (Dr. phil., University of Bremen, 1984) is a member of the Labor Migration Project at the University of Bremen. He has worked on nineteenth-century labor movements in Britain and is currently researching nineteenth-century labor migration from Britain and Germany to the United States.

Index

Abruzzo, emigrants from, 239n

Acculturation, 27; in America, 15, 149, 228; in Vienna, 57; of Hungarians in America, 191

Adamic, Louis, 202, 215–16, 218, 245

Africa, 224; Italian immigration to, 106. *See also* Italy

Agricultural workers, 16–17; in Eastern Europe, 242–43, 259; in Ireland, 264, 273, 287; in Italy, 12; in Sweden, 170. *See also* Wages

Aigues-Mortes: massacre of Italian immigrants in, 115

Alger, Horatio, 5

Alliance Israélite Universelle, 45

Alsace: migrants to Paris from, 39

Amazzonia, L', 231

America, 1, 3, 12. *See also* Acculturation; Democratic Party; El Dorado; Living conditions; Technology; Wages

—anti-myth of: 225

—as bitter land: 229, 232–33

—Catholics in: 204

—Constitution: 6

—contract labor in: 244

—depressions in: 14, 205–09, 215–16, 265, 267

—emigrant expectations of: 1, 180

—as Golden Land: 244

—image of: 1–3, 6–17, 20–27, 28n, 44, 66, 84, 91, 111, 126, 135, 138, 160–61, 180–81, 224–26; in Austria, 64; in Budweis, 78n; in Croatia, 207–08, 245; in Denmark, 162–63; in Eastern Europe, 24, 245–46; in England, 6, 127, 131–32, 134–38, 156–57n; in Europe, 180; in Galicia, 87, 246; gender specific, 8; in Germany, 6–7, 22; in Hungary, 6, 25, 181–82, 184–86; in Ireland, 26, 265–78, 283–85, 287; Italian, 107, 109, 111–14, 121–25, 229–32; messianic, 222; in Norway, 161, 163; in Poland, 86–94, 246; of skilled workers, 161, 165–66; in Slovenia, 25, 199, 201–06, 215–16; in Slovenian labor press, 211–13; among South Slavs, 212; in Sweden, 160–74, 175n; among technicians, 161, 165–67; in union newspapers, 12; among women, 8, 15; in Yugoslavia, 201, 202, 217

—Irish influence in: 265

—land in, 6, 15, 85–87, 142, 202, 204–05

—as land of freedom: 6, 111, 170, 182, 213, 220n, 228, 246

—as land of snakes: 26, 202, 268, 276, 282

—lynching in, 231

—money in: 10–11, 88, 90–91, 202–03, 207, 247

—restrictionism in: 27, 216–17, 223, 232

American Federation of Labor, 14–15; Irish influence in, 265

Amerykanie (Łembiński), 94

Ameriški Slovenec, 208